Adobe®

InDesign® CS2

HANDS-ON TRAINING

Includes Exercise Files & Demo Movies

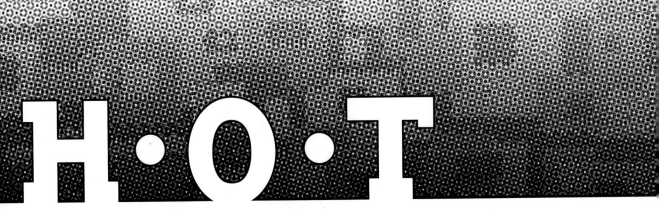

H·O·T

Brian Wood

Adobe InDesign CS2 | H·O·T
Hands-On Training

By Brian Wood

lynda.com/books | Peachpit Press
1249 Eighth Street • Berkeley, CA • 94710
800.283.9444 • 510.524.2178 •
510.524.2221 (fax)
http://www.lynda.com/books
http://www.peachpit.com

lynda.com/books is published
in association with Peachpit Press,
a division of Pearson Education
Copyright ©2006 by lynda.com

ISBN: 0-321-34872-9

0 9 8 7 6 5 4 3 2 1

Printed and bound in the
United States of America

H•O•T | Credits

Original Design: Ali Karp, Alink Newmedia (alink@earthlink.net)

Editor: Karyn Johnson

Copyeditor: Barbara McGowan

Production Coordinator: Myrna Vladic

Compositors: Rick Gordon, Deborah Roberti

Beta testers: Adam Fischer, Jan Kabili

Proofreader: Liz Welch

Cover Illustration: Bruce Heavin (bruce@stink.com)

Indexer: Julie Bess, JBIndexing Inc.

H•O•T | Colophon

The original design for *Adobe InDesign CS2 H•O•T* was sketched on paper. The layout was heavily influenced by online communication—merging a traditional book format with a modern Web aesthetic.

The text in *Adobe InDesign CS2 H•O•T* was set in Akzidenz Grotesk from Adobe and Triplex from Emigre. The cover illustration was painted in Adobe Photoshop and Adobe Illustrator.

Dedication

To my wife, business partner, and best friend—Wyndham.
You are my constant inspiration.

Adobe InDesign CS2 | H•O•T _____ Table of Contents

Introduction

A Note from Lynda

In my opinion, most people buy computer books to learn, yet it is amazing how few of these books are actually written by teachers. Brian Wood and I take pride in the fact that the authors of this book are experienced teachers familiar with training students in this subject matter. The book is filled with carefully developed lessons and exercises to help you learn InDesign CS2.

Our target audience for this book is beginning- to intermediate-level print designers. The premise of the hands-on exercise approach is to get you up to speed quickly with InDesign CS2 while actively working through the lessons in the book. Reading about a product is important, but actually using the product and getting measurable results is even more valuable. Our motto is, "Read the book, follow the exercises, and you'll learn the product." I have received countless testimonials to this fact, and it is our goal to make sure it remains true for all of our hands-on training books.

Many exercise-based books take a paint-by-numbers approach to teaching. Although this approach works, it's often difficult to figure out how to apply those lessons to a real-world situation, or to understand why or when you would use the technique again. What sets this book apart is that each lesson contains the background information and insights into each given subject, which are designed to help you understand the process as well as the exercise.

At times, pictures are worth a lot more than words. When necessary, we have included short QuickTime movies to show any processes that are difficult to explain with words. These files are located on the **INDESIGN CS2 HOT CD-ROM** inside a folder called **movies**. It's our style to approach teaching from many different angles, because we know some people are visual learners, others like to read, and still others like to get out there and try things. This book combines a lot of teaching approaches so you can learn InDesign CS2 as thoroughly as you want to.

This book didn't set out to cover every single aspect of InDesign CS2. The product manual and many other reference books are great for that! What we saw missing from the bookshelves was a process-oriented tutorial that taught readers core principles, techniques, and tips in a hands-on training format.

I welcome your comments at **indesignhot@lynda.com/**. Please visit our Web site at **http://www.lynda.com/**. The support URL for this book is **http://www.lynda.com/info/ books/indesignhot/**.

Brian and I hope this book will raise your skills with InDesign. If it does, we will have accomplished the job we set out to do!

Lynda Weinman

NOTE | About lynda.com/books and lynda.com

lynda.com/books is dedicated to helping designers and developers understand design tools and principles. lynda.com offers hands-on workshops, training seminars, conferences, on-site training, training videos, training CDs, and "expert tips" for design and development. To learn more about our training programs, books, and products, visit our Web site at **http://www.lynda.com**.

About Brian

After graduating from art school many years ago, Brian worked in print production at Eddie Bauer, where he became interested in teaching. Years later he found himself training for Adobe and then broke out on his own, co-founding eVolve Computer Graphics Training Inc. in Seattle (**http://www.evolveseattle.com**), a company he and his wife, Wyndham, own and run together. A long-time QuarkXPress user, Brian was finally swayed over to the InDesign side of the fence when version 2.0 came out. Although he still uses Quark once in a while when a job requires it, he has never looked back since making the transition to InDesign.

Acknowledgments from Brian

I started training almost by accident. In 1998, my boss at Eddie Bauer asked me to teach some of my co-workers Photoshop 5.0. It was the typical trial by fire, and I can only imagine how painful it was for my "students" to watch me fumble my way through explanations. I quickly realized that being able to use software well doesn't translate into being able to teach it well. Since then, I've had many opportunities to hone my teaching skills—primarily in a class or seminar format, which is to say, verbally.

When I accepted the assignment to write this book, I had no idea what a challenge it was going to be. It soon became clear that translating my teaching skills into written form was a more daunting task than I had realized.

All in all, it has proven a very rewarding experience, and one I never could have completed without the incredible input from **Lynda Weinman**. In addition to providing great insight, she was genuinely excited about what I was doing, even at 10 p.m. on a Sunday night.

I also couldn't have done this without **Garo Green**, who guided and supported me throughout the process.

And to **Sharon Swanson**, who designed the book's exercise files, thank you for making this book as visually appealing as it is. It is always an honor to work with someone as talented as you are.

I would also like to thank my wife, **Wyndham Wood**, who, in addition to running our company in my near-absence while I wrote this book, acted as my in-house editor and tester, elevating the quality of the book considerably. Thank you, Wyn.

I also owe a huge thank you to the beta testers and copy editors who did a great job of taking the book to yet another level.

And finally, a big thank you to the production team for making it look so good.

I would also be remiss if I didn't thank my many friends at Adobe, whose work, sense of humor, and support has enriched my own career on professional and personal levels.

How This Book Works

The book has several components, including step-by-step exercises, commentary, notes, tips, warnings, and movies. Step-by-step exercises are numbered, and filenames and command keys are bolded so they pop out more easily. When you see italicized text, it signifies commentary.

- Whenever you're being instructed to go to a menu or to multiple menu items, it's stated like this: **File > Open**.

- URLs are in a bold font: **http://www.lynda.com/**.

- Macintosh and Windows interface screen captures: The screen captures in the book were taken on a Macintosh, as I do most of my design work and writing on a Mac. I also own and use a Windows computer, and I noted important differences when they occurred.

What's on the CD-ROM?

Exercise Files and the InDesign CS2 HOT CD-ROM

The files required to complete the exercises are located inside a folder called **exercise_files** on the **InDesign CS2 HOT CD-ROM**. These files are divided into chapter folders, and you should copy each chapter folder to your Desktop before you begin the exercises for the chapter. Unfortunately, when files originate from a CD-ROM, under some Windows operating systems, it defaults to making them write-protected, meaning that you cannot alter them. You will need to alter them to follow the exercises, so please read the "Making Exercise Files Editable on Windows Computers" section below.

Bonus Exercises on the InDesign CS2 HOT CD-ROM

The **InDesign CS2 HOT CD-ROM** includes a folder called **bonus_exercises**, which contains several PDF files with bonus exercises you'll find useful when learning InDesign CS2.

QuickTime Files on the InDesign CS2 HOT CD-ROM

The **InDesign CS2 HOT CD-ROM** includes a folder called **movies**, which contains several QuickTime tutorial movies for some of the exercises in this book. These movies are intended to help you under-stand some of the more difficult exercises in this book by watching me perform them. If you like these movies, you should definitely check out the **InDesign CS2 for the Web Training Essentials** CD-ROM at **http://www.lynda.com**, which contains several hours worth of QuickTime movies about how to use InDesign CS2.

Making Exercise Files Editable on Windows Computers

By default, when you copy files from a CD-ROM to a Windows 2000 computer, they are set to read-only (write protected). This causes a problem with the exercise files because you need to edit and save some of them. To remove the read-only property, follow these steps:

Note: You do not need to follow these steps if you are using Windows XP Home Edition or Windows XP Professional Edition.

1. Open the **exercises_files** folder on the **InDesign CS2 HOT CD-ROM**, and copy one of the subfold-ers (such as **chap_02**) to the **Desktop**.

2. Open the **chap_02** folder you copied to the **Desktop**, and choose **Edit > Select All**.

3. Right-click one of the selected files, and choose **Properties** from the shortcut menu.

4. In the **Properties** dialog box, click the **General** tab. Turn off the **Read-Only** option to disable the read-only properties for the selected files in the **chap_02** folder.

Making File Extensions Visible on Windows Computers

By default, you cannot see file extensions, such as .indd, on Windows computers. Fortunately, you can change this setting!

1. Double-click the **My Computer** icon on your **Desktop**.

*Note: If you (or someone else) have changed the name of the icon, it will not say **My Computer.***

2. Select **Tools > Folder Options**. The **Folder Options** dialog box opens automatically.

3. Click the **View** tab.

4. Turn off the **Hide extensions for known file types** option. This makes all file extensions visible.

InDesign CS2 System Requirements

This book requires that you use either a Macintosh (Mac OS X v10.2.8 or later) or Windows 2000 or XP. You will also need a color monitor capable of 1024 × 768 resolution and a CD-ROM drive. Here are the minimum system requirements you need to run InDesign CS2.

Macintosh

- PowerPC G3, G4, or G5 processor

- Mac OS X v10.2.8 through v10.4.1

- 256 MB RAM (320 MB recommended)

- 870 MB available hard disk space

- 1024 × 768 monitor resolution with 16-bit video card (24-bit screen display recommended)

- CD-ROM drive

- QuickTime 6 required for multimedia features (included in Mac OS X)

- For Adobe PostScript Printers: PostScript Level 2 or PostScript 3

- Internet or phone connection required for product activation

Windows

- Intel Pentium III or 4 processor

- Microsoft Windows 2000 with Service Pack 3 or Windows XP

- 256 MB RAM (320 MB recommended)

- 850 MB available hard disk space

- 1024 x 768 monitor resolution with 16-bit video card (24-bit screen display recommended)

- CD-ROM drive

- QuickTime 6 required for multimedia features (included in Mac OS X)

- For Adobe PostScript Printers: PostScript Level 2 or PostScript 3

- Internet or phone connection required for product activation

Getting Demo Versions of Software

If you'd like to try the software programs used in this book, you can download demo versions from the Adobe Web site at **http://www.adobe.com/**.

I

Getting Started

| Why Use InDesign? |
| Creative Suite 2 and InDesign CS2 |
| InDesign for QuarkXPress Users |
| InDesign for PageMaker Users |
| What's New in InDesign CS2 |

---

chap_01

InDesign CS2
HOT CD-ROM

Welcome to lynda.com's *Adobe InDesign CS2 Hands-On Training*. I'm very excited to author this book for several reasons. First and foremost, ever since hearing Lynda herself speak at an event several years ago, I have been using lynda.com products. They consistently provide the most comprehensive learning experience of any of the graphic software manuals I have found. Second, as someone who has been in the graphics industry since day one of my professional career, I have seen many software tools come and go, but never have I been so willing to sing the praises of a program as I am about InDesign. I truly enjoy working in this program, and given recent industry trends and hearing the feedback from my own students, a lot of people seem to agree with me. I hope you enjoy learning the program as much as I did.

Now it's time to get started. In this chapter, I'll offer a glimpse of some of the uses for InDesign, including new features for InDesign CS2, and a look at some of the similarities between this program and QuarkXPress as well as Adobe PageMaker.

Why Use InDesign?

That's a good question. Most of us go through our day using the computer as a tool for just about everything from updating our calendars to checking the latest sports scores. When it comes to writing e-mail or getting online, we know which application to turn to. What about when it comes to making that first brochure or drawing a logo? The answer may not be quite as easy, although often it boils down to using the tool that best suits the purpose at hand.

In the graphics world, programs like those found in Adobe's Creative Suite—InDesign, Photoshop, Illustrator, GoLive, and Acrobat—are essential to your daily work. Each of the tools in the Creative Suite 2 offers optimal functionality in a certain area. Yes, there is crossover between the applications—for instance, say you're creating a logo for a new client. Depending on what the design entails and what it's going to be used for, you could create that artwork in Photoshop or Illustrator, or even in both.

InDesign is essentially Adobe's answer to page layout. Adobe InDesign CS2 is a professional-level layout program that can create anything from a single business card to a brochure, large manual or catalog, and beyond. The program gives you a considerable amount of creative freedom, so you can create your best layouts using features like setting columns, placing images of all sorts and types, using master pages and style sheets for speed and accuracy, and much more—all subjects we'll explore throughout this book.

I've often been asked questions like, "Why not just use Microsoft Word?" or "I use Publisher—it suits my needs." My personal favorite is, "I don't have time to learn new software. I've got a deadline." I understand the mind-set—I was caught up in it myself years ago. It's true, we're busy. We have dead-lines. But now that I've seen in my own work how much time I save every day by using a more efficient and flexible software tool, I can't help but ask, "Would you be willing to learn something new and maybe stumble through two or three projects if it made your life easier and your workload more manageable in the long run?" Put that way, most people say yes.

In this book, we are going to see the power of InDesign CS2's many page layout features. By the end of this book, you should be able to answer the question "Why use InDesign?" for yourself.

For those of you using Word, Publisher, or even Illustrator for page layout, InDesign offers amazing typographic control, templates, and the ability to place and manipulate objects with little effort.

As an InDesign user with more than 12 years of prior QuarkXPress use, and a few years of PageMaker sprinkled in the early years, I now realize how many work-arounds I used to rely on to get my work done, and how comfortable I once was with the shortcomings of other page layout programs. Back in 1999, when InDesign 1.0 dropped, I was skeptical and immediately rallied behind QuarkXPress, with-out even giving InDesign a chance. Slowly, and with much prodding from a colleague at the time, I gave it a chance. To my amazement, as I navigated the program, I found myself saying, "It'd be nice if Quark would do that." No matter how much I enjoy and appreciate InDesign, however, it's worth mentioning that no program is infallible. In my opinion, InDesign CS2 comes as close to page layout perfection as I've seen up to this point.

Creative Suite 2 and InDesign CS2

With the release of the Creative Suite 2, you will witness a workflow more streamlined than the first release of the Creative Suite, and certainly more so than the many other piecemeal options out there. All the applications that come with it are well suited, these days, to working together. InDesign is only one piece of this puzzle. All the products are now more tightly integrated to make it easier to share files and program settings.

Several new features and improvements have been added to the suite. Some of those improvements include:

- Color swatches that can be shared among Photoshop, Illustrator, and InDesign.

- Improved PDF (Portable Document Format) file creation.

- More consistent out-of-the-box color management (including the ability to synchronize the color management settings of all CS2 applications via controls in the Adobe Bridge).

- The Adobe Bridge, which builds on the features of the File Browser in Photoshop CS (and ultimately replaces it), has been written from the ground up for performance and flexibility. It's a stand-alone application that frees up Photoshop to process images while you work in the Adobe Bridge and vice versa. It's highly extensible and will be the hub for automation and file management across the entire Creative Suite 2.0.

- Version Cue 2.0 (new version) manages files and versions as a single user or in a small workgroup. You can integrate it with the Adobe Bridge to manage files for your InDesign and Creative Suite projects.

All these features, plus a slew of other features that will be discussed throughout the book, are sure to make it easier and more enjoyable for you to work.

InDesign for QuarkXPress Users

For those of you who are currently using, or have used, QuarkXPress, switching to InDesign CS2 doesn't need to be a traumatic experience. In this section, I am going to reveal some of the steps that Adobe has taken to minimize the time and effort involved in making that transition.

For starters, Adobe has created an online guide for users considering switching from QuarkXPress to InDesign. On that page, you'll find firsthand accounts, tutorials, and documents guiding you through the conversion process. This page can be found on Adobe's Web site at **http://www.adobe.com/ products/indesign/conversion.html#quark**. In this section, I will lay out some of the similarities and differences, but I will concentrate on the things that are inside InDesign meant to make your transition comfortable.

Converting QuarkXPress Documents to InDesign CS2

When making that first leap over to InDesign, you need to think about how many legacy QuarkXPress files you have and what you want to do with them. This is one of the hardest questions that has to be answered before jumping in. I've been to a fair amount of companies making the switch and am always asked the easiest way to get their existing QuarkXPress documents into InDesign.

To translate a QuarkXPress file into an InDesign CS2 file, Adobe instructs you to open QuarkXPress 3.0–4.11 documents within InDesign. Notice the QuarkXPress versions? If you have QuarkXPress 5 documents, you will need to save back to version 4.x. If you have version 6.x documents, you may have a bit more trouble. Since QuarkXPress 6.0 doesn't save back to version 4.x files, Adobe's conversion guide tells you that you must first save back to QuarkXPress version 5.x; then from version 5.x, you can save to version 4.x. Quite the process, if you ask me.

Also, the larger the document, the longer it will take to translate, and the more likely that there will be differences between the QuarkXPress version of the document and InDesign's translation of it. Depending on your system resources, you may need to divide documents of very large file size into several smaller documents within Quark before opening them in InDesign. This same principle also applies to longer documents with dozens, and perhaps hundreds, of pages.

While I, and many of my students, have had success with this process, the unfortunate reality is that it won't always work. Your files from QuarkXPress may or may not open correctly in InDesign CS2, and there simply are no guarantees. Adobe suggests alternative methods such as copying/pasting to get text (minus formatting) from a QuarkXPress file into InDesign, saving the page as EPS (Encapsulated PostScript) or PDF to place in InDesign as a picture, XML (Extensible Markup Language) exporting from QuarkXPress and importing into InDesign CS2, and more. These are all viable options, but again, like all software itself, nothing is perfect.

Let's step through the conversion process by opening a Quark file directly in InDesign CS2.

1. Select a document by going to **File > Open** and choosing the QuarkXPress document to be translated.

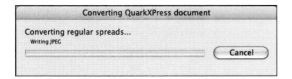

2. A dialog box appears alerting you that the translation to an InDesign CS2 document is occurring.

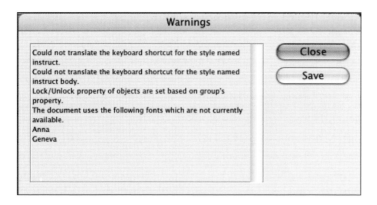

3. A third dialog box most likely appears warning of things that went gone wrong in the translation process.

You will run across a host of things that will not translate well. You will likely see problems with fonts, links, locked objects, and style shortcuts, among other things. Before opening any QuarkXPress document within InDesign, I recommend verifying that the links within the Quark document are correct, and that all the linked images are in one folder.

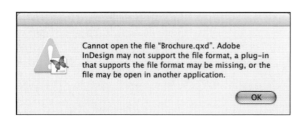

*Since QuarkXPress version 5.x and up will not be converted, if you attempt to do so, you will see a dialog box explaining that InDesign CS2 may not have the required plug-in or that the document may be opened in another application. When you click **OK**, InDesign basically gives up and you are left without a translated document.*

Translating Terminology Between QuarkXPress and InDesign

There is a fair amount of new terminology in InDesign compared with QuarkXPress. The following table translates QuarkXPress terminology into InDesign CS2. Discovering these differences (and similarities) is critical to understanding how InDesign thinks and acts.

QuarkXPress and InDesign Terminology	
QuarkXPress Term	**InDesign CS2 Term**
Project/layout	Document
Item	Object
Box	Frame
Item tool	Selection tool
Content tool	Direct Selection and Type tools
Get Picture/Get Text	Place
Frame	Stroke
Style sheets	Styles
Runaround	Text wrap
Background color	Fill
Collect for output	Package
Picture usage	Links
Tools palette	Toolbox
Lists	Table of contents
Space/align	Align
Normal style sheet	Default text attributes
XTensions	Plug-ins

Workspace

Workspace refers to the toolbars, palettes, and menus that make up the usable area of the program. Between QuarkXPress and InDesign CS2, there are definite differences, and some similarities. First, both programs have menus, palettes, and a toolbar (referred to as the **Toolbox** in InDesign). Like InDesign CS, InDesign CS2 can be made to look like QuarkXPress with a few modifications. If you look below, you can see the workspaces after making a few changes, like undocking the **Control** palette (which mirrors the Measurement palette in QuarkXPress) and undocking the palettes on the side of the work area and only showing some of the them. This may make you feel a bit more at home at the outset.

InDesign CS2

InDesign CS2 made to look like QuarkXPress

InDesign has a palette that bears a striking resemblance to the Measurement palette in QuarkXPress. It's called the **Control** palette. For QuarkXPress users, you can undock this palette and move it to the bottom of the screen where Quark has the Measurement palette by default.

The Toolbar in QuarkXPress also has an equivalent in InDesign CS2; it's called a **Toolbox**. They're the same idea; InDesign just offers a few more tools to work with. Also, in the **Toolbox** in InDesign CS2, do you notice the two boxes (circled above) with an X and without? These tools can work the same as in QuarkXPress. You can use the box (InDesign calls it a frame) with the X for pictures and the one without for text! InDesign gives you several more ways to get your text and pictures on the pages, but we'll get into that a bit later on.

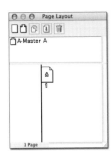

QuarkXPress 6   InDesign CS2

Palettes in general are similar between QuarkXPress and InDesign CS2 in form and function. For instance, the **Pages** palette in InDesign CS2 is comparable in function to the Page Layout palette in QuarkXPress, the **Swatches** palette in InDesign CS2 works similarly to the **Color** palette in QuarkXPress, and so on.

InDesign CS2 actually has many more palettes than QuarkXPress, so it's important to find those you know. Once you get into the program, you may find that you will be accessing more palettes in InDesign CS2 than you did in QuarkXPress. This is a good thing—an indication that you are tapping into InDesign's incredible potential.

Shortcuts

✓ Default
Shortcuts for PageMaker 7.0
Shortcuts for QuarkXPress 4.0

What about shortcut keys? I've talked to many students who fear a vast decrease in productivity because they assume they will no longer be able to use the QuarkXPress shortcut keys they have used for so many years. Luckily for all of us Quark users, Adobe anticipated that and came up with a solution to get you over the initial transition. In InDesign CS2, we can use QuarkXPress shortcut commands. You will find this option under **Edit > Keyboard Shortcuts**. In the **Keyboard Shortcuts** dialog box, you can choose which set to use. There is an option for QuarkXPress 4.0.

Preferences for QuarkXPress Users

Before you begin working full steam in InDesign CS2, there are a few preference settings you will need to be aware of as a QuarkXPress user. First, open the preferences in InDesign under **Edit > Preferences > General** (Windows) and **InDesign > Preferences > General** (Mac). Here is a listing of preferences you may want to look at and why they are important.

Preferences for QuarkXPress Users	
Preference	**Reason**
Type > Apply Leading to Entire Paragraphs	With QuarkXPress, leading is applied as a paragraph format (it affects an entire paragraph). But InDesign, by default, treats leading as a character format (it only affects lines in the paragraph or more you have selected). Turn this preference on if you would like it to more closely mirror QuarkXPress.
Composition > Text Wrap > Text Wrap Only Affects Text Beneath	In QuarkXPress, runaround on images only affects the text if the picture is above the text. In InDesign, it doesn't matter whether the image is underneath the text or not. Turn this on to more closely mirror QuarkXPress.
Guides & Pasteboard > Color	Change the colors of your margin guides and guides to more closely match those in QuarkXPress.

InDesign for PageMaker Users

PageMaker users switching to InDesign CS2 also have options to make the transition easier.

As they did for QuarkXPress users, Adobe published an online guide for PageMaker users moving to InDesign. On that page, you'll find firsthand accounts, tutorials, and documents guiding you through the conversion process. You can find this page on Adobe's Web site at **http://www.adobe.com/ products/indesign/conversion.html#pagemaker**.

Converting PageMaker Documents to InDesign CS2

As with QuarkXPress conversions, it is important to think about how many legacy PageMaker files you have and what you intend to do with them. Once again, Adobe tells us that we can directly open a PageMaker 6+ document within InDesign. Larger documents will likely take longer to translate and may be more prone to produce discrepancies between the PageMaker document and InDesign's translation of it. Breaking a larger and/or longer file into multiple smaller PageMaker files before opening it in InDesign can decrease these discrepancies.

The unfortunate reality is, this process won't always work. Files from PageMaker may or may not open correctly in InDesign CS2. When file conversion doesn't work optimally, Adobe again suggests other methods, such as copying/pasting to get text (minus formatting) from a PageMaker file into InDesign, saving the page in EPS (Encapsulated PostScript) or PDF (Portable Document Format) format to place it in InDesign as a picture, and more.

Let's step through the conversion process by opening a PageMaker file directly in InDesign CS2.

1. Select a document by going to **File > Open** and choosing the PageMaker document to be translated.

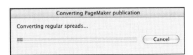

2. A dialog box will be displayed showing that the translation to an InDesign CS2 document is in process.

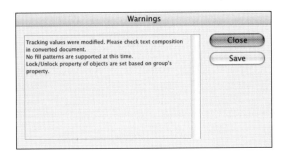

3. A dialog box will most likely appear warning of things that went gone wrong in the translation process.

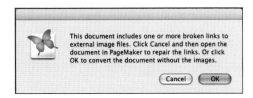

You will run across a host of things that will not translate well. Most of the time you will see problems with fonts, links, locked objects, and style shortcuts, among other things. One tip for converting PageMaker files is to make sure that the linked images are all in the same folder and that the links are correct in PageMaker.

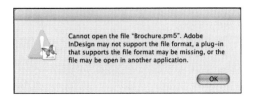

Since PageMaker versions previous to 6 will not be converted, if you attempt to do so, you will see a dialog box explaining that InDesign CS2 may not have the required plug-in or that the document may be opened in another application.

Translating Terminology Between PageMaker and InDesign	
PageMaker Term	**InDesign Term**
Publication	Document
Colors palette	Swatches palette
Printer styles	Print presets
Linking options	Links palette
Styles	Paragraph, character, and nested styles
Crop tool	Position tool
Rounded corners	Corner effects
Build booklet	InBooklet SE
Align command	Align palette
Expert tracking	Tracking

Workspace

Workspace refers to the toolbars, palettes, menus and the like that make up the usable area of the program. Between PageMaker and InDesign CS2, there are definite differences, and some similarities. Both programs have menus, palettes, and a toolbar (referred to as the **Toolbox** in InDesign).

To make PageMaker users feel more at ease, InDesign CS2 has a toolbar specifically for PageMaker users. It's called the **PageMaker toolbar**. Unlike InDesign CS, which required a special PageMaker plug-in pack to access this toolbar, InDesign CS2 makes the **PageMaker toolbar** readily available—no plug-in needed. This is a great bonus for those of us making the switch from PageMaker, because the toolbar contains the shortcuts and tools that PageMaker users are familiar with.

Even as a QuarkXPress user, I like the PageMaker toolbar because it gives me shortcuts to commonly used features and palettes in the program. It also allows you to create bulleted and numbered lists, and to add or delete pages from your document easily. We will discuss this toolbar in more detail in Chapter 2, "*Interface.*"

Shortcuts

In every program, you are likely to adopt some of the shortcut keystrokes that speed up your work process. In PageMaker and InDesign CS2, some of those widely used shortcuts vary. This can cause some unnecessary fumbling to remember what the new ones are in InDesign CS2. As with QuarkXPress, PageMaker users can also set their program preferences to match those they used in PageMaker.

By going to **Edit > Keyboard Shortcuts** and choosing from the list of shortcut sets, you can see that shortcuts for PageMaker 7.0 are available. We will discuss how to set your shortcuts in more depth in Chapter 2, "*Interface.*"

```
✓ Default
  Shortcuts for PageMaker 7.0
  Shortcuts for QuarkXPress 4.0
```

New Features in InDesign CS2

InDesign CS2 has an amazing number of new features, making the program even easier and more productive. The chart below shows the critical new features of the program in relation to InDesign CS. This may be helpful for those of you trying to decide whether or not to upgrade. For those of you new to InDesign altogether, this chart may give you an idea of the program's overall capabilities. To view a full list of new features, you can also visit Adobe's Web site at: **http://www.adobe.com/products/ indesign/newfeatures2.html**.

New Features in InDesign CS2

Feature	Description
Welcome Screen	The Welcome Screen is now common among all the Adobe applications within the Creative Suite 2 (CS2). When you first launch the program, you are greeted by this dialog box. The Welcome Screen is great for finding out about new features, tutorials, and cool extras that are on the install disk. It also allows for quick access to creating new documents, opening existing documents, and showing where to find templates. You'll learn more about the Welcome Screen in Chapter 2, "*Interface.*"
New keyboard shortcuts	In InDesign CS, the PageMaker plug-in pack offered several advantages, like using your PageMaker 7.0. Now, in InDesign CS2, the PageMaker features from the plug-in pack are installed automatically. You'll learn more about keyboard shortcuts in Chapter 2, "*Interface.*"
Adobe Bridge	The Adobe Bridge is a file browser that will work across all the Adobe Creative Suite 2 applications. Using the Adobe Bridge, you will be able to track content, add metadata, browse for files, and much more. When you open the Adobe Bridge, you also gain access to tips and tricks, the Adobe User Forums, templates, and more. You'll learn more about the Adobe Bridge in Chapter 3, "*Setting Up Documents.*"
Save backward to InDesign CS	Save InDesign CS2 documents for use in InDesign CS by exporting as the Exchange file format. You'll learn how to save backward-compatible files in Chapter 14, "*Output and Export.*"
Drag and drop text editing	Drag and drop selected text into another text frame, document, or page, or into the Find/Change dialog box. You'll learn how to drag and drop text in Chapter 4, "*Working with Text.*"
Dictionary management	Reference more than one user dictionary across a workgroup. Create unique dictionaries, and import or export word lists. You'll learn more about dictionary management in Chapter 4, "*Working with Text.*"
Dynamic spell checking	When turned on, InDesign checks spelling as you type and offers alternative spellings. You'll learn more about dynamic spell checking in Chapter 4, "*Working with Text.*"

continues on next page

New Features in InDesign CS2 *continued*	
Feature	**Description**
Automatic text correction	A preference setting that gives InDesign the power to correct capitalizations and misspellings from a dictionary that you provide. You'll learn more about automatic text correction in Chapter 4, "*Working with Text.*"
Quick apply	Search any and all available styles (paragraph, character, object) and apply them to text or graphics. You'll learn how to quickly apply formatting in Chapter 6, "*Type Styles.*"
Unformatted paste	When pasting text from other programs or from within an InDesign document, paste without its original formatting. It will assume the formatting of the text frame you paste into. You'll learn how to paste unformatted text in Chapter 4, "*Working with Text.*"
Overset text indicator	In the **Story Editor**, view any overset text. The overset text is indicated by the red sideline and the overset container separating it from the visible text. You'll learn more about the overset text indicator in Chapter 6, "*Type Styles.*"
WSIWYG font preview	Preview the font family from the **Type** menu, **Control** palette, or **Character** palette. You'll learn more about WYSIWYG font preview in Chapter 4, "*Working with Text.*"
Footnotes	Apply footnotes within text, controlling their numbering, appearance, etc. Also, import footnotes from Word, RTF, InDesign, and Tagged Text files. You'll learn how to create footnotes in Chapter 13, "*Long-Document Tools.*"
Text formatting enhancements	New Features for Indents, Paragraph Alignments, Hyphenations, Lists, and Inline graphics (anchored objects). You'll learn more about text formatting enhancements in Chapter 5, "*Typography in InDesign.*"
Styles	Select a subset of styles when loading them from another InDesign document. Overwrite or rename duplicate styles. You'll learn more about styles in Chapter 6, "*Type Styles.*"
Color management improvements	Maintain common color settings throughout the Creative Suite applications. You'll learn more about color management improvements in Chapter 14, "*Output and Export.*"

continues on next page

New Features in InDesign CS2 *continued*	
Feature	**Description**
Swatches	Save swatches to an external file that can be shared between documents. You'll learn more about how to export swatches in Chapter 7, "*Working with Color.*"
Layer visibility	When placing PSD (Photoshop format) files, you can define which layers will be visible, choose from layer comps, and choose to override or use the saved layer visibility states from Photoshop, if the file is edited in Photoshop. You'll learn more about layer visibility in Chapter 8, "*Bringing in Graphics.*"
Multipage PDFs	PDF files can be placed into an InDesign document one page at a time or multiple pages at once. Separate layers from a layered PDF can also be made visible or hidden when placing the file. You'll learn more about placing multipage PDFs in Chapter 8, "*Bringing in Graphics.*"
Anchored objects	InDesign now has the ability to place Anchored Objects in line with text. These are great for sidebars and callouts within the text. The anchored object (image, etc.) travels with the text as it moves in the text frame. You'll learn more about anchored objects in Chapter 8, "*Bringing in Graphics.*"
Object styles	Object styles allow users to apply object-level formatting to things like frames, text and more. They are similar to paragraph and character styles but can apply to objects. You'll learn more about Object styles in Chapter 9, "*Vector Artwork.*"
Transformations	Repeat a transformation on an object, such as scale or rotate, or apply several transformations at once. You'll learn to use transformations in Chapter 9, "*Vector Artwork.*"
Fill content proportionally	Fit a placed image into its frame without any white space left between it and the frame. It is in addition to the other Fitting menu commands. You'll learn how to fill content proportionally in Chapter 8, "*Bringing in Graphics.*"

continues on next page

New Features in InDesign CS2 *continued*	
Feature	**Description**
Frame-based grids	Until now, a baseline grid had to be set at the document level. InDesign CS2 allows you to set up a baseline grid for a single text frame. Also, your baseline grid can be measured from the top of the margin instead of the top of the page. You'll learn more about frame-based grids in Chapter 13, "*Long-Document Tools.*"
Locking column guides	Column guides can lock independently from the ruler guides. You will learn how to lock the column guides in Chapter 4, "*Working with Text.*"
Frame shapes	InDesign now supports the ability to change the shape of frames. You will learn more about changing frame shapes in Chapter 9, "*Vector Artwork.*"
Data merge enhancements	InDesign allows you to put placeholders on master pages. This allows you to update data fields automatically.
QuarkXPress Passport support	InDesign CS2 now supports the ability to open and convert QuarkXPress Passport documents. You will learn how to do this in Chapter 3, "*Setting Up Documents.*"

After looking at the new features of InDesign CS2, it's time to get into some hands-on experience. Starting with your workspace in Chapter 2, this book will take you through the program, showing you not only how the program works but also why it functions as it does.

2

Interface

| The Welcome Screen | Interface Overview |
| The Toolbox | Toolbox Fly-Out Menus | InDesign Palettes |
| Collapsing and Grouping Palettes |
| Moving and Resizing Docked or Collapsed Palettes |
| Moving the Control Palette | Moving the PageMaker Toolbar |
| Resetting and Saving Workspace Settings |

chap_02

InDesign CS2
HOT CD-ROM

With the advent of the Creative Suite 2, Adobe has given each of the suite's individual programs a consistent interface. For those of us who are used to being productive in a program like Photoshop, moving to a program like InDesign and getting right to work is much easier, mainly due to the consistent tools, workspace resets, and palettes among the Creative Suite 2 programs. This chapter will take you through the interface and how it can be used to your advantage when working within InDesign CS2 and among the Creative Suite 2 programs.

The chapter begins with an introduction to the menus and toolbars and works its way through palette positioning. You will learn how this program's interface can resemble other layout programs, discover how to reset your workspace, and save your preferred workspace layout. You will also learn how to create keyboard shortcuts.

Consider this chapter a necessary path on the journey to your understanding of InDesign CS2. Many of us jump forward, ignoring these most basic concepts. But an effective understanding of how to make the tools work for you is essential in working smarter, not harder, within InDesign CS2.

The Welcome Screen

Most of the Creative Suite 2 programs open upon launch with the Welcome Screen, which gets you started in the program. InDesign CS had a welcome screen as well, but it only appeared after you installed the available PageMaker plug-in pack, so many of us didn't see it.

The Welcome Screen is an effective tool to get a jump on opening a document or creating a new one, or even finding a template to start your project with. It offers a listing of new features with InDesign CS2, some helpful tutorials, and a list of cool extras that the program either comes with or can perform.

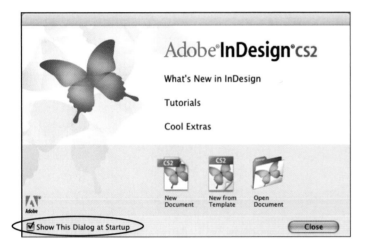

To use the Welcome Screen, you need to select an option. The screen then disappears until you launch the program again (it displays on program launch).

Note: If you click **What's New in InDesign**, you need to have an Internet connection. It takes you to the Adobe Web site. Clicking **Tutorials** takes you to tutorials in the Adobe Help Center, and clicking **Cool Extras** requires a PDF reader like Adobe Reader to view it, but it shows you some extra features.

Note: If you close the Welcome Screen, you can always open it up again by choosing **Help >
Welcome Screen.**

If you decide not to have the Welcome Screen appear every time the program is launched, turn off the **Show This Dialog at Startup** option in the lower-left corner of the Welcome Screen.

If you click the **New from Template** selection, you are taken into the **Adobe Bridge**. The Adobe Bridge software is a file browser used across the Creative Suite 2 with InDesign CS2. This allows you to search for files, work with projects, view tips and tricks, and more.

When taken to the Adobe Bridge (it will launch), you will be able to search for, preview, and launch templates that come with InDesign CS2, as well as templates you have created. Templates are used to start typical design projects. InDesign comes with templates for business documents, brochures, and more. Use the Adobe Bridge application to browse, search for, add, and delete templates, and more. The templates live in C:\Program Files\Common Files\Adobe\Templates\InDesign (Windows) or MacintoshHD:Library/Application Support/Adobe/Templates/InDesign (Mac).

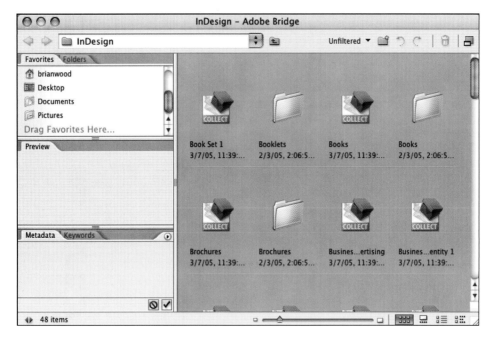

Note: Several of the Adobe Bridge functions require an Internet connection to reach.

Interface Overview

In this chapter, you are going to explore the interface of InDesignCS2. InDesign hasn't changed much since version 3 (CS), but a few new palettes have made their way into the InDesign CS2 palette mix. As I mentioned in Chapter 1, if you are new to InDesign but have used other Adobe applications like Illustrator or Photoshop, you will feel relatively comfortable with the tools and palettes in general.

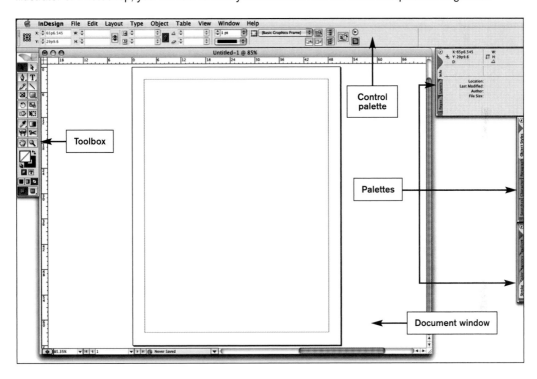

Opening InDesign CS2 opens the **Control** palette, **Toolbox**, and several default palettes. You can change how this interface appears, and will do so throughout this chapter. If you have used any other Adobe application, namely Illustrator or Photoshop, you will notice a similarity in the workspace layout, **Toolbox**, and palettes.

Tip: At times you will want to temporarily hide all the palettes to see the document window by itself. Pressing the **Tab** key hides all the palettes and the **Toolbox.** If you want to just hide the palettes, press **Shift+Tab**. Pressing **Shift+Tab** again causes the palettes to reappear in the workspace.

The Toolbox

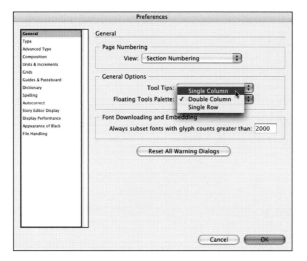

The **Toolbox** in InDesign CS2 resides in the upper-left corner of the workspace and can be moved around the workspace using the bar at the top. The InDesign CS2 **Toolbox** is very similar to that of InDesign CS. The only modification is the addition of the **Position** tool, and that was available in the PageMaker plug-in pack for InDesign CS.

Note: When you click the InDesign **Butterfly** icon at the top of the **Toolbox**, you are taken to the InDesign homepage of the Adobe Web site. Each tool in the **Toolbox** also has a shortcut associated with it that can be found in the tooltip that shows when you hover over the tool.

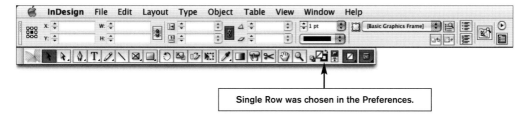

Single Row was chosen in the Preferences.

Tip: The **Toolbox** can be changed in shape to either a double column of tools, a single row of tools, or a single column of tools. For those of you who are PageMaker users, the single row of tools is familiar. You can set the **Toolbox** in **Edit > Preferences > General** (Windows) or **InDesign > Preferences > General** (Mac) under the **Floating Tools Palette** drop-down menu.

Toolbox Fly-Out Menus

When working with the **Toolbox** in InDesign CS2, you'll notice that many of the tool buttons have small arrows in the lower-right corners (circled below). Click, hold down your mouse button, and pause over a tool with an arrow, and a fly-out menu appears. These fly-out menus show more tools that are either similar to or subsets of the main tools on the **Toolbox.**

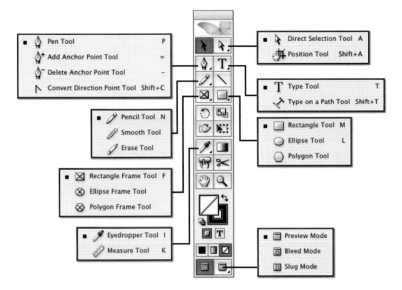

Tip: Taking a look at the fly-out menus, if you look to the right of the tool name, you see a shortcut to invoke the tool itself. For instance, look at the **Pen** tool above. If you look to the right of the words "**Pen Tool,**" all the way at the right edge of the box, you'll see the letter "**P.**" This is the shortcut for the tool itself.

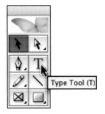

The main tools in the Toolbox also have shortcut keys associated with them. To access a shortcut, hover over a tool, and you see a tooltip show up. It gives you the name of the tool as well as a letter in parentheses. This is the shortcut you can key in when you want to reach that tool.

InDesign Palettes

Palettes in InDesign are very interesting, indeed. In most applications, you are fighting for your virtual life to keep your work area cleared of palettes. You usually only want them when they are necessary. InDesign is no different. Thankfully, though, the Adobe engineers put some serious thought into all their Adobe apps and decided to make it easier for us to keep things orderly.

InDesign palettes allow us to control the workspace and access certain features such as creating colors and working with pages. They come in several forms. At the top of the screen is the **Control** palette, which allows you to access features that depend on what you have selected.

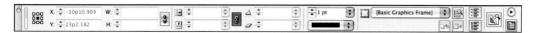

On the right side of the screen, you see groups of palettes collapsed. InDesign has a lot of palettes, so Adobe has come up with a way to enable them to dock and collapse on the side of the screen in groups. To view a certain palette, click its tab. If the palette was collapsed, it slides out to come into view.

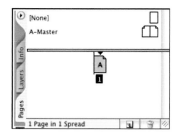

Your palettes can be opened from the **Window** menu and are organized in alphabetical order, with several hidden under arrows. In the next few exercises, you are going to learn how to control the InDesign palettes effectively.

I. ——————————**Collapsing and Grouping Palettes**

InDesign palettes are docked on the side of the workspace by default. You need to be able to access them, hide them, and generally work with them to make your life easier. InDesign lets you hide them, pull them out of their groups, or dock them into different groups. To start out with the palettes in their default locations, choose **Window > Workspace > Default** from the menus to reset the workspace to its default position. You will learn more about this feature in Exercise 5, "Resetting and Saving Workspace Settings," later in this chapter.

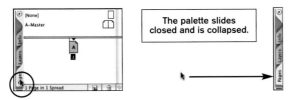

1. In InDesign, click the **Pages** palette tab once. You will see the palette group collapse onto the side of your workspace or open if it was already collapsed.

Note: *To see another palette, you can click its tab. For instance, if you collapsed the **Pages** palette by clicking on the **Pages** tab and then wanted to see the **Info** palette, click the **Info** tab, and the group will open again with the **Info** palette up front.*

Note: *The palettes shown here are examples where a document is open (without a document some of the palettes, such as the **Pages** palette, appear to be blank). You do not have to have a document open to proceed through these exercises.*

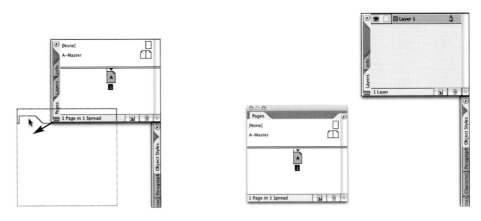

2. In InDesign, if you'd like to remove a palette from the side of the workspace, you need to remove it from its group. Drag the **Pages** palette by its tab into the workspace. Place the freed palette anywhere you'd like within your workspace. This gives you a single palette that can be moved into another group, kept by itself, or docked in another group.

Tip: To open and close a palette completely, first you need to pull it out of its group. Then you can click the close button. The close button on the Mac is the red button located in the upper-left corner of most palettes. On the Windows platform, the top bar is blue and the close button is an **X** located in the upper-right corner.

Most of you will want to dock your palettes back onto the side of the workspace in an existing group or on their own after you've pulled them out.

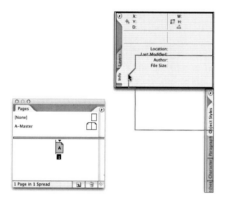

3. You are going to take the **Pages** palette and group it into the palette group you pulled it from in the previous exercise. Click the **Pages** tab, and drag the palette over the top of the group with the **Info** palette. The palette turns into an outline, and the tab turns vertically. Let go of the tab at this point. You just grouped the **Pages** palette back with the **Info** and **Layers** palettes.

Something interesting to note is the order in which your palettes appear. As you drag palettes into a group on the side of the workspace, the newest addition appears at the top of the group. To change this order, you can drag each of the palettes out and drag them back in one at a time.

4. Next you'll collapse a palette on the side of the workspace outside an existing group. Drag the **Pages** palette by its tab out of the palette group containing the **Info** and **Layers** palettes.

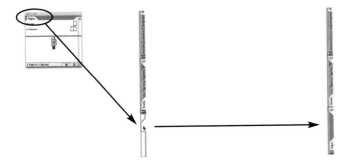

5. Drag the **Pages** palette to an empty area on the side of the workspace. Get it close to the edge of the workspace (you'll need to go pretty far over toward the edge of your screen if your program is maximized). The palette appears in outline form and goes vertical. Let go, and the **Pages** palette is collapsed by itself on the side of the workspace.

*Note: Depending on the size of your screen, there may not be room enough to collapse the **Pages** palette on the side of the workspace.*

 MOVIE | Collapsing and Grouping Palettes

To learn more about docking and undocking palettes, check out **palettes.mov** in the **movies** folder on the **InDesign CS2 HOT CD-ROM**.

TIP | Collapsing Palettes on the Left Side of the Workspace

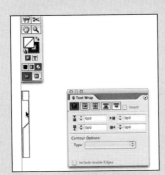

You can also collapse palettes on the left side of your workspace. I do this all the time with some palettes like the **Text Wrap** palette (**Window > Text Wrap**), for instance. It works the same way as Step 4. The only difference is that you need to drag it below the **Toolbox** if you have it on the left side of the workspace in the default location.

TIP | Docking Palettes Vertically

Another great way to dock palettes that is consistent with Photoshop and Illustrator is to dock palettes vertically.

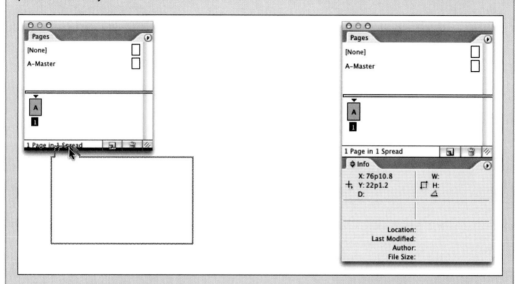

Palettes that are not docked or collapsed can be docked vertically. Click and drag a palette by the tab (such as the **Info** palette) to the lower edge of another palette. A black line will appear indicating that the palette will be docked. Release the mouse and the palettes are docked vertically. To undock either palette, click and drag either of the tabs away from the group.

Moving and Resizing Docked or Collapsed Palette Groups

You may, at times, want to change the order of the palette groups located on the side of the workspace, or they may be overlapping a bit. In this short exercise, you will move those docked groups around.

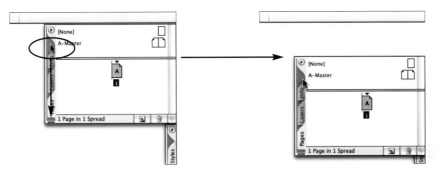

1. To move a docked group, click within the gray area of the palette group (it can be collapsed or not at this point), and drag it up or down to move its position on the side of the workspace.

There is going to come a time when your palette groups are overlapping, or you want to see more of a docked palette. InDesign allows you to resize palette groups.

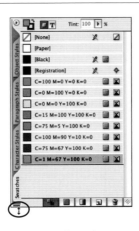

2. Place your cursor over the lower-left edge of the palette group containing the **Swatches** palette. A double arrow appears when you hover over the line.

Note: *If the **Swatches** palette is still collapsed, click the **Swatches** tab to open it.*

3. Click and drag to change the size of the **Swatches** palette group.

Tip: *By resizing the palette groups, you can fit quite a few of them vertically on your screen if your monitor is resolution challenged.*

3. —————————Moving the Control Palette

The **Control** palette in InDesign is where most of your object and text formatting can take place. It's contextual, so when you click an object or text, the **Control** palette displays the attributes for whatever is selected. The Creative Suite 2 has provided a **Control** palette in all its major applications. The **Control** palette is docked at the top of the screen under the menus by default. You can move it, undock it, and move it again, depending on your work style and preferences.

The **Control** palette is just one of the many places you can go to find formatting, but it's the closest at hand. In this exercise, you will learn how to dock and undock the **Control** palette.

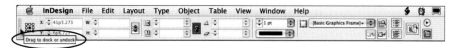

1. Place your cursor over the left edge of the **Control** palette. You see a vertical bar (not to be confused with the blue bar on the left side of the **Control** palette on Windows). Hover over this, and a tooltip appears explaining that you can drag to dock or undock the **Control** palette.

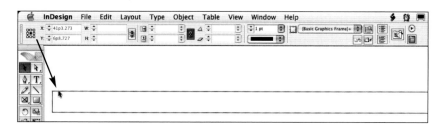

2. Click and drag, pulling the **Control** palette away from the menus above it.

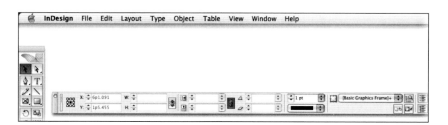

3. Place the **Control** palette wherever you like.

*Note: To move the **Control** palette around the workspace, you can drag it by the bar at the left edge (this is the blue bar on Windows and the gray bar on a Mac). To dock it back up top, click the vertical bar (once again, not to be confused with the blue bar on the left side of the **Control** palette on Windows), and drag it underneath the menus.*

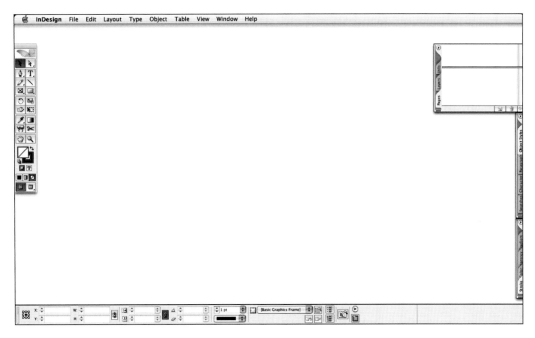

Note: The *Control* palette can be docked either at the top of the screen or at the bottom, which gives you a bit more flexibility when it comes to your workspace options.

TIP | Moving the Control Palette Another Way

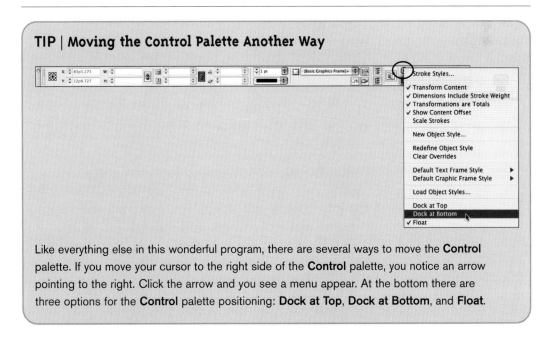

Like everything else in this wonderful program, there are several ways to move the **Control** palette. If you move your cursor to the right side of the **Control** palette, you notice an arrow pointing to the right. Click the arrow and you see a menu appear. At the bottom there are three options for the **Control** palette positioning: **Dock at Top**, **Dock at Bottom**, and **Float**.

4. ——————————Moving the PageMaker Toolbar

For those of you who are switching or have switched to InDesign from PageMaker, the transition can be a little rough. Any efficiency you may have had in PageMaker suddenly seems as if it's gone out the window. Well, Adobe has some help for you in the form of the **PageMaker** toolbar.

The **PageMaker** toolbar mimics a toolbar in PageMaker–complete with similar tools and functions. This toolbar made its first appearance in InDesign back in version CS with the installation of the PageMaker plug-in pack. Now it comes in InDesign CS2 by default. In this exercise, you will learn where to find it and how to move it around the workspace.

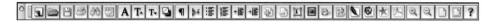

1. To open the **PageMaker** toolbar, choose **Window > PageMaker Toolbar**.

Even though the PageMaker toolbar looks very much like the Control palette, it actually shares only a few features, like font size. The PageMaker toolbar is meant for those who are transitioning from PageMaker, but it can be very useful for opening palettes and per-forming other functions, like creating lists.

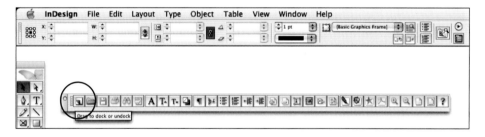

2. To move the **PageMaker** toolbar in the workspace, drag it by the bar at the left end of the palette. The bar on the Mac has a dot, which is how you close the toolbar. On the Windows platform, the bar is blue and there is an **X** to close the toolbar.

3. As with the **Control** palette, you can dock the **PageMaker** toolbar at the top, below the menus (also below the **Control** palette if it's showing). Drag the toolbar by the small vertical "gripper" bar at the left end of the toolbar. This is just to the left of the **New Document** icon. If you hover over it, you'll see a tooltip that says "Drag to dock or undock."

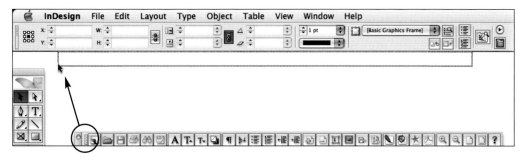

4. To dock the **PageMaker** toolbar under the **Control** palette, click on the small vertical bar and drag it to the top of the workspace (below the **Control** palette if it's showing).

Tip: You can actually drag the toolbar to the top, right, left, or bottom of the workspace, and InDesign will dock it!

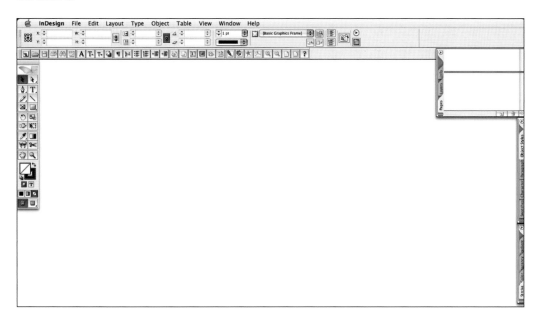

*The **PageMaker** toolbar is now fully docked at the top of the workspace, below the **Control** palette.*

TIP | Resetting Your Workspace

One of the worst things about working in a program like InDesign is that at some point or another, you're going to get your palettes in such a state that you'll wish they could magically go back to where they started from. Well, they can.

InDesign gives you the ability to reset your workspace. It essentially sets the workspace up so that all your toolbars and palettes go back to their factory default positions. Here you'll learn how to accomplish that.

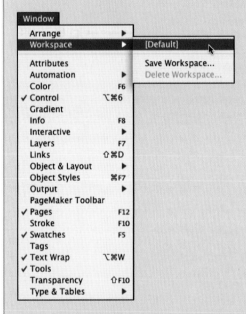

Choose **Window > Workspace > [Default]**, and your workspace resets itself. You may want to do this every time you start, for a clean workspace slate, because InDesign remembers where your palettes were when you closed and opens the same palettes in the same locations next time you launch InDesign.

5.———————Resetting and Saving Workspace Settings

Most of the time, I prefer to set my workspace to mirror my work style for a given project. I group certain palettes together, dock them on both the left and right sides of the workspace, and show my **PageMaker** toolbar at times. This means that moving these palettes around where I need them could be a big time waster. Fortunately, in InDesign you can set up what palettes are open and their positions and then save your workspace. Then you can click a button or use a shortcut to make your workspace go back to the way you originally set it up! In this exercise, you'll learn how to do just that.

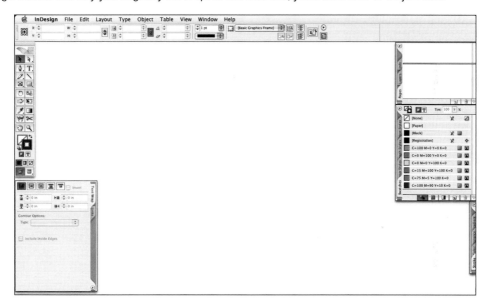

1. Set up your workspace to reflect how you want to work with your toolbars and palettes. The different palettes that are available are located under the **Window** menu.

*In the above illustration, the **Text Wrap** palette (**Window > Text Wrap**) and the **Links** palette (**Window > Links**) have been docked on the left side of the workspace.*

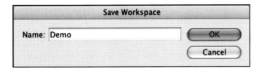

2. To save your workspace so you can reset it, choose **Window > Workspace > Save Workspace**. In the **Save Workspace** dialog box, type a name in the **Name** field, and click **OK** to accept it.

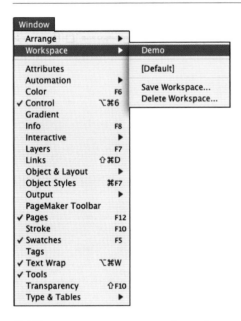

3. Whenever you want to reset the workspace to this saved custom configuration, choose **Window > Workspace > Demo (the name of your workspace)**.

Saving workspaces is great for those of us who have multiple users on a single computer!

Working with Palette Menus

InDesign CS2 has an abundance of palettes and menus, all to hold the large amount of program features. Within those palettes and toolbars, InDesign has features that are hidden under pop-up menus.
These pop-up menus are referred to as palette menus. Some of the features found in these menus are
found nowhere else in the program. One such palette menu that holds a lot of features is the **Pages**
palette menu.

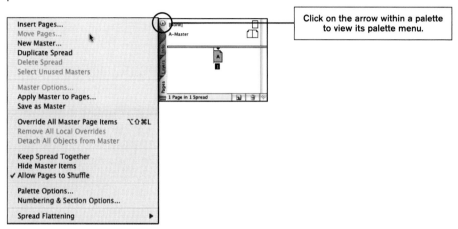

Click on the arrow within a palette
to view its palette menu.

All palettes have some sort of palette menu, including the **Control** palette, the **Toolbox**, and all the
docked palettes. Each palette (including the **Control** palette) allows access to the palette menu
either through the upper-left corner or upper-right corner, depending on whether the palette is
docked or collapsed.

InDesign Keyboard Shortcuts

Most programs have shortcuts, or ways to use your keyboard instead of your mouse to speed up
processes. InDesign is no exception. Not only does InDesign give you the option of using shortcuts,
but you can also change them to suit your needs. Also, if you are coming in from either PageMaker or
QuarkXPress, you might be concerned about losing productivity time if you are a shortcut user. Well,
fear not. InDesign lets QuarkXPress and PageMaker users leverage the shortcuts from those applications.

In this section, first you will learn how to change your shortcuts to match either PageMaker or
QuarkXPress, and then you will learn how you can customize your shortcuts to suit your needs.

BONUS EXERCISE | Customizing Your Keyboard Shortcuts

To learn how, check out **shortcuts.pdf** in the **bonus_exercises** folder on the **InDesign CS2 HOT CD-ROM**.

TIP | Using PageMaker or QuarkXPress Shortcuts in InDesign

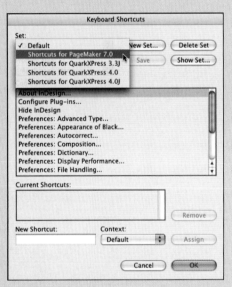

1. For those of us coming from either Adobe PageMaker or QuarkXPress, take heart. To use your shortcuts choose **Edit > Keyboard Shortcuts**.

2. Choose the program you'd like to use the shortcuts for from the **Set** pop-up menu.

3. Click **OK**.

This makes the general shortcuts the same as either PageMaker or QuarkXPress (depending on which you choose). There will be differences between some of the less widely used shortcuts, however.

TIP | Seeing All Your Shortcuts

Most likely you will see the keyboard shortcuts in the menus, next to the commands. But some shortcuts don't jump out at you, like the ones for changing your leading value and for increasing the size of your text. By choosing **Edit > Keyboard Shortcuts**, you can click the **Show Set** button (make sure you have the set you use chosen first from the **Set** pop-up menu).

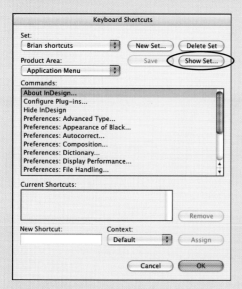

InDesign opens a list of all its features as a text file. This list will be pretty large because it contains all the features and commands, even if they don't have keyboard shortcuts assigned to them. This can be annoying at times, especially when you are looking for that one keyboard shortcut for, say, leading. You'll have to scroll through or find it through a **Find** or **Search** command in the text editor.

Tip: Here's how I handled my shortcuts. After I assigned any and all keyboard shortcuts I thought I might use, I went through the list in the text file and deleted any that didn't have relevance to what I do, or just didn't have a keyboard shortcut assigned. I then came up with a much-improved list that I printed and laminated as a quick reference for myself.

Now you've set up your workspace and learned how to use some aspects of the program's interface to your advantage. In the next chapter, you will learn how to set up a document using the first of several page layout projects that will take you through this book and InDesign CS2.

3

Setting Up Documents

chap_03

InDesign CS2
HOT CD-ROM

InDesign CS2 gives you options to create a multitude of different document types—business cards, bound textbooks, posters, advertisements, and many more. Each document type requires a unique approach, which is why document settings are so important.

In this chapter, you will learn how to set up documents for various document types, including how to control some of the more important application preferences in document setup. In addition, you will begin to understand how to navigate InDesign's document creation process using important tools such as guides, grids, and rulers. InDesign CS2 handles some of these tools differently from other page layout programs, like QuarkXPress and Adobe PageMaker, so understanding how InDesign handles these tools is critical in learning to work efficiently in the program from the start.

Opening InDesign Documents from Previous Versions

To convert previous versions of InDesign documents to the current version, simply choose **File > Open** to open the file.

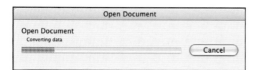

You need to keep a few things in mind when you do this, however:

- When you convert a document, you may see an alert message asking if you want to use the exception word list in the user dictionary or the one in the document. To maintain document integrity, you may need to keep the document's dictionary.

- If third-party plug-ins were used to create a document, check with the manufacturer of that plug-in to see if an update is available that is compatible with InDesign CS2. Otherwise, when the file is opened, any features applied with that third-party plug-in could be lost.

- Library files created in earlier versions of InDesign will open and convert in InDesign CS2. You will be asked to rename the library and save it to a location.

- Previous versions of InDesign, including CS.x, 2.x, and 1.x, can't open InDesign CS2 documents directly. That makes sense, since past versions of InDesign could not have predicted the new features in CS2. To work with CS2 files in older versions of the program, save the InDesign CS2 document in INX format (you will learn more about the INX format in Chapter 14, "*Output and Export*").

Opening QuarkXPress Files

InDesign can convert document and template files from QuarkXPress 3.3 or 4.1x. InDesign can also convert document and template files from QuarkXPress Passport 4.1x files, so you don't have to save Passport files as single-language files first. To open a QuarkXPress file, choose **File > Open** within InDesign CS2. If your QuarkXPress file is newer than 4.1x, you need to save backward-compatible documents. That can be quite a chore if you have QuarkXPress 6.x because you have to save back to 4.1x in two stages (from 6.x to 5.x, then from 5.x to 4.1x).

When you open a QuarkXPress file, InDesign converts the original file information to native InDesign information. Here are some things to look out for:

- To accurately convert text wrapping (known as runaround in QuarkXPress) applied in QuarkXPress, choose **Edit > Preferences > Composition > Text Wrap Only Affects Objects Beneath** (Windows) or **InDesign > Preferences > Composition > Text Wrap Only Affects Objects Beneath** (Mac).

- QuarkXPress color profiles are not recognized by InDesign CS2.

• Text and graphics links from QuarkXPress are preserved and appear in the Links palette.

Note: Embedded graphics—those added to the original document using the **Paste** command—are not converted.

• InDesign doesn't support OLE or Quark Xtensions. If you used them and then attempt to convert the file, either the picture won't show up or the file won't convert.

• QuarkXPress 3.3 HSB colors are converted to RGB, and colors from the color library are converted based on their CMYK values.

• QuarkXPress 4.1 HSB and LAB colors are converted to RGB, and colors from the color library are converted based on their RGB/CMYK values.

• To see a conversion chart showing what happens to Quark files, go to the Adobe Web site at **http://www.adobe.com/support/techdocs/329065.html**.

Opening a QuarkXPress Document or Template

Before opening a QuarkXPress document in InDesign CS2, Adobe recommends saving the file and all the links in the same folder. You should also make sure all the links in the QuarkXPress file are updated. Once those things are done, follow these steps:

1. Close the QuarkXPress document if it's open in Quark.

2. In InDesign, choose **File > Open**.

3. In the **Open a File** dialog box, choose a QuarkXPress file and click **Open** (on the Windows platform if the file doesn't appear, choose **QuarkXPress [3.3-4.1x]** from the **Files of Type** pop-up menu).

4. A dialog box usually appears to warn you about some problem. If you click **Close**, the dialog box disappears and you are faced with the newly converted file. If you click **Save**, InDesign saves the warning message into a text file. This isn't usually necessary, but you might want to refer back to the initial warning sometime to see what needs to be fixed. Some of the more common error messages you are likely to see are that the document is missing fonts (they are not installed on your machine), image links are broken, and certain types of grouped or locked objects are not recognized by InDesign.

Opening PageMaker Files

InDesign can convert document and template files from PageMaker 6.0 and later. When you open a PageMaker file, InDesign converts the original file information to an InDesign file.

Before opening the document in InDesign, you may want to try some of these tips:

• Make sure that all PageMaker documents and their links are copied to your hard disk before opening them in InDesign.

- Before converting the file in InDesign, open the file in PageMaker and do a **Save As** (instead of Save). You can use the same filename and replace the previous file. By using **Save As** instead of Save, you clear extraneous data from the file, which can facilitate the conversion to InDesign.

- Make sure that all necessary fonts are available in InDesign.

- Repair broken graphics links in the PageMaker publication.

- If you have a problem converting a large PageMaker document, divide it into smaller sets of pages and convert each document individually. This will isolate the problem.

A longer list of tips is available on Adobe's Web site at **http://www.adobe.com/support/techdocs/ 324329.html**. The site also displays a lengthy chart showing how different features from PageMaker translate to InDesign. The chart is divided into six sections: Publication Settings, Preferences, Page Layout Features, Text Attributes, Color, and Graphics and Objects. It's a fairly long list, but I recommend looking through it.

If you cannot open a corrupt PageMaker document in PageMaker, try opening it in InDesign. InDesign can recover most documents that PageMaker cannot open.

Opening a PageMaker Document or Template

As with a QuarkXPress conversion, before opening a PageMaker document in InDesign CS2, Adobe recommends saving the file and all the links in the same folder. You should also make sure all the links in the PageMaker file are updated. Once you've taken care of those items, you're ready to follow these instructions:

1. Close the PageMaker document if it's open in PageMaker.

2. In InDesign, choose **File > Open**.

3. In the **Open a File** dialog box, choose a PageMaker file and click **Open** (on the Windows platform if the file doesn't appear, choose **PageMaker [6.0-7.0]** from the **Files of Type** pop-up menu).

4. A dialog box usually appears to warn you about some problem. If you click **Close**, the dialog box disappears and you are faced with the newly converted file. If you click **Save**, InDesign saves the warning message into a text file. This isn't usually necessary, but you might want to refer back to the initial warning sometime to see what needs to be fixed. Some of the more common error messages you are likely to see are that the document is missing fonts (they are not installed on your machine), image links are broken, and certain types of grouped or locked objects are not recognized by InDesign.

I. _____**Setting Initial Preferences**

InDesign CS2 comes with a standard set of default preferences. For instance, by default, InDesign sets all your measurements to picas. The good news is that InDesign CS2 gives you the freedom to set preferences like measurements to suit your work style. While it may be tempting to get into the program right away, I highly recommend taking some time at the beginning to set your preferences to suit your needs. It can save you a lot of time in the long run. You can start by changing the units of measurement from picas to inches, since at least some of you are more comfortable working with inches. Remember, all the preferences are yours to tailor to your liking, so if you prefer picas, by all means leave that preference as is. This is just an exercise to introduce you to the process of customizing the program's preferences.

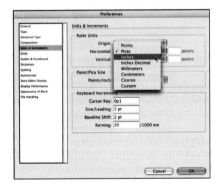

1. Choose **Edit > Preferences > Units & Increments** (Windows) or **InDesign > Preferences > Units & Increments** (Mac) to display the **Units & Increments** options.

Note: Setting your preferences in InDesign can be tricky. If you try to set a preference for global use—in other words, if you want all your InDesign documents to be measured in inches, not picas, from now on (for every new document)—close all documents first. If an InDesign file is open, the program assumes you want to apply the preference changes only to the open document. If no InDesign document is open when you change preferences, the program assumes you want to apply the changes globally.

2. In the **Ruler Units** section, select **Inches** from both the **Horizontal** and **Vertical** fields to set inches as your working measurement unit.

3. Click **OK**. You're now ready to move to the next exercise and set up your document.

Note: Many more preference settings are in this dialog box. You will look at them later in the book as their various functions are put into context.

The preferences you set here allow you to work in inches rather than picas throughout the exercises. In the next exercise, you will set up your initial document and learn about the different settings involved.

2. Creating a New Document

With your preferences in place, you can begin your first document. In this exercise, you will set up a new document, addressing all the settings that have the potential to make each document unique.

The first step is to create a document. As in most other programs, this function is found in the **File** menu. InDesign does provide a few more options under **File > New** than many other programs do. For now, however, you will concentrate on creating a document.

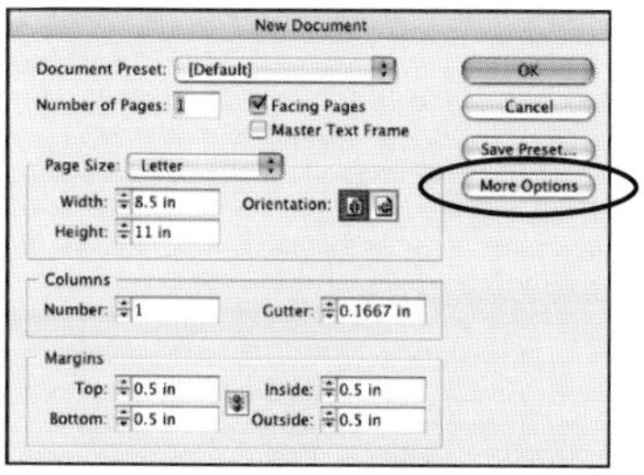

1. Choose **File > New > Document** to open the **New Document** dialog box.

Note: *Notice the* ***More Options*** *button? Click it and you see the dialog box expand a bit at the bottom, adding a few more items for you to look at. The button then changes to* ***Fewer Options.***

This section of the chapter reviews the settings in the ***New Document*** *dialog box. We'll wait until the end of the exercise to explore the* ***Document Preset*** *options. First, you will learn about* ***Number of Pages, Facing Pages,*** *and* ***Master Text Frame.***

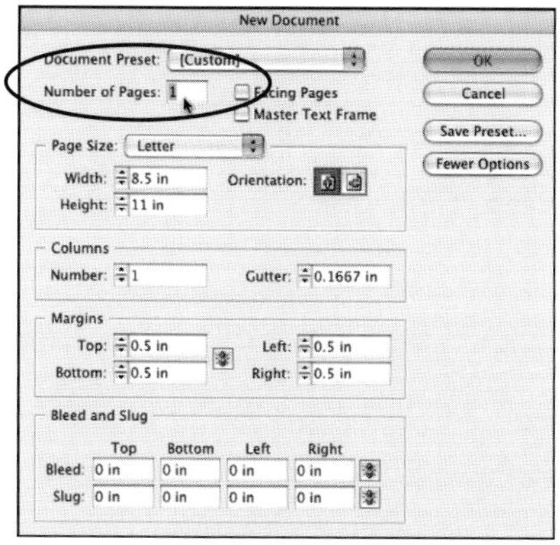

2. Leave the **Number of Pages** at the default setting of **1**. The **Number of Pages** setting enables you to decide how many pages you'd like to start with.

Tip: *You can add pages easily once the document is open. You will learn more about that in Chapter 10,* "Pages, Master Pages, and Layers."

---

3. **Facing Pages** is an important setting that we'll look at in later chapters. Deselect the check box to the left of **Facing Pages** for now. You are going to create a single-page document, so you don't need it on.

*Tip: Using InDesign's **Facing Pages** setting, you can create a document that has left and right pages facing each other in a double-page spread. A good example is a bound book (like this one) or a saddle-stitched magazine. You should deselect this option if you plan to have each page stand alone (or if you are creating a single-page document). Another reason you might want to turn this option off is to have a bleed in the gutter between pages in a spread.*

4. Leave **Master Text Frame** deselected for this document.

*Note: The **Master Text Frame** setting can be useful, but only in certain instances. If this box is checked, InDesign places a single large text frame on the master page (which will be covered in Chapter 10, "Pages, Master Pages, and Layers"), allowing you to see a text frame on every page of your document as soon as you start. This can be good, but it can also be problematic when dealing with master pages. This will be discussed when we get into master pages. For now, turn it off.*

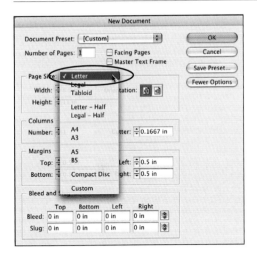

5. From the **Page Size** pop-up menu, choose **Letter** to create an 8.5 × 11-inch document. Those page dimensions are automatically preset when you choose the **Letter** option.

*Note: Notice the **Custom** option in the **Page Size** pop-up menu? To set up a document that has unique page dimensions, you can simply type the width and height into the fields directly below the **Page Size** pop-up menu. The **Custom** option shows up automatically from the **Page Size** pop-up menu.*

6. The next step is to set the page orientation. The orientation determines which side of the page is at the top, bottom, left, and right. You're probably familiar with the two available options, portrait and landscape. **Portrait** is the default orientation setting; leave it that way.

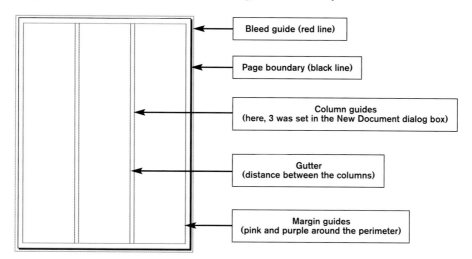

Bleed guide (red line)

Page boundary (black line)

Column guides
(here, 3 was set in the New Document dialog box)

Gutter
(distance between the columns)

Margin guides
(pink and purple around the perimeter)

The rest of the settings are best shown visually, using the image above. The document dimensions are represented by the page boundary (black line) surrounding the page.

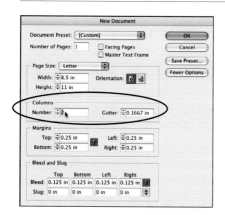

7. In the **Columns** options, change **Number** to **3** and **Gutter** to **0.1875 in.** (If you are using units other than inches, see the **Tip** sidebar "Unit Conversion Made Easy," on page 51.)

*The columns are guides that are drawn on the page, splitting it up into either a single column (which is the default) or multiple columns (depending on how many columns you want to divide pages into). The **Column** setting is applied to all the pages in your document. At the moment, you are creating a single-page document, so that isn't an issue that you need to consider.*

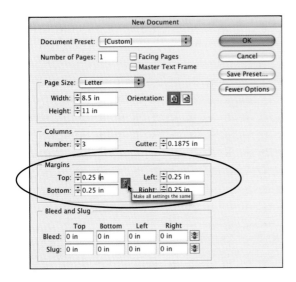

8. By default, all margins are set to 0.5 inch, which is useful in discouraging you from placing objects like images and text at the edge of the document. Change the top margin to **0.25 in**. With the cursor in the **Top** margin field, click the **Broken Link** ( ) icon to make all four margin settings the same.

*The **Margins** options, which are below the **Columns** options that were just discussed, are particularly important for documents that you want to print. The **0.25 in** setting tells you to stay one-quarter inch from the edges so you can print this document on your desktop printer or any other output device that can't image to the page edge. Margin settings can serve other purposes, but for now, leave them as they are.*

*Tip: InDesign gives you a leg up when setting margins. If you type in a value in one of the margin fields and click the **Broken Link** icon ( ) all the margins become the same, and the **Broken Link** icon changes to the **Link** icon ( ). It's a great way to save time and ensure consistency.*

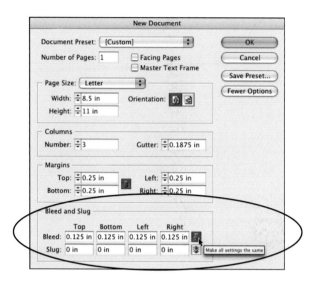

9. Click **More Options**, and the **Bleed and Slug** settings become visible at the bottom of the dialog box. In the **Top** field, type **0.125**. (If you set up your preferences using inches as your units, then just type **0.125**. If the units are something other than inches, you need to type **0.125 in**—notice the inch mark. The measurement units are then converted into your chosen unit when you click another field.)

10. Click the **Broken Link** icon to the right of the **Bleed and Slug** settings to make all the **Bleed** settings the same.

This one-eighth inch (or however much you need) is referred to as the bleed. Bleed guides are simply lines drawn one-eighth inch off the edge of the page (or whatever you set them to). With the bleed guides set, you can pull your pictures and text to set points outside the normal boundaries of the page to ensure that you have a little room for error in the trimming process.

Bleeds can be useful in a variety of circumstances. For instance, if you are creating a magazine cover in InDesign and you want to cover the entire front page with a photo, you need to use bleeds. If you place the image on the page, making sure it covers the entire page from edge to edge and corner to corner, you may run into problems when you see the final printed piece. That magazine cover is cut out of a large sheet run on a commercial press, and the cutting is never perfect. As a result, some magazine covers are cut tighter than others. To avoid this, make sure that any objects (your cover picture, in this case) are always pulled beyond the edge of the page just a little bit—usually one-eighth inch. This provides a safety net for that cutting margin of error

Note: *The bleed is typically set only around the edges of the page that are going to have a bleed.*

11. You are not going to use the document's slug area in this project, so for now, leave all of the **Slug** fields set at **0 in**. You will use slugs in a later project.

Not to be confused with the slimy creature you might find in your garden, a slug is an area you can add to any side of a document to convey useful information such as creation date, modification dates, colors, and fonts. A slug can be printing or nonprinting, and the slug guides allow you to determine the size and location of the slug. When you set slug guides in the **New Document** *dialog box, the guides appear off the edge of the page (many people choose to place them off the bottom edge of the page). The information won't print unless you check a box in the* **Print** *dialog box instructing InDesign to print the slug. The size of the slug depends on how much information you anticipate needing to include in it.*

12. Keep the **New Document** dialog box open for the next exercise, in which you will learn how to save the presets you just created.

NOTE | What Is a Slug?

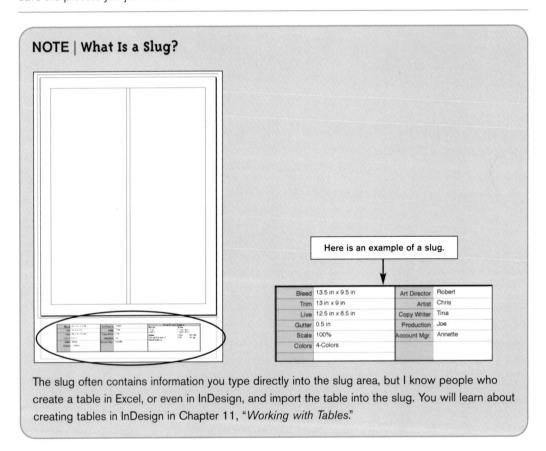

Here is an example of a slug.

Bleed	13.5 in x 9.5 in		Art Director	Robert
Trim	13 in x 9 in		Artist	Chris
Live	12.5 in x 8.5 in		Copy Writer	Tina
Gutter	0.5 in		Production	Joe
Scale	100%		Account Mgr.	Annette
Colors	4-Colors			

The slug often contains information you type directly into the slug area, but I know people who create a table in Excel, or even in InDesign, and import the table into the slug. You will learn about creating tables in InDesign in Chapter 11, "*Working with Tables.*"

TIP | Unit Conversion Made Easy

Let's say that you set the units in the program preferences (see "Setting Initial Preferences" earlier in this chapter) to picas, and, for whatever reason, you now need to set the gutter size in a new document to inches. InDesign lets you make the change directly in the **Gutter** field.

Note: The instructions that follow work in almost every dialog box that uses unit measurements.

1. Let's say you are working in picas, and you are given measurements in inches for the gutter. In the **New Document** dialog box, set the number of columns to **3**.

2. Type **0.1875 in** (you could also type in **.1875in**—without a zero or a space) in the **Gutter** field. Press **Enter** or **Return**.

3. InDesign automatically converts inches to the default units (picas, in this example).

Tip: A tip within a tip, who would've thought? To select any field in any InDesign dialog box or palette, you don't need to highlight the field. Instead, you can simply click the field name—in this case, **Gutter**—and InDesign automatically places the cursor in the field and highlights its contents so you can make any necessary changes.

Here is a chart showing the conversion units.

To get these units:	Type any of these after the number:
Inches	i, in, inch, or "
Picas	p
Points	pt
Millimeters	mm

3. _____Saving Document Presets

In the previous section, you created a new document using settings in the **New Document** dialog box. Now you are almost ready to start working on the file. Before clicking **OK** in the **New Document** dialog box, we need to discuss one final item–the **Save Preset** button. **Save Preset** allows you to retain document settings so you can easily create the same type of document again. You can save one set of presets or many.

If you do save your document settings, InDesign keeps that setting name in the **New Document** dialog box under the **Document Preset** pop-up menu.

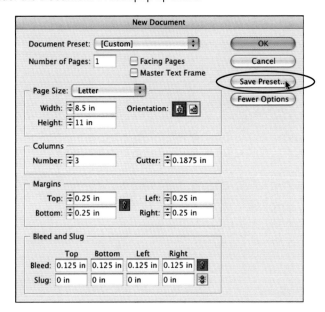

1. In the **New Document** dialog box still open from the previous exercise, click **Save Preset**.

2. Name the preset by typing into the **Save Preset As** field. I usually name it according to the document's dimensions and purpose. Click **OK**.

3. Now select the preset you just created from the **Document Preset** pop-up menu, and click **OK**.

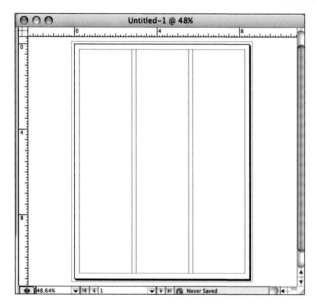

4. You have just created an InDesign document. Keep the file open. Next you will learn how to save an InDesign file.

*Note: After saving a preset, if you choose it from the **Document Preset** pop-up menu and change any of its properties, the **Document Preset** field automatically switches to **Custom.** That's just InDesign's way of letting you know that you have strayed from one of the saved presets.*

TIP | Creating Custom Page Sizes

Note: This tip isn't for the faint of heart. I recommend that anytime you change things in the application folder itself, you make copies of the original files, just in case.

If you are constantly having to change page sizes, or if your company uses a set standard that deviates from the page sizes preset by InDesign, you can add your own. This feature may be a bit off the beaten path for some of you, but it can be very useful, especially since InDesign lets you share custom page sizes with other users.

First, make sure InDesign is closed. Then go to the InDesign application folder. Once in the application folder, open the **Presets** folder. Within the **Presets** folder, InDesign holds a variety of files that it uses for things like the shortcut sets you have saved, your saved workspaces, and your custom page sizes. You see a text file named **New Doc Sizes**. Double-click that file to open it. It should launch a text editor, such as Wordpad or Notepad. If it doesn't, you need to open it within a text-editing program like Microsoft Word.

The text file has instructions on how to add your own page size presets. I added a page size called "**Certificate**" with a page dimension of 11 × 9 inches.

Save the text file and close it. *(**Don't rename it or move it.**)*

Relaunch InDesign, and create a new document using **File > New**. In the **Page Size** pop-up menu in the **New Document** dialog box, you see the preset you saved in the **New Doc Sizes** file earlier.

There it is! You can share this text file, as long as the other users place it in the same location on their computers and replace the text file that is already in the **Presets** folder.

Saving InDesign Files

With the new document you created in the last exercise still open, you will now learn how to save it. InDesign has a working file format referred to as the indd (InDesign Document) file format. Like Microsoft Word's .doc files and Photoshop's .psd files, indd is a native file format.

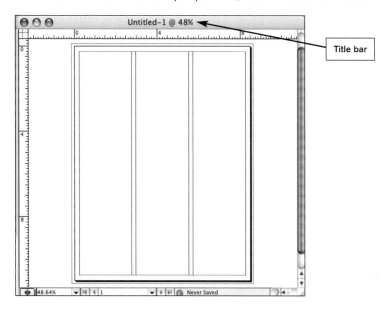

Title bar

At the top of your document, you see the **title bar**. Every time you create a new document, it is an untitled document.

At the bottom of the document is the **status bar**. When you first create a new document, you see the words "**Never Saved**" in the status bar, warning you that you haven't saved your file. The main purpose of the status bar, however, is to track versions and alternates relating to the **Adobe Bridge** and **Version Cue**. The Adobe Bridge will briefly be discussed later in this chapter and Version Cue CS2 is out of the scope of this book.

1. Choose **File > Save As**.

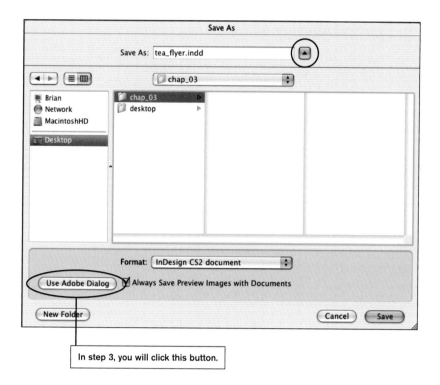

In step 3, you will click this button.

2. In the **Save As** dialog box, click the arrow to the right of the **Save As** field and choose the **chap_03** folder on your **Desktop**. Name the file **tea_flyer.indd**. Don't save the file yet; keep the **Save As** dialog box open for the next step.

Note: The extension .indd is not always necessary. However, it may become necessary if you need to transfer files across platforms—between Macintosh and Windows or the other way around. Just in case, I prefer to leave the extension in the filename.

*Note: The **Always Save Preview Images with Documents** check box is selected by default. To see a preview of your document before opening it in the **Adobe Bridge** dialog box or using the **Adobe Dialog** (or in the Windows Explorer in Windows when **Thumbnails** are chosen or in the **Finder** on the Mac), leave this box checked. It adds a few kilobytes of size to your file. You can control exactly how much size it adds in your InDesign preferences.*

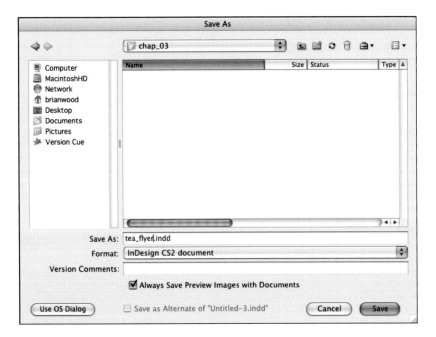

3. Click **Use Adobe Dialog** in the lower-left corner of the **Save As** dialog box. (In the illustration above, the Use Adobe Dialog Box has already been selected.) The **Save As** dialog box changes to show features that allow you to work with its application called **Version Cue** more effectively. In Version Cue, you can create projects that track your files, keep any versions for you, and allow others to access your files if you so desire.

*The **Use Adobe Dialog** button is a new feature of InDesign CS2. Adobe has created its own dialog box to more easily work with the Version Cue application for file sharing and project work. If you don't have the entire Creative Suite 2 and you don't utilize Version Cue CS2, this dialog box won't offer you any added benefit.*

4. Making sure your file is going into the folder named **chap_03** on your **Desktop**, click **Save**.

5. ——————Navigating through InDesign

Now that your document is created and you're ready to begin working, you need to be able to navigate through the program by zooming and moving. InDesign offers many ways to zoom into and out of the page and to move the page within the document window. In this exercise, using the **tea_flyer.indd** file from the previous exercise, you are going to zoom in and out and move the page around.

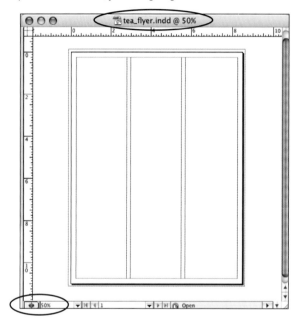

With your document open, look at the title bar and notice the name of the file (**tea_flyer.indd**), the at sign (@), and then a percentage. The percentage is the zoom percentage. Looking at the left corner of the status bar, you will also notice a percentage, which should be about the same number as what you see in the title bar, just a little more exact. These are two places you can see the zoom percentage.

To zoom in and out of the document, you use the **Zoom** tool located in the **Toolbox**.

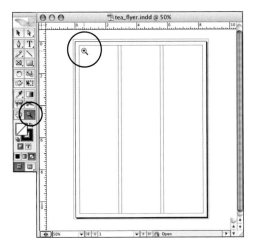

To zoom in:

1. Select the **Zoom** tool from the **Toolbox**. On the page, click once.

Note: When you click, InDesign zooms in on the page, making the document bigger in the window by an incremental percentage. As you continue clicking, InDesign continues to zoom into the document, bringing the point where you are clicking to the center of the document window.

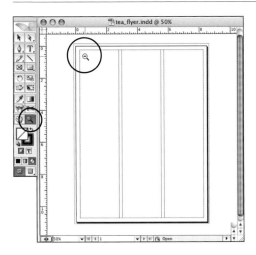

To zoom out:

2. To zoom out and make the document smaller in the document window, select the **Zoom** tool from the **Toolbox**. While pressing the **Alt** (Windows) or **Option** (Mac) key, click once on the page. InDesign zooms out by increments at the same percentage as it did when you zoomed in.

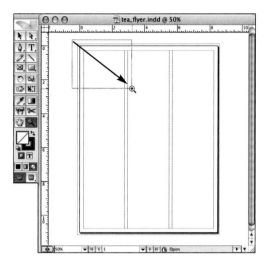

To zoom in on a selected area:

3. With the **Zoom** tool selected, you can also zoom into a selected area. Click the desired area, hold down the mouse key, and drag the cursor, making a selection box. Whatever appears in that box enlarges, making that specific area expand into the entire document window.

Note: This click-and-drag technique does not work well for zooming out!

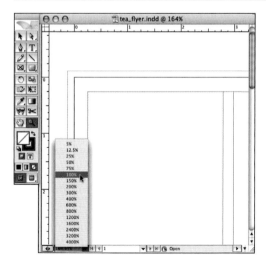

4. You can also change the view percentage by choosing a value from the **View** text box in the left corner of the status bar. Choose **100%**, or type **100** (or any number) directly into the field to the left of the arrow, and press **Enter** or **Return**.

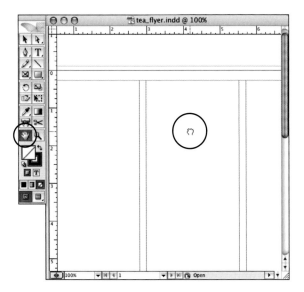

5. Select the **Hand** tool from the **Toolbox**. Click somewhere on the page, hold down the mouse key, and move the cursor. Notice the hand that appears actually grabs the page when you move the cursor. Unlike the typical horizontal and vertical scroll bars, the **Hand** tool gives you virtually the same flexibility you would have if you picked a piece of paper up with your own hands.

*Tip: The shortcut to get to the **Hand** tool is the **spacebar**. With any other tool selected, hold the spacebar down and the hand appears. The effect is only temporary, however. When you let go of the spacebar, you are back to the tool you had selected.*

6. Keep the document open for the next exercise.

TIP | Other Ways to Zoom

InDesign CS2 offers many ways to zoom. Here are some that I think are the best:

1. To zoom in using the **Zoom** tool while any other tool is selected: **Ctrl+spacebar** (Windows) or **Cmd+spacebar** (Mac).

2. To zoom out using the **Zoom** tool while any other tool is selected: **Ctrl+Alt+spacebar** (Windows) or **Cmd+Option+spacebar** (Mac).

3. To zoom in or out using key commands: **Ctrl++** or **Ctrl+−** (Windows) or **Cmd++** or **Cmd+−** (Mac). The plus (+) key zooms in, and the minus (-) key zooms out.

4. To fit the page in the document window: **Ctrl+0 (zero)** (Windows) or **Cmd+0 (zero)** (Mac). This command is also found under **View > Fit Page in Window**. Another way to fit the page in the document window is to double-click the **Hand** tool in the **Toolbox**.

5. To zoom to 100 percent: Double-click the **Zoom** tool in the **Toolbox**.

NOTE | InDesign's Pasteboard

When you zoom out far enough to see the first page of an open document, you see a few things in the document window. First, InDesign has a white area outside the page area referred to as the **pasteboard**. This area is nonprinting, which means you can put anything out there—notes to coworkers, pictures for later use, or pasted text, for instance.

From experience, I recommend keeping the pasteboard as clean as possible. When you print your file, it's just good practice to clear the pasteboard. If nothing else, your printer will thank you for it.

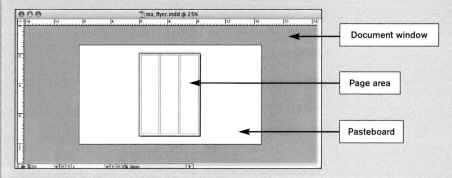

For each page or spread (set of two or more pages), InDesign automatically adds a pasteboard.

TIP | Setting the Pasteboard Size

Setting the pasteboard size to match your working style can be very helpful. By default, InDesign creates an inch of pasteboard above and below every page, and a much larger area to the right and left of your document. This can be limiting. Every now and then, if I want a little more space to work with above and below a document, I'll change what's called the **Minimum Vertical Offset** to a larger number. There is no option allowing you to increase the (horizontal) width of the pasteboard.

To increase the vertical height of the pasteboard, choose **Edit > Preferences > Guides & Pasteboard** (Windows) or **InDesign > Preferences > Guides & Pasteboard** (Mac). Notice the **Pasteboard Options** area at the bottom of the dialog box. Changing the **Minimum Vertical Offset** to **12 in** causes InDesign to place the pasteboard 12 inches above and below the page area. This gives you more room to work.

Note: Watch out how much you decide to add to the height of the pasteboard. The more you add, the more vertical space between the pages it has as well. When you learn about adding pages in Chapter 10, "*Pages, Master Pages and Layers,*" this will make more sense.

What Are Guides?

Guides are nonprinting horizontal and vertical lines that you create to make it easier to align objects on the page. They can save a lot of time if there are multiple objects on a page that need to be evenly and/or consistently aligned to each other, or to the page. An object can be "snapped" to a guide, meaning that the edge of the object is pulled to the guide when the object is within a certain distance from that guide.

InDesign, like other page layout applications, makes it easy for you to line up objects using guides. As with other page layout programs, guides are created in InDesign by clicking and dragging off the horizontal and vertical rulers.

The one major difference between InDesign and other page layout applications is how guides are deleted. In page layout applications like PageMaker or QuarkXPress, you get rid of guides by dragging them toward a ruler (basically, dragging them off the page area). In InDesign, however, guides are treated like objects. To delete objects on a page, you select them and press the **Delete** key. The same practice applies to guides in InDesign. In this exercise, you will place a few guides and see how they interact with the page.

6.——————————**Working with Rulers and Guides**

Many people use rulers to figure out where objects are on the page and to determine the scale. When rulers are turned on, they appear along the x-axis at the top of the page and along the y-axis on the left side of the page.

In this exercise, you will learn how to work with rulers and set guides, using the document from the previous exercise.

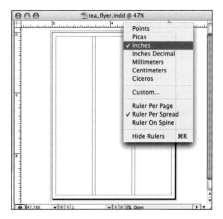

1. With the rulers showing by default, **right-click** the horizontal ruler (for Mac users with a one-button mouse, **Control-click** works just as well). A contextual menu appears. **Inches** should be selected automatically because they are the units you chose in the preferences earlier in the chapter. Keep that setting, but this is another way to change the units for this document only.

*The guides and rulers should be showing by default. If they are not, choose **View > Rulers** to show the rulers and **View > Grids & Guides > Show Guides** to see any guides you will create later.*

Note: *Changing units on the horizontal ruler only changes the units for the horizontal ruler. To change both rulers, you need to perform the same step on the vertical ruler as well.*

The units you chose for the document appear on the rulers. This means that if you've created your document from scratch, the rulers should reflect the preference you set for the measurement units in the "Setting Initial Preferences" exercise. This also means that when someone hands you a document to work on, the ruler units that person chose come with the document. For example, you might work on a file created by someone who works in picas, but you prefer to work in inches. You change the measurement units from picas to inches without causing any of the guides, grids, or objects to move. The only thing that changes is the unit on the rulers.

Note: *The units you select for the horizontal ruler are where the tabs, margins, indents, and other measurements get their units from.*

Tip: *A shortcut method for changing the units on both the horizontal and vertical rulers within a document is to press* **Ctrl+Alt+Shift+U** *(Windows) or* **Cmd+Option+Shift+U** *(Mac). This cycles through the unit possibilities. (Sometimes it's hard to tell which one is which.)*

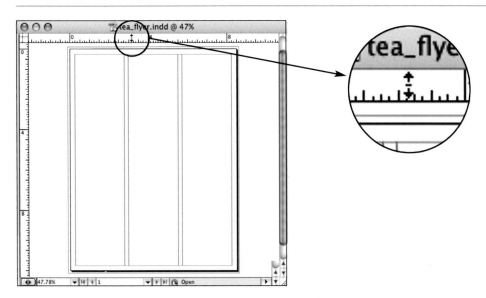

2. With the rulers showing on the page (if you don't see them, you can access them through **View >**
Show Rulers), click and drag off the horizontal ruler to create a horizontal guide.

Note: *To create a horizontal guide, drag off the horizontal ruler from the top of the document. To create a vertical guide, drag off the vertical ruler from the left side of the document window. You can place as many guides on the page as you need.*

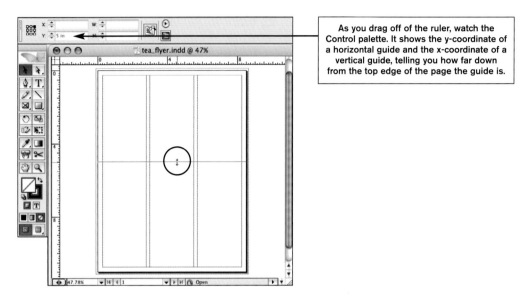

As you drag off of the ruler, watch the Control palette. It shows the y-coordinate of a horizontal guide and the x-coordinate of a vertical guide, telling you how far down from the top edge of the page the guide is.

3. Drag the guide out onto the page. Before letting go of the mouse, check the **Control** palette to see the position of the guide relative to the top edge of the document. Let go of the mouse when the **Y** field of the **Control** palette shows **5.25 in**.

Note: When the guide is selected, it is blue. When the guide is deselected, it is aqua by default.

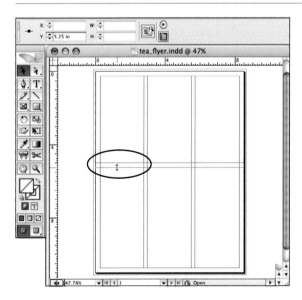

4. Guides are easy to manipulate once they are placed on the page. With the **Selection** tool, click and drag the guide to reposition it on the page.

*Tip: As you drag a horizontal or vertical guide on the page, hold down the **Shift** key to snap the guide to the closest increment on the ruler.*

*Removing guides is even easier than placing them. In most page layout applications, removing guides from the page requires that you select the guide and drag it off the page in the direction of the rulers. InDesign treats guides like objects. To delete a guide, select it with the **Selection** tool, and press the **Delete** key. To remove several guides at once, **Shift+click** all of them or drag across them with the **Selection** tool and press **Delete**.*

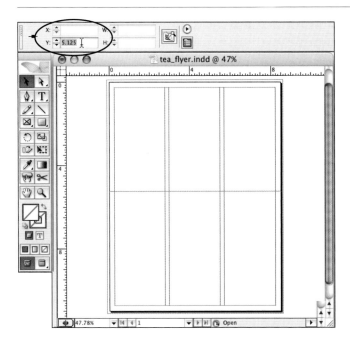

5. You can also set a guide into position "by the numbers." With the guide selected, go to the **Control** palette. Set the **Y** value at 5.125 inches from the top of the page by highlighting the number in the **Y** field and typing **5.125**. Press **Return** or **Enter**.

*Note: InDesign automatically inserts the units (such as "in" for inches) when you press **Return** or **Enter** or if you use the **Tab** key.*

*Tip: To select the text in any field, click the field name (such as **Y**) in the **Control** palette.*

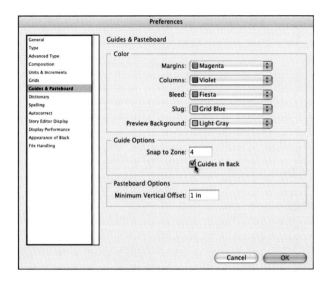

6. Choose **Edit > Preferences > Guides & Pasteboard** (Windows) or **InDesign > Preferences > Guides & Pasteboard** (Mac).

*The **Preferences** dialog box lets you control two aspects of guides: the **Snap to Zone** and whether they are placed in front or back of the document's content. The **Snap to Zone** can be important if you work with tight or loose tolerances. This setting determines how close to a guide you can get before the object snaps (is pulled to) the guide. Leaving the **Snap to Zone** set at **4** (pixels) is a good place to start. If you want InDesign to pull the object to the guide when an object is farther away from the guide—more than 4 pixels from the guide, in this case—set the **Snap to Zone** at a larger number so that you don't have to come as close to a guide to get the object to snap.*

__Guides in Back__ is very useful when you don't want guides to interfere with your design. Selecting this option pushes guides behind the document content, while still allowing objects to snap to them.

7. Click **OK** to close the dialog box without making any changes.

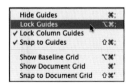

8. Choose **View > Grids & Guides > Lock Guides**.

The last step in creating guides is to decide whether you want to lock them or not. Because InDesign treats guides as objects that you can easily delete, you could delete them accidentally. That's why I prefer to lock guides after placing them and unlock them only when I need to make changes to them.

*Tip: Don't forget that a lot of menu items can be found in the contextual menus by **right-clicking** (Windows) or **Control-clicking** (Mac). Also, locking guides doesn't mean you can't add new ones. InDesign lets you drag guides off the rulers and position them; once you let go, the new guides are locked like the rest!*

9. Choose **File > Save** and close the document.

TIP | Changing Guide Options

InDesign has a few other useful options for guides. One of the features to take advantage of is changing the color of guides. The aqua color, which is the default color of a guide once it is set on a page, can be hard to see, in my opinion.

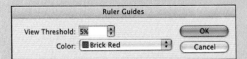

To change the color of your guides, choose **Layout > Ruler Guides**, and you see a dialog box that allows you to do two things: change the color of guides on the page and change the view threshold.

The color of the guides works in several ways:

1. If you have any guides selected, any changes you make within the **Ruler Guides** dialog box will apply only to the guides you have selected when you make the changes. Any new guides you create will default to the previous color. (You can select more than one guide by either **Shift+clicking** on each with the **Selection** tool or dragging across with the **Selection** tool.)

2. If you change the color of your guides by choosing **Layout > Ruler Guides** with no guides selected, the new color you choose will be applied to any *new* guides you create on the page.

The other feature in the **Ruler Guides** dialog box is **View Threshold**. When you set **View Threshold** at 50%, for example, the guides temporarily disappear when the **View** text box is set anywhere between 1% and 49% (to find out what the **View** text box is, return to the earlier section titled "Navigating through InDesign").

This makes guides disappear from view when you zoom out so you can get a clear view of the overall design and layout. The guides are still in the document layout, just not visible at the specified zoom level. Using the **View Threshold** setting, you can determine at what point the guides become temporarily invisible. The **View Threshold** setting only affects *either* new guides created after it is set or any guides that were selected on the page.

TIP | Adding or Removing Guides Quickly

InDesign has another great feature that allows you to quickly lay a grid of guides on the page for all sorts of possible guide arrangements. I use these to lay out a series of business cards on a page or a biography sheet where I have rows of pictures and text to place on the page.

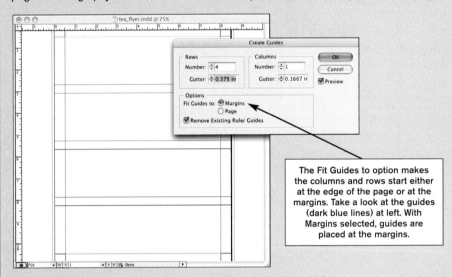

The Fit Guides to option makes the columns and rows start either at the edge of the page or at the margins. Take a look at the guides (dark blue lines) at left. With Margins selected, guides are placed at the margins.

Choose **Layout > Create Guides**. The dialog box that opens allows you to set a series of rows and/or columns on the page, complete with gutters (the distance between the columns or rows). Also, remember to check the **Preview** box to see how the guides appear on the page.

The **Options** settings within the **Create Guides** dialog box create guides that either ignore or factor in your margin settings. The **Options** settings also let you remove existing guides (such as the guide you placed in the previous exercise at 5.125 inches). This last option is a great way to clear guides quickly!

NOTE | Adding Guides by Clicking

There's an even faster way to add guides, for those of you who like to buzz the program at near lightning speed, as I do. Not many people even know about this one, in fact.

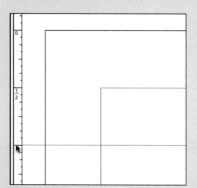

With the rulers showing (choose **View > Show Rulers** if you don't see them), double-click either ruler to put a guide on the page. Double-clicking on the horizontal ruler gives you a vertical guide, and double-clicking on the vertical ruler gives you a horizontal guide. The best trick is to hold the **Shift** key down to snap the new guide to the ruler tick marks.

NOTE | Disabling or Hiding the Guides

InDesign lets you turn off the snap-to function of your guides and allows you to easily hide the guides so they don't interfere with your design when you don't need them. Choose **View > Grids & Guides > Hide Guides** to temporarily hide them (you can still snap objects to them, even when they're hidden). Choose **View > Grids & Guides > Snap to Guides**. A check mark to the left of either one of these indicates that this function is enabled.

BONUS EXERCISE | Working with Grids in InDesign

To learn how, check out **grids.pdf** in the **bonus_exercises** folder on the **InDesign CS2 HOT CD-ROM**.

7. ──────────Changing the Zero Point in InDesign

Now that you can work with guides and rulers effectively, you may want to place an object a set distance from, say, the bottom of the page. If you're good with numbers and like to do math, that's great. But for the rest of you, InDesign offers an easier way. The horizontal and vertical rulers converge at what is called the **zero point**—where the zero on the x-axis meets the zero on the y-axis. InDesign lets you move the zero point to any place within the document window.

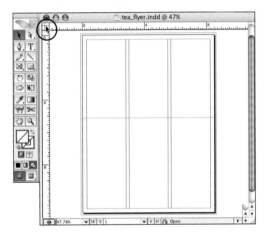

1. Open **tea_flyer.indd** from the **chap_03** folder on your **Desktop**. Notice that the default zero point is located at the upper-left corner of any page.

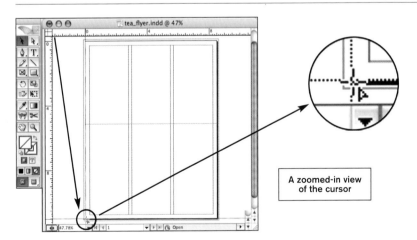

A zoomed-in view
of the cursor

2. To change the location of the zero point, click and drag out from the "crosshairs" (that's what they look like to me). You see vertical and horizontal dotted lines. Release the mouse when you come to the lower-left corner of your page. The zero point (0,0) is now at that location.

Note: Sometimes you will open a document with a zero point that is not set at the default position (InDesign saves the zero point position with the file). You can revert the zero point back to the default position in the upper-left corner by double-clicking on the "crosshairs" at the convergence of the rulers.

Tip: You can get a zero point on each page of a spread (a spread is a set of two facing pages). To do this, **right-click** (Windows) or **Control-click** (Mac with a one-button mouse) on the horizontal or vertical ruler. Choose **Ruler per Page.** The rulers start over at each new page and allow you to set the zero point for a right page and a left page separately.

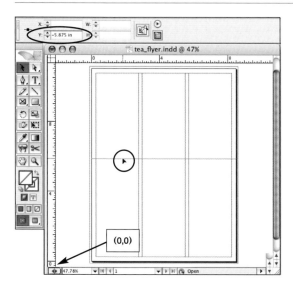

3. With the **Selection** tool, select the horizontal guide already on the page from the previous exercise. Look at the **Y** field in the **Control** palette to see where your guide is on the page.

Because the zero point was moved to the lower-left corner, the locations of all the objects on the page (including guides) are now relative to the lower-left corner. Double-clicking on the "crosshairs" again causes the zero point (where the rulers start) to return to the default position at the upper-left corner of the page.

4. Close the file without saving. In the next exercise, you will learn how to create a document from the templates that come with the program.

8._____Starting from an InDesign Template

Not only can you turn your creative vision into a masterpiece using the incredible functionality that comes with this program, but also InDesign can enhance, or even stimulate, your creative juices with templates. I can honestly say that compared with most other programs, InDesign has taken templates to a whole new level. InDesign's templates are light-years ahead of those available in other programs I have seen. The templates function found in InDesign CS2 was available with the PageMaker plug-in pack from InDesign CS. They now come standard with this version.

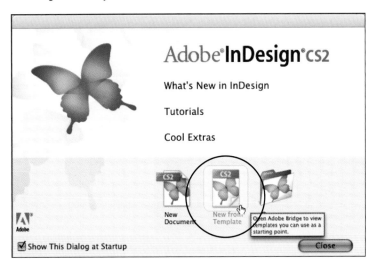

1. To access InDesign's templates, go to the **Welcome Screen** by choosing **Help > Welcome Screen**. From the **Welcome Screen**, click **New from Template**.

Note: At this point, InDesign CS2 launches the ***Adobe Bridge****—a separate application that installs when you install InDesign CS2. It is a great companion to InDesign because it can remain open and lets you browse for files, drag and drop pictures into InDesign CS2, view templates, and much more!*

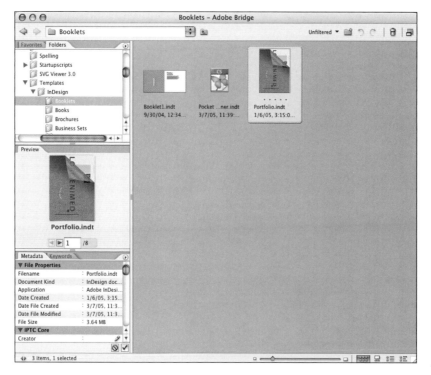

The Adobe Bridge is a great addition to InDesign CS2. You can browse your hard drive for files, view and work from templates, and drag pictures and other files into InDesign CS2.

2. You are taken to a folder containing templates within the Adobe Bridge application. Choose a template file from the many templates listed, and double-click to open the template in InDesign CS2.

Note: The InDesign template files have an extension of .indt.

3. Once the file launches in InDesign, choose **File > Save As**, and save it to your **Desktop** or another location to work on. You can now edit it to suit your needs.

4. Close the file.

In this chapter, you discovered how to create different types of documents using preferences, and how to begin working with a new document using guides, grids, and rulers. This foundation will be very helpful as you move through the program's more advanced features like placing text on the page and basic text formatting, all of which you will learn in Chapter 4.

4

Working with Text

| Typing Text on the Page | Applying Character Formatting |
| Working with Fonts | Placing Text |
| Creating Multiple Columns with a Single Text Frame |
| Threading Text | Unthreading Text Frames |
| Applying Paragraph Formatting | Checking Spelling |

chap_04

InDesign CS2
HOT CD-ROM

In my opinion, Adobe has raised the bar on people's expectations in some areas, and one great example is how type is handled by graphic software programs like the Creative Suite applications. Starting with the first release of the Creative Suite in 2003, all three of the major Adobe applications—InDesign, Illustrator, and Photoshop—began sharing a common type "engine." This common engine is also present in Creative Suite 2 and allows for easier transfer of text among the applications.

In this chapter, you will begin exploring the different ways of bringing type into InDesign from programs such as Microsoft Word and Excel, as well as options for typing directly in InDesign documents. Text formatting, as well as columns and other important text and typography features, will also be covered.

Controlling type is central to effective page layout, so this chapter will provide you with essential skills.

Working with Text Frames

Compared with those of other layout applications, InDesign CS2's text capabilities provide an interesting mix of features from PageMaker, QuarkXPress, and a few others.

Before you can format text, it is important to consider how to get words onto the page. InDesign provides you with several ways of doing this. In the next few exercises, you are going to concentrate on getting text into the program, first by typing text directly into an InDesign document and then by bringing text in from applications such as Word and Excel. But before you start, you need to understand the relationship between text and frames in InDesign.

The single most important thing to remember is that all text needs to be inside a **frame**. What is a frame? Some programs call them boxes (QuarkXPress) or even text blocks and frames (PageMaker). A **frame** is a box that contains the text. The frame itself won't print, just the frame's content. To print the frame edges, you need to assign a border (called a **stroke** in InDesign) or background fill color. In the first exercise, you are going to type a headline onto the page. Later you will learn to "place" text from an outside source that will provide the bulk of the document's content.

NOTE | Working with Frames

Frames in InDesign come in a few flavors, each intended to hold a specific type of content. There are **graphic**, **text**, and **unassigned** frames. The content of graphic and text frames is self-evident, but what about unassigned? Unassigned frames are used for "other" types of content, such as a color fill for a background or color bar behind text.

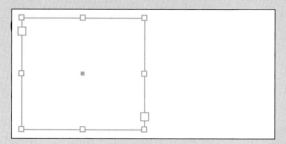

While the content types differ, all three types of frames share a common structure. Select a frame with the **Selection** tool from the **Toolbox.** and you see its **bounding box.** Along the edges of the bounding box are eight square points, called **text frame handles**, evenly spaced around the frame. The bounding box allows you to reshape and/or resize the frame. When you select a text frame, you see the bounding box and text frame handles, but you also see two other square points in the upper-left and lower-right corners of the selected frame. These are the **in port** and **out port**, respectively. These two ports allow you to **thread** (flow or link) text between frames. You will learn how to thread text in Exercise 5, "Threading Text," later in this chapter.

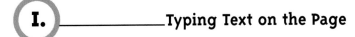

I. ——————————**Typing Text on the Page**

For the first exercise, you will type a headline and position it on the page.

1. Copy the **chap_04** folder from the **InDesign CS2 HOT CD-ROM** onto your **Desktop**.

2. From the **chap_04** folder, open the file **tea_flyer_final.indd**. This is the final piece, as it will look when you have completed the exercises in this chapter. You will place the text on the two pages, having it flow from page to page and editing the text using character and paragraph formatting. The graphics will already be on the page when you start the first exercise. You will learn how to place graphics in Chapter 8, "*Bringing in Graphics.*" To see how to create the background images you see here, look for the Tip, "Creating a Background Image," toward the end of Chapter 8. Close the file once you've had a look at it.

*Note: The **Missing Fonts** dialog box may appear when you open this file. If it does, change the font(s) by choosing **Find Font** and replacing the font(s) with a version of Arial or Helvetica. To learn more about this process, visit Exercise 1 of Chapter 5, "Typography in InDesign."*

*Note: A **Missing Links** dialog box may appear. Click the **Don't Fix** button for this file. You will learn how to fix missing links in Chapter 8.*

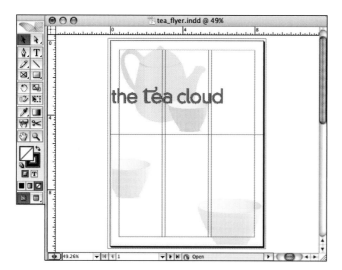

3. In InDesign CS2, open **tea_flyer.indd** from the **chap_04** folder on your **Desktop**.

Note: This is the document you began setting up in Chapter 3, "Setting Up Documents." There are some images on this page around which text will be placed. You will learn how to place background images you see in this chapter in the last exercise of Chapter 8, "Bringing in Graphics."

InDesign offers several ways to work with text. To type text directly into an InDesign document, you need to create a frame (or use one that's already on the page) and type your headline into it.

4. Select the **Type** tool from the **Toolbox**.

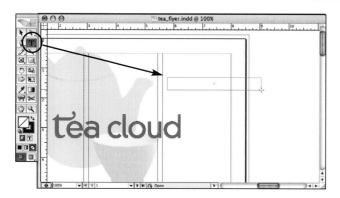

5. With the **Type** tool selected, click and drag to create a rectangular shape to type the text into.

As soon as you let go of your mouse button, a cursor shows up in the frame. This creates an empty text frame. You can now begin to type into the text frame you just created.

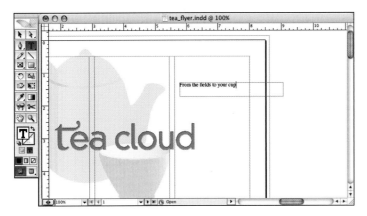

6. With the cursor in the text frame, type "**From the fields to your cup**."

*Note: The default setting for type is either **Times New Roman, 12 pt** (Windows) or **Times Roman, 12 pt** (Mac). You will learn how to change this in the next exercise.*

*Tip: Notice that the text frame you just created has a visible border around it. This is referred to as the **frame edge.** Frame edges don't print. They just show you where the frame is. If you prefer not to see the frame edges, you can temporarily turn off frame edges. With the cursor in the text frame, choose **View > Hide Frame Edges**. To show them again, choose **View > Show Frame Edges**. For this exercise, I recommend turning them back on so that you can easily find frames while working on the document.*

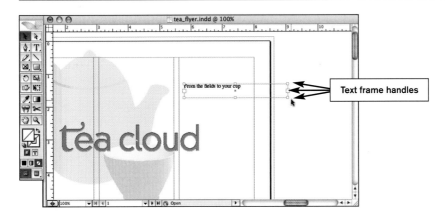

7. You may need to resize the text frame so it's not quite so big. Select the **Selection** tool (black arrow) from the **Toolbox**. If you can't see the **text frame handles**, click anywhere inside the frame to select it. Select the lower-right handle, and click and drag toward the center of the frame to make it a little smaller.

8. Choose **File > Save** to save the file. Keep it open for the next exercise.

Basic Character Formatting

Once you have placed text inside a text frame, you most likely will want to change its properties from the default settings. In the next exercise, you will adjust the character formatting for the text frame you added in the previous exercise. In InDesign (as in most other page layout applications), character formatting consists of options such as font, font size, leading, kerning, tracking, and more.

InDesign makes most of the text formatting palettes readily available in your workspace. The main palette for formatting text is the **Control** palette. The **Control** palette is contextual, meaning that it shows different formatting options depending on what is selected on the page. For a quick refresher of the palettes and where they are, visit Chapter 2, "*Interface.*"

The Control Palette's Character Formatting Controls

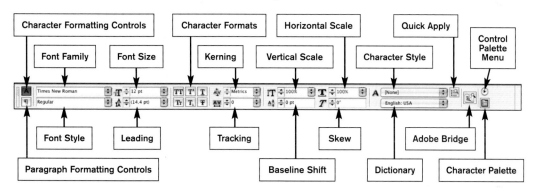

Character Formatting Controls and Functions	
Control	**Function**
Character Formatting Controls button	Shows all character (text) formatting
Font Family field	Sets (and previews) the font family
Font Size field	Sets font size
Kerning field	Adjusts the space between two letters
Vertical Scale field	Adjusts the height of selected text
Horizontal Scale field	Adjusts the width of selected text
Character Style field	Applies a character style (character styles are covered in Chapter 6, "*Type Styles*")
Quick Apply button	Quickly finds and applies a character, paragraph, or object style when you type in part or all of its name
	continues on next page

Character Formatting Controls and Functions *continued*	
Control	**Function**
Control Palette Menu button	Opens a menu offering more character formatting options
Paragraph Formatting Controls button	Switches the palette to show the Paragraph Formatting controls
Font Style field	Sets bold, italic and other styles within the chosen font family
Leading Field	Adjusts the distance vertically between lines in a paragraph
Tracking field	Adjusts the spacing between more than two letters (such as in a headline)
Baseline Shift field	Changes the vertical position of type
Skew field	Applies a fake italic
Dictionary field	Applies the language dictionary for checking spelling and more
Adobe Bridge button	Jumps to the Adobe Bridge
Character Palette button	Opens the same formatting as the Control palette character formatting, but in a floating palette
Character Format Buttons	
All Caps	Changes the selected type to all capitals
Superscript	Text appears above the baseline and is smaller in size
Underline	Underlines selected text
Small Caps	Forces text to change to the small version of capitals
Subscript	Text appears below the baseline and is smaller in size

Another place to find text formatting is in the **Character** palette, which can be opened by choosing **Type > Character**. This palette contains all the same formatting as the **Control** palette, but it comes in a palette that can be docked in your workspace. I prefer to use the **Control** palette because it's out of the way and appears automatically at the top of my workspace.

2. —————————Applying Character Formatting

In the last exercise, you learned how to create and resize text frames. You also typed text directly into that frame. In this exercise, you will learn how to apply character formatting to that text.

1. With **tea_flyer.indd** open from the previous exercise, you are going to apply some charac-ter formatting to the text created in the previous exercise. Zoom in to the newly created text (from the previous exercise) using the **Zoom** tool in the **Toolbox**.

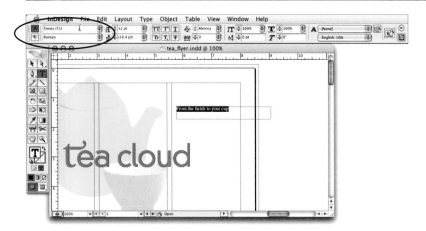

2. With the **Type** tool selected from the **Toolbox**, select the text by clicking and dragging until it becomes highlighted. In the illustration, the left end of the **Control** palette is circled to show you where it is located. As mentioned before, this palette offers contextual settings, meaning its content changes depending on what is selected. With text selected, character and paragraph formatting settings automatically appear.

*Tip: With the **Type** tool, you can also select text by double-clicking to select a word, triple-clicking to select a line, and quadruple-clicking to select a whole paragraph. Click five times on the text and you can select all the text in the text frame.*

3. Click the **Character Formatting Controls** button in the **Control** palette to show the **Character Formatting** controls, or use the **Character** palette found under **Type > Character**.

Note: *To refresh your memory about the character formatting settings in the **Control** palette, visit the **Control** palette section earlier in this exercise.*

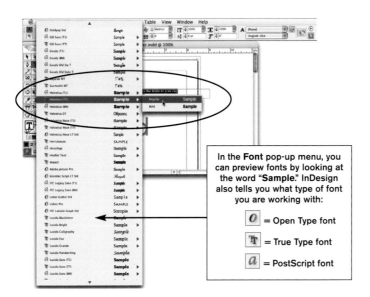

In the **Font** pop-up menu, you can preview fonts by looking at the word "**Sample.**" InDesign also tells you what type of font you are working with:

O = Open Type font

Tt = True Type font

a = PostScript font

4. Choose **Arial** (Windows) or **Helvetica** (Mac) from the **Font Family** pop-up menu on the **Control** palette. On the Mac platform, a lot of the font families also have an arrow to the right of the word "**Sample**" in that menu. This is where you can choose a **font style** such as bold or italic. Choose **Regular** if you see it to the right of the font family **Helvetica**. On the Windows platform, you will choose the font style from the **Font Style** menu in the **Control** palette.

*If there is another **font family** you'd rather use, experiment a little! Also, not all font families will have an arrow to the right of the word "Sample." This is because some of the font families only have one style, such as regular, built into them.*

Note: *New in InDesign CS2 is the ability to preview a **Font Family** from the **Control** and **Character** palettes, as well as by choosing **Type > Font**!*

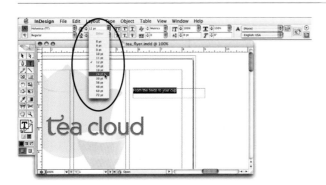

5. With the text selected, choose **24 pt** from the **Font Size** pop-up menu.

Type Size field

Note: *Most InDesign palette fields (such as the **Type Size** field) have two arrows to the left of the field, and arrow(s) to the right (depending on your platform). The arrow to the right produces a pop-up menu of font size choices (in this instance). The arrows to the left of the field change the value in the field incrementally. You can also type a value into any field.*

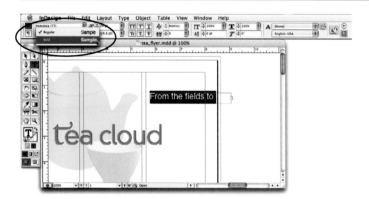

6. The next step is to change the type to **bold** by selecting it from the **Font Style** menu, circled in the illustration. Those of you who have used Word, QuarkXPress, or other publishing tools will immediately begin looking for a **B** button for bolding text or an **I** button for italicizing text. InDesign doesn't offer those buttons. When you use those buttons in a program like Word, you are letting Word change the font when the file is printed. This is considered to be "faux" bolding or "faux" italicizing, because it takes a nonbolded or nonitalicized font and alters it. InDesign, instead, looks for the correct font style within a font family from which you can choose bold and italic. The catch here is that the font family has to have the font style built in. For example, with certain versions of Helvetica, regular and bold are available, but not italic.

Don't panic! This is a good thing! InDesign is a professional-level page layout tool. For years, printers have been scolding people who use faux styling because it can often result in longer printing times and sometimes even crashes the software at the printer if you overuse it.

*Some of you may use shortcuts for bold or italic in other programs. In InDesign, the shortcut for bold is **Ctrl+Shift+B** (Windows) or **Cmd+Shift+B** (Mac). This bolds any text that is selected if the bold font style is present in the font family. For italic text, substitute **I** for **B**.*

Note: *If you do use the shortcut for bold or italic but you don't have that font style in the font family, you may run into some trouble. InDesign won't let you do it, or worse yet, it may highlight the text in pink to let you know that it can't perform your request, because that font style is not available in that particular font family.*

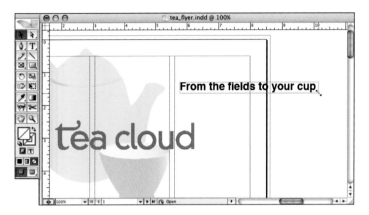

7. With the text set at **24 pt**, you may notice a **red plus sign** in the text frame. This indicates that there is too much text for the size of the frame. The excess text is called **overset text**. To fix it, you need to resize the frame. Use the **Selection** tool to select the text frame (you can click anywhere in it). You then see the text frame handles. Select a corner handle, and make the frame larger by dragging away from the center.

Tip: If you want to see the text as you resize a frame, select a text frame handle, hold down the button on your mouse for a second or two, and then drag. InDesign CS2 shows you a live preview of the content of the frame as you resize.

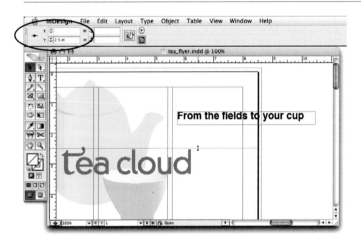

8. To put the text frame into place, position a horizontal guide on the page at **2.5 inches** from the top edge of the page. As you learned in Chapter 3, "*Setting Up Documents*," you can do this by moving the cursor to the ruler at the top of the document window and then clicking and dragging down from the ruler. When you release the mouse button, a horizontal guide appears. With the guide still selected, in the **Control** palette, type **2.5** into the **Y** field.

*Note: If a horizontal guide doesn't appear, choose **View > Show Guides**. You may also wish to lock the guides so they won't move. Choose **View > Grids & Guides > Lock Guides** to lock them.*

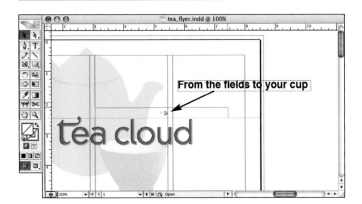

9. Using the **Selection** tool, click inside the text frame, hold down the mouse button and drag it into position, as you see in the illustration for this step.

*Note: Notice that the black arrow turns into a white arrow in Step 9? The cursor from the **Selection** tool (black arrow) will turn white when the frame you are dragging comes close to a guide (margin, column, or page guide). If you let go when the arrow is white and positioned near a guide, the frame snaps to the closest guide!*

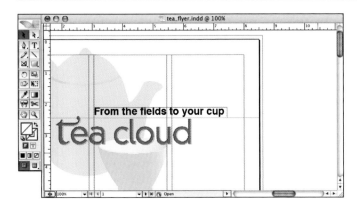

10. Save the changes and leave the file open for the next exercise, where you will place text from another application.

NOTE | InDesign CS2 and Fonts

How to manage fonts is a subject you may deal with while using InDesign. Although this topic is too big to cover fully here, having a basic understanding of different font types as they relate to InDesign CS2 may prove helpful.

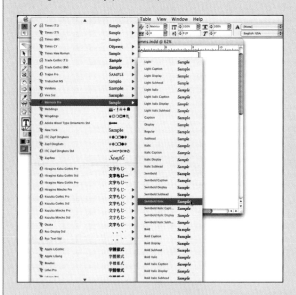

InDesign CS2 offers a broad selection of fonts. InDesign can handle **Open Type** fonts, **PostScript** fonts, and **True Type** fonts. To see what type of fonts are available to you, select the **Type** tool and click on the font family pop-up menu in the **Control** palette (or **Character** palette). The icon to the left of each font in this menu represents the font type. Below is a listing of the font types supported by InDesign and some of the differences between them.

Open Type fonts: Open Type fonts are relatively new to the industry. They contain more Glyphs than True Type or PostScript fonts and are easily shared across platforms. Glyphs are commonly used type symbols, like the copyright symbol (©) or a bullet point. InDesign also supports features such as ligatures—characters that consist of two or more letters or characters joined together, like "æ"—and more. Open Type fonts are also contained in a single font file.

PostScript fonts: PostScript fonts are composed of two files commonly referred to as screen and printer font files. You generally need both files to print with. They typically have an extension of .pfm and .pfb (Windows) or .ffil and .lwfn (Mac).

True Type fonts: True Type is a single font file with a file extension of .ttf typically. These are mainly used in the Windows operating system but are now becoming more accepted as fonts appropriate for design.

TIP | Resizing Text Frames Automatically

Text frames can easily be manipulated with the **Selection** tool, and won't print unless you put a stroke (border) on them (which you will learn to do in Chapter 7, "*Working with Color*"). It is good practice, however, not to make text frames bigger than they need to be. I resize my frames continuously as I'm working so that they are as small as possible. This can make it easier for you to select text frames on the page. An easy way to do this is to select the text frame with the **Selection** tool, then choose **Object > Fitting > Fit frame to content**. This will make your text frames as small as possible!

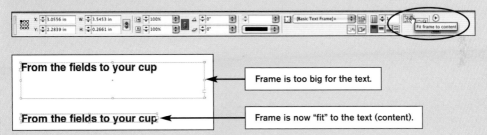

From the fields to your cup ← Frame is too big for the text.

From the fields to your cup ← Frame is now "fit" to the text (content).

You can also accomplish this by **right-clicking** (**Control-clicking** on the Mac) on a text frame and choosing **Object Fitting > Fit frame to content** or clicking the **Fit Frame to Content** button on the **Control** palette with the **Selection** tool active.

TIP | Changing Character Formatting Without Selecting Text

Here's a way for you to save some serious time. If you have a text frame with uniform formatting (that is, all the text in the frame uses the same font, size, etc.), you can change character or paragraph formatting without selecting text.

1. With the **Selection** tool, select the text frame for the text "**From the fields to your cup.**"

2. With the text frame selected, choose the **Type** tool from the **Toolbox**.

3. The **Control** palette will show the character formatting settings if the **Character Formatting Controls** button (instead of the Paragraph Formatting Controls button) is chosen at the far left end of the palette. Choose a new font family or other character formatting, and the text will change!

Text Import Options for Plain Text Files Explained

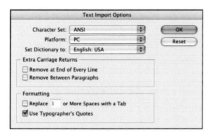

As you will learn in the next exercise, to place text in the document from an external text file, you choose **File > Place**. Selecting the **Show Import Options** check box in the **Place** dialog box causes the **Text Import Options** dialog box to appear. This dialog box gives you control over some appearance and formatting settings before the text is placed on to the page. The chart below explains **Text Import Options** dialog box options.

Text Import Options and Results	
Option	**Result**
Character Set	Specifies the computer language character set, such as ANSI, Unicode, or Windows CE, that was used to create the text file. It defaults to the character set that corresponds to the default language set in InDesign.
Platform	Allows you to choose which platform the text was created on (to avoid changing special characters).
Set Dictionary to	Shows the more than 13 languages that can be used for spell checking (this can be set later if necessary).
Extra Carriage Returns	Contains two options: **Remove at End of Every Line** allows you to remove extra returns in documents like e-mails that are saved as text files and later placed into InDesign. **Remove Between Paragraphs** allows you to remove all paragraph returns so that you can decide where they go once the text is in InDesign.
Formatting	Offers options allowing you, for instance, to fix a gross misuse of spacebar spaces to line up text with tabs. The **Use Typographer's Quotes** option replaces feet and inch marks with curly quotes.

Note: The **Text Import Options** dialog box is contextual, which means the options vary depending on what type of text file you are placing (for instance, a Word document or a plain text file, among others).

3. ——————Placing Text

Sometimes you will need to bring text into InDesign CS2 from another program, like Word. InDesign CS2 can place text in ASCII, plain text, Word, RTF (Rich Text Format), Excel, and tagged text formats. If you are working with text in another application, I recommend saving it in one of these file formats before placing the text in InDesign.

When placing text onto a page, InDesign provides a very helpful feature called **Show Import Options**. As you will see in this exercise, **Show Import Options** allows you to tell InDesign how to handle the formatting applied to the text in the original application, like Word. This can be very helpful because it saves you from having to remove formatting applied to the text in another program.

1. With **tea_flyer.indd** open from the previous exercise, click the **Selection** tool in the **Toolbox**.

*If this is the first exercise you are joining, open the file **tea_flyer.indd** from the **chap_04** folder you copied onto your **Desktop** from the **InDesign CS2 HOT CD-ROM**.*

*Note: The **Missing Fonts** dialog box may appear when you open this file. If it does, change the font(s) by choosing **Find Font** and replacing the font(s) with a version of Arial or Helvetica. To learn more about this process, visit Exercise 1 of Chapter 5, "Typography in InDesign."*

*In the first exercise, "Typing Text on the Page," you learned how to create a frame and type text into it. When you place text from a program like Word, you don't have to make a text frame first. When you place the text, InDesign automatically generates a frame for your text. The frame that it creates is the width of the column guides you set in your document. You can, of course, create a frame first and then place the text in it, but why not let InDesign do it for you? This is one of the major advantages of setting up **column guides** when you first create a document, as you did in Chapter 3, "Setting Up Documents."*

2. Choose **Edit > Deselect All** (or click on the pasteboard) to deselect all your content.

Note: Before placing text, always take notice of any frames that are selected. If frames are selected when you place text, the content of the selected frame (even an object or picture frame) can be replaced by the new text you are placing. For this reason, it's always a good idea to deselect before placing any new content on a page.

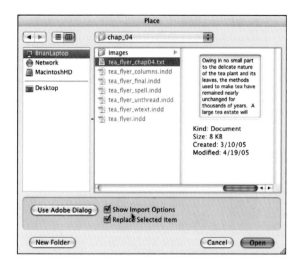

3. Choose **File > Place**. In the **Place** dialog box, select **tea_flyer_chap04.txt**. Click the **Show Import Options** check box. Click **Open**.

*Note: On the Windows platform, the **Place** dialog box shows only the importable files. If you want to see all the files in the folder, choose **All Files** from the **Files of Type** menu, and the dialog box shows all the files you see in the illustration for this step.*

*In the **Place** dialog box on the Mac platform, InDesign previews the text file you are placing. Also, when placing text files of any kind, select the **Show Import Options** check box and then click **Open**. The **Text Import Options** dialog box opens, allowing you to change how the text is formatted and to choose what is brought in.*

*In the **Place** dialog box, the **Replace Selected Item** option was available in previous versions. It can serve as an alternative to what was described in Step 2 of this exercise because it is possible to replace the content of any selected frame with the new content you are placing. You can deselect this option when placing content and it will serve the same as deselecting all objects on the page. It will not allow InDesign to replace any selected text.*

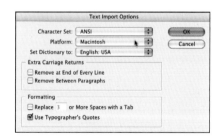

4. Choose **Macintosh** in the **Platform** field (this text file was created on a Mac) and click **OK**.

*Note: The **Missing Fonts** dialog box may appear when you place this text file. If it does, change the font(s) by choosing **Find Font** and replacing the font(s) with a version of Arial or Helvetica. To learn more about this, visit Exercise 1 of Chapter 5, "Typography in InDesign."*

*While it's great to have this option, not all of us are going to know what platform our text was created on. If you leave this at the default, you won't harm your file. If it's the wrong platform, it might change some of your special characters like quotes, bullets, and such. For more information on other options inside the **Text Import Options** dialog box, read the chart that follows this exercise.*

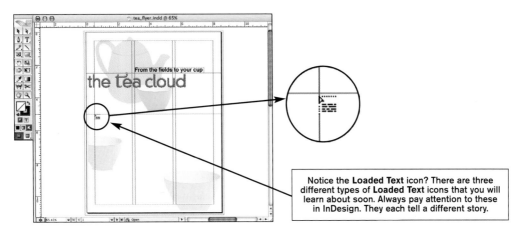

Notice the **Loaded Text** icon? There are three different types of **Loaded Text** icons that you will learn about soon. Always pay attention to these in InDesign. They each tell a different story.

5. Position the **Loaded Text** icon (⊞) in the first column, at a point level with the horizontal guide. The **Loaded Text** icon is an indication that you have text to place. You see the **Loaded Text** icon with a white arrow. This means that it will snap the newly created text frame against the horizontal guide and the left column guide, stopping the frame at the bottom margin guide. Now click. The text should be placed within the confines of the column and margin guides.

The margin and column guides you set up in this document in the last chapter are now serving a purpose. InDesign is smart—it uses the margin and column guides to create text frames for you in columns. As you progress further in this book, you will see some amazing features involving these guides and how the program places text on pages.

*Tip: If you clicked and the text appears on the page within a frame, congratulations! You've succeeded. But what happens if you place the wrong text file or if you accidentally click into an existing text frame and replace the text that was there? These are very common mistakes because they're all too easy to make, even for experienced InDesign users. Never fear. You don't have to delete and start over. Choose **Edit > Undo Place**, or press **Ctrl+Z** (Windows) or **Cmd+Z** (Mac). InDesign CS2 can undo almost anything, including placing text! If you undo after placing your text, you are brought back to the **Loaded Text** icon, and the text you accidentally replaced will reappear. Feel free to place the text elsewhere. If it was the wrong text file, undo a second time, and InDesign takes away the **Loaded Text** icon.*

6. Choose **File > Save** and then close the file.

TIP | Placeholder Text

Inim doloreet nullandre feum
atin henismo dolesectem nulland
reriure volenim digna aciduis adit
lore consequisim esto od

The placeholder text won't make any sense, and spell checking it will give you a headache, but it's great for mocking up your layout, determining text fitting, and so on.

You may not have text when starting a document, and that can make it difficult to envision the final layout. InDesign provides placeholder text to use while the real thing is being written.

With the cursor in a text frame that you created, choose **Type > Fill with Placeholder Text**. Nonsensical words, sometimes referred to as Lorem ipsum text, or "greeking," will fill the text frame from top to bottom. Placeholder text can be styled and moved around like regular text, which makes it very helpful in determining how the text will function within the design.

NOTE | Watch the Loaded Text Icon

When placing text or working with any objects in InDesign, always pay attention to your cursor. When placing text, the **pointer** will turn into a **Loaded Text** icon. This icon can be telling in several ways. If you place the cursor at a point on the page where there are no frames or objects, you see the **Loaded Text** icon. If you place your cursor over an existing frame (text or other content type), you see the **Loaded Text** icon with parentheses around it. Finally, if you place the **Loaded Text** icon within snapping range of a guide, you see a third icon. This third icon is a white arrow with a black outline that indicates that the frame you are about to place will snap to the guide you have come near.

Always look for these three icons. They can alert you to potential missteps, such as placing text into the wrong frame or type of frame.

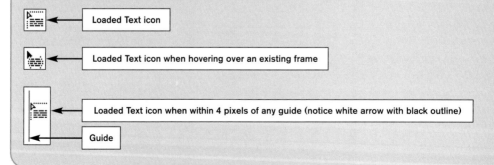

Loaded Text icon

Loaded Text icon when hovering over an existing frame

Loaded Text icon when within 4 pixels of any guide (notice white arrow with black outline)

Guide

4. _____Creating Multiple Columns with a Single Text Frame

Many of you will create newsletters, flyers, brochures, annual reports, and other documents that require more than a single column of text. InDesign CS2 gives you several ways to create columns, each with its own purpose. In this exercise, you are going to create multiple columns within a single text frame using the text you placed in the previous exercise. I use this option when I have columns of text that are the same width and generally the same height.

1. Open **tea_flyer_columns.indd** from the **chap_04** folder on your Desktop.

*Note: The **Missing Fonts** dialog box may appear when you open this file. If it does, change the font(s) by choosing **Find Font** and replacing the font(s) with a version of Arial or Helvetica. To learn more about this, visit Exercise 1 of Chapter 5, "Typography in InDesign."*

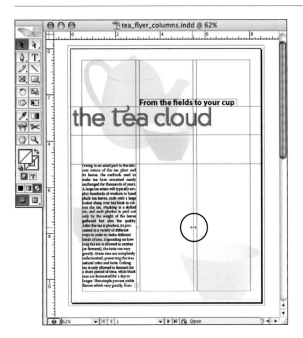

2. With the **Selection** tool, select the text frame of the body text. The text frame handles appear all around the frame. As you learned earlier, these square points allow you to resize the text frame. Select the text frame handle on the right side of the frame, and pull open the frame to the next column guide. It will snap into place when it gets close enough to the guide.

Tip: If you are resizing a text frame, you generally only see the frame edge, not the text inside as you resize it. If you select a text frame handle and hesitate for a second or two before you begin moving your cursor, InDesign will redraw the text (the text will be visible) within the text frame as you resize!

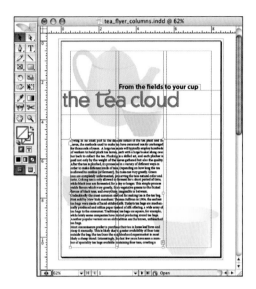

3. Once you've resized the text frame, release the mouse. The text should fill the newly resized text frame.

*Note: In the last step, with the text frame on the page, you can see a red plus sign (⊞) in the lower-right corner of the frame. This is called the **Overset Text** icon. This happens when the text frame is too small for placed text. You will learn how to correct that in the next exercise.*

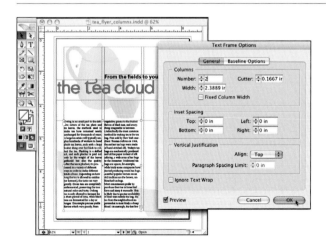

4. The next step is to create two columns in the text frame. With the text frame still selected, choose **Object > Text Frame Options**. The **Text Frame Options** dialog box appears. On the **General** tab, in the **Columns** section, choose **2** for **Number** of columns, and set the **Gutter** to **0.1667 in**. Click **OK** to close the **Text Frame Options** dialog box. This will split the single text frame into two columns with a distance of 0.1667 inch between the columns.

Tip: Use this option typically when you have several same-sized columns to place on the page.

Note: When you set the **Gutter** within the **Text Frame Options** dialog box, you were asked to set it at **0.1667 in.** The reason for this was to match the column gutter width that you set for the document in the last chapter. Using set standards for gutter widths isn't required, but it does help to maintain consistency.

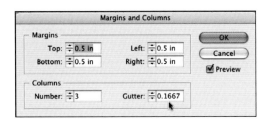

Tip: If you set a column gutter when you first created your document and you can't remember what it is, choose **Layout > Margins and Columns.** InDesign shows you the document's margin and column measurements in the **Margins and Columns** dialog box.

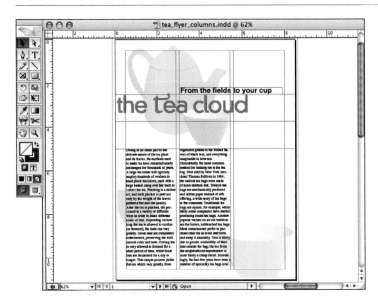

5. Choose **File > Save**, and keep it open. We will use this same file for the next exercise.

NOTE | Understanding Text Frame Column Settings

By selecting a text frame and choosing **Object > Text Frame Options**, you can access the **Text Frame Options** dialog box. The settings in this dialog box are great for creating evenly spaced, multiple-column text frames. They are useful in other instances as well. For example, let's say you are working on a product catalog, and you need to have all your columns set at width of 3 inches.

Using the settings in the **Text Frame Options** dialog box, you can create a single text frame and easily set each of the two columns at 3 inches.

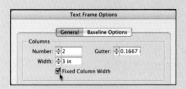

Option	Function
Number	Sets the number of columns you want to split your text frame into.
Gutter	Sets the distance between the columns.
Width	Sets fixed-width columns (at 3 inches, for example).
Fixed Column Width	Maintains the width of any new columns added to the text frame. All column widths are fixed at the **Width** setting.

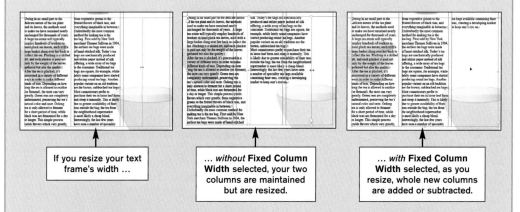

If you resize your text frame's width …

… *without* **Fixed Column Width** selected, your two columns are maintained but are resized.

… *with* **Fixed Column Width** selected, as you resize, whole new columns are added or subtracted.

You can save a lot of time by checking the **Fixed Column Width** option listed under **Object > Text Frame Options** if you are working on longer documents with lots of consistently sized columns on each page.

What Is Text Threading?

Text **threading** is what some programs refer to as text linking or flowing. InDesign refers to text frames that have text flowing between them (from one to the next) as **threaded text frames**. Threading frames can be very important when you work with multipage or large-sized documents that require text to continue on more than one page.

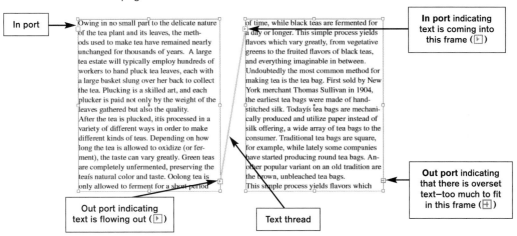

Text Threading Options	
Term	**Definition**
In port	Shows a connection to another text frame. Typically, this indicates the first text frame in the thread.
In port indicating thread from previous frame	Shows a connection to a previous frame.
Out port	Used to thread text to another frame. If there is no blue arrow icon in it for a specific frame, that means that the text is not flowing or connecting to another frame and that the text is fitting within it.
Out port indicating thread to next frame	Indicates that a text thread has been created, flowing text to another text frame.
Text thread	When **View > Show Text Threads** is selected, and a text frame that is part of a thread is selected as well, this line indicates the connection or thread between frames.
Out port indicating overset text	Overset text, indicated by the **Overset Text** icon (⊞), means that the text frame is too small to fit all the text.

5. ——————Threading Text

Threading in InDesign is an important feature that will require time to grasp and fully understand. In the last exercise, you placed a text file and created two columns of text. But there is still overset text in the frame, as indicated by the **Overset Text** icon (⊞) showing in the lower-right corner of the text frame. This overset text needs to go into the third column on the page.

To achieve this, you could create a frame with three columns and resize the frame to fit the page. But the third column needs to start higher on the page (right below the word "**cloud**" in the Tea Cloud logo), so this won't work. The best solution is to thread the text into a third column, which is what you will learn to do in this exercise.

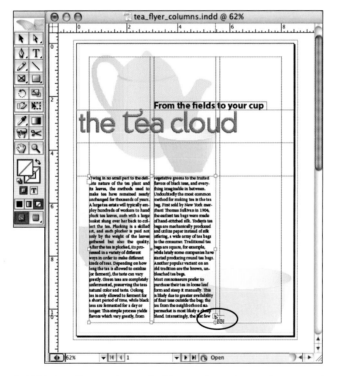

1. With **tea_flyer_columns.indd** open from the previous exercise, select the **Selection** tool from the **Toolbox** and select the text frame. Next click the plus (⊞) in the **out port** of the text frame. The **Loaded Text** icon appears (as you saw in Exercise 3, "Placing Text"). Your job is to flow the text into an existing frame or make a new frame from scratch.

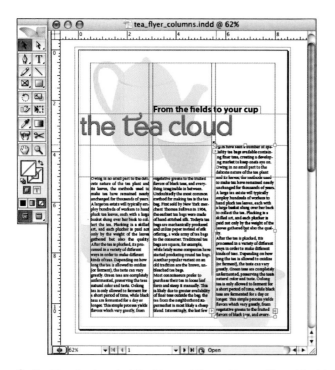

2. Position the **Loaded Text** icon at the guide positioned just below the "**d**" in the word "**cloud**" on the left side of the third column, and click. A new text frame (with the text flowed into it) will automatically appear. This is how you can create a thread from one text frame to another.

The frame spans from the horizontal guide to the bottom margin guide. When you click with the ***Loaded Text*** *icon, InDesign assumes you want to place text and automatically creates a frame for you. InDesign uses the horizontal guide to determine the height of the column and uses the column guides and margin guides to determine the width of the column. Notice that even with a third column, there is still overset text. The next step teaches how to deal with the remainder of the overset text.*

3. With the third column still selected, choose **View > Show Text Threads**. You will see a line connecting the two-column frame with the new third column—the frame that InDesign just created for you. In the remainder of this exercise, you will learn how to thread the rest of the text onto the second page of the document using a method called **semi-autoflow** text threading.

Note: *To view these text threads, you need to have one or more of the text frames selected with the* ***Selection*** *tool.*

Once the text is threaded, you can move the frames on the page or between pages, and InDesign keeps the frames linked and threaded.

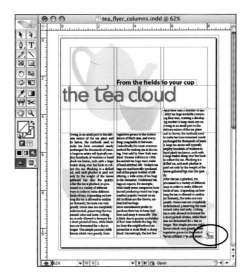

4. The next objective is to get the overset text to flow onto the next page of this document. With the **Selection** tool still selected, click on the third-column text frame to select it. A red plus appears in the lower-right corner of the frame. Click on the **Overset Text** icon in the **out port** of the text frame to get the **Loaded Text** icon.

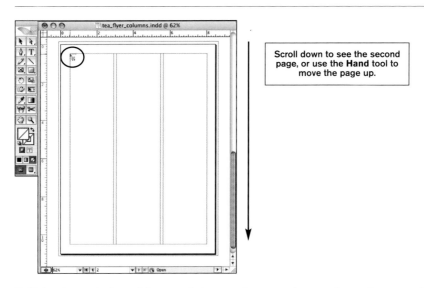

Scroll down to see the second page, or use the **Hand** tool to move the page up.

5. Using the vertical scroll bar, scroll down to the second page of your document. The document that you've been working with, **tea_flyer_columns.indd** from the **chap_04** folder on your **Desktop**, will have the two pages in it already. In Chapter 10, "*Pages, Master Pages, and Layers*," you will learn how to add pages to a document.

6. After scrolling down to see the second page, press the **Alt** key (Windows) or **Option** key (Mac), and the **Loaded Text** icon changes to the **Semi-autoflow** icon (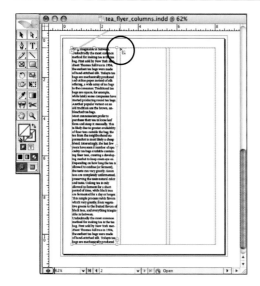). ***Don't let go of the key for a few steps!*** At the very top of the first column, click. InDesign creates a text frame the size of the column.

7. With the **Alt** key (Windows) or **Option** key (Mac) still held down from Step 6, you should still see the **Semi-autoflow** icon. Click the top of the next column. Let go of the **Alt** key (Windows) or **Option** key (Mac).

*Using **semi-autoflow** is a great way to place text on the page and flow it where you want it to go. You can control how the text is placed. And it's much faster than selecting the **out port** indicating overset text and choosing the next frame for how many frames it takes to get all the text to appear on the page.*

*Note: You may be surprised at what happens when you release the **Alt** key (Windows) or **Option** key (Mac). When you let the key go, InDesign assumes that you have one more text thread to create. You see the **Loaded Text** icon (). In theory, when you use semi-autoflow, you should release the **Alt** key (Windows) or **Option** key (Mac) before the last text frame is threaded. If you thread all your frames and then release the key, just select another tool from the **Toolbox**, and InDesign stops threading.*

Tip: If your threads get out of hand (it's OK, it happens to all of us), you may be best served by placing your text again. Trying to unravel a seriously tenacious thread can take more time than it's worth. Starting a new one is often the more efficient option. InDesign provides you with a hefty supply of undo commands, so stepping backward using an undo command can be the best option.

8. Choose **File > Save** and close the file.

NOTE | Different Types of Text Threading

InDesign text threading can be accomplished in several different ways. In addition to threading two frames together and the semi-autoflow method you have just learned, there are two more methods for flowing text onto your pages. Semi-autoflow is helpful because it makes the process quicker, but there are two other text threading methods: autoflow and fixed-page text autoflow. At the end of this exercise, the Tip titled "How to Autoflow Text" describes how autoflow works. Also, in Chapter 10, "*Pages, Master Pages, and Layers,*" you will learn more about how to thread text using the autoflow and fixed-page text autoflow methods with your master pages for super-fast text placement!

This chart explains the different methods for placing text and flowing.

Icon	Method	Shortcut Key	Functionality
	Manual text flow	None	Threads text one frame at a time. This method requires that you first select the out port of a text frame and then click another frame or have InDesign create one for you.
	Semi-autoflow	**Alt** (Windows) or **Option** (Mac) + **Loaded Text** icon	Works like manual text flow except that you don't have to constantly click the out port to load the cursor every time. You can just hold down the Alt key (Windows) or Option key (Mac) and click on text frames (or have InDesign create them by clicking) until all the text appears on the page.
	Autoflow	**Shift** (Mac or Windows) + **Loaded Text** icon	Places text by adding pages and text frames until all of your text is on your pages.
	Fixed-page text autoflow	**Alt+Shift** (Windows) or **Option+Shift** (Mac) + **Loaded Text** icon	Places text by adding text frames until all the text is on your pages. This method stops text threading when it reaches the last page of your document (even if text is still overset).

TIP | Threading Text to an Existing Text Frame

So far you've learned how to thread text to a column and allow InDesign to make a text frame for you. While this is a speedy solution, it may not work with some templates.

A lot of companies use preexisting company templates to start a new document. Often these templates include text frames intended to facilitate placing text on the page. In cases like that, you need to place text and flow it into existing text frame(s), rather than having InDesign create a new frame for you.

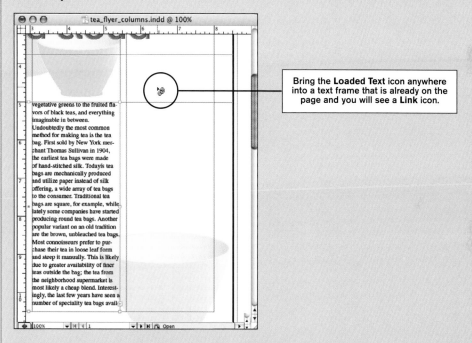

Bring the **Loaded Text** icon anywhere into a text frame that is already on the page and you will see a **Link** icon.

This type of threading works the same way as it did in the previous exercise, with one small difference. Choose the **Overset Text** icon (⊞) in the **out port** of the text frame that has the overset text. Bring your cursor anywhere into the text frame that is already on the page, and you see a **Link** icon (⧉). Click to flow the text and thread (link) the text frames together!

MOVIE | Threading Text

To learn more about the various methods for threading text, check out **threading.mov** in the **movies** folder on the **InDesign CS2 HOT CD-ROM**.

TIP | How to Autoflow Text

In the previous exercise, you learned how to flow your text by threading frames together using the semi-autoflow method. This is a great feature of text threading, but there may come a time when even semi-autoflow just isn't efficient enough. For instance, say you have a Word document that's 30 or more pages long and you need to place that text into an InDesign document quickly and easily. The semi-autoflow method would allow you to thread across all the pages, but it would require that the pages already be there. It would also require you to go to every one of those pages to thread the text. Here's where autoflow steps in.

Autoflow works much the same as regular text threading, with the exception of a shortcut key.

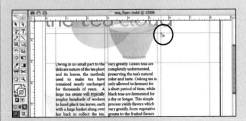

Choose **File > Place** to get your text document onto the page. In a column, hold down the **Shift** key, and you see the **Autoflow** cursor (⌘). Click in a column (to make a text frame the size of the column) or anywhere on the page.

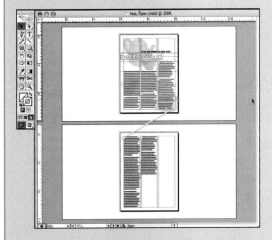

InDesign creates as many text frames as necessary to show all the text.

Tip: If you only have 2 pages in your InDesign document and you autoflow a 30-page Word or other text document, InDesign adds as many pages as it needs to get all the text threaded and showing in the document!

6. ————————Unthreading Text Frames

There may be times when you need to unthread text frames to flow the text somewhere else. One of the great features in InDesign is that it treats the text frame and the actual text as separate entities, so if you delete a text frame that is threaded to other text frames, the text itself won't be deleted. Instead, it will either be flowed into remaining text frames or be treated as overset text.

This short exercise shows you how to unthread two frames without having to delete one of the frames.

1. Open **tea_flyer_unthread.indd** from the **chap_04** folder on your **Desktop**. This document is identical to what you were working on before, saved in its final state.

*Note: The **Missing Fonts** dialog box may appear when you open this file. If it does, change the font(s) by choosing **Find Font** and replacing the font(s) with a version of Times or a comparable font. To learn more about this, visit Exercise 1 of Chapter 5, "Typography in InDesign."*

2. Scroll to the second page using the vertical scroll bars or the **Hand** tool.

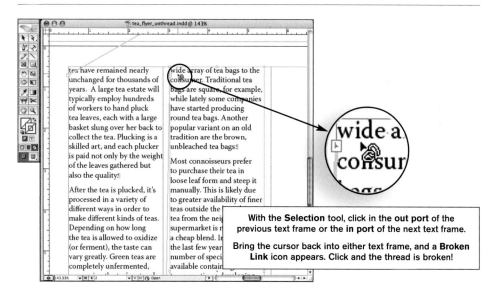

With the **Selection** tool, click in the out port of the previous text frame or the in port of the next text frame.

Bring the cursor back into either text frame, and a **Broken Link** icon appears. Click and the thread is broken!

3. On the second page of the **tea_flyer_unthread.indd** document, choose the second-column text frame with the **Selection** tool. To unthread (unlink) two frames, click the **in port** of the second frame. With the **Loaded Text** icon, click in either of the text frames that the thread is going between. You see a **Broken Link** icon ( ), indicating that you are about to unthread these two frames.

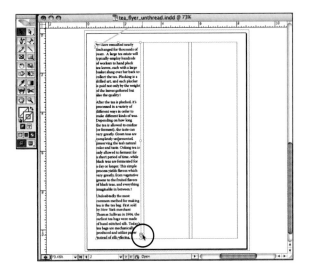

The text frames are now unthreaded, but both frames are still there, and your text is pulled back into the previous text frame, where you now see an **Overset Text** *icon (⊞). Now you can thread the overset text onto another page or into another column.*

Tip: *You can also double-click on the* **out port** *of the first text frame or the* **in port** *of the second text frame and achieve the unlinking in one step!*

4. Close the file without saving.

Basic Paragraph Formatting

Paragraph formatting, like character formatting, is at the heart of InDesign's typography capabilities. InDesign, like most other programs that allow for typographic control, has split your formatting up into two types—character formatting and paragraph formatting—for a reason. Character formatting is applied at the character level, whereas paragraph formatting is applied at the paragraph level. In other words, paragraph formats can be applied by simply placing your cursor in a paragraph (the formatting applies to the whole paragraph), whereas character formatting only applies to whatever text is selected.

The Control Palette's Paragraph Formatting Controls

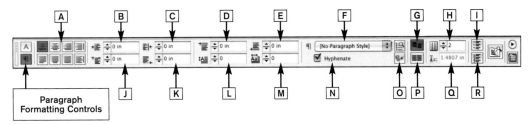

Paragraph Formatting Controls

Paragraph Formatting Controls and Functions	
Control	**Function**
Paragraph Formatting Controls button	Shows all paragraph formatting
A Paragraph alignment buttons	Set the horizontal alignment for a paragraph
B Left Indent field	Sets the amount a paragraph is indented from the left edge of the text frame
C Right Indent field	Sets the amount a paragraph is indented from the right edge of the text frame
D Space Before field	Sets the amount of space before a paragraph
E Space After field	Sets the amount of space after a paragraph
F Paragraph Style Applied field	Offers paragraph style options and shows which style is applied
G Do Not Align to Baseline Grid button	Does not lock text to the baseline grid, which is used to align columns of text and appears on the page like ruled notebook paper
H Number of Columns field	Allows for multiple columns in a single text frame
I Bulleted List button	Applies a bullet and indent to a selected paragraph
J First Line Left Indent field	Used for first line indents of paragraphs and for hanging indents
K Last Line Right Indent field	Useful for pushing the last line in from the right edge of the text frame
L Drop Cap Number of Lines field	Determines how many lines the drop cap drops down (that is, how many lines tall it is)

continues on next page

Paragraph Formatting Controls and Functions *continued*

Control	Function
M Drop Cap One or More Characters field	Determines how many characters are going to be included in the drop cap
N Hyphenate check box	Hyphenation is turned on by default; this option allows you to turn it on or off
O Clear Local Overrides button	Wipes local formatting off of text; works in conjunction with paragraph styles
P Align to Baseline Grid button	Locks text to the baseline grid
Q Horizontal Cursor Position field	Displays where your cursor is in the text relative to the left edge of the text frame
R Numbered List button	Applies a number and indent to a selected paragraph

NOTE | Control Palette vs. the Paragraph and Character Palettes: Which to Use?

As you have seen, InDesign offers several different ways to do the same thing. While many of you will enjoy the freedom the program gives you to work according to your own style, some of you who are new to InDesign might not be immediately clear on the advantages of the various options available to you. One example is whether to use the **Control** palette or the **Character** and **Paragraph** palettes. I tend to prefer the **Control** palette for some very basic reasons: it contains most of the formatting from both the **Character** and **Paragraph** palettes, it's docked out of the way, and there's only one control palette instead of two separate palettes. That said, the important thing is to use what is most comfortable for you, so which palette(s) you use most often is ultimately up to you. In the next chapter, "*Typography in InDesign*," you will see one formatting option that is available in the **Paragraph** palette and not in the **Control** palette (Adobe Single-line Composer), but for the most part, the functionality available in the **Control** palette is simply the sum of the options in the **Character** and **Paragraph** palettes.

7. ——————Applying Paragraph Formatting

In Exercise 2, "Applying Character Formatting," you learned how to apply some of the basic character formatting options, and in this exercise, you are going to learn how to apply some of the standard paragraph formats using the **Control** palette.

1. Open **tea_flyer_wtext.indd** from the **chap_04** folder you copied to your **Desktop** from the **InDesign CS2 HOT CD-ROM**. Select the **Type** tool from the **Toolbox**, and on the first page of this document, place your cursor in the first paragraph of the first column of text.

*Note: The **Missing Fonts** dialog box may appear when you open this file. If it does, change the font(s) by choosing **Find Font** and replacing the font(s) with a version of Times or another suitable font. To learn more about this, visit Exercise 1 of Chapter 5, "Typography in InDesign."*

2. With the cursor in the text, choose **Edit > Select All** or press **Ctrl+A** (Windows) or **Cmd+A** (Mac). With the text selected, click the **Paragraph Formatting** button on the **Control** palette. In the **Space After** field, specify a value of **0.125 in** using the arrow keys to the left of the **Space After** field, or type the number directly in the field.

*You are going to be applying some paragraph formatting to all the text within the threaded frames. **Edit > Select All** selects not only the text in the frame your cursor is in but also all the text within the threaded frames. Because all the text is selected, when you apply this formatting, it affects all of the text in the story.*

*Space After is a great feature for setting how much space will come after a paragraph return. I occasionally still use a hard return to insert space between paragraphs, but I find it more efficient to use **Space After** (and **Space Before**, which functions similarly, just adding space before a paragraph instead of after). These features are not only quick and easy to use; they can also be added to **Paragraph Styles**, as needed. (You will learn about styles in Chapter 6, "Type Styles.")*

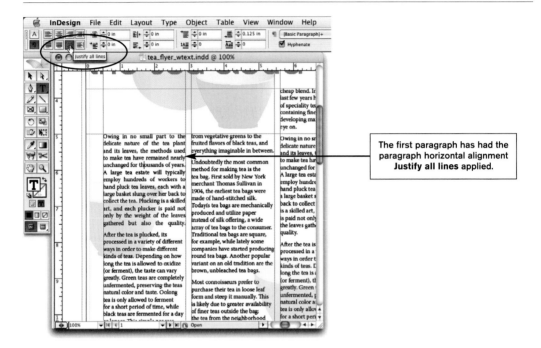

The first paragraph has had the paragraph horizontal alignment **Justify all lines** applied.

3. The next objective is to change the alignment of the first paragraph. Choose **Edit > Deselect All** to deselect the text. With the **Type** tool, place the cursor inside the first paragraph and click the **Paragraph Formatting Controls** button on the **Control** palette.

4. Click the **Justify all lines** button on the left end of the **Control** palette with **Paragraph Formatting Controls** selected.

*There are eight horizontal alignment methods for paragraphs, and each one has its own special purpose. The **Justify all lines** alignment is useful when you need to force a paragraph of text to fit into the column like a "block" of text that is aligned with both edges of the text frame. This alignment method may remind you of a newspaper layout.*

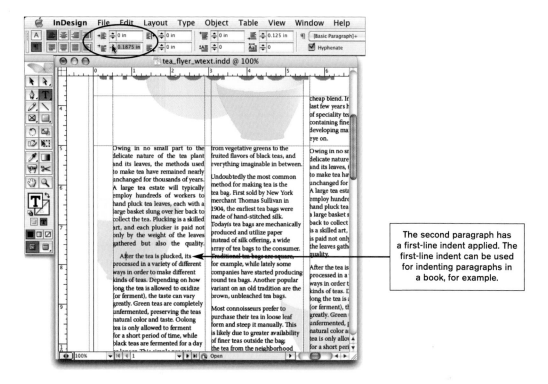

The second paragraph has a first-line indent applied. The first-line indent can be used for indenting paragraphs in a book, for example.

5. Other basic paragraph formats you will be using include indents. With the **Type** tool selected, click in the second paragraph that starts with "**After the tea**." In the **Control** palette (with **Paragraph Formatting Controls** still selected), you see settings for left, right, and first-line indents. Using the arrows to the left of the **First Line Left Indent** field, click the up arrow to increase the value to **0.1875 in**. Notice that the first line indents relative to the left edge of the text frame.

*In addition to using the up and down arrows to the left of the **First Line Left Indent** field, you can type a number directly into the field. Left indent is used in many books and other long documents, but it is also used to create bulleted and numbered lists.*

6. Choose **File > Save**, and then close it.

BONUS EXERCISE | Dragging and Dropping Text in InDesign

To learn how, check out **drag_drop.pdf** in the **bonus_exercises** folder on the **InDesign CS2 HOT CD-ROM**.

---

8. Checking Spelling

Like many other programs that handle text, InDesign CS2 has a spell-checking feature. InDesign supports 20 or so languages (including some regional dialects), which means the program has multiple dictionaries built in. As a result, it is important to use the proper dictionary, particularly when bringing text in from other programs. You will learn more about this in the Note, "Choosing Your Dictionary for Foreign Languages," following this exercise.

If you choose **Edit > Spelling > Check Spelling**, InDesign highlights misspelled or unknown words, words typed twice in a row (such as "it it"), and words with possible capitalization errors in the document. The **Check Spelling** dialog box allows you to change those highlighted words or leave them as is. By default, hyphenation and spelling rules are based on the dictionary for the language specified for the text. You can create user dictionaries, use multiple dictionaries to spell check or hyphenate a document, and import or export word lists saved in a plain text file.

InDesign CS2 has also added features like **Dynamic Spelling** and **Autocorrect**, both found in word processing applications and higher-end e-mail programs. You will learn how to enable and use these features in the section titled "Autocorrect and Dynamic Spelling" following this exercise.

1. Open the file **tea_flyer_spell.indd** from the **chap_04** folder on your **Desktop**.

*Note: The **Missing Fonts** dialog box may appear when you open this file. If it does, change the font(s) by choosing **Find Font** and replacing the font(s) with a version of Times or a suitable font. To learn more about this, visit Exercise 1 of Chapter 5, "Typography in InDesign."*

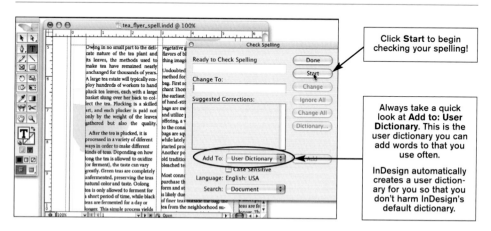

Click **Start** to begin checking your spelling!

Always take a quick look at **Add to: User Dictionary**. This is the user dictionary you can add words to that you use often.

InDesign automatically creates a user dictionary for you so that you don't harm InDesign's default dictionary.

2. With the **Type** tool, click in the first column of text. You may need to zoom in a bit using the **Zoom** tool from the **Toolbox**. Choose **Edit > Spelling > Check Spelling** or press **Ctrl+I** (Windows) or **Cmd+I** (Mac). Click **Start** in the **Check Spelling** dialog box that appears to begin spell checking.

Note: Make sure the cursor is in the text you are going to spell check. InDesign won't spell check anything unless the cursor is in the associated text.

Tip: Place the cursor at the beginning of the story if you wish to check all of it. Otherwise, InDesign will start from where the cursor is. If you start at the cursor point but want to spell check the whole story, InDesign gives you a quick fix. When it has finished checking from the cursor point, a dialog box appears that allows you to tell it to start at the beginning of the text. If you have selected text in your page before choosing **Edit > Spelling > Check Spelling**, pay attention to the **Search** drop-down menu in the **Check Spelling** dialog box. Your choices are **All Documents** (spell check all open documents), **Document**, **Story**, **To End of Story**, and **Selection**.

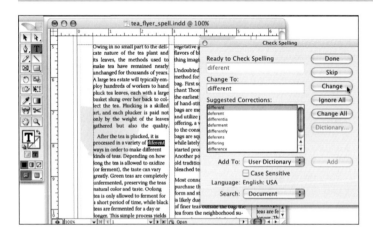

The **Done** button closes the **Check Spelling** dialog box, and **Skip** tells InDesign to skip the word in question.

3. Once started, InDesign flags the word "**diferent**." In the **Check Spelling** dialog box, click on the correct option in the **Suggested Corrections** field ("**different**"), and then click **Change**. InDesign CS2 moves on to the next word that it considers to be misspelled.

*Note: The word "**diferent**" that it flags may be in another location on your page. That's OK.*

*Change All corrects all occurrences of the word "**diferent**." This option is very useful for words that are typically misspelled or miscapitalized. For instance, I am constantly capitalizing the "O" in "You" when it starts a sentence (slow hand-eye coordination, I guess). Change All would catch and repair all those occurrences, freeing me from having to change them one by one. Ignore and Ignore All are useful if you run across a word (such as "Jurassic") and you don't want InDesign to flag it anymore; you can ignore each occurrence as it comes up or click Ignore All to, well, ignore all instances of the word. The Ignore and Ignore All commands are used in lieu of having to add the word to your dictionary.*

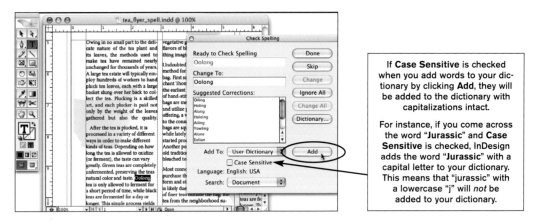

If **Case Sensitive** is checked when you add words to your dictionary by clicking **Add**, they will be added to the dictionary with capitalizations intact.

For instance, if you come across the word "Jurassic" and **Case Sensitive** is checked, InDesign adds the word "**Jurassic**" with a capital letter to your dictionary. This means that "jurassic" with a lowercase "j" will *not* be added to your dictionary.

4. Next, InDesign flags the word "**Oolong**." Add it to your dictionary by clicking **Add**. InDesign then moves on to the next suspect word.

*Clicking the **Add** button in the **Check Spelling** dialog box tells InDesign to add that word to your dictionary and make that word accessible for any document you work on from here on out. I add words like "**PageMaker**" and "**EPS**" because I use them in most of my handouts (and in this book).*

*The **Check Spelling** dialog box has been reworked a bit in InDesign CS2. Clicking the **Add** button used to take you to a separate window. In InDesign CS2, it automatically adds and continues on its merry way. If you wish to see the list of words you have added up to this point, click the **Dictionary** button in the **Check Spelling** dialog box.*

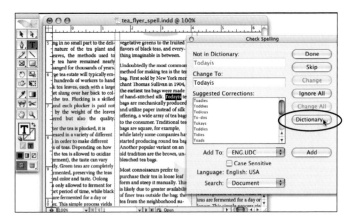

5. "**Todayis**" will most likely appear as the next suspect word. Ignore this word and click the **Dictionary** button in the **Check Spelling** dialog box. This allows you to see the word "**Oolong**" added to the dictionary in the previous step and to add another word you know you will run across while spell checking.

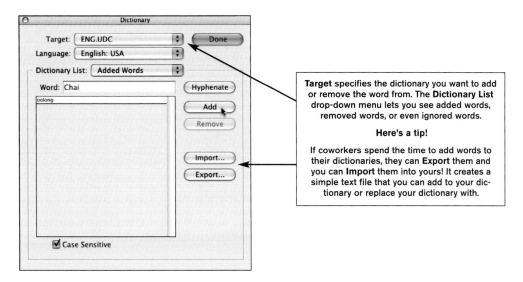

Target specifies the dictionary you want to add or remove the word from. The **Dictionary List** drop-down menu lets you see added words, removed words, or even ignored words.

Here's a tip!

If coworkers spend the time to add words to their dictionaries, they can **Export** them and you can **Import** them into yours! It creates a simple text file that you can add to your dictionary or replace your dictionary with.

6. In the **Dictionary** dialog box, type "**Chai**" in the **Word** field. Click the **Case Sensitive** check box to maintain its uppercase status (so it will flag it during spell checking if the word isn't capitalized). Click the **Add** button to see it added to your dictionary.

*The **Dictionary** dialog box is a great place to go if you have a number of words you know you want to add without having to "run across" them while spell checking. Some companies create their own dictionaries specific to their industry.*

7. Click the **Done** button to close the **Dictionary** dialog box and return to the **Check Spelling** dialog box.

8. Click the **Done** button in the **Check Spelling** dialog box to finish spell checking.

*There are more words that it will flag, but click **Done** to stop spell checking.*

9. Save your document by choosing **File > Save**, and then close it.

NOTE | Choosing a Dictionary for Foreign Languages

For most of you, running a spell checker will be pretty routine. However, if you place foreign language text files, or ASCII text files, you may need to pay more attention. In the **Text Import Options** dialog box (accessed by choosing **File > Place** and clicking the **Show Import Options** check box), make sure the correct dictionary is selected in the **Set Dictionary to** field. Choosing a dictionary is important if you want InDesign CS2 to provide accurate spell checking.

If your document includes foreign language text, there are three or more ways to change the dictionary to match your text language. Each of these methods affects the language at the selected text level, document level, or the application level:

1. **Selected text:** Select the text and use the **Language** pop-up menu (labeled **[No Language]**) in the **Character Formatting** controls in the **Control** palette or **Character** palette to specify the language for that text.

2. **An entire document:** To change the default dictionary for a specific document, choose **Edit > Deselect All** (or click in an open area of your document), and then choose the language from the **Language** pop-up menu (labeled **[No Language]**) in the **Character Formatting** controls in the **Control** palette or **Character** palette.

3. **All new documents:** Change the default dictionary used in InDesign by choosing the language from the **Language** pop-up menu (labeled **[No Language]**) in the **Character Formatting** controls in the **Control** palette or **Character** palette with no documents open.

TIP | Autocorrect and Dynamic Spelling

Two great new features in InDesign CS2 are **Autocorrect** and **Dynamic Spelling**. **Autocorrect** allows InDesign to automatically correct words as you type them. For instance, if you type "teh," InDesign instantly changes it to "the." Enabling **Dynamic Spelling** tells InDesign to underline potentially misspelled words as you type and allows you to access a contextual menu with possible spelling corrections.

To turn these features on for an open document, choose **Edit > Spelling > AutoCorrect** and/or **Dynamic Spelling**. To turn these features on globally, you will need to set your program preferences. First, you need to close all open documents.

continues on next page

TIP | Autocorrect and Dynamic Spelling *continued*

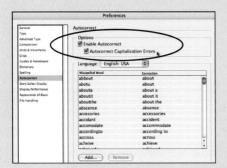 

In the **Autocorrect** panel of the **Preferences** dialog box **[Edit > Preferences > Autocorrect** (Windows) or **InDesign > Preferences > Autocorrect** (Mac)], click the **Enable Autocorrect** check box. To turn on **Dynamic Spelling** globally, keep all documents closed and choose **Edit > Preferences > Spelling** (Windows) or **InDesign > Preferences > Spelling** (Mac) and click the **Enable Dynamic Spelling** check box. Turning these settings on globally is great if you expect to use these features routinely.

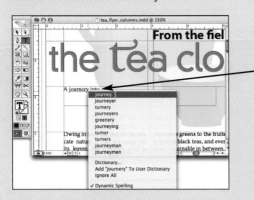

Right-clicking (Windows) or Ctrl+clicking (Mac) takes you to a list of word hints. This also allows you to add the word to your dictionary on the fly.

With **Dynamic Spelling** turned on, you can now create a text frame and begin typing. **Dynamic Spelling** will indicate misspelled words by a red wavy underline. You can correct spelling errors by **right-clicking** (Windows) or **Ctrl+clicking** (Mac) on a potentially misspelled word. If you type words in different languages, select the text and assign the correct language.

In this chapter, you learned the basics of text manipulation in InDesign CS2, including typing text directly into a document, placing text from external programs like Microsoft Word, creating text threads, and much more. The good news is, this is just the beginning. In the next chapter, you will learn some of the more advanced text features in InDesign CS2—features that give you optimal creative flexibility in working with text.

5

Typography in InDesign

Finding and Replacing Missing Fonts	Applying Leading
Applying Kerning	Working with Tracking	Drop Caps
Setting Tabs	Creating Bulleted and Numbered Lists
Working with Glyphs	Changing Type Case
Find/Change in Text

chap_05

InDesign CS2
HOT CD-ROM

The result of styling and arranging the look of text is often referred to as typography. Coming from programs like QuarkXPress and PageMaker, it's refreshing to see InDesign CS2's typographic power. Thanks to its wide range of typographic capabilities, InDesign CS2 allows you to focus on great design, rather than on software limitations. In the last chapter, you learned how to place text and apply basic paragraph and character formatting. In this chapter, you will learn how to use several of InDesign's more advanced typography features, including fine-tuning text with leading, kerning, and tracking, and stylizing text with drop caps, paragraph rules, and lists. You will also dive into everyone's perennial favorite—tabs. All these features are integral to creating well-designed, stylized text.

Character vs. Paragraph Formatting

Paragraph and character formatting are at the heart of InDesign's typographic capabilities. Character formatting, which includes choosing the font, font size, kerning, tracking, and more, is applied at the character level, whereas paragraph formatting, which includes the alignment, indent, spaces before and after, and more, is applied at the paragraph level. While paragraph formats can be applied by placing the cursor in a paragraph (the formatting applies to the whole paragraph), character formatting is only applied to the selected text.

In the previous chapter (Chapter 4, "*Working with Text*"), you learned about some of the differences between character and paragraph formatting. In this chapter, those differences will become even more distinct.

I. ——————————Finding and Replacing Missing Fonts

In this chapter, you will learn about InDesign CS2's more advanced typographic features. First, you will learn about the one of the fundamental, although not always straightforward, components of typography—fonts. In the first exercise, you will learn how to handle files that use fonts you don't have.

1. Open **tea_product_begin.indd** from the **chap_05** folder on your **Desktop**.

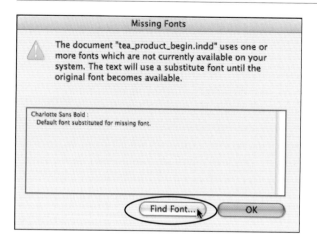

2. When the document opens, a dialog box titled **Missing Fonts** appears. As you work in the program, expect to see this fairly often (everyone does). Click **Find Font** to open the **Find Font** dialog box.

*The **Missing Fonts** dialog box alerts you to the fact that you have just opened, or are using, a document that uses fonts that aren't installed on your system. The reality is, most people are faced with font issues from time to time—it's almost unavoidable because fonts have a significant impact on output. The **Missing Fonts** dialog box may show more than one font. That's all right.*

Note: *If you open a document that uses the PostScript Type 1 version of a font and you have the True Type version of that same font (or vice versa), InDesign tells you that the font is missing. **When InDesign is missing a font, it substitutes the missing font with an available font.** As in other programs, a font change can cause InDesign to flow text differently.*

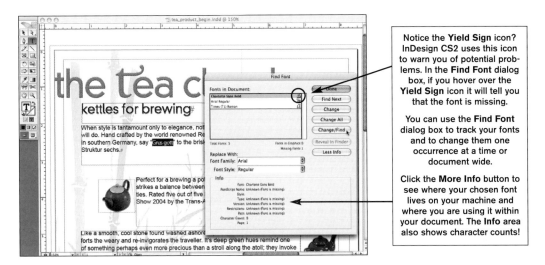

Notice the **Yield Sign** icon? InDesign CS2 uses this icon to warn you of potential problems. In the **Find Font** dialog box, if you hover over the **Yield Sign** icon it will tell you that the font is missing.

You can use the **Find Font** dialog box to track your fonts and to change them one occurrence at a time or document wide.

Click the **More Info** button to see where your chosen font lives on your machine and where you are using it within your document. The **Info** area also shows character counts!

3. The **Find Font** dialog box is where you can keep track of what fonts are being used where in a document, and you can change the fonts used in the document. In this dialog box (which you can also open by choosing **Type > Find Font**), click **Charlotte Sans Bold** in the **Fonts in Document** list.

*Note: If you see several fonts listed in the **Missing Fonts** dialog box, a **Yield Sign** icon appears to the right of the names of each font in the **Find Font** dialog box. You can replace those fonts as well if you choose to.*

4. In the **Replace With** section, select **Arial** as the **Font Family** and **Regular** as the **Font Style**.

*Note: If you don't have **Arial**, select **Helvetica**, **Times Roman**, or **Times New Roman**.*

*The **Replace With** section tells InDesign to replace the font you chose from the **Fonts in Document** list in Step 3 with Arial (or another font if you don't have Arial).*

5. Before replacing the missing font with another, you need to see where it appears in your document. Click the **Find First** button (the illustration above shows a **Find Next** button. The **Find Next** button appears after the first time you click the **Find First** button). InDesign highlights where the first bit of text that is supposed to be using Charlotte Sans Bold, the font that is missing. The text "**Grus gott**" should be highlighted because it is the first occurrence of the font Charlotte Sans Bold.

6. Click **Change/Find** to change the text that is highlighted to Arial Regular.

*There are three methods for changing a font: **Change**, **Change All**, and **Change/Find**. **Change** changes just the highlighted text to the **Replace With** font you chose. **Change All** changes all the text in the entire document that uses the font Charlotte Sans Bold to Arial Regular (this is referred to as a global font change). **Change/Find** changes the first occurrence of Charlotte Sans Bold and then it finds the next occurrence of Charlotte Sans Bold in the document, so you can decide what to do in each instance.*

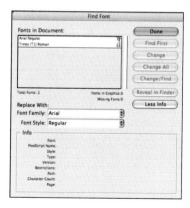

7. Once the occurrence of the missing font is changed to Arial Regular, the search should be complete and the **Find Fonts** dialog box should show no more **Yield Sign** icons. Click **Done**.

Once again, if you have more than one font missing, it's because either Times Roman or Arial Regular is not available for InDesign to use. Feel free to change any other missing fonts to a version of Times.

Note: *In Chapter 6, "Type Styles," you will learn about paragraph and character styles. When using the **Find Font** dialog box to replace a font, you need to take into account any styles you've created.*

8. Leave this file open for the next exercise.

TIP | Missing Fonts in Your Document

Everyone at some point or another clicks **OK** when first opening a file and being faced with the **Missing Fonts** dialog box you saw at the beginning of this exercise. When you click **OK** in that dialog box, InDesign does a few things. First, it substitutes the font with a font that is available on your system and that it considers to be similar to the original missing font.

InDesign also adds a pink highlight to all the text for which it has replaced a missing font.

Note: *If you work in **Preview** mode, InDesign does not show you the pink highlighting!*

continues on next page

TIP | Missing Fonts in Your Document *continued*

Select the **Type** tool from the **Toolbox**, place the cursor in any text that has pink highlighting, and look at the **Control** palette. Click the **Character Formatting Controls** button (A) on the left end of the **Control** palette if it's not already selected. In the **Font Family** and **Font Style** fields, you see the font name and/or style name in brackets. The brackets are another way InDesign tells you that the text you have selected (or have the cursor in) is missing the original font.

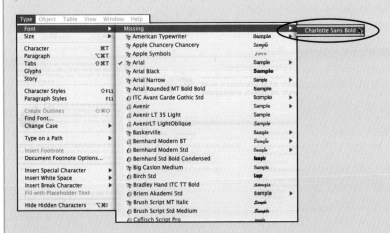

In addition to the pink highlights and bracketed font name, InDesign has a third way of alerting you to missing fonts. Choose **Type > Font > Missing**, and you see a list of all the fonts in the document that are being used in the document but can't be found on your system by InDesign.

The image of the **Type > Font > Missing** menu in this Tip only shows the **Charlotte Sans Bold** font. If you had other missing fonts, they would appear here as well.

Working with Leading, Kerning, and Tracking

Now that you can handle fonts in InDesign, you are ready to learn how to control **leading**, **kerning**, and **tracking**. These features are often used for copyfitting (fitting all of the text on the page), as well as for design elements like headlines (letter spacing), and more.

What Are Leading, Kerning, and Tracking?

The vertical space between lines of type is called **leading**. Leading is measured from the baseline of one line of text to the baseline of the line *above* it. Baselines are not visible by default.

If you've always dreamed of being free to combine earnest decor with unparalleled craftsmanship, then be sure to consider our set entitled Blue Flowers™. Each is hand painted with a different type of flower in celebration of the vibrant diversity and beauty of nature, the arrangements of which are changed seasonally.

All text sits on invisible baselines (like ruled paper). The distance between those baselines is the leading.

InDesign automatically sets the leading at 120 percent of the size of the font to which leading is applied.

Leading is automatically applied to all paragraphs. Without leading, text lines would be bunched together. InDesign automatically sets the leading at 120 percent of the size of the font. For example, if a paragraph is using 12-pt type, InDesign automatically sets the leading at 14.4 pt (120 percent of 12 pt). This means that the larger the font size, the larger the automatic leading value.

The horizontal space between two letters is called **kerning**. In short, kerning is measured in $^1/_{1000}$ em, a unit of measure that is relative to the type size. Every pair of letters in a font has a set distance between them, such as *t* and *h* in the word *the*. This is called a **kern pair**. You will learn how to adjust kerning in the following exercise.

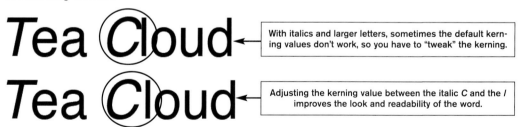

With italics and larger letters, sometimes the default kerning values don't work, so you have to "tweak" the kerning.

Adjusting the kerning value between the italic *C* and the *l* improves the look and readability of the word.

Adjusting the horizontal space between more than two letters (such as a word or headline) is called **tracking**. Some refer to this as "loosening" or "tightening" a selection of text. Tracking is also measured in $^1/_{1000}$ em, a unit of measure that is relative to the type size.

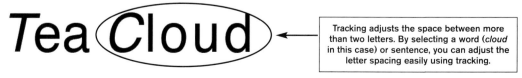

Tracking adjusts the space between more than two letters. By selecting a word (*cloud* in this case) or sentence, you can adjust the letter spacing easily using tracking.

Working with Leading in InDesign CS2

Leading works similarly in InDesign CS2 as it does in other applications. There is automatic leading, which is preset at 120 percent of the type size. You can also either choose a **Leading** value from a drop-down menu or type a value directly into the **Leading** field. Whichever method you choose, **Leading** values are measured in point sizes, so if you set 12 pt leading on 12 pt type, there will be no space between the lines of text in your paragraph.

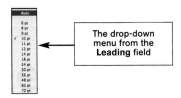

The drop-down menu from the **Leading** field

The difference between InDesign's leading and that of other page layout applications is how InDesign applies leading by default.

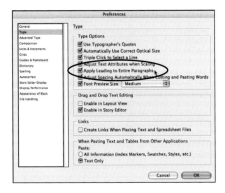

Unlike many other page layout programs, which apply leading to all the text in a paragraph, regardless of how much of the paragraph is selected (even if the cursor is just placed in a paragraph), InDesign applies leading only to the text that is selected. At the outset, it will take time to get accustomed to this if you have been working with leading in other page layout applications.

To set *how* leading is applied, choose **Edit > Preferences > Type** (Windows) or **InDesign > Preferences > Type** (Mac) and select the **Type** category from the left side of the dialog box. In the **Type Options** area, check the box next to **Apply Leading to Entire Paragraphs**. This sets the leading for the open document to apply to the whole paragraph, even if you just place the cursor in it. I would suggest checking that box so you can easily apply leading to entire paragraphs. Click **OK** to close the **Preferences** dialog box.

Tip: If you are coming from QuarkXPress, having this option checked may be more comfortable because that is how QuarkXPress deals with leading. If you want to set this preference globally, close all open documents, and then set the leading preference.

2.————————**Applying Leading**

Before learning about leading, you first need to place text. The text you place at the beginning of this exercise you will also use for several other exercises later in the chapter, when you will learn to apply kerning and tracking as well.

1. With **tea_product_begin.indd** open from the previous exercise, choose **File > Place**. From the **chap_05** folder on the **Desktop**, select **product_list.txt** from the **text** folder and click **Open**.

*Note: As you learned in Chapter 4, "Working with Text," if **Show Imports Options** is checked in the **Place** dialog box, the **Show Import Options** dialog box appears. If you see that dialog box, just click **OK**. The features within that dialog box are not relevant in this particular exercise.*

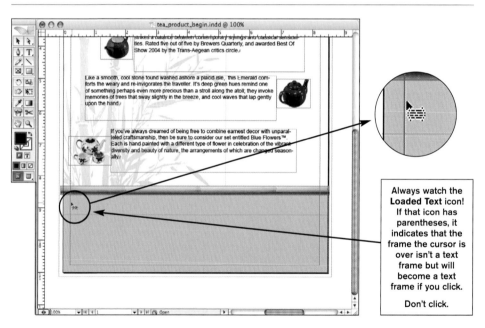

Always watch the **Loaded Text** icon! If that icon has parentheses, it indicates that the frame the cursor is over isn't a text frame but will become a text frame if you click.

Don't click.

*With the **Loaded Text** icon, you are going to place the text in the greenish-colored frame at the bottom of the page. If you bring the cursor into that frame, you notice the icon change. The parentheses indicate that you are about to convert the frame you are hovering over into a text frame. I suggest creating a new frame.*

*If you drag a horizontal guide on the page and bring the **Loaded Text** icon with parentheses close to it, it won't matter that you are hovering over a frame that can be converted. The **Loaded Text** icon with parentheses turns into the **Loaded Text** icon without parentheses, which indicates that InDesign will create a new text frame.*

Tip: Watch the **Control** *palette at the top of the screen to see where the guide is. If you hold the* **Shift** *key down while dragging the guide (you can even hold down the* **Shift** *key after beginning to drag the guide out), the guide snaps to whole-unit measurements on the rulers.*

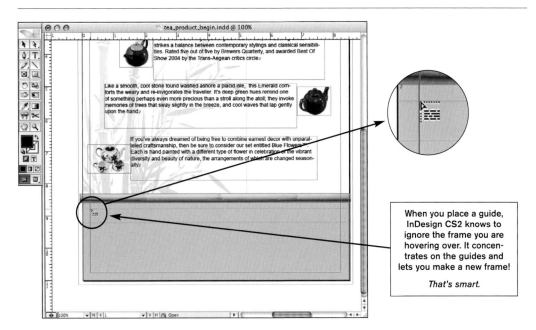

When you place a guide, InDesign CS2 knows to ignore the frame you are hovering over. It concentrates on the guides and lets you make a new frame!

That's smart.

2. If you don't see rulers in the document window, choose **View > Show Rulers**. With the **Loaded Text** icon, drag a horizontal guide from the horizontal (top) ruler. Drag the guide down to **8.7 in** from the top edge of the page. Once the guide is in place, bring the **Loaded Text** icon to the point where the guide you just drew and the left margin guide meet. Click to place the text.

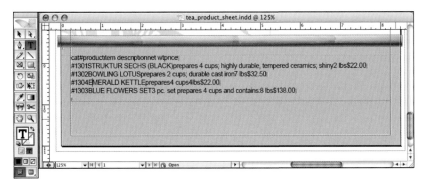

The text should be placed within a frame that InDesign creates to fit within the margin guides, starting vertically at the guide you created in Step 2 of this exercise.

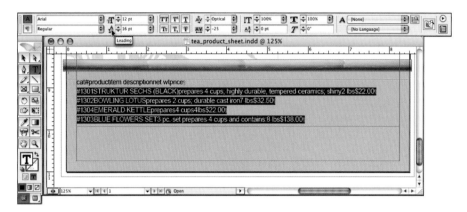

3. With the **Type** tool selected from the **Toolbox**, select all the text you just placed except for the first line by clicking and dragging across the text or by choosing **Edit > Select All** or by pressing **Ctrl+A** (Windows) or **Cmd+A** (Mac). Make sure that the hidden characters are showing by choosing **Type > Show Hidden Characters**. This gives visual feedback to help you determine what is a paragraph, soft return, and so on.

4. From the **Character Formatting** controls of the **Control** palette (or if you prefer, you can use the **Character** palette found under **Type > Character**), type **16** into the **Leading** field.

5. Choose **File > Save**. The next few exercises will build on what you have just done, so keep the file open.

*Leading is a great way to control exactly how your text looks. It's also a great way to fit a lot of copy into a smaller space or even fill a lot of space with a little copy. This is referred to as **copyfitting**. In the next exercise, you will learn how to use kerning to control the spacing between some of the letters within the text on the page.*

3. —————————Applying Kerning

In this next exercise, you will adjust some problem areas within the text using kerning.

1. The file **tea_product_begin.indd** should be open from the previous exercise.

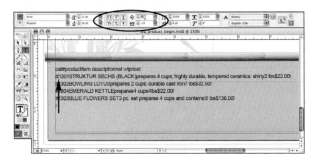

2. With the **Type** tool selected, place the cursor between the **#** (pound sign) and the **1** in **#1301**. To adjust the space between these two characters, from the **Character Formatting** controls in the **Control** palette (or from the **Character** palette) choose **75** from the **Kerning** drop-down menu.

*Note: A positive value increases the space, whereas a negative number decreases the space. You can also use the two smaller arrows to the left of any of the **Character Formatting** controls to increase the values by smaller increments.*

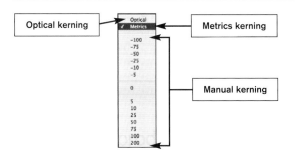

*Note: Kerning in InDesign can be **Optical**, **Metrics**, or **Manual**. **Metrics** is the default kerning that is built into the font. **Optical** kerning adjusts the spaces between letters based on the shape of the letters. This is more visually based than the "numbers" approach used by **Metrics**. **Manual** kerning is a more free-form option that lets you adjust the spacing between letters according to your sensibilities. In the last step, you changed the kerning manually, so neither **Metrics** nor **Optical** will be checked in the **Kerning** menu.*

3. Save the document and keep it open for one more exercise. In the next exercise, you will learn about tracking.

Working with Tracking

Now that you have a better handle on kerning, you are ready to learn how to adjust **tracking**, or the spacing between two or more letters. In fact, you are going to adjust the spacing between all the letters in the first paragraph. Tracking is great for adjusting headlines and trying to fit lines of text into a column.

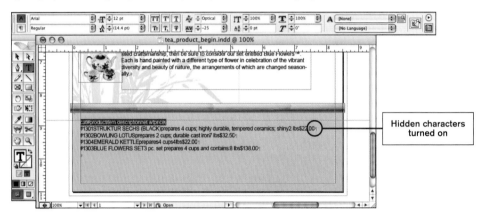

Hidden characters turned on

1. Still working in the **tea_product_begin.indd** document from the previous exercise, use the **Type** tool to select the first paragraph of the text you placed, starting with the word "**cat**." The first line of the text is a paragraph all to itself.

*Note: Make sure you can see **hidden characters**. If not, choose **Type > Show Hidden Characters**.*

Tip: You don't have to drag through the text to select the paragraph. You can select an entire paragraph by quadruple-clicking it (clicking it four times). Also, double-clicking text selects a word, and triple-clicking selects the line the cursor is in.

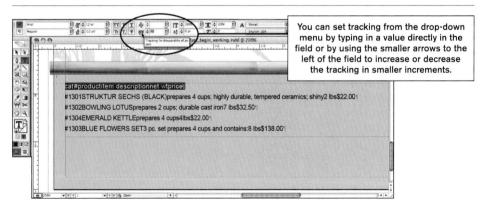

You can set tracking from the drop-down menu by typing in a value directly in the field or by using the smaller arrows to the left of the field to increase or decrease the tracking in smaller increments.

2. From the **Control** palette (or the **Character** palette), type **40** in the **Tracking** field.

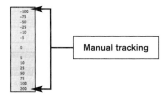

Manual tracking

*Note: All tracking in InDesign is **Manual**. With **Manual** tracking, you can adjust the spacing between selected letters using your own judgment. A positive value increases the distance between the selected letters, and a negative value decreases the distance between the selected letters.*

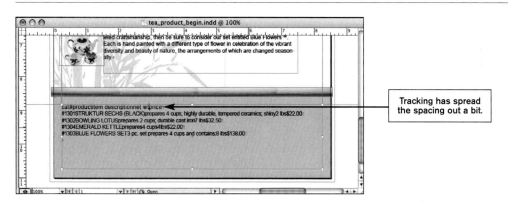

Tracking has spread the spacing out a bit.

3. Save the file and keep it open for the next exercise, in which you will learn how to apply drop caps.

Preferences for Leading and Kerning Keyboard Shortcuts

Below are the preference settings for Keyboard Increments in InDesign CS1 (the previous version of InDesign).

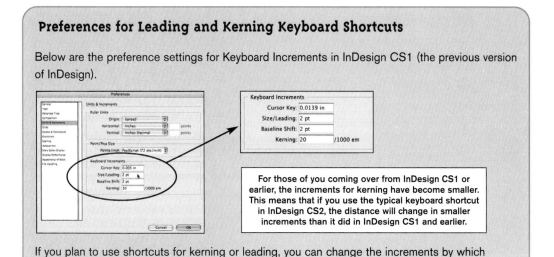

For those of you coming over from InDesign CS1 or earlier, the increments for kerning have become smaller. This means that if you use the typical keyboard shortcut in InDesign CS2, the distance will change in smaller increments than it did in InDesign CS1 and earlier.

If you plan to use shortcuts for kerning or leading, you can change the increments by which they change by choosing **Edit > Preferences > Units & Increments > Keyboard Increments** (Windows) or **InDesign > Preferences > Units & Increments > Keyboard Increments** (Mac).

TIP | Leading, Kerning, and Tracking Shortcuts

Here are some of the more widely used typography shortcuts within InDesign CS2. If you want to see a complete list of these shortcuts, return to Chapter 2, "*Interface.*"

Leading, Kerning, and Tracking Shortcuts	
Function	**Shortcut**
Increase leading	**Text: Text: Alt+Down Arrow** (Windows) or **Option+Down Arrow** (Mac)
Increase leading × 5	**Text: Text: Alt+Ctrl+Down Arrow** (Windows) or **Option+Cmd+Down Arrow** (Mac)
Decrease leading	**Text: Text: Alt+Up Arrow** (Windows) or **Option+Up Arrow** (Mac)
Decrease leading × 5	**Text: Text: Alt+Ctrl+Up Arrow** (Windows) or **Option+Cmd+Up Arrow** (Mac)
Decrease kerning/tracking	**Text: Alt+Down Arrow** (Windows) or **Option+Left Arrow** (Mac)
Decrease kerning/tracking × 5	**Text: Text: Alt+Down Arrow** (Windows) or **Option+Cmd+Left Arrow** (Mac)
Increase kerning/tracking	**Text: Option+Right Arrow** (Mac) or **Text: Alt+Down Arrow** (Windows)
Increase kerning/tracking × 5	**Text: Text: Alt+Down Arrow** (Windows) or **Option+Cmd+Right Arrow** (Mac)

Drop Caps

Much of typography is meant for mechanical tasks like copyfitting text into a newspaper or magazine layout, but it has an artistic side as well. One example of artistic typography is the drop cap, which you will learn to use in this next exercise. You've probably seen it used in a book or magazine, where the first letter of a paragraph is formatted in a very large point size. That letter is called a drop cap.

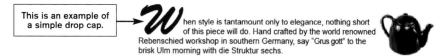

This is an example of a simple drop cap.

*W*hen style is tantamount only to elegance, nothing short of this piece will do. Hand crafted by the world renowned Rebenschied workshop in southern Germany, say "Grus gott" to the brisk Ulm morning with die Struktur sechs.

The drop cap format can be applied to one or more characters in a paragraph. InDesign starts with the first character of a paragraph (whatever that may be) and works its way into the first line, depending on how many characters you tell it to format as drop caps.

1. Scroll to the top of the document **tea_product_begin.indd**, which you used in the last exercise, or you can open it from the **chap_05** folder you copied to your **Desktop** from the **InDesign CS2 HOT CD-ROM**.

2. Using the **Type** tool from the **Toolbox**, place the cursor in the first paragraph that starts with, "**When style is**."

Don't forget! *You learned in Chapter 4, "Working with Text," that if you want to apply para-graph formatting to a single paragraph, simply place the cursor anywhere in it. Then choose your formatting, and paragraph formatting will be applied to the whole paragraph!*

3. Click the **Paragraph Formatting Controls** button (![¶]) in the **Control** palette (or use the **Paragraph** palette), and increase the value in the **Drop Cap Number of Lines** field to **2** using the up arrow to the left of the field.

4. With the cursor still in the paragraph from the previous steps, click the **Paragraph Formatting Controls** button (![¶]) in the **Control** palette (or the **Paragraph** palette), and increase the value in the **Drop Cap One or More Characters** field to **4** by using the up arrow to the left of the field. Notice that the entire word "**When**" appears enlarged instead of only one character. Change the **Drop Cap One or More Characters** value back to **1**.

*There are two parts to a drop cap: **Drop Cap Number of Lines** and **Drop Cap One or More Characters**. Drop Cap Number of Lines instructs InDesign how many lines tall the first character should be "dropped." The **Drop Cap One or More Characters** tells InDesign how many characters, starting from the first in the paragraph, to include in the drop cap.*

5. Next you will use kerning to adjust the space between the drop cap and the adjacent text. With the **Type** tool, place the cursor after the "**W**" in the first paragraph. Switching to the character formats by choosing the **Character Formatting Controls** button in the **Control** palette (or from the **Character** palette) enter **20** in the **Kerning** field by manually typing it into the field or using the arrows to the left of that field.

*Note: Even though you adjusted the kerning between what looks like the drop cap and the "**h**" in the word "**When**," InDesign adjusts the space between the drop cap and the letter to the right of it on each line.*

6. Select the "**W**" with the **Type** tool and adjust the font size in the **Control** palette (or **Character** palette) to **21** pt.

Adjusting the font size of a drop cap allows you to raise the height of the letter(s) above the height of the first line of the paragraph. This can be great if used to raise the ascenders (the part of a lower-case character b, d, f, h, k, l, and t that extends above the height of lowercase letters) above the first line to give the drop cap a more "natural" look.

7. Save the file and close it.

What Is Hyphenation?

I remember starting out in the graphics field and listening to those with much more experience than I talk about "the art of typography." This "art" involves some of the features you have already learned—font selection, justification, kerning, tracking, leading—as well as some new ones like hyphenation. Together, these features control the look and feel of text. Many design experts say that that "good" typography should be "invisible" to the reader, which I interpret as a recommendation for neat, clean type that doesn't have jarring word hyphenations or "rivers" of white space running through it.

***

BONUS EXERCISE | Working with Text Hyphenation

To achieve "neat and clean" hyphenated (broken) words requires you to control the hyphenation of text. To learn how, check out **hyphenate.pdf** in the **bonus_exercises** folder on the **InDesign CS2 HOT CD-ROM**.

***

Working with Tabs

The spacebar just may be the most overused key on the keyboard. Many people use it to align words and sentences. To these people, I highly recommend tab therapy. Plodding away on the spacebar is a highly imprecise way to align text. **Tabs** allow you to control the placement and alignment of lists and words with ease. Tabs can also be saved within a paragraph style (you'll learn more in Chapter 6).

Many of you are probably familiar with the **Tab** key on your keyboard, which can be used to indent text, for instance. What is often less evident is how to control **tabs**. Every time you press the **Tab** key, InDesign looks at the horizontal ruler and moves the text to the next half-inch mark (or equivalent if you have your units set differently). This can be jarring because, depending on where the text starts before you add tabs, it will be clear that tabs move text by different distances at different times. This is best explained through experience. By pressing the **Tab** key and looking at the horizontal ruler. you can see exactly where the tab stopped. **Tab stops** are the mechanism with which you control tabs. In this exercise, you are going to use tabs to align the text at the bottom of **tea_product_begin.indd** into neat, organized categories.

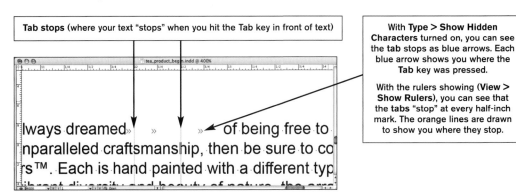

Tab stops (where your text "stops" when you hit the Tab key in front of text)

With **Type > Show Hidden Characters** turned on, you can see the **tab stops** as blue arrows. Each blue arrow shows you where the Tab key was pressed.

With the rulers showing (**View > Show Rulers**), you can see that the **tabs** "stop" at every half-inch mark. The orange lines are drawn to show you where they stop.

The Tabs Palette

This palette, found under **Type > Tabs**, allows you to set **tab stops**, or how and where text stops after you press the **Tab** key. The ruler along the bottom edge of the **Tabs** palette has a zero starting point on the left end. This zero ruler corresponds to the left edge of the text frame.

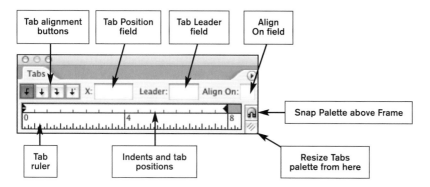

Tabs Palette	
Option	**Functionality**
Tab alignment buttons	Determine how the text aligns to the tab placed before it.
Tab Position field	Relative to the left edge of the text frame, the **Tab Position** field indicates how far the tab will go.
Tab Leader field	A tab leader is a repeated character (of your choosing) between the tab and the text that follows it. An example is a restaurant menu that looks like this: Salad. $2.95
Align On field	When you click a tab alignment button (**Left-Justified, Center-Justified, Right-Justified**, or **Align to Decimal**), you can tell InDesign to stop the text at a specific character, like a dollar sign ($), by typing that character into the **Align On** field.
Snap Palette above Frame	This positions the **Tabs** palette above the text frame the cursor is in.
Indents and tab positions	This is where tab stops and indents are created.
Tab ruler	This ruler lines up with the text frame, with the zero on the ruler lining up with left edge of the text frame.

Choosing Tab Alignment

Choosing one of the tab alignment buttons is the first step to controlling tabs. Each of these buttons has a particular purpose. Placing the cursor in front of the text you are going to tab over and then pressing the **Tab** key causes the text to move. Where it moves and how it aligns on the tab stop is up to you. There are four tab alignment buttons for aligning text to the tab stop: **Left-Justified**, **Center-Justified**, **Right-Justified**, and **Align to Decimal**. The following chart shows examples of the same tab stop position, each one using a different alignment method.

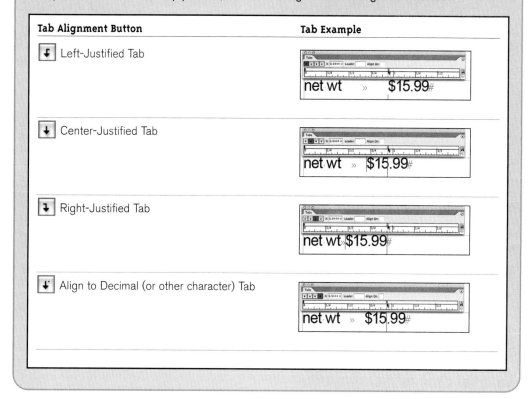

Tab Alignment Button	Tab Example
Left-Justified Tab	net wt » $15.99
Center-Justified Tab	net wt » $15.99
Right-Justified Tab	net wt »$15.99
Align to Decimal (or other character) Tab	net wt » $15.99

6. _____ Setting Tabs

In this exercise, you will learn how to set and use tabs. Tabs may not be the most exciting or creative part of page layout, but they are a necessary evil and one of the most misunderstood features of page layout programs.

1. Open **tea_product_tabs.indd** from the **chap_05** folder you copied onto your **Desktop**.

*After opening the document, the **Missing Fonts** dialog box may appear. Click the **Find Font** button, and replace the missing fonts. For a refresher on how to deal with missing fonts, refer to the first exercise of the chapter.*

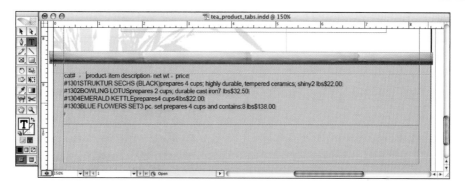

2. You are going to put some tabs into your text and then control how and where the tabs stop (that's why they are called tab stops). With the **Type** tool, click between "**cat#**" and "**product**" and press **Tab** on your keyboard. Place tabs between "**product**" and "**item description**," between "**item description**" and "**net wt**," and between "**net wt**" and "**price**."

Note: The reason for placing tabs in the text and then controlling how they work is so that you can see how to change the text tabs as you go. Of course, you could set the tab stops first and then place the tabs in the text.

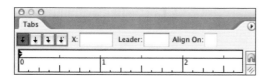

3. Open the **Tabs** palette by choosing **Type > Tabs**.

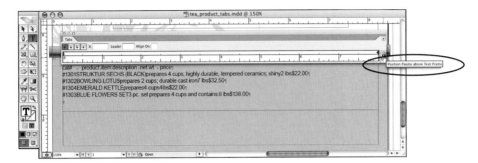

4. Place the cursor in the text frame at the bottom of the page with the **Type** tool. With the **Tabs** palette open in your workspace, click the **Magnet** icon on the right side of the **Tabs** palette to automatically position the **Tabs** palette horizontally with the text frame that the cursor is in.

*Note: The **Magnet** icon won't always give you the desired effect! If the text frame you are going to place tabs into is too close to the top of the document window, InDesign won't have enough room to move the **Tabs** palette into position above the text frame. Notice in my example picture in Step 3, I have some space between the text frame and the top of the document window.*

*The great thing about the **Tabs** palette is that it doesn't even have to be near the text your are applying tabs to. When you set tabs in the next few steps, you will notice a line extending down into your text. That line is showing you where the tab will line up. So although it's not necessary, it's nice to have the **Tabs** palette above the text you are working on. You can always drag the **Tabs** palette into position if the **Magnet** icon isn't working!*

5. With the cursor in the text frame, choose **Edit > Select All**, or press **Ctrl+A** (Windows) or **Cmd+A** (Mac).

*The first step is to determine where you want the tabs to go and how you want them to work. The reason for selecting all the text in the text frame is so that as you set the tabs, the formatting will apply to all the paragraphs in that frame at once. The positions of the tabs you placed with the **Tab** key in the first paragraph will be saved in all these paragraphs. You just have to add the actual tabs using the **Tab** key later on!*

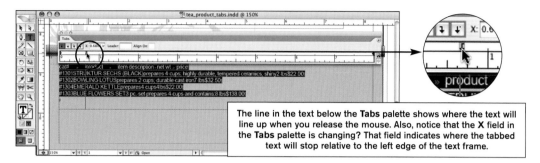

The line in the text below the **Tabs** palette shows where the text will line up when you release the mouse. Also, notice that the X field in the **Tabs** palette is changing? That field indicates where the tabbed text will stop relative to the left edge of the text frame.

6. From the **Tabs** palette, click the **Left Justified** tab alignment button. In the **Tab** area above the ruler, click and place a tab at approximately **0.68 inch**. Once you click to place the tab, you can click and drag it into position.

*Note: Tab placement is either done numerically using set values or, as in this case, visually. As you move the tab into position, a line will show up beneath the **Tabs** palette within the text. This line indicates where the text will stop within the text frame. As you set **tab stops** in the **Tabs** palette, the text will shift position to reflect the new **tab stops.** However, the number of tab stops needs to match the number of **tabs** inserted with the **Tab** key. So, if you set the first tab stop, this will only apply to the first tab inserted with the **Tab** key. In Step 2 of this exercise, you pressed the **Tab** key four times, placing four tabs into the first paragraph. In Step 6, you controlled the positioning of the first tab with a **tab stop**. You will now place the same type of left-justified tab for the three remaining **tab stops** that need to be set.*

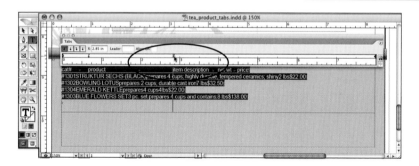

7. With the text still highlighted, click the **Left-Justified** tab alignment button in the **Tabs** palette, click in the **Tab** area above the ruler (where your first tab is showing up) and drag into position. The **X** field in the **Tabs** palette should read something like **2.85 in** when selected. The text beginning with "**item description**" should move so that the "**i**" in "**item**" lines up with the second tab you set.

*Note: Tabs placed in the **Tabs** palette can be very fluid. They can be moved at any time, as long as the cursor is in text (or multiple paragraphs are selected) and the **Tabs** palette is open. Simply click the existing tab above the **Tabs** ruler and drag it into its new position!*

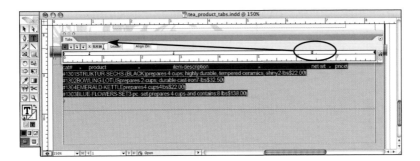

8. For the third tab, click the **Left-Justified** tab alignment button again, and then click in the **Tab** area above the **Tabs** ruler to set the tab to the right of the second tab you just set in Step 7. With the tab still chosen, select the text in the **X** field in the **Tabs** palette and type **6.4**. Press **Enter** or **Return** to apply it.

*Note: By placing a tab in the **Tabs** palette and then typing a value in the **X** field, you are setting the tab to stop at an exact position from the left edge of the text frame. This can give you very precise control of text positioning.*

Note: The tab you just set has a gray box behind it, telling you that it is the selected tab. If you choose another tab alignment, the selected tab changes, depending on which of the four types of tab alignments you chose. Always pay attention to which tab is selected before moving on!

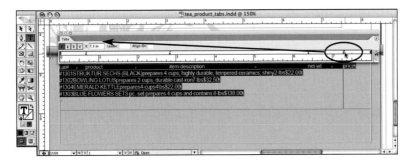

9. Place the fourth tab using the same you used for the first two tabs you set (visually). Click the **Left-Justified** tab alignment button, and place the tab in the **Tab** area above the **Tabs** ruler in the **Tabs** palette by clicking. Position it so that the **X** field in the **Tabs** palette reads **7.3 in** or so (doesn't have to be exact).

*Note: Notice how only the first paragraph is moving as you add tabs in the **Tabs** palette? Don't forget, you haven't actually pressed the **Tab** key and placed the tabs into the rest of the paragraphs. You will do that soon.*

*In the next step, you will add a little flair to the tabs using the **Align to Decimal** tab alignment button to place periods between the "**net wt**" text and the "**price**" text.*

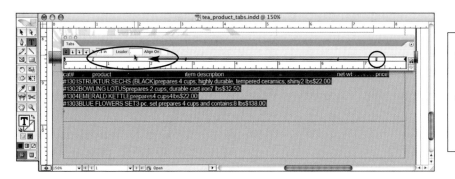

You can change any tab at any time. Simply select the tab from above the **Tabs** ruler and set either the **X**, **Leader**, or **Align On** field.

10. With the **Type** tool still active, select the fourth tab (the one you just set in Step 9) from the **Tabs** palette. In the **Leader** field in the **Tabs** palette, type a **period (.)** and press the **spacebar**. You see dots appear between the "**net wt**" text and the "**price**" text. This is referred to as a **dot leader**.

*Tip: The period (.) may be sufficient for you, but sometimes the periods are too close together. You can adjust the space between the repeating periods by pressing the spacebar in the **Leader** field. You also can use a character other than the period, such as an underscore (_) to create a solid line.*

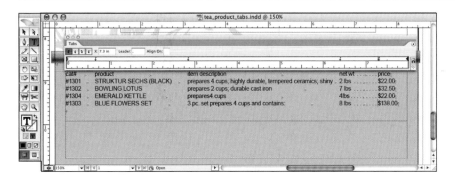

11. Now that the tabs are set, keep the **Tabs** palette open. You will need it in the next step. For now, in each paragraph, place tabs by placing the cursor and pressing the **Tab** key between the **cat#** and the **product name** (capitalized), between the **product name** (capitalized) and the **item description**, between the **item description** and the **net wt**, and between the **net wt** and the **price** for each paragraph. There should now be four tabs in each paragraph.

*Note: Setting tabs in the **Tabs** palette can save time if you select all the paragraphs at once. Remember, you still have to place the tabs into the text using the **Tab** key.*

12. After all the tabs have been placed, the text should begin to look more organized. With the **Type** tool, select all the paragraphs except for the first.

This line illustrates how the **Align On** feature works. The character in the **Align On** field tells InDesign to align the tab with the character specified in that field. In this case, the tab is aligned with the decimal point in the dollar values at the far right.

The **Align On** field can accept numerous characters—symbols like the dollar sign ($), letters, and many others!

13. In the **Tab** area above the **Tab** ruler, select the fourth tab, which is affecting the tab for **price**. With that tab selected, click the **Align to Decimal** tab alignment button in the **Tabs** palette. This changes what type of tab the fourth tab is.

*Note: If the **Tabs** palette isn't visible, choose it from **Type > Tabs**.*

You just changed the properties of a tab you set up earlier in this exercise. Editing the tab stops will become more important the more you work with tabs.

*Note: When you click the **Align to Decimal** tab alignment button, InDesign automatically puts a period (.) into the **Align On** field. InDesign knows to look at all the selected paragraphs and stop the text that follows the tab (positioned at the price list) to align on the period (decimal).*

Click and drag the tab stop to the right. Position it over the "price" text.

This changes the position of the tab for the selected paragraphs only.

14. With the cursor, move the **Align to Decimal** tab you just converted in the **Tabs** palette to the right on the **Tabs** ruler.

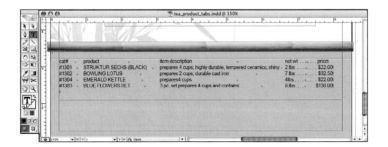

15. Save and close the file. In the next exercise, you will learn how to make lists.

TIP | Speed and Consistency with Tabs

Using tabs can seem tedious at times, but InDesign CS2 does try to make the process a little easier.

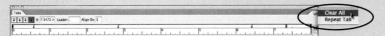

At the right end of the **Tabs** palette is the **Tabs** menu (click the palette menu arrow). The **Tabs** menu has two options: **Clear All** and **Repeat Tab**. **Clear All** is self-explanatory. It clears all the tabs set for a particular paragraph or all selected paragraphs. **Repeat Tab** is great for creating evenly spaced tabs multiple times without having to re-create them each time. Select a tab first, then choose **Repeat Tab**.

NOTE | Removing Tabs

Removing tabs is as easy as placing them.

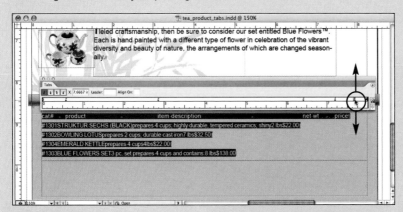

With the cursor in a paragraph (or in a block of selected paragraphs), open the **Tabs** palette by choosing **Type > Tabs**. With the cursor, select the tab you want to remove by clicking it in the **Tabs** ruler. Click and drag away from the **Tabs** ruler.

Your tab is now gone, by simply dragging it off the **Tabs** ruler!

 ## MOVIE | Setting and Using Tabs

To learn more about setting tabs, check out **tabs.mov** in the **movies** folder on the **InDesign CS2 HOT CD-ROM**.

What the Bullets and Numbering Dialog Box Options Mean

The **Bullets and Numbering** dialog box is big. In most cases, it offers more options than most people need. In this exercise, you will focus on the most commonly used features in this dialog box.

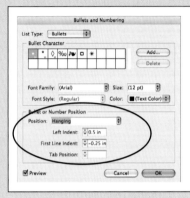

- If you've always dreamed of being free to combine earnest decor with unparalleled craftsmanship, then be sure to consider our set entitled Blue Flowers™. Each is hand painted with a different type of flower in celebration of the vibrant diversity and beauty of nature, the arrangements of which are changed seasonally.

A **Hanging Position** creates the list style presented above. The bullet or number character hangs outside the text (at left).

The **Left Indent** pushes the whole paragraph in from the left side. The **First Line Indent** brings the first line of the list back toward the left with a negative value. This way the bullet or number character "hangs."

- If you've always dreamed of being free to combine earnest decor with unparalleled craftsmanship, then be sure to consider our set entitled Blue Flowers™. Each is hand painted with a different type of flower in celebration of the vibrant diversity and beauty of nature, the arrangements of which are changed seasonally.

A **Flush Left Position** provides a different list style (shown above). The bullet or number character is positioned within the body of the text.

The **Left Indent** pushes the whole paragraph in from the left side. The **First Line Indent** is set to zero. When using a **Flush Left Position**, the **Tab Position** field is available. You can use this field to adjust the distance between the bullet or number character and the text.

7. _____Creating Bulleted and Numbered Lists

Next you will learn about lists. In past versions of InDesign, lists were created by indenting the paragraph and creating a hanging indent for the first line—a tedious process. With the PageMaker plug-in pack, however, InDesign CS could create bulleted and numbered lists with the click of a button.

InDesign CS2 has pulled all the features from the PageMaker plug-in pack, including one-click list creation, and rolled them into the program (no plug-in pack required in this version). In this exercise, you will learn how to create numbered and bulleted lists and how to change them to match design criteria.

1. Open **tea_product_lists.indd** from the **chap_05** folder you copied to your **Desktop** from the **InDesign CS2 HOT CD-ROM**. Zoom into the bottom part of the page using the **Zoom** tool. That is where you will make a bulleted list.

*Again, if you encounter the **Missing Fonts** dialog box when opening this file, click the **Find Font** button and replace the missing font with a suitable font. For a refresher on this, refer to the first exercise of the chapter.*

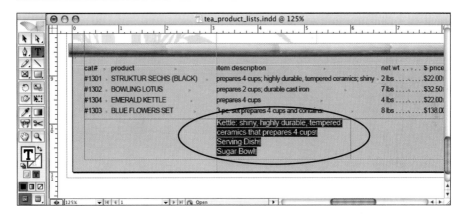

2. With the **Type** tool active, click inside the frame that contains the text starting with "**Kettle: shiny, highly durable**," and choose **Edit > Select All**, or press **Ctrl+A** (Windows) or **Cmd+A** (Mac) to select all the text in the frame. In the next step, you will change the font size, so the text needs to be selected.

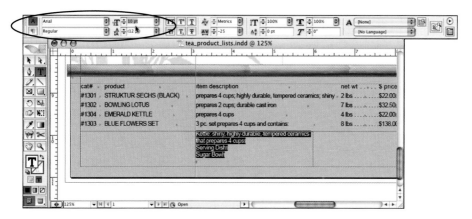

3. Make sure that **Arial Regular** (or another font family if this is not available) is chosen from the **Character Formatting** controls of the **Control** palette (or from the **Character** palette). Also, choose **10 pt** from the **Font Size** pop-up menu if it isn't set to that size already.

*Tip: To decrease or increase the font size, select the text and press **Ctrl+Shift+<** or **Ctrl+Shift+>** (Windows) or **Cmd+Shift+<** or > (Mac); < will increase font size and > will decrease font size. These are very handy shortcuts.*

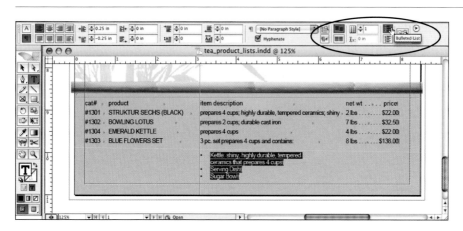

4. With the text still selected, click on the **Bulleted List** button from the **Paragraph Formatting** controls in the **Control** palette.

*Bulleted and numbered lists are created in exactly the same way. Either place the cursor in a single paragraph or select more than one paragraph at a time and click either the **Bulleted List** or **Numbered List** button from the **Paragraph Formatting** controls in the **Control** palette.*

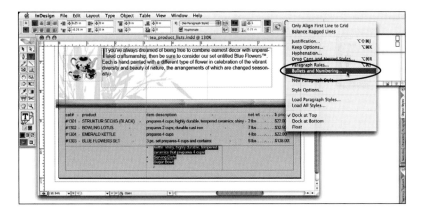

5. Next you will learn how to control the appearance of the list formatting. Bullets and numbers in a list are not objects and cannot be selected or edited directly in the InDesign document. This can only be achieved in the **Bullets and Numbering** dialog box. With the bulleted text still selected, choose **Bullets and Numbering** from the **Control** palette menu (in the **Control** palette, the **Paragraph Formatting Controls** button needs to selected for this option to appear). This causes the **Bullets and Numbering** dialog box to open.

*Tip: There are two other ways to access the **Bullets and Numbering** dialog box—from the **Paragraph** palette menu and with the keyboard shortcut. To use the shortcut, press the **Alt** (Windows) or **Option** (Mac) key and click the **Bulleted List** or **Numbered List** button (depending on which kind of list was applied).*

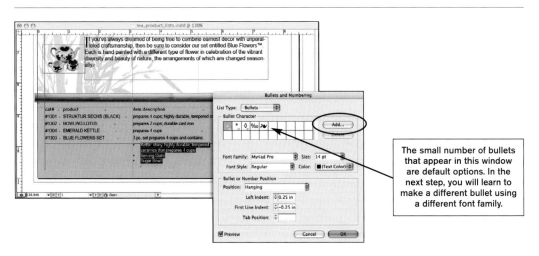

The small number of bullets that appear in this window are default options. In the next step, you will learn to make a different bullet using a different font family.

6. With the **Bullets and Numbering** dialog box still open from the previous step, the **List Type** should be set to **Bullets**. Click the **Add** button to create a new type of bullet. This opens the **Add Bullets** dialog box you will use in the next step.

*The **Bullet Character** options you see at the beginning of Step 6 show a few default bullet types. If you want to use one of them, feel free. Just click the bullet you would like to use and click **OK**. The bullet is then applied to the list.*

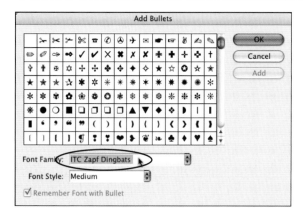

7. In the **Add Bullets** dialog box, choose **ITC Zapf Dingbats** (or another font family if this is not available) from the **Font Family** pop-up menu, and choose **Medium** from the **Font Style** menu.

*Note: This affects the appearance of the bullet character. You can always come back into the **Bullets and Numbering** dialog box later to change any of these settings.*

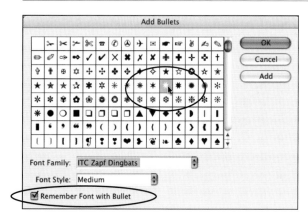

8. Choose a character from the list of characters that appears in the **Font Family** you just selected. The check box for **Remember Font with Bullet** should already be checked; leave it that way.

*Note: Checking **Remember Font with Bullet** means that you will need to send the font with the file if you are sending it to a printer or outside party. I would suggest not checking this option if you are using a fairly standard bullet (•) or number because almost all fonts include those characters.*

9. In the **Add Bullets** dialog box, click OK to add the selected bullet to the list of bullets that appears in the **Bullets and Numbering** dialog box. The **Add Bullets** dialog box will also close, returning you to the open **Bullets and Numbering** dialog box.

*Tip: Click the **Add** button in the **Add Bullets** dialog box to add several bullets at once. When finished adding, click **OK** to exit the **Add Bullets** dialog box.*

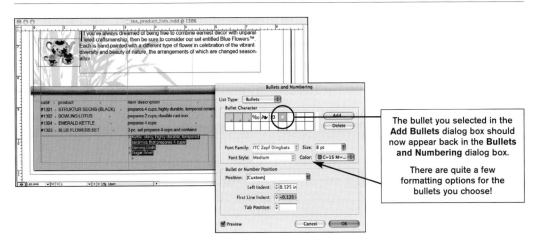

The bullet you selected in the **Add Bullets** dialog box should now appear back in the **Bullets and Numbering** dialog box.

There are quite a few formatting options for the bullets you choose!

10. In the **Bullets and Numbering** dialog box, the new bullet point now shows up in the **Bullet Character** table of bullet points. Select it. Change the size of the bullet character in the **Size** field to 8 pt (if it isn't already that size). Choose the red color from the **Color** pop-up menu. Select the **Preview** check box to preview the changes you made to the list.

11. Choose **File > Save** and keep the file open for the next exercise.

*Note: Adding a new bullet point to the **Bullets and Numbering** dialog box is file specific, so the new bullet will be saved only with the active document.*

TIP | Converting Bulleted or Numbered Lists to Editable Text

As mentioned previously, the bullets and numbers created with the **Bulleted List** and **Numbered List** buttons are not editable directly on the page. Open the **Bullets and Numbering** dialog box to edit them.

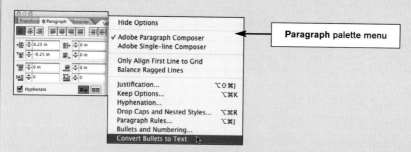

Paragraph palette menu

To move, edit, and change the bullet directly on the page, select the list created with the **Bulleted List** or **Numbered List** button. Open the **Paragraph** palette by choosing **Type > Paragraph**, and choose **Convert Numbering to Text** or **Convert Bullets to Text** (depending on what type of list is was that you created) from the **Paragraph** palette menu.

*As mentioned in Chapter 4, the **Paragraph** palette has a few options that the **Control** palette doesn't have. This is one of them!*

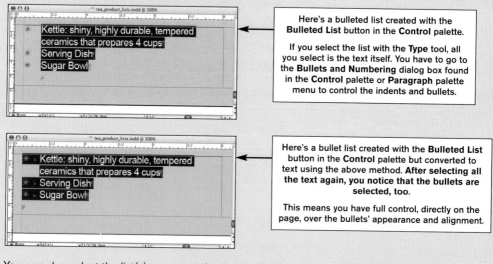

Here's a bulleted list created with the **Bulleted List** button in the **Control** palette.

If you select the list with the **Type** tool, all you select is the text itself. You have to go to the **Bullets and Numbering** dialog box found in the **Control** palette or **Paragraph** palette menu to control the indents and bullets.

Here's a bullet list created with the **Bulleted List** button in the **Control** palette but converted to text using the above method. **After selecting all the text again, you notice that the bullets are selected, too.**

This means you have full control, directly on the page, over the bullets' appearance and alignment.

You can also select the list(s) you created using the **Type** tool and **right-clicking** (Windows) or **Control-clicking** (Mac) the selection. Then select **Convert Numbering to Text** or **Convert Bullets to Text** (once again, depending on the type of list you are creating).

Paragraph Rules

Paragraph rules can be used for something as simple as underlining text or as complex as creating a colored box beneath a headline. There are two types of paragraph rules: **Rule Above** and **Rule Below**. **Rule Above** places a rule (or line) above a paragraph, and **Rule Below** places a rule below a paragraph.

Like a smooth, cool stone found washed ashore a placid isle, this Emerald comforts the weary and re-invigorates the traveller.#

At left is an example of both a paragraph rule above and a paragraph rule below.

You can apply either one or both to a single paragraph!

Since paragraph rules are a kind of paragraph formatting, they apply to a single paragraph only.

> **BONUS EXERCISE | Using Paragraph Rules in InDesign**
>
> To learn how, check out **rules.pdf** in the **bonus_exercises** folder on the **InDesign CS2 HOT CD-ROM**.

8. ————————Working with Glyphs

Working with fonts and special characters in other page layout programs can be a real challenge. In fact, when I first started in the graphics industry and I needed to use a bullet point or trademark, I would open a file that had one in it and copy/paste it into the new document.

InDesign offers a lot of flexibility in working with these types of characters. As a matter of fact, several menu items and a palette are devoted to what are called **Glyphs. Glyphs** are the characters and symbols like registration marks (®), trademarks (™), and bullet points (•) that are contained within font families.

In this exercise, you will apply several different **Glyphs** to text.

1. Using **tea_product_lists.indd** from the last exercise, you will replace the "**o**" in "**Grus gott**" found in the first paragraph starting with "**When style is**" with the proper accented letter. Select just the lowercase "**o**" in the word "**gott**."

From the **Show** pop-up menu, you can choose **Alternates** for the character you chose in the **Glyphs** palette or the entire font.

Open Type fonts will have a lot more Glyphs to choose from!

The **Mountain** icons make the character previews either smaller or larger!

2. Choose **Type > Glyphs** to open the **Glyphs** palette.

InDesign gives you the option to choose another font family from the pop-up menu at the bottom of the **Glyphs** palette.

3. Make sure **Arial** is selected from the **Font Family** pop-up menu at the bottom of the palette. Scroll in the **Glyphs** palette to find the "ö" character, which is the correct character for the language. Double-click the character. The "o" you had selected in the word is replaced with the new "ö" character!

In the next few steps of the exercise, you will learn how to save frequently used characters in a defined Glyph set that you can access at any time!

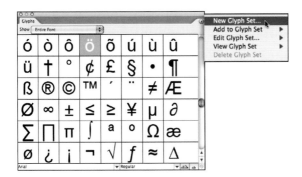

4. Choose **New Glyph Set** from the **Glyphs** palette menu.

5. When the **New Glyph Set** dialog box opens, type **teacloud**. Click **OK**. That new **Glyph** set is now saved.

Note: New Glyph sets stay with InDesign and are not tied to any one document. So even if a document is open when a new Glyph set is created, that Glyph set will be available globally, in all documents.

6. With the new **Glyph** set saved, select the same **Glyph** you chose in Step 3 (the "ö" character). From the **Glyphs** menu, choose **Add to Glyph Set > teacloud**.

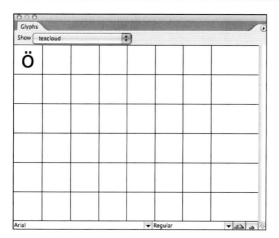

7. From the **Glyphs** palette, choose **teacloud** from the **Show** pop-up menu. This allows you to view all the **Glyphs** (only one, so far) saved in the **teacloud Glyph** set. The next time you need to use that same **Glyph**, this is where you will find it. Close the **Glyphs** palette.

8. With the "ö" **Glyph** in place on the page and a new **Glyph** set created, choose **File > Save** and close the document.

9. —————————Changing Type Case

Change Case is a frequently used feature in type formatting. This feature can change type from lower-case to uppercase and more.

1. Open **teacloud_case.indd** from the **chap_05** folder on your **Desktop**.

*Note: You may come across the **Missing Fonts** dialog box. If you do, change the font by choosing **Find Font** and replacing the font with a version of Arial or Helvetica. For a refresher on this, refer to the first exercise of the chapter.*

*The file **teacloud_case.indd** is similar in appearance to the file you have been using throughout this chapter.*

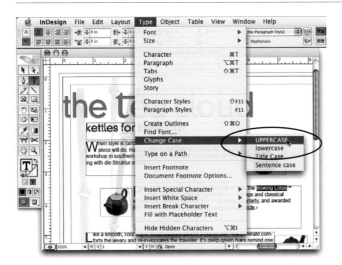

2. With the Type tool selected from the Toolbox, select the text **"Bowing Lotus"** from the second paragraph on the page.

3. Choose **Type > Change Case > UPPERCASE**.

*The menu items found under **Type > Change Case** preview each of the formatting options. **Title Case** puts an initial cap on each word, and **Sentence Case** puts an initial cap on the first word of each sentence.*

*Tip: All the **Change Case** options can also be accessed in a contextual menu by selecting the text to change and **right-clicking** (Windows) or **Control-clicking** (Mac) over the text.*

4. The final text is all UPPERCASE. Save the file and close it.

This can be particularly useful when placing unformatted text or copying text from an e-mail and pasting it into InDesign.

Sampling Text Formatting

To Adobe Photoshop and Illustrator users, the **Eyedropper** tool is a way to sample color and use it elsewhere. In InDesign, the **Eyedropper** tool can sample color, type formatting, transparency, and drop shadows, as well as any strokes (borders) or fills of frames. A note of warning, though. While helpful in many circumstances, this tool can also lead to formatting problems if used improperly. To learn about the **Eyedropper** tool, view the movie below.

MOVIE | Using the Eyedropper Tool to Sample and Apply Formatting

To learn about using the **Eyedropper** tool to copy formatting and apply it to other type, check out **eyedropper.mov** in the **movies** folder on the **InDesign CS2 HOT CD-ROM**.

BONUS EXERCISE | Custom Underlining and Strikethrough Formatting Options

To learn how to change the appearance of an underline or a strikethrough applied to text, check out **underline.pdf** in the **bonus_exercises** folder on the **InDesign CS2 HOT CD-ROM**.

IO. ——————————Find/Change in Text

InDesign CS2 offers a **Find/Change** feature for finding text you are searching for or finding text and then replacing it with something else. This feature is great for replacing special characters, text, and more. In this exercise, you will find and replace some problematic quotation marks (") in an InDesign document.

1. Open the file **tea_findchange.indd** from the **chap_05** folder on your **Desktop**.

*Note: You may come across the **Missing Fonts** dialog box. If you do, change the font by choosing **Find Font** and replacing the font with a version of Arial or Helvetica. For a refresher on this, refer to the first exercise of the chapter.*

2. Select the **Type** tool from the **Toolbox**, and then choose **Edit > Find/Change**.

3. In the **Find/Change** dialog box, you need to tell InDesign to find the ¥ character and change it to the quotation mark ("). Since you may not know how to type the ¥ character, copy it from the document and paste it into the **Find What** field in the **Find/Change** dialog box. With the **Type** tool, select the ¥ character next to the phrase "**Grus gött**" in the first paragraph copy and paste it into the **Find What** field.

*You can also type words or characters directly into the **Find What** field.*

4. With the **Type** tool, place the cursor in the **Change to** field and type in a quotation mark.

*The **Find/Change** dialog box can also be used to locate and/or replace formatting options like tabs, spaces, and so on. To the right of the **Find What** and **Change to** fields is a single arrow pointing to the right (▶). Place the cursor in the **Find What** or **Change to** field and then click the arrow. The menu that appears allows you to choose from some of the more typical find-and-change characters, such as tabs, bullets, copyright symbols, and a lot more.*

5. Choose **Document** to search all of the text in this document.

*The **Find/Change** feature can search selected text or an entire story (which consists of the text frame your cursor is in and any threaded frames or overset text outside the frame), to the end of a story (which begins searching where your cursor is in the text frame), and all documents (which searches all open documents). Always pay attention to this option because InDesign makes a choice for you based on where your cursor is (or isn't) and what is selected in the document.*

6. Click **Find Next** to find the first instance of the ¥ character in your document.

7. Click **Change/Find** to change the first instance and have InDesign find the next instance.

*You have several options for changing what InDesign finds. The **Change** button changes the first instance it finds and stops. **Change All** changes all the instances of the ¥ character to the quotation mark ("). **Change/Find** is a little safer because it tells InDesign to change the instance that's highlighted and go find the next one. This allows you to view each instance of the found character and change it (or not) on a case-by-case basis. If you come across an occurrence of the found character that you want to keep as is, click **Find Next** to tell InDesign to skip to the next occurrence.*

8. Click **Done** to close the **Find/Change** dialog box.

9. Save the document and close it.

This is one of the longer chapters in this book thanks to all the text formatting features in InDesign CS2. Congratulations on getting through it. You've covered a wide range of topics from spacing lines using leading to controlling how underlines look. The next chapter dives into paragraph and character styles and how to use them to your advantage.

6

Type Styles

| Creating Paragraph Styles Manually |
| Creating Paragraph Styles from Text | Applying Paragraph Styles |
| Editing Paragraph Styles | Basing Paragraph Styles |
| Creating Character Styles Manually and from Text |
| Applying Character Styles | Creating Nested Styles |
| Using the Story Editor |

chap_06

InDesign CS2
HOT CD-ROM

You've seen some of the amazing typographic control that InDesign CS2 provides. Now you will learn how InDesign type styles (often referred to as style sheets in other programs) can help maintain consistency within documents and make text formatting more efficient. As with so many features, when compared to other page layout programs, InDesign takes styles to a whole new level.

In this chapter, you will learn how to make and use paragraph and character styles, and then how to share them between documents.

The Paragraph Styles Palette

A **paragraph style** is a saved set of formatting attributes that can be applied to a given paragraph (or several paragraphs). Because a paragraph style can be applied with a click or two, using styles can save a lot of time when the same set of formatting attributes need to be applied throughout a document. One example is a magazine article or a catalog that uses standard formats for headings, footers, and so on. The default style for all new documents is called the **Basic Paragraph** style. This style is what InDesign applies to all text in a new document. This is why new documents always use **Times Roman** or a font similar to that. The **Paragraph Styles** palette is where style formatting for paragraph styles is saved for individual documents.

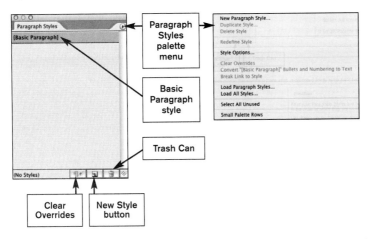

The **Paragraph Styles** palette has several buttons, each of which is described briefly in the following table.

Paragraph Styles Palette	
Feature	**Function**
Basic Paragraph Style	Applies the default type styling to text. All paragraph styles live here and are listed in the order they were created.
Clear Overrides button	Wipes out any formatting that is applied to text after the paragraph style is applied.
Paragraph Styles palette menu	List of features for paragraph styles.
New Style button	Creates a new paragraph style from selected text.
Trash Can	Deletes any selected paragraph styles.

The **Paragraph Styles** palette shown above may look different from yours because it was undocked from the side of the screen by clicking and dragging on its tab.

I. ————————— **Creating Paragraph Styles Manually**

In this lesson, you will learn how to create your own paragraph styles using the **Paragraph Styles** palette and unformatted text. Paragraph styles contain both paragraph and character formatting and affect an entire paragraph when applied. In this first exercise, you will create a paragraph style for body text.

1. Copy the **chap_06** folder from the **InDesign CS2 HOT CD-ROM** to your **Desktop**.

2. In InDesign CS2, open **tea_mag_begin.indd** from the **chap_06** folder on your **Desktop**.

Note: When the InDesign file opens, it may warn you that fonts are missing. If this dialog box appears, choose **Find Font** to see which font it is looking for. Replace any missing fonts before opening the file with **Times Roman** or a similar font. If the text is highlighted in pink, this also indicates that a font is missing. Choose **Type > Find Font** to find and replace the font.

3. Click the **Paragraph Styles** tab to open the palette from the side of your screen. If you don't see the palette docked on the side of the workspace, proceed to **Type > Paragraph Styles** to open it.

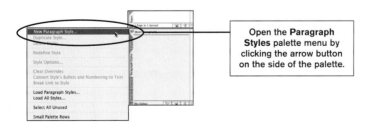

Open the **Paragraph Styles** palette menu by clicking the arrow button on the side of the palette.

4. To create a paragraph style manually, deselect the text and text frames with the **Selection** tool by choosing **Edit > Deselect All**. Open the **Paragraph Styles** palette menu by clicking the arrow button (▶) on the upper-right corner of the **Paragraph Styles** palette. Choose **New Paragraph Style**.

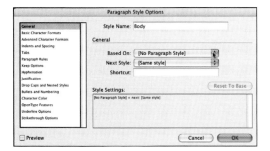

5. The **Paragraph Style Options** dialog box opens. Name the style **Body** in the **Style Name** field.

Notice all the formatting options on the left side of the dialog box? A paragraph style contains almost all the paragraph and character formatting that InDesign has to offer!

6. Choose **No Paragraph Style** from the **Based On** pop-up menu.

Based On *is a feature that allows InDesign to build new styles from existing ones. This means that, by default, styles will start with the **Basic Paragraph** formatting and build on that. Choosing **No Paragraph Style** from the **Based On** pop-up menu tells InDesign that any formatting applied to that text stands alone. You will learn more about **Based On** later in this chapter.*

7. From the formatting options on the side of the **Paragraph Style Options** dialog box, choose **Basic Character Formats**. In the **Font Family** pop-up menu choose **Adobe Garamond Pro** (that font should come with InDesign). If that font is missing on your system, use a similar font that is available. Choose **12 pt** for the font size. Click **OK** to close this dialog box and accept the changes.

*Creating a style this way can be time consuming. With no text selected, it starts the style settings out with default formatting. The style categories on the left side of the **Paragraph Style Options** dialog box can make it more difficult to find things like text alignment.*

8. Choose **File > Save** and leave this document open for the next exercise, where you will learn to make a paragraph style from text that is formatted in the document.

2. ─────────────**Creating Paragraph Styles from Text**

In this lesson, you will learn how to create paragraph styles using the **Paragraph Styles** palette and formatted text. This method is preferred because you can use the **Control** palette and text shortcuts to format text the way you want before committing to a paragraph style. You are going to format text for a headline and then create a style from the formatted text. InDesign will copy the formatting from the text, give it a name, and allow you to apply that style to other text.

When working with paragraph styles, it is a good idea to show hidden characters. This allows you to see where a paragraph begins and ends, which can prevent unpleasant surprises. To show hidden characters, go to **Type > Show Hidden Characters**.

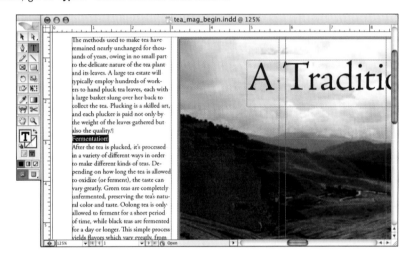

1. With **tea_mag_begin.indd** open from the last exercise, select the text "**Fermentation**" in the first column of text with the **Type** tool.

You can triple-click to select the line. Make sure the paragraph symbol is selected as well!

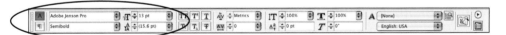

2. Using the **Character Formatting** controls of the **Control** palette, change the **Font Family** to **Adobe Jensen Pro**, the **Font Style** to **Semibold**, and **Font Size** to **13 pt**.

*If you don't have the fonts used in this step of the exercise, try **Verdana Bold** or **Arial Bold** instead.*

3. From the **Paragraph Formatting** controls of the **Control** palette (or from the **Paragraph** palette), click the **Center** alignment button. Also, change the **Space Before** and **Space After** to **0.125 in** by using the arrows to the left of the fields (or by typing the numbers directly into the fields).

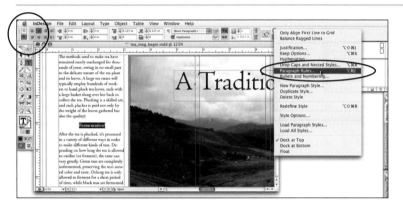

4. Choose **Paragraph Rules** from the **Control** palette menu.

*Make sure the **Paragraph Formatting Controls** button is chosen in the **Control** palette.*

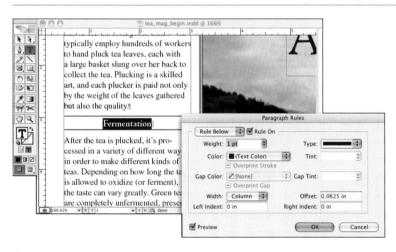

5. In the **Paragraph Rules** dialog box, choose **Rule Below** from the pop-up menu to create a rule (line) below the paragraph. Check the box to the left of **Rule On** after choosing the rule type. Change the **Offset** (the distance between the rule and the text) to **0.0625 in**. Keep this dialog box open for the next step.

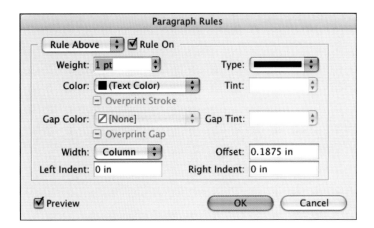

6. Now choose **Rule Above** and select the check box to the left of **Rule On** to activate the rule. Change the **Offset** for the **Rule Above** to **0.1875 in**. Click **OK** to close the **Paragraph Rules** dialog box and apply the rules above and below to the selected paragraph.

You learned about paragraph rules in the previous chapter. In this case, you are applying both kinds of paragraph rules to a paragraph.

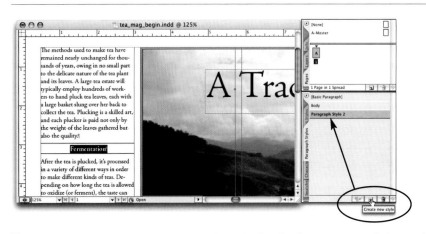

7. With the "**Fermentation**" paragraph selected, click the **Create new style** button in the **Paragraph Styles** palette. **Paragraph Style 1** (or some other number) appears in the palette. Double-click **Paragraph Style 1** in the **Paragraph Styles** palette to name it.

*Every paragraph style will be numbered in succession and listed in the **Paragraph Styles** palette that way. I recommend naming styles to keep track of their purpose.*

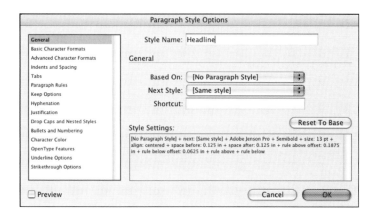

8. Type **"Headline"** for the **Style Name** in the **Paragraph Style Options** dialog box. Click **OK**.

*The **Style Settings** area at the bottom of the **Paragraph Style Options** dialog box shows all the formatting it picked up from the paragraph that was selected.*

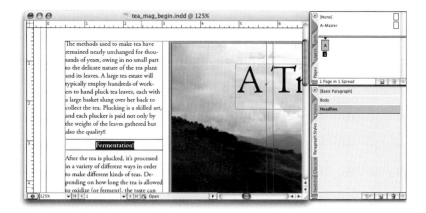

9. Save the file and keep it open for the next exercise, where you will apply the **Headline** style you just created.

*With the dialog box gone, the text looks the same, but there is now a paragraph style named **Headline** in the **Paragraph Styles** palette. The style is highlighted because the text used to create the style is highlighted. Creating paragraph styles from already-formatted text copies the formatting of the original text into the style definition and automatically applies the style (**Headline**, in this case) to the original text (the "**Fermentation**" headline, in this instance). Next you are going to learn how to apply paragraph styles to other text in the document.*

3. ─────────────**Applying Paragraph Styles**

In the previous two exercises, you created a **Body** paragraph style and a **Headline** paragraph style. In this exercise, you will apply them to text, starting with the **Body** paragraph style.

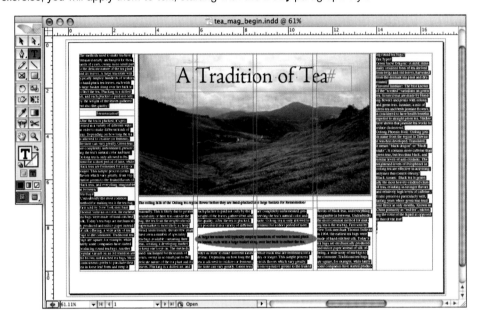

1. With the **tea_mag_begin.indd** document open from the last exercise, you can now apply the **Body** and **Headline** paragraph styles. Place the cursor in the first column of text and choose **Edit > Select All**. This selects all the text so that you can apply the **Body** paragraph style.

*In the previous exercise, you created the **Headline** paragraph style. It was applied to the "**Fermentation**" text in the first column. You are going to apply the **Body** style to all the text, including "**Fermentation**." Why? Because when you apply styles, it makes sense to apply the style that is used most throughout the document (like body text), first. You do this by selecting all the text and applying the **Body** style. Then you can go back through the text and apply the style for the headlines. It makes it a bit more efficient when applying styles.*

*Note: When you apply the **Body** paragraph style to text that already has a paragraph style associated with it (the "**Fermentation**" headline you created in the previous exercise), InDesign removes the old paragraph style (**Headline**) and applies the new one (**Body**).*

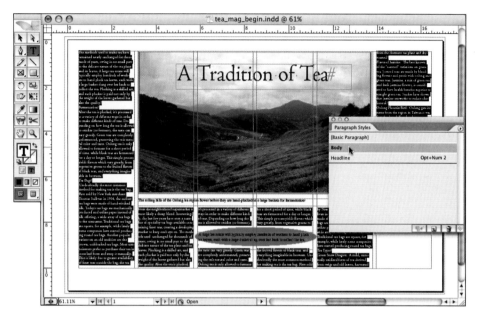

2. From the **Paragraph Styles** palette, choose **Body**. The text should change in appearance.

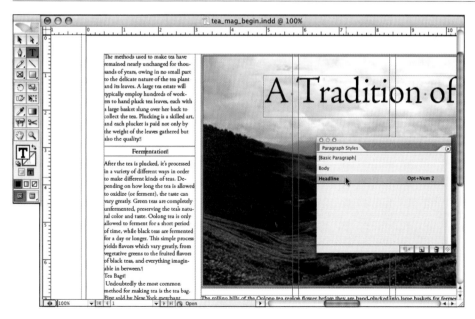

3. Place the cursor in the "**Fermentation**" headline. Click the **Headline** style in the **Paragraph Styles** palette, and the formatting appears.

*Tip: Once again, when working with paragraph styles, it's a good idea to show hidden characters. To view them, choose **Type > Show Hidden Characters.** Applying a paragraph style is as simple as putting the cursor in a paragraph and clicking on the style name in the **Paragraph Styles** palette. If hidden characters are not visible, it is too easy to accidentally place the cursor in the wrong paragraph.*

*In the next step, you will apply the **Headline** paragraph style to another headline using a different method.*

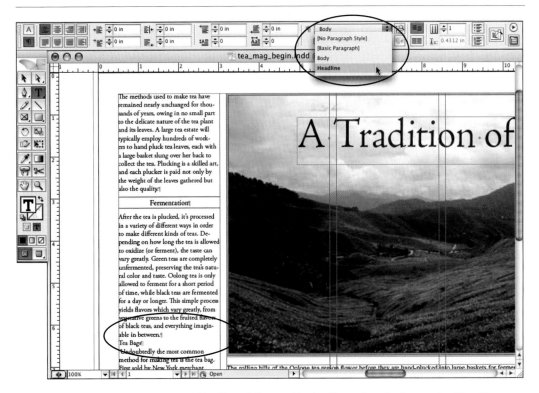

4. With the cursor in the paragraph "**Tea Bags**" (located in the first column), choose the **Headline** style from the **Paragraph Style** list in the **Control** palette. The paragraph should now be formatted with the **Headline** style!

5. Choose **File > Save** and close the document.

TIP | Using Shortcuts to Apply Paragraph Styles

Applying keyboard shortcuts to paragraph styles is one of the easiest ways to apply paragraph styles. Once a shortcut is assigned to a paragraph style, you can apply it by placing the cursor in a paragraph and pressing the assigned shortcut keys. If you would like to try this, you can use the **tea_mag_begin.indd** file from the previous exercise.

1. Double-click the style in the **Paragraph Styles** palette that you'd like to assign a shortcut to.

Warning: When editing styles (including assigning shortcuts), be careful! If you double-click to open the **Paragraph Style Options** dialog box, InDesign automatically applies that style to any paragraphs your cursor is either in or has selected. I always deselect before editing a paragraph style.

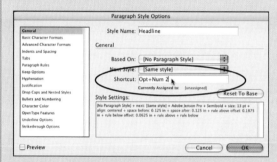

2. In the **Paragraph Style Options** dialog box, place the cursor in the **Shortcut** field. Choose a shortcut by pressing the keys on your keyboard. InDesign alerts you if that shortcut is already in use.

Note: InDesign limits the keys that can be used for a shortcut. **Ctrl**, **Alt**, and/or **Shift** (Windows) or **Cmd**, **Option**, and/or **Shift** (Mac) must be used in combination with a number on the keypad (not the numbers running along the top of your keyboard). **Option+2** (Mac) was used in this example. InDesign also shows the shortcut In the **Paragraph Styles** palette so you don't have to remember it!

Note: On some laptops, like the Mac PowerBook, you need to press the **Num Lock** key to access the "keypad" on the keyboard.

4. _____Editing Paragraph Styles

One critical advantage of using paragraph styles is the ability to update the formatting in paragraphs that use paragraph styles by editing the style definition. This saves enormous amounts of time and is one of the major reasons paragraph styles are so commonly used.

In this exercise, you are going to learn how to edit paragraph styles several different ways.

1. Open **tea_mag_edit.indd** from the **chap_06** folder on your **Desktop**. Using the **Zoom** tool, zoom into the first column on the left.

*Note: When the InDesign file opens, it may warn you that fonts are missing. If this dialog box appears, choose **Find Font** to see which font it is looking for. Replace it before opening the file with **Times Roman** or a similar font. If the text is highlighted in pink, this also indicates that a font is missing. Choose **Type > Find Font** to find and replace the font.*

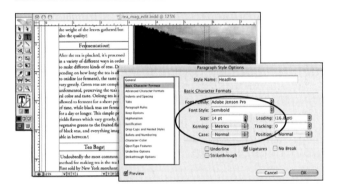

2. Select the **Type** tool, place the cursor in the headline "**Fermentation**," and double-click the style name **Headline** in the **Paragraph Styles** palette. The **Paragraph Style Options** dialog box shows all the paragraph and character formatting that a style can hold. Click the **Preview** check box in the lower-left corner, and move the dialog box out of the way to see the changes take place immediately. Click the category **Basic Character Formats** to edit those formats. Change the size of the text to **14 pt**. To accept the changes, click **OK**.

*Editing styles this way doesn't require that the **Preview** check box be on. If it were off and you clicked **OK**, the new formatting would be applied. The **Preview** check box is just a great way to see the formatting applied to the text before you commit by clicking **OK**. Another great feature in the **Paragraph Style Options** dialog box is the **Cancel** button. This may seem obvious, but by clicking **Cancel**, you can reject the changes that you made and maintain the appearance of the text.*

Editing styles this way can be a great time-saver. There are other ways to change styles, though, and you will learn one of those ways in the next few steps.

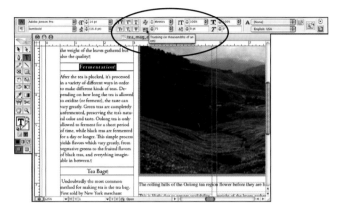

3. Select "**Fermentation**" with the **Type** tool. In the **Character Formatting** controls of the **Control** palette, change the **Tracking** value to **75**. This spreads the headline out a bit.

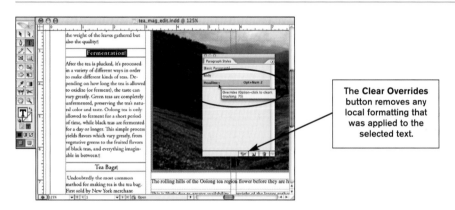

The **Clear Overrides** button removes any local formatting that was applied to the selected text.

4. Look at the **Paragraph Styles** palette, and you notice a plus sign (+) next to the **Headline** name. Hover over the style name. A tooltip indicates that the text that uses this style has been changed (**tracking: 75**), but that change is not reflected in the style definition. This is referred to as **local formatting**. Using local formatting is fine. InDesign is just letting you know that there is a discrepancy between the style and the text to which it was applied.

Tip: There may come a time when you have applied local formatting (like the tracking in this example) and you don't want it anymore. Or you have been given an InDesign document that someone else created and you are to edit. You place the cursor in some text only to find that someone used paragraph styles but then went in and applied local formatting. In both of these cases, you may want to get rid of any formatting except for the style applied. To get rid of the local formatting in the "Fermentation" headline, select the paragraph and click the Clear Overrides button at the bottom of the Paragraph Styles palette. This button can also be found on the Control palette when Paragraph Formatting controls are selected. If you do click this button at this point to see it in action, choose Edit > Undo to continue with the exercise.

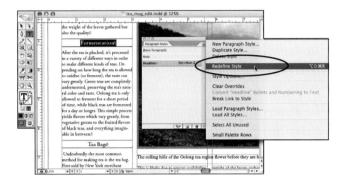

5. With the "**Fermentation**" headline still selected, choose **Redefine Style** from the **Paragraph Styles** palette menu to update the definition based on the text selected on the page. This change should ripple through all the other headlines on the page that use this paragraph style.

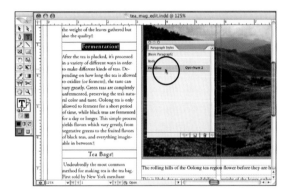

6. The plus sign (+) is now gone from the **Headline** style in the **Paragraph Styles** palette. Choose **File > Save** and keep the file open for the next exercise. You will next learn how to base paragraph styles on each other.

NOTE | Replacing Fonts in Text That Uses Styles

When replacing fonts in the **Find Font** dialog box, I would like to alert you to a potential problem. If you have created styles in a document (or a document you have received is using them), and you replace fonts in the **Find Font** dialog box, the **Find Font** dialog box replaces the fonts in the document and treats the changes as local formatting. This means that it ignores your type styles and replaces the fonts. The next time you go to work in the document, you will most likely have to update your type styles to mirror the newly replaced fonts. For this situation, you should open the **Find Font** dialog box, and find the first occurrence of a font that is missing, then close the **Find Font** dialog box and open the **Paragraph Styles** palette and see which style is applied, then edit the style directly.

5. ——————Basing Paragraph Styles

It is not uncommon to have several styles with similar definitions. For instance, for a magazine article, there may be two subhead styles. Both use identical formatting, except subhead 2 uses smaller text. Instead of creating two subhead styles from scratch, you can use a feature called **Based On** to create the subhead 2 style. After creating the subhead 1 style, you use **Based On** to tell InDesign to use all the formatting from subhead 1 to create a new style with all of the same formatting except font size.

Using the **Based On** feature creates an association between the subhead 1 and subhead 2 styles. If edits are made to any of the shared characteristics (everything but font size) in the subhead 1 style (this only works one way), the shared formatting in the subhead 2 style is simultaneously changed. The associations formed by the **Based On** feature can be extended to several styles all based on each other. **Based On** is enormously helpful when a series of styles need to have the same look, with a few differences among them. The **Based On** feature can also be used in several ways. You are going to focus on the simplest method.

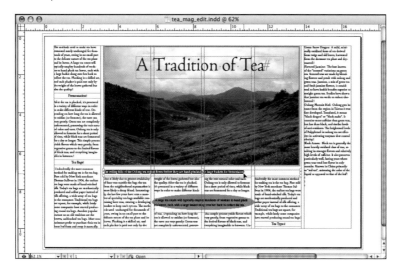

1. With the **tea_mag_edit.indd** open from the last exercise, select the subhead below the picture with the **Type** tool.

2. With the text selected, apply **Center** alignment from the **Paragraph Formatting** controls on the **Control** palette.

3. From the **Character Formatting** controls in the **Control** palette, change the **Font Family** to **Adobe Jensen Pro**, the **Font Style** to **Semibold Italic** (or some kind of italic), and the **Font Size** to **16 pt**.

As always, if you don't have this Open Type font, substitute it with something that looks good to you. Just make sure the font family you choose has an italic in **Font Style***.*

4. With the text still selected, create a new paragraph style from the **Paragraph Styles** palette by clicking the **Create New Style** button at the bottom of the palette. Double-click your new paragraph style listed in the **Paragraph Styles** palette to open the **Paragraph Style Options** dialog box.

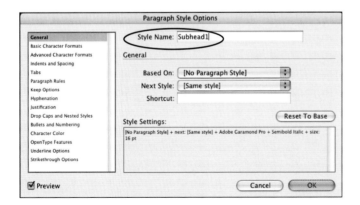

5. In the **Paragraph Style Options** dialog box, name the style "**Subhead1**." Make sure that the **Based On** setting is set to **No Paragraph Style**. Click **OK** to close the dialog box.

Note: This is the style that the **Subhead2** *style you will create in the next few steps will be based on.*

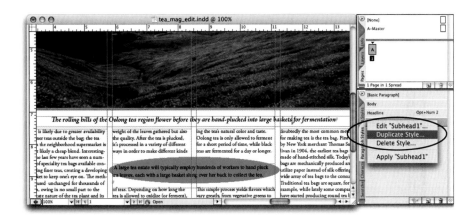

6. Right-click (Windows) or **Control+click** (Mac) directly on the **Subhead1** style in the **Paragraph Styles** palette, and a contextual menu shows up. Choose **Duplicate Style**.

*You are going to duplicate the **Subhead1** style and change some of its attributes. This is one way to make a paragraph style base itself on another. A different way to access the **Duplicate Style** command and the others you see in the contextual menu is to open the **Paragraph Styles** palette menu by clicking on the arrow button (⊙) in the **Paragraph Styles** palette.*

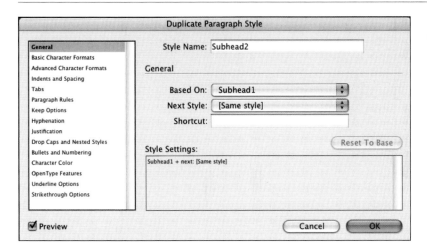

7. In the **Duplicate Paragraph Style** dialog box, name the style **Subhead2**. Also, make sure that the **Based On** setting is **Subhead1**.

*Next you will instruct InDesign to start with the **Subhead1** formatting and change a few things to make this new style slightly different.*

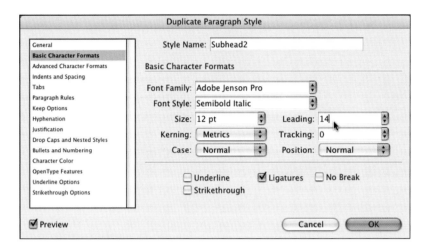

8. Choose **Basic Character Formats** from the formatting options on the left side of the **Duplicate Paragraph Style** dialog box. Change the **Size** to **12 pt** and the **Leading** to **14 pt**.

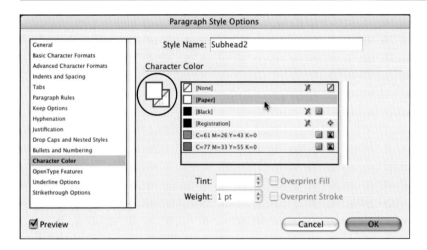

9. Next you will change the text color, because the **Subhead2** paragraph style is going to be used on text that is over the green oval. Click the **Character Color** option on the left side of the **Paragraph Style Options** dialog box. Choose **Paper** as your color. Click **OK**.

*Note: Since you haven't yet learned how InDesign CS2 handles color (you will get to that in the next chapter), just know that **Paper** is white. Also, make sure that the box that is circled in the figure above (this controls the text fill) is selected and therefore appears in front of the box with the red slash through it.*

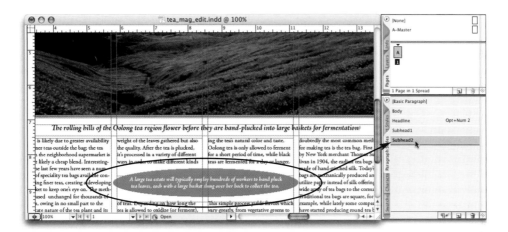

10. Place the cursor in the text on top of the green oval. Apply the **Subhead2** style by clicking on it in the **Paragraph Styles** palette.

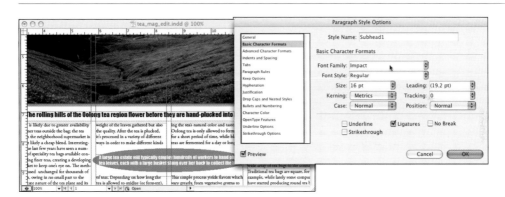

11. Now, for the **Based On** moment you've been waiting for! Choose **Edit > Deselect All**. Double-click the **Subhead1** paragraph style in the **Paragraph Styles** palette. From the **Basic Character Formats** options, change the font to **Impact** or something similar. Click the **Preview** check box, and move the **Paragraph Style Options** dialog box out of the way to see to see how the changes affect the text. Click **OK** to close the dialog box and apply this change.

*This is a nice way to maintain consistency among the subheadlines in the document. And if any formatting common to both styles is changed in **Subhead1**, that formatting is automatically updated in the **Based On** style, **Subhead2**!*

12. Save and close the file.

Next you will learn how to create character styles and then move on to applying them.

TIP | Using Next Style in Paragraph Styles

Next Style is an underused feature of paragraph styles. In the document you are using, **Next Style** would be helpful because every headline is followed by body copy. **Next Style** can automate the application of the **Body** style after each instance of the **Subhead1** or **Subhead2** style.

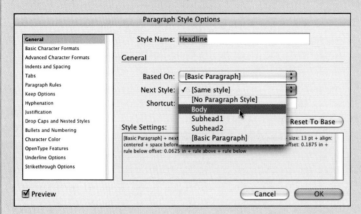

Double-click the **Headline** style in the **Paragraph Styles** palette to open the **Paragraph Style Options** dialog box. Choose **Headline** style (which always comes before **Body**) from the **Style Name** pop-up menu, and then choose **Body** from the **Next Style** pop-up menu. Click **OK**.

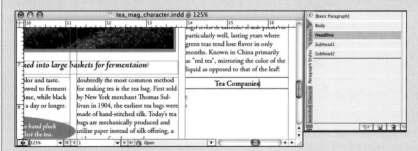

In a text frame, type in a headline and apply the **Headline** style. Press **Enter** or **Return** and start typing. The **Body** style is automatically applied to the paragraph that directly follows the chosen **Headline** style!

TIP | Using Quick Apply to Apply Styles

Using **Quick Apply** is an easy way to apply styles when several styles are being used in a single document. This is a new feature in InDesign CS2 and a great one for saving time.

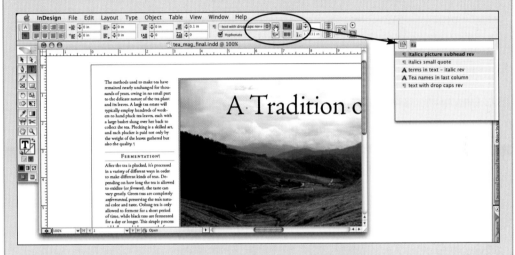

1. Place the cursor in a text frame, or select the text or frame to which you want to apply a style.

2. Choose **Edit > Quick Apply**, click the **Quick Apply** button (circled above) in the **Control** palette, or press **Ctrl+Enter** (Windows) or **Control+Return** (Mac).

3. Start typing the name of the style. As you type, styles appear in a list that narrows down the more you type.

4. When the desired style appears, press **Enter** or **Return**.

Shortcuts for Quick Apply:

- To apply a paragraph style and remove any local overrides, press **Alt+Enter** (Windows) or **Option+Return** (Mac).

- To apply a paragraph style and remove local overrides and character styles, press **Alt+Shift+Enter** (Windows) or **Option+Shift+Return** (Mac).

- To apply a style and leave the Quick Edit list displayed, press **Shift+Enter** or **Shift+Return**.

What Are Character Styles?

Character styles are similar to paragraph styles in that they facilitate consistent formatting. Unlike paragraph styles, however, character styles only apply to individual words or letters. For instance, if you need to apply distinct formatting to a company name throughout a document, character styles will prove tremendously useful.

Note: To apply paragraph styles, you placed the cursor in the text and chose the paragraph style to apply. A character style is applied by selecting the text first and then the character style.

The Character Styles Palette

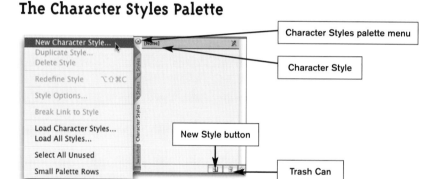

The **Character Styles** palette has several buttons, each of which is described briefly in the following table.

Character Styles Palette	
Feature	**Function**
Character Style	All character styles live here and are listed in the order they were created.
Character Styles palette menu	List of features for character styles.
New Style button	Creates a new character style from selected text.
Trash Can	Deletes any selected character styles.

Note: The **Character Styles** palette shown above may look different from yours because it was undocked from the side of the screen by clicking and dragging on its tab.

In the next two exercises, you will learn how to create character styles using the **Character Styles** palette and both unformatted and formatted text. Character styles contain only character formatting and affect only selected text when applied. In this first exercise, you will create a character style for terms.

6. ——————Creating Character Styles Manually

In this first exercise on character styles, you will make a character style from scratch.

1. Open **tea_mag_character.indd** from the **chap_06** folder on your **Desktop**. This document looks the same as the previous exercises, but it has paragraph styles applied already.

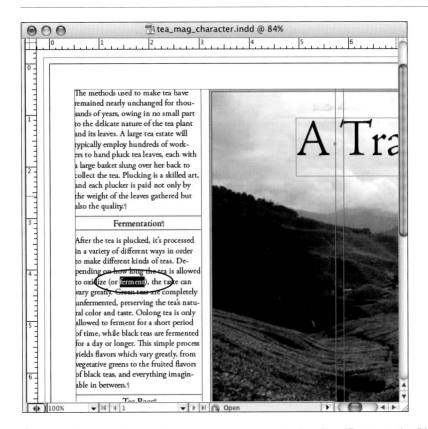

2. Locate the word "**ferment**" in the paragraph after the headline "**Fermentation**." You are going to create a character style that you can apply to specific terms in the document such as this word. Do not select the word. It is selected in this case to show you where it is located.

*Note: The word "ferment" does not need to be selected to proceed. If text is selected—specifically, formatted text—InDesign may pick up that formatting and add it to the character style you are creating. It is highlighted above to show its position on the page. If any text is selected, choose **Edit > Deselect All**.*

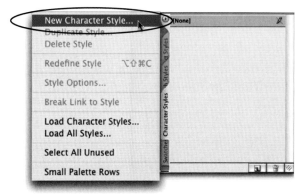

3. Creating a character style is very similar to creating a paragraph style. Open the **Character Styles** palette menu and choose **New Character Style**.

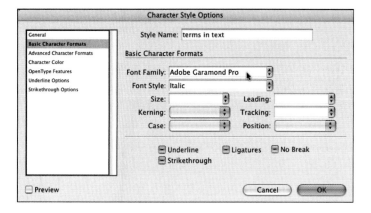

4. In the **Character Style Options** dialog box, name the style "**terms in text**" in the **Style Name** field.

5. Click the **Basic Character Formats** options on the left side of the dialog box to see the formatting options. Choose **Adobe Garamond Pro** for the **Font Family** and **Italic** for the **Font Style**. Click **OK** to close the dialog box and save the style. Once the style is created, you have to apply it to text. You will do that later in this chapter.

6. Save the document and keep it open for the next exercise.

As with paragraph styles, creating a character style this way can be time consuming, especially if you have to hunt for the formatting you want to apply from the style categories on the left side of the **Character Style Options** *dialog box. In the next exercise, you will learn how to create a character style from text that is already formatted on the page.*

7. ———————Creating Character Styles from Text

In the previous exercise, you created a character style from scratch. In this exercise, you'll learn what it takes to create a character style from text that is already formatted on page. InDesign will "pick up" (copy) the formatting from highlighted text and save it into a character style.

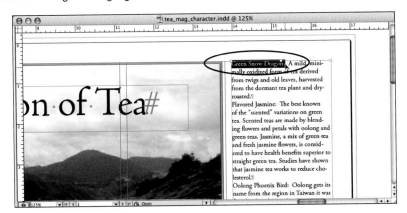

1. In the file **tea_mag_character.indd** still open from the previous exercise, use the **Zoom** tool to zoom in to the text on the page that begins "**Green Snow Dragon**". This should be in the last column on the right, at the top of the page. If it is at the bottom of the previous column, don't worry. Select the text.

Don't forget to work with hidden characters showing. They can be viewed by choosing **Type > Show Hidden Characters.**

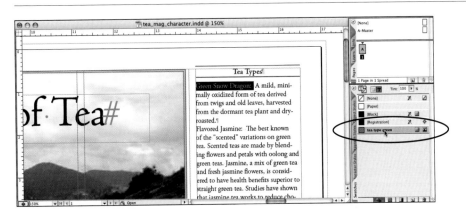

2. With the words "**Green Snow Dragon**" selected, open the **Swatches** palette from the right side of the workspace. You haven't gotten to colors yet (that's in the next chapter), so for now, click the color "**tea type green**" to apply it.

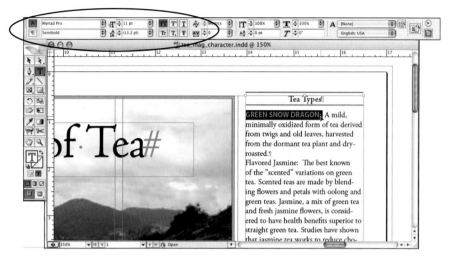

3. With "**Green Snow Dragon**" still highlighted from the previous step, use the **Control** palette to change the **Font Family** to **Myriad Pro**, change the **Font Style** to **Semibold**, and set the **Font Size** to **11 pt**. Then click the **All Caps** button (TT).

As always, choose a different font if you don't have the ones mentioned in this exercise.

*Tip: To avoid having to manually change the formatting options in the **Control** palette from character to paragraph, use this shortcut: **Ctrl+Alt+7** (Windows) or **Cmd+Option+7** (Mac). This toggles the formatting options from character to paragraph and back!*

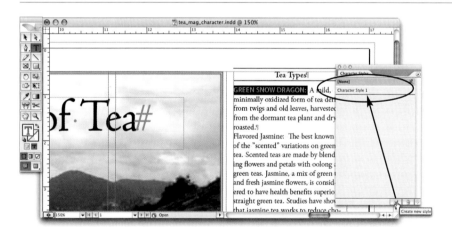

4. After changing the formatting of the text, keep it selected. You are going to create a character style that can be used elsewhere. With the **Character Styles** palette open, click the **Create new style** button at the bottom of the palette.

5. Double-click **Character Style 1** to open the **Character Style Options** dialog box.

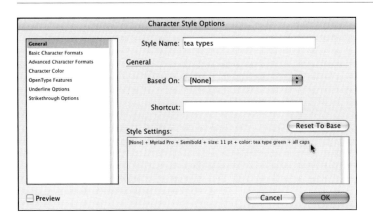

6. Rename the character style "**tea types**." Leave this dialog box open for the next step.

Note: Earlier in this chapter, you learned how InDesign can "pick up" or copy formatting from format-ted text to create new styles. Character styles work differently. With character styles, when you use selected text to create a new style, InDesign only adds the changed formatting options to the style definition. What does that mean? For example, say you apply the **Body** *paragraph style to the main paragraph and then decide to italicize proper names (which you already did). Once the names are italicized, you decide to make a new character style that includes the italic font style. The definition of the new character style will only include the italicized character formatting, because a paragraph style has already been applied to the text. Essentially, the paragraph style outranks the character style, so InDesign only includes "local formatting" (in this case, the italic font style) in the character style defi-nition. The blank fields in the* **Character Style Options** *dialog box indicate that these options are not included in the new character style. InDesign looks to the* **Body** *paragraph style (in this example) to fill in these blanks.*

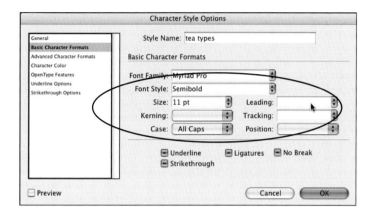

7. Choose **Basic Character Formats** from the formatting options listed on the left side of the dialog box. Notice that the leading doesn't have a value in the field? A paragraph style called **Body** was already applied to this text. InDesign doesn't bother to put any of that formatting in the character style because it is already in the paragraph style. If leading (or any missing attribute) needs to be in the character style definition, select a value in the **Character Style Options** dialog box, and InDesign will add it to the definition. This is only useful if you are going to use this character style in a paragraph with a different paragraph style applied.

*Why would any "missing" attributes need to be in the character style? If you decided to use a character style (the **tea types** character style, for instance) in another paragraph with a different paragraph style applied, it would only make the selected text italic! So any missing attributes would have no effect on the new paragraph.*

8. Click **OK** to close the dialog box.

9. The **tea types** character style is now created and already applied to your text. Save the file and keep it open for the next exercise, in which you will apply this character style to other tea names in the document.

8. —————————Applying Character Styles

Character styles are applied by selecting text and then applying the character style. This is because a character style only employs character formatting. It lets you use the character formatting for a single character or most of a paragraph. Character styles are helpful for things like prices, Web site addresses, company names, or any letter, word, phrase, or character formatting that needs to be consistent within a paragraph.

In this short exercise, you will apply the **tea types** character style you created in the previous exercise to other tea names.

1. With **tea_mag_character.indd** open from the previous exercise, use the **Zoom** tool to zoom into the top of the last column on the page, if you aren't already there.

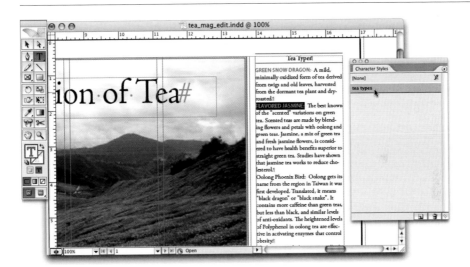

2. With the **Type** tool, highlight the text "**Flavored Jasmine**" on the page.

3. Open the **Character Styles** palette and click the **tea types** style. The selected text should be formatted!

*Note: Editing character styles works the same way as editing paragraph styles. Either double-click the character style name to edit the options, or edit the text on the page and redefine the character style in the **Character Styles** palette menu.*

*Tip: As with paragraph styles, character styles can be assigned a keyboard shortcut. After deselecting, double-click a character style name and type a keyboard shortcut using the **Shortcut** field. The keyboard shortcut needs to use **Ctrl, Alt**, and/or **Shift** (Windows) or **Cmd, Option**, and/or **Shift** (Mac) plus a number on the keypad.*

*Note: When it comes to creating shortcuts for styles on some laptops, such as the Mac PowerBook, you need to press the **Num Lock** key to access the "keypad" in the keyboard.*

4. Save the file and close it.

What Are Nested Styles?

Nested styles first appeared in InDesign CS. They allow for efficiency when consistently applying paragraph and character styles to multiple layers of text. For instance, the document you have been working on in this chapter has several paragraphs describing tea types. Each of these paragraphs includes the name of the tea, which is always followed by a colon and then a description of the tea type. The final text might look like that pictured below.

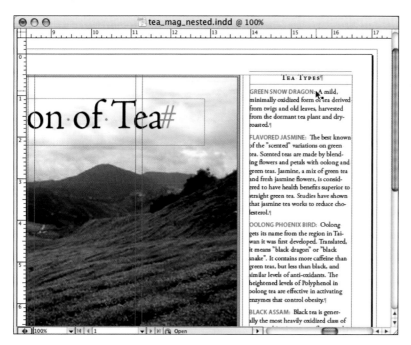

This text requires both paragraph and character formatting. Because these paragraph and character styles are consistently applied to the text in the same sequence, this is a perfect opportunity to take advantage of nested character styles.

Using a **nested character style**, you can tell InDesign to apply a paragraph style (which you will make for the general formatting of the tea type text) and then to apply a character style for the tea type name up to the first colon (in this case) in each paragraph. Since each of these tea type paragraphs starts with the name of the tea and then a colon, it will be advantageous to use a nested character style.

To create a nested character style, you need to do three things:

1. Create a paragraph style.

2. Create a character style for the text that needs to be styled differently from the rest of the paragraph.

3. Nest the character style in the paragraph style.

You accomplished the first two steps in the previous exercises. You will learn about the third step in the next exercise.

FLAVORED JASMINE: The best known of the "scented" variations on green tea. Scented teas are made by blending flowers and petals with oolong and green teas. Jasmine, a mix of green tea and fresh jasmine flowers, is consid-

To understand how InDesign interprets nested styles, take a look at the picture above. InDesign always starts from the first letter of the paragraph and says, "From here, marching to the right, what character styling do you want to use?" In this example, the first word, "**Flavored**," through the colon (:) character needs to use the **tea name** character style. After applying that style, InDesign applies the paragraph formatting to the rest of the paragraph. InDesign "nests" character styles within the paragraph style and automatically applies them at set points within the text—again, always moving from left to right.

However, while InDesign has a built-in "reading" order, you need to tell InDesign how you want it to apply the nested character style(s). This is done in the **Paragraph Style Options** dialog box (which opens when you double-click a paragraph style name).

9. ——————————Working with Nested Styles

In this exercise, you are going to create nested styles. Using the character style **tea types** you created in the previous exercises, you will instruct InDesign to apply that formatting at the same time that you apply a paragraph style to the text.

1. Open **tea_mag_nested.indd** from the **chap_06** folder on your **Desktop**, and use the **Zoom** tool to zoom into the last column (which contains the tea type text "**Green Snow Dragon**" and "**Flavored Jasmine**" on the right side of the page).

All the documents look alike in this chapter. Don't worry, you aren't seeing double.

Note: When the InDesign file opens, it may warn you that fonts are missing. If this dialog box appears, choose Find Font to see which font it is looking for. Replace any missing fonts before opening the file with Times Roman or a similar font. If the text is highlighted in pink, this also indicates that a font is missing. Choose Type > Find Font to find and replace the font

In the next step, you will see how to remove character formatting that is applied to text—a nice feature to know. Then you'll build a nested style.

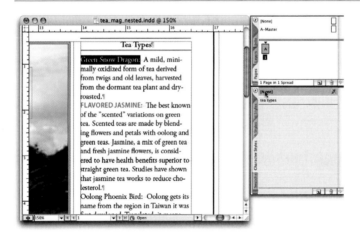

2. Open the **Character Styles** palette. A character style named **tea types** already exists, and two of the tea names on the page already have that character style applied to them. With the **Type** tool, select the text "**Green Snow Dragon:**" and click the **None** character style in the **Character Styles** palette. Now select "**Flavored Jasmine:**" in the next paragraph and select the **None** style again.

When the None character style is applied, the formatting from the tea types character style is removed. The None character style strips off formatting from character style formatting previously applied.

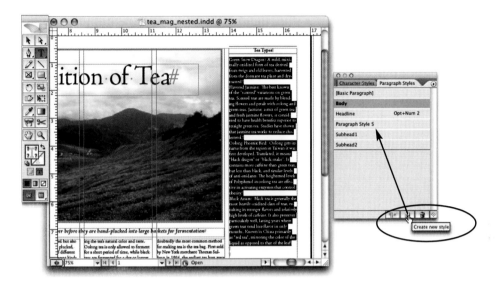

3. Now that the text has no character style applied to it, you need to make a paragraph style for the text. With the cursor in the text, select the four tea type paragraphs, starting with the paragraph that begins "**Green Snow Dragon.**" With the **Paragraph Styles** palette open, click the **Create new style** button at the bottom of the palette. Double-click the "**Paragraph Style (#)**" for the next step.

*Note: For this step, you can change how the text looks by changing the **Font Family**, **Font Size**, and so on.*

*Notice in the **Paragraph Styles** palette that the **Body** paragraph style is applied to the selected text? That's OK; it was already in the file. You are making a new paragraph style for this section of text because you don't want the nested style to apply to all of the body text.*

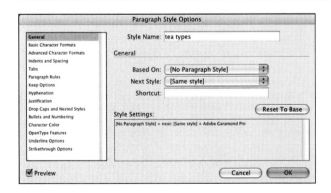

4. In the **Paragraph Style Options** dialog box, name the style **tea types**, and choose **No Paragraph Style** from the **Based On** pop-up menu. Click **OK** to close the dialog box. The **tea types** paragraph style will now be applied to all the selected text.

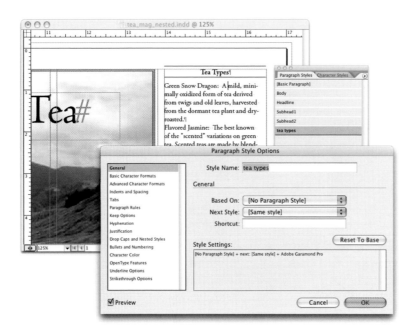

5. Now that the **tea types** paragraph style is created and applied, and the character style **tea types** is already created, place the cursor in the first paragraph, starting with "**Green Snow Dragon.**" In the **Paragraph Styles** palette, double-click the **tea types** paragraph style to open the **Paragraph Style Options** dialog box.

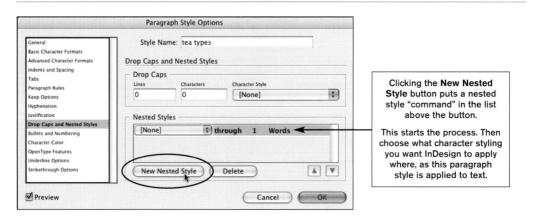

Clicking the **New Nested Style** button puts a nested style "command" in the list above the button.

This starts the process. Then choose what character styling you want InDesign to apply where, as this paragraph style is applied to text.

6. In the **Paragraph Style Options** dialog box, select the **Drops Caps and Nested Styles** options on the left side. Click the **New Nested Style** button. In the next step, you will control the nested style.

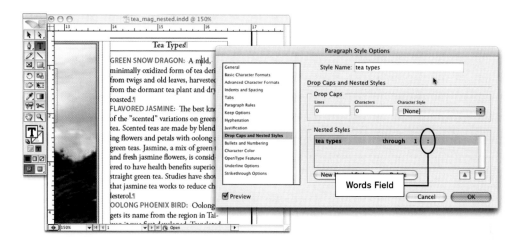

7. In the **Nested Styles** section, click **None** to see a menu containing the **tea types** character style in this document. Choose **tea types** to apply the character style formatting. Working from left to right, make sure "**through**" is showing, and then type a colon (**:**) in the **Words** field and click elsewhere to accept these changes.

*You have just instructed InDesign to apply the **tea types** character style from the first character through (including) the colon when the **tea types** paragraph is applied. In the **Paragraph Style Options** dialog box, you are giving InDesign instructions on how to apply character formatting from left to right. You can apply as many nested styles to a single paragraph as your design sensibilities can handle. Since you are only applying one, when InDesign applies the character style through the colon, it will stop and wait for you to tell it what to do next with another nested style. If there are no more nested styles to apply, InDesign will apply the paragraph style to the rest of the paragraph.*

8. Click the **Preview** check box if it isn't already selected, and move the **Paragraph Style Options** dialog box out of the way to see the changes happen immediately! Click **OK** to close the dialog box and apply your nested style.

9. Save the document and close it.

NOTE | Nested Style Options

In the **Paragraph Style Options** dialog box, the **Nested Style** settings appear by choosing the **Drop Caps and Nested Styles** section. Here is an explanation of each of the settings associated with nested styles found.

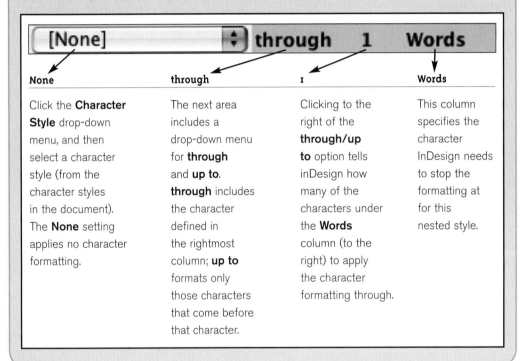

None	through	I	Words
Click the **Character Style** drop-down menu, and then select a character style (from the character styles in the document). The **None** setting applies no character formatting.	The next area includes a drop-down menu for **through** and **up to**. **through** includes the character defined in the rightmost column; **up to** formats only those characters that come before that character.	Clicking to the right of the **through/up to** option tells inDesign how many of the characters under the **Words** column (to the right) to apply the character formatting through.	This column specifies the character InDesign needs to stop the formatting at for this nested style.

 MOVIE | Nested Styles

To learn more about **Nested Styles**, check out **nestedstyles.mov** in the **movies** folder on the **InDesign CS2 HOT CD-ROM**.

BONUS EXERCISE | Sharing Styles Between InDesign Documents

To learn how, check out **share_styles.pdf** in the **bonus_exercises** folder on the **InDesign CS2 HOT CD-ROM**.

IO. _____Using the Story Editor

Features and options like styles, the spell checker, and viewing hidden characters and missing fonts make editing text in InDesign straightforward. There are times, though, when editing is more complicated because, for instance, text that needs editing is threaded across multiple pages. By placing the cursor in the story (a story consists of all the text contained in a series of threaded frames), and opening the **Story Editor**, you can see and edit all the text in all the threaded frames simultaneously. In this short exercise, you will learn how to use the **Story Editor**.

1. Open **tea_mag_final.indd** from the **chap_06** folder on your **Desktop**, and place the cursor in the first column of text.

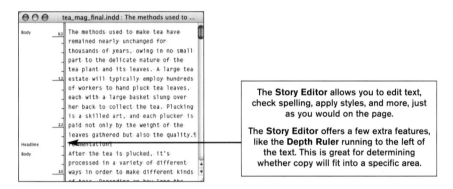

The **Story Editor** allows you to edit text, check spelling, apply styles, and more, just as you would on the page.

The **Story Editor** offers a few extra features, like the **Depth Ruler** running to the left of the text. This is great for determining whether copy will fit into a specific area.

2. Open the **Story Editor** by choosing **Edit > Edit in Story Editor**.

*When you edit text in the **Story Editor**, the changes automatically appear in the document. Using **right-click** (Windows) or **Control+click** (Mac) in the **Story Editor** is a great timesaver when you need to check spelling, insert special characters, and more. When determining how type flows on the page, however, it's better to work in the layout. InDesign also doesn't preview styles in the **Story Editor**.*

3. Choose **Edit > Edit in Layout** to close the **Story Editor** and return to the layout.

This is a great feature for copywriters and copy editors who only deal with the copy in a layout.

*Tip: If you don't like the appearance or functionality of the **Story Editor**, you can change it. Choose **Edit > Preferences > Story Editor** (Windows) or **InDesign > Preferences > Story Editor Display** (Mac) to edit the cursor, the background color, and more!*

4. Close the file without saving.

Congratulations, you are now experienced with InDesign CS2's many type features! That is no small accomplishment. In the next chapter, you will learn how to create and work with colors.

7

Working with Color

| Creating a CMYK Color Using the Color Picker |
| Creating a Color Using the Color Palette |
| Saving Colors in the Swatches Palette |
| Creating a Tint | Creating a Spot Color |
| Applying a Stroke |

chap_07

InDesign CS2
HOT CD-ROM

Color is one of the most exciting elements of good design, and InDesign provides many ways to create color for use in print or even Web work.

In this chapter, you will learn the different ways to create color. From sampling a color from a picture imported into InDesign from another program, to mixing one in the Swatches palette, InDesign has something for everyone.

As you proceed through this chapter, I encourage you to pay special attention both to the exercises and the tips and sidebar notes. Color is a large and complex topic unto itself, and the notes and tips in this chapter provide useful details that will help produce color output that meets your expectations.

Color Modes in InDesign CS2

When producing color for printing, you can use different types of color in a program like InDesign. Each type of color affects color output differently.

Before delving into how InDesign handles color, however, it is important to address the two ways color can be produced on a press: as **spot** color or **process** color (also called **process build** color). **Spot** is a generic term that can describe any premixed color—that is, a color premixed before being used on a press—although many people associate spot colors with colors produced by companies like Pantone®. A spot color is used in printing when you must have an exact color (in a logo, for instance) or when a process color can't produce the desired color (such as a deep blue or fluorescent-appearing color). Spot colors are a great way to achieve consistency when printing. But it is important, to talk to your print service provider about spot colors because they *can* be more expensive to print than CMYK process colors. **Process build** colors, on the other hand, are created by "mixing" several inks together directly on the printed page as it is being printed.

The colors you will use on text, frames, shapes, and vector graphics in InDesign CS2 can be created in one of several color modes. A **color mode** is the type of model that is used to create color. InDesign CS2 can work with three major color modes, which are defined here:

1. **RGB:** Composed of red, green, and blue, these colors represent the range of color a computer monitor can display. RGB color is most appropriate in Web pages and onscreen presentations.

2. **CMYK:** CMYK represents cyan (C), magenta (M), yellow (Y), and black (K). These are the four inks used in typical printing processes. The four inks mix together to form the range of colors that can be printed.

3. **Lab:** Lab is a color mode that is used by some professional photographers and graphics professionals who want to maintain color consistency from program to program. In printing, Lab mode is converted to CMYK, so many people just use CMYK throughout, instead of beginning with Lab and converting to CMYK.

The Color Picker

One of the newest ways to make color in InDesign CS2 is from the **Color Picker** dialog box. This is accessed from a number of places, as you will learn in the first exercise. The **Color Picker** is a dialog box that has been in Adobe Illustrator and Photoshop for many versions and finally has made its way into InDesign CS2. It's a very visual way of picking colors. The most widely used method for accessing the **Color Picker** is to double-click the color **Fill Box** at the bottom of the **Toolbox**. See the next section titled "**Stroke and Fill**" for an image of the **Fill Box**.

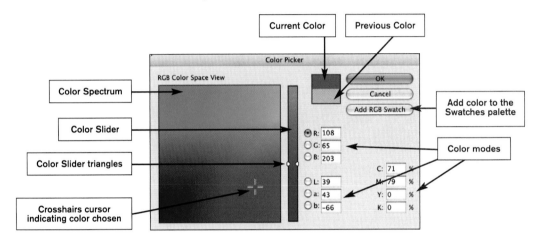

Color Picker Options	
Feature	**Function**
Color Spectrum	When you choose a color mode (CMYK, RGB, or Lab), this area displays the range of color available in that color mode.
Color Slider	Used to choose how much of a color is applied. If you chose red from the RGB color mode, dragging the Color Slider triangles higher up adds red, and dragging the triangles down on the Color Slider removes red from the color chosen in the Color Spectrum.
Color Slider triangles	Click and drag to change how much of a single color (red, green, blue, etc.) is added to the final blended color.
Current Color	Displays the color that has been selected from the Color Spectrum.

continues on next page

Color Picker Options *continued*	
Feature	**Function**
Previous Color	Shows the last color chosen from the Color Spectrum. Click it to use it again.
Add RGB Swatch button	Adds this color to the Swatches palette to be saved with this document and used again.
Color mode fields	When selected, indicates which color mode is used to create the color in the Color Spectrum. **Note:** Later in this chapter you will learn how to make a swatch. You can save a color as a swatch from this dialog box by clicking **Add RGB Swatch**. Whichever color mode field is selected (in other words, if the cursor was in a CMYK field in the Color Picker dialog box) the button would change to **Add CMYK Swatch**.

Stroke and Fill

Text, frames, shapes, and certain types of graphics can have color applied in InDesign. InDesign categorizes color applied to objects as stroke or fill.

The **stroke** refers to the border or outline color of a frame, shape, text, or graphic. The **fill** refers to the inside color of a frame, shape, text, or graphic. When working with color in InDesign, you usually need to tell InDesign whether to apply color as stroke and/or fill *before* the color is applied. The general process of applying color is described here:

1. Select the frame, shape, text, or graphic to which you want to apply the color.

2. Choose whether you want to change the stroke or the fill. You will learn how to do this in the exercises that follow.

3. Apply the color to the object. You will learn how to do this in the exercises that follow.

The **Toolbox**, pictured below, is one place to find the stroke and fill options in InDesign.

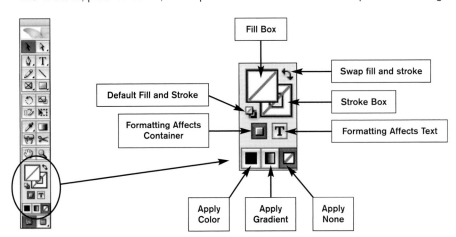

Toolbox Color Options	
Feature	**Function**
Fill Box	When selected, this option tells InDesign to fill a frame with color.
Stroke Box	When selected, this option tells InDesign to change the color of the stroke of an object.
Swap Fill and Stroke	If color is applied to either stroke or fill (or both), this switches the colors (stroke for fill and fill for stroke) on an object.
Default Fill and Stroke	Sets the Fill Box to None and the Stroke Box to black.
Formatting Affects Container	For a selected frame, this button makes the Fill and Stroke boxes affect the frame.
Formatting Affects Text	For a selected frame, this button makes the Fill and Stroke boxes affect the text within the frame.
Apply Color	Click this button to apply the last color used.
Apply Gradient	Click this button to apply a generic gradient.
Apply None	Click this button to remove color. (Set the color to None.)

I. ————————Creating a CMYK Color Using the Color Picker

In this first exercise, you will create your first color, a CMYK color (used for printing), in the **Color Picker**.

> **1.** Open **javaco_poster.indd** from the **chap_07** folder on your **Desktop**. The document will be blank except for several guides on the page, which you will use to create the color frames that make up a good deal of the poster.
>
> *Throughout the exercises in this chapter, you will open and close several palettes. For most of the steps, the palettes are undocked and sitting next to the object you will be working on. Remember that you can always return the palettes to their default locations by choosing* **Window > Workspace > Default**.

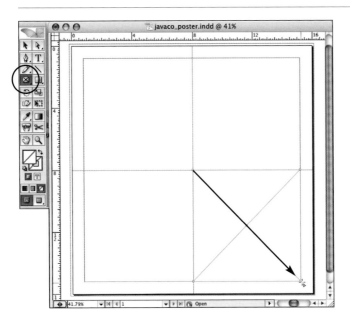

> **2.** Select the **Rectangle Frame** tool from the **Toolbox**. From the center of the page (where the guides meet) hover the cursor over the page until a small white arrow appears next to the crosshairs cursor. This arrow indicates that the next frame that is drawn will snap to the guides already on the page. Drag the cursor to the lower-right corner of the margin guides. A small white arrow appears once again when the cursor is within snapping distance of the margin guides. Release the mouse and a frame appears.
>
> *There are two types of frame-drawing tools in InDesign: the* **Rectangle Frame** *tool and the* **Rectangle** *tool. They both draw frames that can hold text or pictures or nothing at all. You chose the* **Rectangle Frame** *tool. The difference between these two drawing tools is discussed in the* **Note** *titled "***Rectangle Frame Tool vs. Rectangle Tool***" at the end of this exercise.*

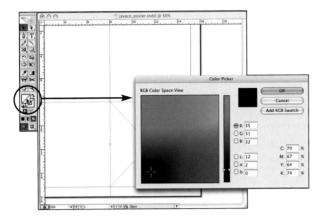

3. The frame should be selected by default; if it is not, choose the **Selection** tool, and click in the middle of the frame to select it. You are going to make your first color using the **Color Picker**. To open the **Color Picker** dialog box, double-click the **Fill Box** in the **Toolbox**.

Note: *This is not the only one way to access the **Color Picker**. Towards the end of Exercise 2, you will learn about another method involving the **Color** palette.*

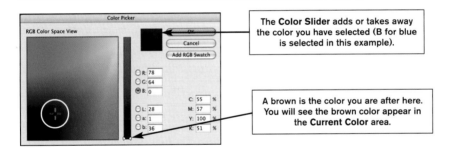

The **Color Slider** adds or takes away the color you have selected (B for blue is selected in this example).

A brown is the color you are after here. You will see the brown color appear in the **Current Color** area.

4. In the **Color Picker** dialog box, you are going to create a light brown color. In the **R** field, type **78**; in the **G** field, type **64**; and in the **B** field, type **0** to create a color similar to the one you see in the illustration above. Click the radio button to the left of **B** (for blue). With the cursor, click and drag in the **Color Spectrum** area to change the color to your liking in the **Current Color** area (don't stray too far from the original). Keep this dialog box open for the next step.

*The **Color Picker** doesn't always work the way you might expect. When you create a color in the **Color Picker** in the RGB color mode (as you did when you chose the **B** (for blue), you see **RGB Color Space View** displayed above the **Color Spectrum**. When you click **OK**, InDesign will generate an RGB color.*

Note: *When you choose a color from a particular color mode, such as **B** for blue, the **Color Spectrum** window displays the range of colors from red to green (the other two colors in the RGB color mode). The **Color Slider** is used to add blue (by dragging up) or take away blue (by dragging down).*

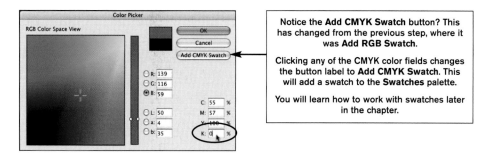

Notice the **Add CMYK Swatch** button? This has changed from the previous step, where it was **Add RGB Swatch**.

Clicking any of the CMYK color fields changes the button label to **Add CMYK Swatch**. This will add a swatch to the **Swatches** palette.

You will learn how to work with swatches later in the chapter.

5. The brown color you just chose is too dark. You could sample a darker brown in the **Color Spectrum**, but that could prove visually challenging (or it might just make you dizzy). To make the color lighter, you will use the **CMYK** color mode. Type **0** in the **K** field and either tab to another field or place the cursor in another field to see the lighter brown. Click **OK** to close the dialog box, and the color will be applied to the frame.

You can use either the RGB or CMYK color mode numbers to change a color. The easiest way to make a color darker or lighter is to change the amount of K (black) in its CMYK value. Decreasing the K value makes a color lighter, and increasing the K value makes a color darker.

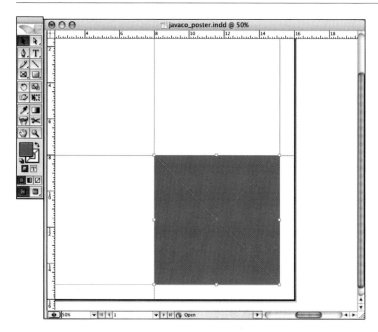

6. Save the file and keep it open for the next exercise.

NOTE | Rectangle Frame Tool vs. Rectangle Tool

There are two types of frame creation tools in InDesign: the **Rectangle Frame** tool and the **Rectangle** tool. After using InDesign for a while, you come to realize that these two tools are mostly interchangeable. In the previous exercise, you used the **Rectangle Frame** tool for one reason only: frames created with the **Rectangle Frame** tool have no stroke and no fill by default. The **Rectangle** tool has a black stroke on frames by default.

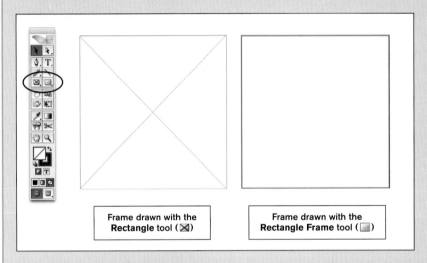

Frame drawn with the
Rectangle tool (⊠)

Frame drawn with the
Rectangle Frame tool (▢)

Frames drawn with the **Rectangle Frame** tool have an "**X**" in them. This "**X**" serves two purposes. The first is to make QuarkXPress users, who are used to seeing an "**X**" in picture boxes, feel right at home in InDesign. The second reason for the "**X**" is to make it easier to mock up a design. Before text and images are even available, frames created with the **Rectangle Frame** tool can be used to hold the place of pictures, and frames drawn with the **Rectangle** tool can hold the place of text. The frames are easily distinguishable because of the "**X**." Frames created with either of these tools can contain text, color, or graphics. They are interchangeable.

The Color Palette

InDesign provides many ways to make color, and each method has specific uses. The two main palettes you will use to create and edit color are the **Color** palette and the **Swatches** palette. The **Color** palette is located under **Window > Color**.

The **Color** palette creates colors that are known as **unnamed colors**. These are the colors used in the document, but usually only in one place or for one object. In Illustrator, these types of colors are referred to as **local colors**. To change the color you have already applied to an object, first you need to select the object, and then you edit the color mix in the **Color** palette. The color change is automatically applied to the selected object.

This works well for a single color used in one object. But to create and edit colors used several times in a document, or to edit all colors from one place, the **Swatches** palette is very useful. You will learn about swatches in an exercise later in this chapter.

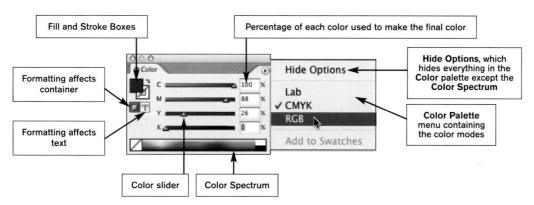

The **Color** palette contains a lot of the same formatting options as the **Toolbox**. This includes the **Stroke** and **Fill** boxes, the **Formatting Affects Text** and **Formatting Affects Container** buttons, and **Last Color**. Color in InDesign CS2 has many redundancies. Once you are comfortable with the different options, I encourage you to choose the method that works best for you.

2. _____Creating a Color Using the Color Palette

In this exercise, you will create another frame and then a color using the **Color** palette.

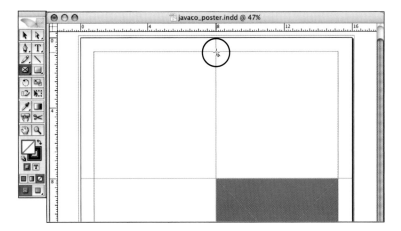

1. With **javaco_poster.indd** open from the previous exercise, choose the **Rectangle Frame** tool. You will create another frame right above the one you created in the previous exercise. From the center of the page (where the center vertical guide and the top margin guide meet), hover the cursor over the page until a small white arrow appears next to the crosshairs cursor.

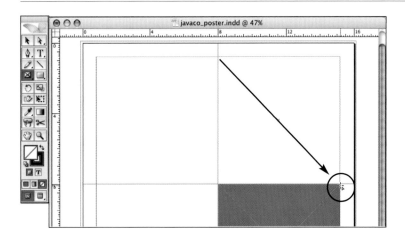

2. Click and drag the mouse to the point where the center horizontal guide and the right margin guide meet. When the white arrow shows up next to the crosshairs cursor, let go of the mouse.

*Tip: If the frame doesn't snap into the guides, choose the **Selection** tool from the **Toolbox**, and resize the frame by selecting it and dragging a corner.*

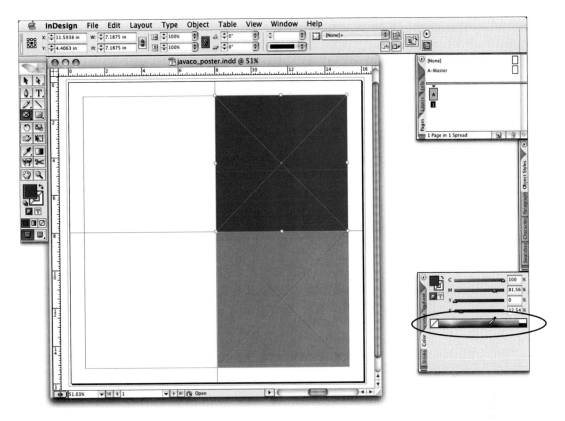

3. Open the **Color** palette that is docked on the side of the workspace by clicking on its tab. With the frame still selected (keep the **Rectangle Frame** tool selected), bring the cursor into the **Color Spectrum** of the **Color** palette. An eyedropper appears. Click a blue color to sample and apply it to the frame selected on the page.

*The **Color Spectrum** is a pretty small area in the **Color** palette, no doubt. After sampling a color, you can edit the color by using the sliders above the **Color Spectrum**. You can also click, hold down, and drag around in the **Color Spectrum** area instead of having to click several times to get the color you want. The sliders jump around, but it is sometimes the easier way to get the color you desire.*

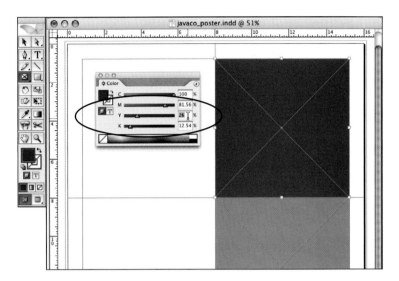

4. Once you've sampled a color, you can edit it numerically by typing directly into any of the color fields. With the frame still selected, double-click the number in the **Y** (yellow) field to the right of the slider and type **26**. Press **Enter** or **Return** to accept. This will add a little more yellow to the color. Keep the frame selected.

Note: The Color palette in this and the next few steps was pulled off the palette group on the right side of the workspace and set on top of the page. You may find the Color palette easier to work with in this location if you need to create or edit several colors.

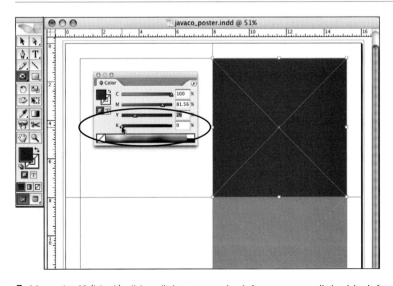

5. Move the **K** (black) slider all the way to the left to remove all the black from the color.

This is another way to change the color mix. When using the CMYK color mode (which is necessary for print work), you are actually mixing the four inks used in the printing process—cyan, magenta, yellow, and black—to achieve the desired color. Each ink can achieve a maximum of 100 percent.

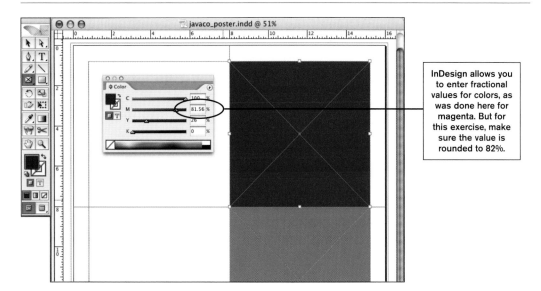

InDesign allows you to enter fractional values for colors, as was done here for magenta. But for this exercise, make sure the value is rounded to 82%.

6. Release the mouse. The color should resemble the blue pictured here. If not, make the values for the **C** (cyan) and **M** (magenta) match **C, 100%** and **M, 82%** (rounded up).

Note: *Many programs round color values (expressed as a percent) to the nearest whole number. InDesign lets you pick a fraction of a percentage for any one ink.*

Tip: *Double-clicking on the **Fill Box** in the **Color** palette opens the **Color Picker** dialog box to give you a bigger visual color field to pick a color from.*

7. Save the file and keep it open for the next exercises, where you will create two more frames and two more colors using different methods.

TIP | Creating a Lighter Shade of a Color in the Color Palette

It is not uncommon to create a color and then use a lighter version of that color in other parts of a design. The lighter version of the color is referred to as a **tint**. The **Color** palette allows you to create a lighter version, or tint, of any color.

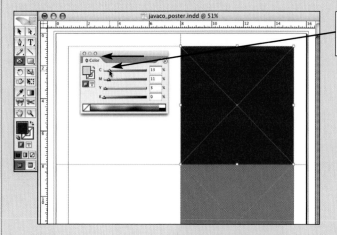

The **C** (cyan) slider is dragged to the left with the **Shift** key held down.

Choose the frame or object that has the color you want to change with the **Selection** tool. Hold down the **Shift** key and with the cursor, click and drag a CMYK slider. To make the color lighter overall, drag the slider to the left. The **Shift** key causes all the color sliders to move together to create a lighter version of the same color.

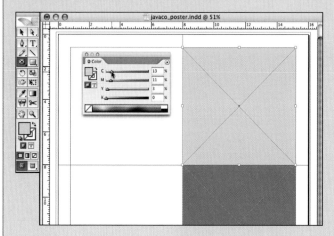

Release the mouse, and the color changes in the object on the page! If you don't like this new color, you can always choose **Edit > Undo Color** to return to the original color.

The Swatches Palette

The **Swatches** palette is yet another place to create and edit color, but it is also the most important because it offers more functionality than the **Color** palette. In the previous exercises, you created unnamed colors in the **Color** palette. Unnamed colors are only used locally, or in one location. Colors created in the **Swatches** palette, however, can be named and saved as swatches. These swatches can then be applied in multiple places, much like paragraph and character styles. When changes are made to a swatch, those changes are automatically applied to the objects that use the (edited) swatch. In Illustrator, colors that behave this way are referred to as global colors. In InDesign CS2, all colors saved in the **Swatches** palette are global colors. The **Swatches** palette is located under **Window > Swatches**.

Any colors created and saved in the **Swatches** palette are only saved with the document that is open at the time. Later in the chapter, you will learn how to share color swatches between documents.

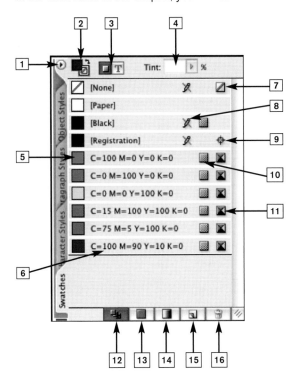

Swatches Palette Options	
Feature	**Function**
1 Swatches Palette menu	Provides extra functionality for swatches.
2 Fill Box and Stroke Box	Determines whether stroke or fill is changed.
3 Object or Text control	Determines whether text or frame is changed.
4 Tint field	Creates a percentage of a color (such as 30 percent tint of blue).
5 Swatch	Color as it appears on screen.
6 Swatch name	Name of color swatch.
7 None	Applies no color (or removes color).
8 Cannot Edit	Indicates that None, Black, and Registration colors cannot be changed.
9 Registration	Indicates color used for printers marks or for lining up separations.
10 Spot or Process	Indicates whether the swatch is spot or process build.
11 Color mode indicator	Indicates whether swatch is composed of CMYK, RGB, or Lab colors.
12 Show All Swatches	Shows all solid, tint, and gradients swatches in the palette.
13 Show Solid Color Swatches	Shows only solid colors in the palette.
14 Show Gradient Swatches	Shows only gradient colors in the palette.
15 Create New Swatch	Creates a new solid-color swatch.
16 Delete Swatch	Removes a swatch from the swatches palette. If the swatch was used in the document, a menu prompts you to replace the color being deleted with another.

3. ——————————Saving Colors in the Swatches Palette

In this exercise, you save as a swatch the color you created in the **Color** palette in the previous exercise. You will also create a CMYK swatch from scratch.

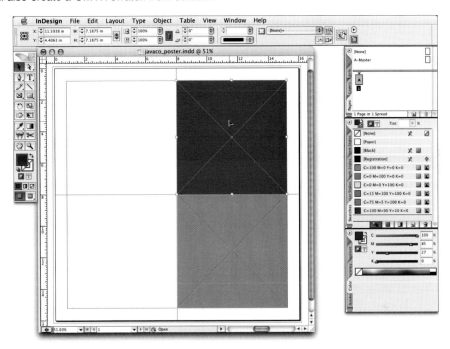

1. With **javaco_poster.indd** open from the previous exercise, open the **Swatches** and **Color** palettes on the side of the workspace by clicking on the appropriate tabs. Select the blue frame you created in the previous exercise with the **Selection** tool.

Throughout the exercises in this chapter, you will open and close several palettes. For most of the steps, the palettes are undocked and sitting next to the object you will be working on. Remember that you can always return the palettes to their default locations by choosing **Window > Workspace > Default**.

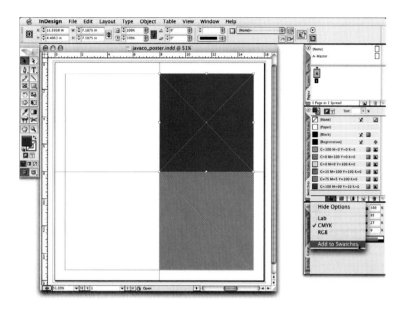

2. The color for the blue frame will appear in the **Color** palette. To use this color elsewhere (make it a global color), you need to make it a swatch. From the **Color Palette** menu, choose **Add to Swatches**. To see the swatch added, proceed to Step 3.

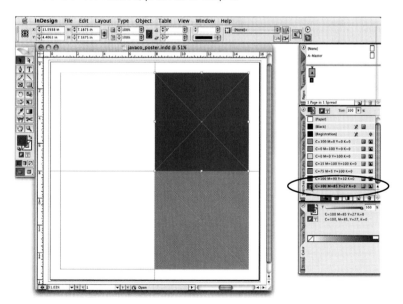

*The color appears in the **Swatches** palette and is now a global color. Do you notice that there are two blue swatches that are very similar? The new swatch has values of C, 100; Y, 85; M, 27; and K, 0.*

*Note: There may be times when you don't know which colors are unnamed and which are swatches. To find out, select a colored object. If an object uses a swatch, the swatch is highlighted in the **Swatches** palette when the object is selected, and the **Color** palette will turn into a tint creator, showing tint percentages of the color (which you can change). If the object has an unnamed color applied, the **Color** palette shows the color sliders so you can edit the color in the selected location. In the illustration for Step 2, the **Color** palette shows that the color for the selected object is a swatch because the tint slider is showing.*

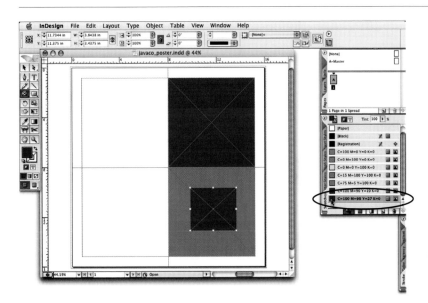

3. Select the **Rectangle Frame** tool from the **Toolbox** and click and drag a rectangle on top of the brown frame. Click the **Fill Box** in the **Toolbox** (to apply the color to the fill of the frame), and in the **Swatches** palette, click the new blue swatch to apply the color to the frame.

Using this second blue frame in the next step, you will see how editing a swatch changes the color wherever it is used in the document.

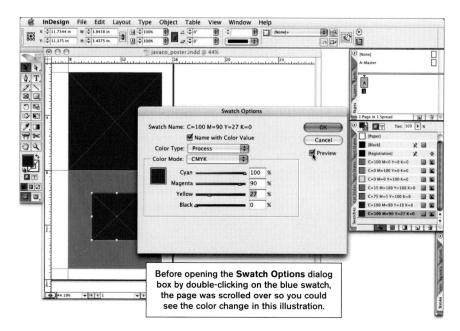

Before opening the **Swatch Options** dialog box by double-clicking on the blue swatch, the page was scrolled over so you could see the color change in this illustration.

4. The next step is to edit the swatch and see it automatically update on the page. This is one of the main reasons for using a swatch (as opposed to an unnamed color). In the **Swatches** palette, double-click the swatch you just created. The **Swatch Options** dialog box opens. In the **Swatch Options** dialog box, which contains some of the same color settings as the **Color** palette, change the **Magenta** percentage by moving the slider to the right until **90%** is displayed in the field. Turn on **Preview** by clicking the **Preview** check box, and move the dialog box out of the way to see the color automatically change in both frames on the page! Click **OK** to accept the changes. Delete the smaller blue frame by selecting it with the **Selection** tool (if it is not still selected) and pressing **Delete**. That frame was created solely to change the color and see it change in multiple places.

Don't forget that the idea behind creating and using a swatch is that once it is applied throughout a document, it changes globally when the swatch color is changed. In this way, because the swatch was applied to the two frames on the page, they will both change color when the swatch color is changed.

Note: *When editing swatches that are used in a document, the objects or text that use the swatch do not need to be selected for the swatch changes to be automatically applied. As a matter of fact, unless you are targeting a certain object, it may be best to deselect before editing swatches.*

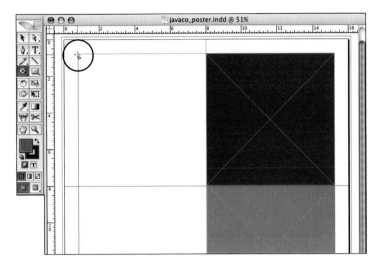

5. Select the **Rectangle Frame** tool from the **Toolbox**. You will now create another frame to the left of the blue frame. In the upper-left corner of the margin guides, hover the cursor over the page until a small white arrow appears next to the crosshairs cursor.

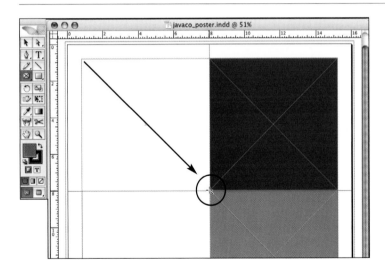

6. Click and drag the mouse to where the center horizontal guide and center vertical guide meet. When the white arrow appears next to the crosshairs cursor, let go of the mouse. A new frame is created.

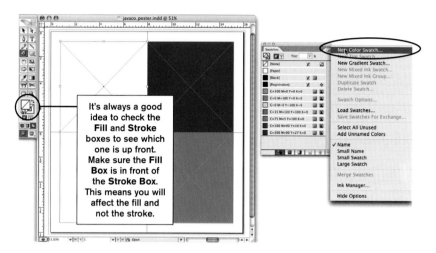

It's always a good idea to check the **Fill** and **Stroke** boxes to see which one is up front. Make sure the **Fill Box** is in front of the **Stroke Box.** This means you will affect the fill and not the stroke.

7. With the upper-left frame still selected, check to make sure that the **Fill Box** is still in front of the **Stroke Box** in the **Toolbox.** Then choose **New Color Swatch** from the **Swatches Palette** menu. You will now create a color from scratch in the **Swatches** palette.

*Tip: To change which box (**Stroke** or **Fill**) is in front using a shortcut, first make sure the cursor is not in text, and then press the **X** key. Whichever box is behind will come to the front! This toggles back and forth every time you press the **X** key.*

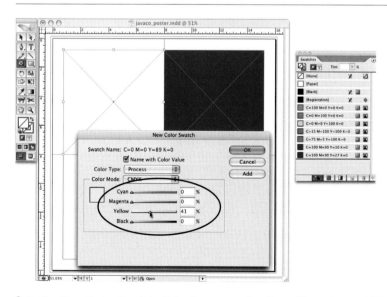

8. In the **New Color Swatch** dialog box, move the **Cyan, Magenta**, and **Black** sliders to the left (until each one reads **0%**). The color will now be a lighter yellow made of just the color yellow. Type **41** or slide the color slider until **Yellow** is set at **41%.**

*Notice all of the settings in this dialog box, like **Color Type** and **Color Mode**, that you haven't touched yet? When a color swatch is created from scratch, InDesign automatically chooses **CMYK** for the **Color Mode** and **Process** for the **Color Type**. Remember, **CMYK** are the four printing inks, and **Process** refers to a process build of colors to create the final color during printing. This is a good default for printed documents.*

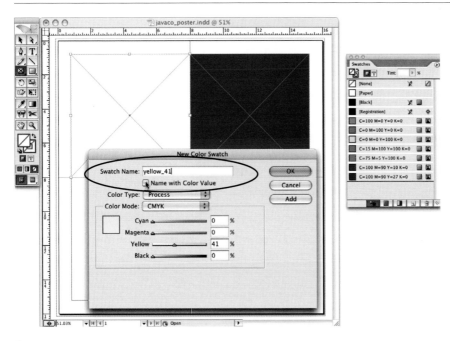

9. Deselect the **Name with Color Value** check box to give the color a name of your own choosing. Type "**yellow_41**" in the **Swatch Name** field. Click **OK**.

*Note: All the colors created in the **New Color Swatch** dialog box are automatically named according to how much of each ink is used to create the swatch (for instance, the name of the swatch you just created comes from the fact that Yellow is set at 41 and the other three colors are set at 0). That can be good because the name appears in the **Swatches** palette and you can easily distinguish colors that look similar. It's not always necessary though. I tend to name the colors according to what they are being used for (such as "**headline_orange**").*

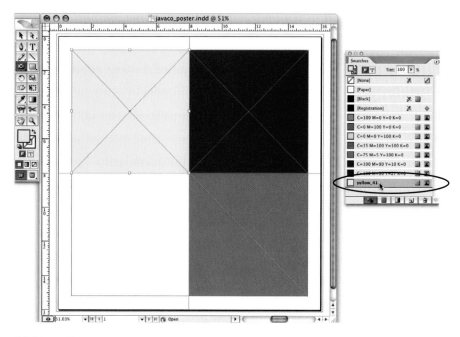

10. The **yellow_41** color is now applied to the frame, and the swatch shows up in the **Swatches** palette.

11. Save the file and keep it open for the next exercise.

TIP | Seeing Color Values in the Swatches Palette

If the cursor hovers over a color name in the **Swatches** palette, InDesign shows a little yellow tooltip that displays how much of each ink is used in that swatch. To see the difference between two colors, hover over each separately to see the color breakdown.

4.——————————Creating a Tint

In this exercise, you will create a tint from the yellow color you created in the previous exercise. A **tint** is a lighter shade of a single color or several combined colors. In this case, the yellow CMYK color swatch is composed of 41 percent yellow. To make a lighter shade of that yellow, you will create a tint.

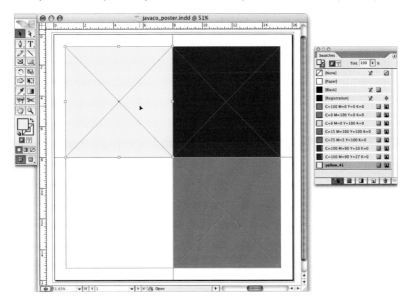

1. With **javaco_poster.indd** open from the previous exercise, use the **Selection** tool to select the frame filled with yellow. Open the **Swatches** palette as well.

Notice that when you select the frame, the swatch named ***yellow_41*** *is selected in the* ***Swatches*** *palette? This is an excellent way to tell which color swatch is applied to which object. If the yellow color had been made with the* ***Color Picker*** *or the* ***Color*** *palette and not saved as a swatch, nothing would be selected in the* ***Swatches*** *palette.*

Note: For this example, the ***Swatches*** *palette was removed from the group docked on the side of the workspace.*

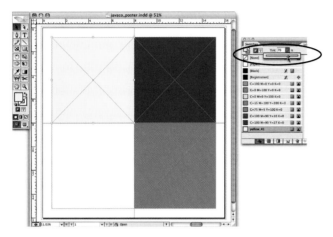

2. With the **yellow_41** swatch selected, you will change the tint of the color. In the **Swatches** palette, click the arrow to the right of the **Tint** field at the top of the **Swatches** palette. A slider bar appears. Drag the slider to the left and stop when it shows **70%** in the **Tint** field. The yellow-filled frame is now filled with the new tint.

*Note: To create the tint, you can also type a value into the **Tint** field and press **Enter** or **Return**.*

*Tints created in the **Swatches** palette are only applied to the selected object. The swatch itself is not changed. If you make a tint that you then want to apply to other objects, save the tint as a swatch, which you will learn how to do in the next step.*

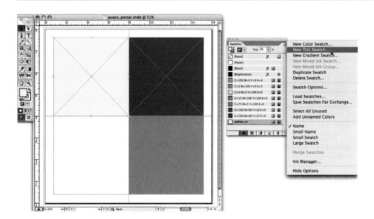

3. Now that the yellow frame shows the yellow tint you just created, it is a good idea to save the tint as a swatch for use later. Making sure the frame is still selected, from the **Swatches Palette** menu, choose **New Tint Swatch**.

*Choosing **New Tint Swatch** tells InDesign to "pick up," or copy, the color and tint and make a new swatch from it.*

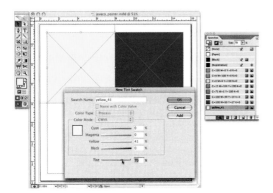

4. In the **New Tint Swatch** dialog box that opens, you see the swatch name of **yellow_41** and the mix of CMYK. The **Tint** field should have **70%** in it. If not, change the value in the field by dragging the slider or typing **70**. Click **OK** to accept and save the swatch.

*Note: The **Swatch Name** and settings are dimmed because you are making a tint of the color, not adjusting the original color swatch.*

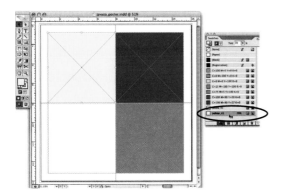

5. The **Tint Swatch** for **yellow_41** now appears as a separate swatch. Notice the "**70%**" to the right of the swatch name? This is a tint of the original color that can now be applied easily to any object.

6. Save the file and keep it open for the next exercise.

*Note: Tint swatches are great because they can be saved and used later. They also work the same as other swatches. Double-clicking on the tint swatch brings up the swatch options you saw in Step 4. If you change the tint percentage, InDesign automatically applies that change anywhere that tint is used! One difference between regular swatches and tint swatches is that a tint swatch is tied to the original color swatch it was created from. So if the original color swatch (**yellow_41** in this example) is deleted, the tint swatch (**yellow_41 – 70%**) is deleted as well. This only works one way, however, so you can delete a tint swatch and rest assured that the original color swatch is still in the **Swatches** palette.*

TIP | Creating Tints in the Color Palette

Tints can also be created in the **Color** palette. This is similar to the tip earlier in the chapter that also dealt with making colors lighter in value in the **Color** palette, but this tip shows you how to create true tints (percentages of color). When a color swatch is created (like the **yellow_41** in the previous exercise), and applied to an object, the **Color** palette turns into a tint maker. In this circumstance, the sole purpose of the **Color** palette is to create a tint for the applied swatch. If you want to try this using the file that is open from the previous exercise, first delete the tint created in the last exercise by clicking on the tint in the **Swatches** palette and clicking on the trash can at the bottom of the palette to delete it.

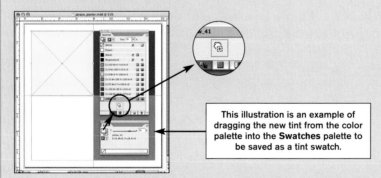

This illustration is an example of dragging the new tint from the color palette into the **Swatches** palette to be saved as a tint swatch.

With the yellow frame selected and the **yellow_41** swatch applied, open up the **Color** palette. When an object with a swatch applied is selected, the **Color** palette is relegated to making tints. It works just like the **Tint** field in the **Swatches** palette, but you also get a cool tint spectrum that you can sample from at the bottom of the **Color** palette. Drag the slider or type in a value, and a new tint is made! To save it as a swatch, drag the **Fill Box** from the **Color** palette into the **Swatches** palette.

The tint is now created and saved as a swatch! Since the frame had the **yellow_41** swatch applied, it named it the same thing but added the "**70%**" because it's now a tint.

TIP | Replacing Colors

If you are using a swatch in the document and you wish to use a different swatch, you can perform a global replacement by deleting the swatch currently in use. InDesign displays a dialog box asking you to pick a color to replace the color you are deleting. This replaces the color globally throughout the document.

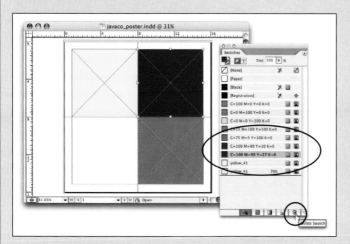

Choose a swatch to delete from those used somewhere in the document. Click the **Trash Can** icon in the lower-right corner of the **Swatches** palette to delete it. If the swatch is being used in that document, the **Delete Swatch** dialog box opens. If not, InDesign simply deletes the swatch.

The **Delete Swatch** dialog box allows you to replace the deleted swatch with another (existing) swatch (you cannot create a new swatch from here), or it replaces the deleted swatch with an unnamed color. After telling InDesign how to replace the deleted swatch, click **OK**. InDesign automatically updates the document according to your instructions.

What Is a Spot Color?

So far in this chapter, you've learned how to create CMYK colors using several different methods. In this exercise, you will create a spot color. **Spot color** is a generic term given to colors that are pre-mixed, or mixed prior to printing. Spot colors are most often used when color accuracy is critical—in a company logo, for example. They are also used because they provide a greater range of color than process build CMYK colors.

The poster you have been creating in this chapter uses only process build CMYK colors, meaning that every color in the poster represents a different mixture of cyan, magenta, yellow, and black inks. This is referred to as a four-color job, because all four inks are required to print it.

A spot color, on the other hand, is a premixed ink that a printer or service provider purchases from a company like Pantone. If a spot color is applied to an object on the page, the printer prints the spot color in the area (or spot) where it is applied on the page—hence the name spot color.

Spot colors require additional work for the printer, who must set up the color on their printer or press. If you plan on using spot colors (sometimes referred to as Pantone colors or PMS colors), be aware that using spot colors may increase the cost to the job. So far, the poster uses four colors (cyan, magenta, yellow, and black). If a spot color is added to the document, it will be a five-color job because five inks—CMYK and the spot color ink—are needed to print it. More often than not, the more inks needed, the higher the printing cost.

Most often you will choose spot colors from a swatch book. The most popular brand of spot colors is Pantone. Their swatch books show the entire collection of premixed Pantone colors. Pantone colors are built into InDesign's color capabilities, so when you find a color you like in the swatch book, you can create the same color in InDesign by choosing the corresponding Pantone number.

Note: Spot colors are best used in documents that will be printed on a commercial press or another print device that can use spot inks (ask your print vendor if you are unsure). Standard office printers do not have spot, or Pantone, colors built into them, so they will automatically convert spot colors into process CMYK colors.

5. ————————Creating a Spot Color

Now that you've created several process colors, it's time to create a spot color. For a review of what spot colors are, see "Color Modes in InDesign CS2" at the beginning of this chapter.

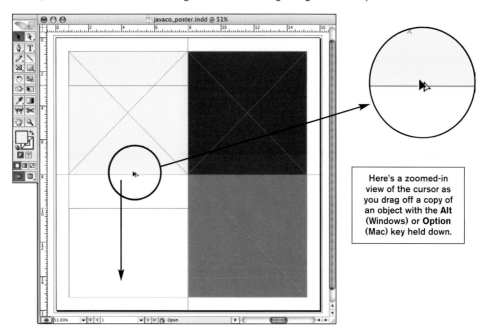

Here's a zoomed-in view of the cursor as you drag off a copy of an object with the **Alt** (Windows) or **Option** (Mac) key held down.

1. With **javaco_poster.indd** open from the previous exercise, select the yellow frame with the **Selection** tool. Hold down the **Alt** (Windows) or **Option** (Mac) key, click the frame, and drag to create a copy. Drag it until the copied frame snaps into the lower-left corner of the margin guides. Next, you will remove the color and fill it with a spot color.

In the previous exercises, you created new frames by drawing them with Rectangle Frame tool. That would have worked fine in this case as well, but holding down the Alt (Windows) or Option (Mac) key while clicking and dragging an object is an easy way to create a copy. You will notice that the arrow turns into a double-arrow when you are dragging off a copy of an object.

Tip: As you drag a copy off of an object, hold down the Shift key to constrain the copy's movements to vertical, horizontal, or diagonal.

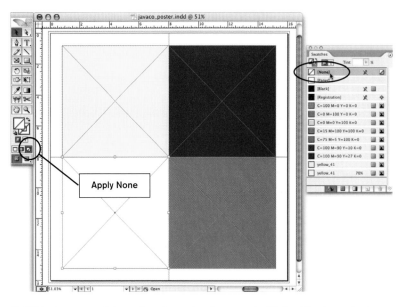

Apply None

2. With the copy of the yellow frame in place, and with it still selected, choose the **Fill Box** from the **Toolbox**. Select the **None** swatch from the **Swatches** palette to remove the (copied) yellow color from the fill.

*Note: A red slash in the **Fill Box** indicates that there is no color in the fill. The fill color can also be removed by selecting the rather small **Apply None** button at the bottom of the **Toolbox.***

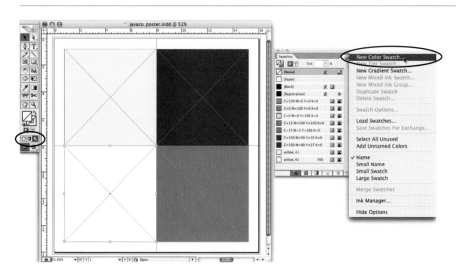

3. With the lower-left frame still selected, choose **New Color Swatch** from the **Swatches Palette** menu. In the next step, you will create a spot color.

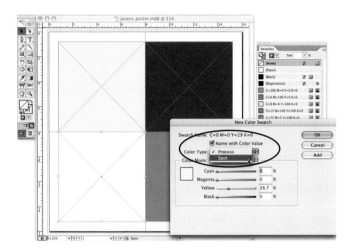

4. Using the **New Color Swatch** dialog box, you will go through three steps to make a spot color. The first step is to choose **Spot** from the **Color Type** pop-up menu.

*Remember, a **process** color is a process build, or a color built from other colors during printing (such as CMYK). A **spot** color, on the other hand, is typically used for premixed inks, such as Pantone or PMS colors.*

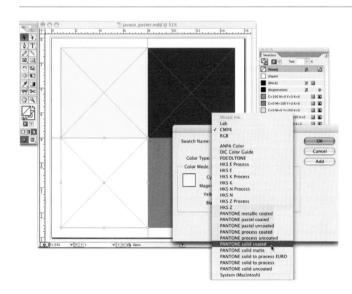

5. The next step is to choose a color library from the **Color Mode** pop-up menu. To this point, CMYK has been the preferred color mode. In this case, you are going to pick a spot color from the Pantone library. Choose **Pantone solid coated**. A list of all possible Pantone colors appears in the **New Color Swatch** palette.

*Note: The **Color Mode** pop-up menu contains many color-matching-system libraries. These libraries are digital "swatch books" that many companies offer to their customers. Once you pick a color system, such as Pantone, the swatch book of colors that they offer appears in the **New Color Swatch** palette in digital form. By choosing **Pantone solid coated**, you are choosing a color made by the company called Pantone. It is a solid color (premixed spot ink) labeled "coated" because of the paper or stock it will be printed on. Coated, matte, and uncoated are different finish types for paper. If in doubt, ask your print vendor which finish is appropriate for the job you are creating. If you are exploring spot colors for the first time, this may seem a little overwhelming, but if you do any kind of printing, you will soon realize that a lot of companies use spot colors in their logos to maintain consistent color, or they use spot colors to achieve a color that CMYK can't make.*

*If you are going to be using spot colors, make sure to maintain consistency when choosing the color library. If you don't know what kind of paper you are printing the document on (coated, matte, or uncoated), don't worry. Just choose the same library for all the spot colors in this document. Even if it's the wrong color library, choosing the same (such as **Pantone solid coated**) throughout is better than using different ones in different places.*

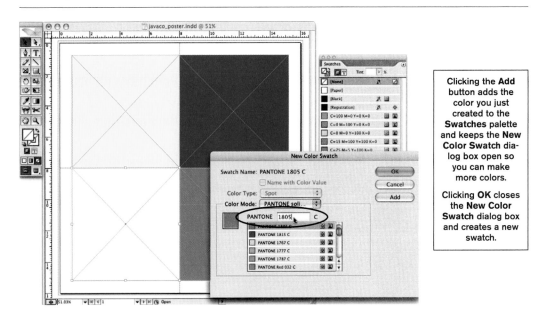

Clicking the Add button adds the color you just created to the Swatches palette and keeps the New Color Swatch dialog box open so you can make more colors.

Clicking OK closes the New Color Swatch dialog box and creates a new swatch.

6. You can scroll down to find a good spot color or type the number into the **Pantone** field. For this exercise, type the color number **1805** in the **Pantone** field. Click **OK** to accept the color and close the **New Color Swatch** dialog box.

The color number you just typed was found in a Pantone swatch book. Swatch books like those created by Pantone have thousands of colors in them. Color numbers differentiate the colors.

Tip: When picking a spot color for a document, don't trust the color that appears on the screen! In fact, every color you create in InDesign may look different when it's printed than it does on a monitor. Unless properly calibrated, a monitor, which displays color using the RGB color mode, can easily distort color. Picking a spot color from a printed swatch book (offered by companies like Pantone) is safer because, unlike a monitor, a swatch book displays how each color prints on paper.

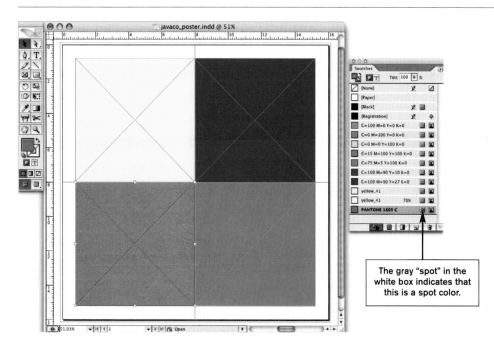

The gray "spot" in the white box indicates that this is a spot color.

7. The Pantone spot color **1805 C** is now in the **Swatches** palette and applied to the frame on the page.

8. Save the file and keep it open for the next exercise.

*Notice the "**C**" at the end of the spot color name? "**C**" stands for "**coated.**" This is the type of paper that may be used to print this poster.*

TIP | Converting Spot Colors to Process Colors

There are times when spot colors need to be converted to process colors, either because the printing costs are too high or because the document is being printed on a device (such as an ink-jet printer) that can't print spot colors. In either case, it is best to convert the spot colors into process CMYK builds in InDesign before printing. If the document is printed with spot colors, the printer or printing device will convert the spot colors to process CMYK builds "on the fly." The result may surprise you, since spot colors offer a much larger color range than process CMYK. It's best to be "surprised" when you are at your desk, not knee-deep in a potentially costly printing process!

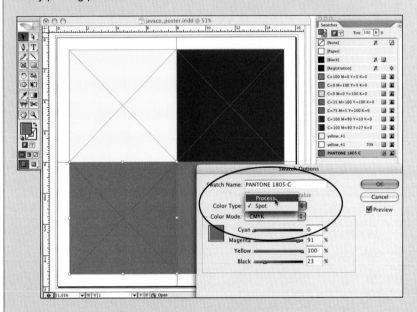

There are only two steps to converting to a CMYK process color from a spot color. Double-click the spot color that will be converted in the **Swatches** palette. Choose **CMYK** from the **Color Mode** pop-up menu, and then choose **Process** from the **Color Type** pop-up menu. Rename the color or keep it the same, and then click **OK**. The spot color is now the closest CMYK color that those four inks can achieve.

Note: After converting a spot color to process, the color may "shift" considerably. This is the "surprise" I referred to at the beginning of this tip. Remember, spot colors offer a greater variety of colors than you can achieve from mixing CMYK together as a process color.

TIP | Bringing Spot Colors in with Graphics

When you place graphics into a document, InDesign picks up the spot colors used in the incoming pictures. If an EPS, PDF, AI or even a PSD file is placed, InDesign will add any spot colors from those placed graphic files to the **Swatches** palette.

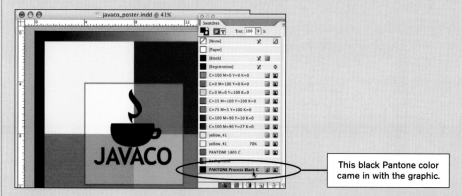

This black Pantone color came in with the graphic.

If you want to place a graphic to see how this works, deselect everything on the page by choosing **Edit > Deselect All**. With the **Selection** tool selected, choose **File > Place**, and select the graphic **cupsteam_spot.eps** from the **images** folder in the **chap_07** folder on your **Desktop**. Click **Open** to place the graphic, and look at the **Swatches** palette when the graphic is placed. This graphic was created in Illustrator and had a spot color applied in that program.

Swatches, like the black Pantone color shown in the illustration, that are added to the **Swatches** palette from imported graphics are saved only as spot colors, not as CMYK colors. Unlike regular swatches, these swatches can't be changed or deleted unless the graphic file is also changed or deleted. However, like other swatches, the swatches added from imported graphics can be applied in other places in the document and remains in the Swatches palette even if the graphic is deleted.

What Are Gradients?

A **gradient** is a color composed of two or more colors that transition from one to the other. Some programs refer to these as blends; others refer to them as gradients. If done right, a gradient can have a great effect on the overall design.

BONUS EXERCISE | Working with Gradients in InDesign

To learn how, check out **gradient.pdf** in the **bonus_exercises** folder on the **InDesign CS2 HOT CD-ROM**.

6. ———————Applying a Stroke

All frames, text, shapes, and lines you create can have both a fill and a stroke. So far, you have created colors and applied them to the fills of frames. Now it's time to add a stroke (border) to a frame.

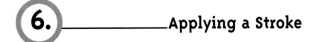

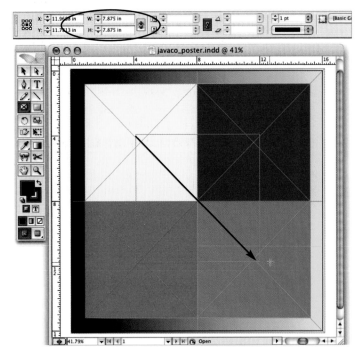

1. With **javaco_poster.indd** open from the previous exercise, select the **Rectangle Frame** tool and holding the **Shift** key down (to constrain its proportions, making it a perfect square), draw a frame in the middle of the page. It doesn't have to be exactly in the center; close is good enough for now. The square in this example is **7.875 in × 7.875 in**.

2. With the frame still selected (you can stay on the **Rectangle Frame** tool), you are going to position the frame exactly in the center of the page. In the **Control** palette, type **8** into the **X** and **Y** fields.

*By default, InDesign always displays the **X** and **Y** values for the position of the center of a selected frame relative to the upper-left corner of the page. The poster is 16 inches across by 16 inches high, so 8 is the exact center for the **X** and **Y** coordinates.*

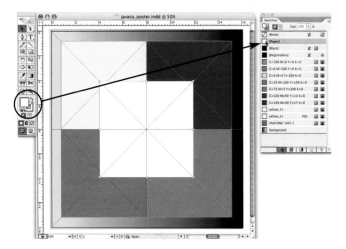

3. With the square frame still selected, choose the **Fill** in the **Toolbox**, and in the **Swatches** palette choose **Paper** (white) as the fill color.

*Paper may be confusing because it doesn't sound like a color. By default, InDesign uses the term "Paper" to refer to the color white. However, you can change the color of **Paper**. First, deselect everything. Next double-click the **Paper** swatch, and then edit the color in the **Swatch Options** dialog box. InDesign previews the document using paper of any color you might print on!*

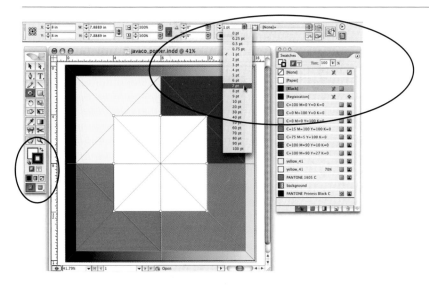

4. Once again, with the square frame still selected, select the **Stroke** tool from the **Toolbox**, and choose the **Black** swatch from the **Swatches** palette to apply a color to the stroke. The stroke also needs to be heavier, so in the **Control** palette, choose **7 pt** from the **Stroke Weight** pop-up menu.

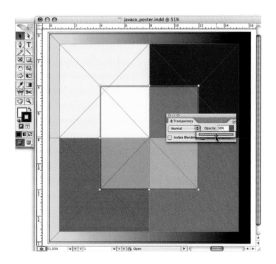

5. Open the **Transparency** palette by choosing **Window > Transparency**. The white frame you just created with the black stroke would look better if it were partially transparent (see-through). With the frame selected with the **Selection** tool, change the **Opacity** in the **Transparency** palette to **50%**. You can either type **50** in the **Opacity** field or click the arrow to the right of the field and use the slider to change the opacity. This affects the opacity of the stroke as well as the fill.

*Transparency is a built-in feature of InDesign and can be used on any object, including text and pictures. In Chapter 12, "Transparency," you will learn more about transparency and the **Transparency** palette.*

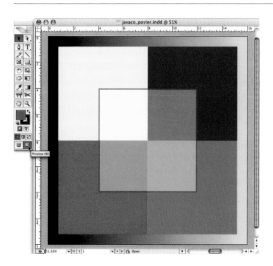

6. Choose **Edit > Deselect All**, or press **Ctrl+Shift+A** (Windows) or **Cmd+Shift+A** (Mac) to deselect all the objects on the page. Click the **Preview** button at the bottom of the **Toolbox** to hide the guides and pasteboard.

7. Save the file and close it.

*The **Preview** button is a great way to take a step back and see how the final piece looks without all the guides, grids, and hidden characters. When finished previewing a document, click the **Normal** button to see the guides, grids, and so on.*

NOTE | RGB for Web or Onscreen Output

You've learned many ways to create colors. When creating a document that will be converted to PDF and used on the Web or an onscreen presentation, you need to convert the colors to RGB (if they weren't originally created as RGB in InDesign). You also need to save all the graphics in the RGB color mode in a program such as Photoshop.

When exporting documents, file formats like PDF allow you to convert graphics and colors to RGB during the conversion process, so you can work in CMYK until you are ready to convert to PDF.

MOVIE | Sharing Color Between Documents

To learn about sharing color between documents, check out **sharecolor.mov** in the **movies** folder on the **InDesign CS2 HOT CD-ROM**.

In this chapter, you learned how to create color using different color modes. You also created tints, and applied and manipulated color gradients. In the next chapter, you will build on this knowledge by learning how to import and manipulate graphics.

8

Bringing in Graphics

| Placing Graphics | Cropping and Scaling Graphics |
| Rotating and Flipping Graphics |
| Editing and Relinking Using the Links Palette | Text Wrap |

chap_08

InDesign CS2
HOT CD-ROM

Now that you have a basic understanding of InDesign's building blocks, including everything from document creation to working with type styles and color, it's time to delve into one of the more exciting elements of the program—working with graphics. You will begin this chapter by placing several types of graphics, and then you will learn a few techniques for finessing them to enhance your designs.

InDesign provides many great ways to manipulate graphics. However, it can't overcome the basic reality of printing graphics—"garbage in, garbage out." To help protect you from this potential pitfall, in this chapter you will also learn what makes a graphic print worthy. While InDesign can't perform miracles on images gone bad, it can help you work faster and smarter with the images you do choose.

InDesign-Accepted Graphic Types

InDesign is a professional page layout application that can accept images and graphics in several file formats. Before delving into the details of each format, however, it is important to have a basic understanding of the two types of graphic files: **raster** and **vector**. Very briefly, a **raster** image is composed of pixels, which are dots (or squares) of color that unify to create an image. Much like an impressionist painting, a raster image viewed up close looks like a mass of individual dots (or squares). Generally, photographs and scanned graphics are raster images. A **vector** image, on the other hand, contains no pixels but uses points and curves that are "drawn" based on complex mathematical equations. As a result, if you zoom into a vector image at a very high percentage, you will see perfectly smooth lines instead of the relatively jagged edges of the pixels in a raster image. Vector images can be created in programs like Adobe Illustrator and Macromedia Freehand and are most often used for logos and illustrations.

Keep these two basic graphic file types in mind as you acquaint yourself with the six file formats you can expect to use while working with graphics in InDesign CS2:

1. **TIFF (Tagged Information File Format; .tif):** TIFF is a raster file format, one of the more common ones for printing. TIFF is referred to as a **cross-application** file format because it can be understood by (imported into) many different types of programs, including Microsoft Word, InDesign, and Photoshop. TIFFs can be generated from digital photos, scanned images, and much more. The general standard for printed resolution of a TIFF file is 300 pixels per inch (ppi).

2. **EPS (Encapsulated PostScript; .eps):** EPS is another common cross-application file format for printing. Unlike TIFFs, however, EPS files are typically vector images, such as logos or illustrations drawn in Illustrator or Freehand.

3. **JPG or JPEG (Joint Photographic Experts Group; .jpg):** JPEG is a raster file format that is primarily intended for the Web and onscreen use (presentations, etc.). Most JPEG files are automatically compressed by removing information (usually color information), which facilitates faster loading times on Web pages. JPEGs can be compressed to varying degrees depending on how the JPEG files are saved in a program like Photoshop. Compressed JPEGs are typically not of sufficient quality for use in print work. When a JPEG has not been overcompressed (the image will look visually better than a JPEG that has been compressed too much), the JPEG can be saved as a TIFF in a program like Photoshop and used for printing, provided it looks good (which probably means it has not been compressed for the Web) and has the proper resolution for printing (300 ppi).

4. **PDF (Portable Document Format; .pdf):** PDFs have been with us for a while now and have the unique advantage of being viewable by anyone with the free Adobe Reader application. A PDF can be placed on a page in InDesign, much like a TIFF, EPS, or JPEG. The primary reason for placing a PDF graphic in InDesign is that when the PDF is created, it keeps the fonts, graphics, and text the same as it was intended initially. For example, if you are creating a monthly magazine that shows the previous month's cover, placing that cover graphic as a PDF would be preferable because the graphic file would appear to be the same as in the application it was originally created.

5. **AI (Adobe Illustrator; .ai):** In addition to the cross-application file formats described above, InDesign can accept some native file formats, including Adobe Illustrator files. Generally speaking, native file formats are intended for use only in the original, or native, application. But InDesign's ability to place several native file formats increases efficiency in some workflows because it omits the need to first save a native file format as a cross-application format like TIFF or EPS.

6. **PSD (Photoshop Document Format; .psd):** PSD is another native file format InDesign accepts. This can be a great time-saver if your print bureau or service provider accepts Photoshop files (check with them first). Placing Photoshop files gives you the added bonus of turning Photoshop layers on and off from within InDesign.

InDesign also accepts other file formats such as PICT, WMF, GIF, and many more. The files listed here are the more widely used file formats. As you proceed through the chapter, you will learn how to place several different file formats.

The Place Dialog Box

Bringing images into InDesign documents is referred to as placing images. The first step to placing a graphic is choosing **File > Place**, which prompts InDesign to bring up the **Place** dialog box.

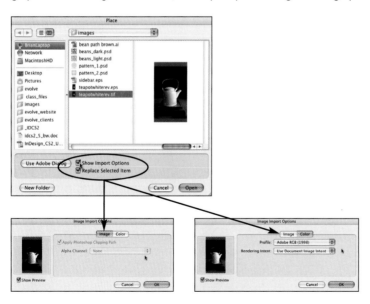

The **Place** dialog box allows you to locate graphics to place into an InDesign document. There are two check boxes in the **Place** dialog box that require some special attention: **Show Import Options** and **Replace Selected Items. Replace Selected Items**, which is checked by default, replaces any selected item on the page with the graphic being placed. When this option is deselected, the new graphic is placed on the page separately from the selected object.

When **Show Import Options** is checked and you click the **Open** button, the **Image Import Options** dialog box appears. This dialog box allows you to tell InDesign how to handle the graphic being placed. The **Image Import Options** dialog box is contextual, meaning that some of the options change depending on the file format of the graphic being placed (TIFF, EPS, PSD, etc.). For example, when you are placing a TIFF file, two tabs appear in the **Image Import Options** dialog box: **Image** and **Color**. When you select the **Image** tab, it shows you whether the TIFF you are placing has a clipping path or alpha channels applied to it. For more information on these options, see the movie called "**Working with Clipping Paths**" discussed at the end of this chapter. Using the **Color** tab, you can control the color management policies for the graphic you are placing. In other words, the **Color** tab helps to ensure that the colors in the graphic print as they appear onscreen. For more information on color management in InDesign, refer to Chapter 14, "*Output and Export.*"

While it is not necessary to use the **Image Import Options** dialog box to place a graphic, using the options can allow for greater control—particularly, flexibility when you're working with image formats like native Photoshop (PSD) files. Precisely how the import options are useful will become clearer as you move through this chapter.

Graphics and Frames

Every graphic placed in InDesign needs to be in a frame (some programs call them boxes). As with a text file in InDesign, you can place a graphic in one of two major ways: InDesign can place the graphic and automatically make a frame, or you can create a frame first and then place the graphic into it.

Regardless of how you place a graphic, however, every graphic in InDesign is always linked to its frame. As a result, anytime the frame of a graphic is repositioned in a document, the graphic inside always moves with it. In this sense, graphics in InDesign are similar to framed pictures hanging on a wall. If you grab the frame to move a picture to another wall, the picture inside automatically comes with it.

However, it is also possible to resize a frame without affecting the graphic inside and to move or resize a graphic *within* its frame. This is where it is important to understand the two basic tools used to move graphics in InDesign: the **Selection** tool and the **Direct Selection** tool.

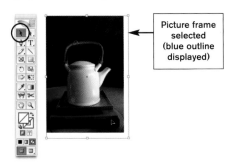

Picture frame selected (blue outline displayed)

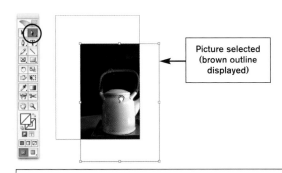

Picture selected (brown outline displayed)

The **Selection** tool, the black arrow, selects the graphic frame and moves it. The **Selection** tool is also used to resize frames.

The **Direct Selection** tool, the white arrow, selects the graphic inside the frame. You can also use the **Direct Selection** tool to reposition the graphic within the frame and resize the graphic.

Simply put, the **Selection** tool moves or resizes the frame of a graphic, and the **Direct Selection** tool moves or resizes the graphic inside the frame. One important distinction is how these tools function when *resizing* a frame or graphic versus *moving* a frame or graphic. Using the **Selection** tool, the frame of a graphic can be resized without affecting the graphic inside. However, when a frame is moved using the **Selection** tool, the graphic inside always moves with the frame. On the other hand, using the **Direct Selection** tool, the graphic inside the frame can be moved and resized without affecting the frame around it.

Linking Graphics vs. Embedding

Because printed graphics need to be high resolution, they tend to be large files. If graphics were viewed at full resolution, working with graphics in InDesign would be significantly slower than it is. To avoid this, when placing a graphic, InDesign always places a low-resolution copy of the graphic. This low-resolution copy is linked to the original graphic file and is often referred to as an **FPO (For Position Only)** graphic, or a **proxy** graphic. This is why some graphics placed in InDesign may not look great onscreen but will still print at a higher quality.

When an InDesign document is output, the program replaces the low-resolution FPO or proxy graphic with the full-resolution graphic. To make this replacement, the InDesign document needs to be linked to the original graphic file. The link between an InDesign document and an original graphic file allows the program to locate the original graphic and replace the FPO copy with the full-resolution original. For the most part, linking is an automatic process, although it does sometimes require updating. You will learn more about this in upcoming exercises.

Embedding a graphic is very different from linking. To embed a graphic, the option must be specifically selected from the **Links** palette menu. Embedding is great for archiving files for storage because it integrates graphic files into the InDesign file, so the graphic elements become part of the document. The downside of embedding graphics is that it increases the size of the InDesign file, making it more difficult, possibly even prohibitive, to send the InDesign file in an e-mail or by some other method. Another difference between linked and embedded graphics is that if you need to perform some editing on an embedded graphic that requires a program like Photoshop to perform, the graphic must first be unembedded, which transforms it into a linked graphic, and then edited in an external program like Photoshop, depending on the graphic file type.

In this chapter, you will learn how to link and embed pictures.

I. ————————Placing Graphics

In the first exercise, you will open a postcard for a coffee and tea company that has the text already on the page but is missing graphics. You will place two images on the page using two different methods.

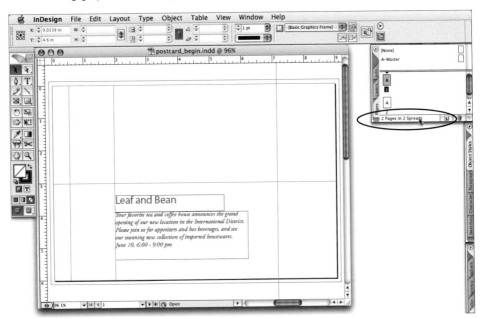

1. Open the file **postcard_begin.indd** from the **chap_08** folder on the **Desktop**. Reset the workspace so that the palettes on the screen are in default position by choosing **Window > Workspace > Default**. This clears the clutter from the workspace and makes it easier to see what you are doing.

*Note: The **Missing Fonts** dialog box may appear when you open this file. If it does, change the font by choosing **Find Font** and replacing the font with a version of Arial or Helvetica. To learn more about this, visit Exercise 1 of Chapter 5, "Typography in InDesign."*

*Notice the **Pages** palette on the right side of the workspace? It tells you that this document consists of two pages. The **Pages** palette, which you will learn about in Chapter 10, "Pages, Master Pages, and Layers," lets you view the pages as well as navigate through a document by going from page to page.*

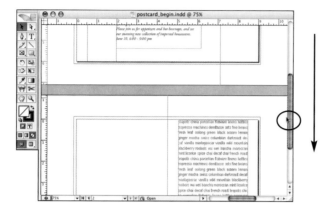

2. To reach the second page in the document, scroll down with the **scroll bar**.

Note: Because the pages are stacked vertically in the document window, you can scroll up and down from page to page using the vertical scroll bar.

*Tip: As you learned in previous chapters, another way to scroll down through the document is to either select the **Hand** tool and click and drag the page up or down to see new pages or hold down the **spacebar** as a shortcut to access the **Hand** tool.*

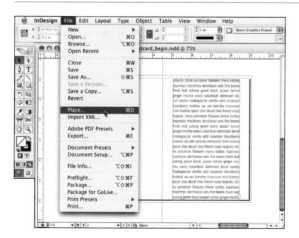

3. To make sure that the graphic you are going to place doesn't replace anything that is selected, choose **Edit > Deselect All**. Choose **File > Place** to place the first graphic on the page.

Note: Deselecting is important because if frames (even text frames) are selected InDesign, by default, replaces the contents with the new graphic being placed! When no frames are selected, InDesign prompts you to indicate where you want the graphic placed once InDesign has loaded the image. This is the technique you will practice in the next few steps.

4. With the **Place** dialog box open, navigate to the **chap_08** folder on the **Desktop** and open the **images** folder inside. Select the graphic **teapotwhiterev.tif** and click **Open**.

The Place dialog box previews the graphic on the Mac and Windows platforms, which is especially helpful if you are unsure of the name or location of the graphic file that needs to be placed.

Note: When placing images, InDesign automatically creates a link between the InDesign file and the original graphic. If a graphic that has been placed in an InDesign document is moved to a new folder or location in a computer network or individual hard drive, the link between the InDesign document and the original graphic is broken. When this happens, InDesign is unable to print the graphic correctly until the link between InDesign and the original graphic (in its new location) is reestablished. I recommend either copying the graphic files ahead of time into a central folder and saving the InDesign file in the same folder or getting in the habit of regularly checking the graphic links in the Links palette, which you will learn about later in this chapter.

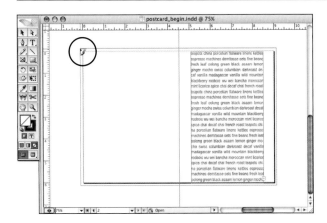

5. With the **Place** dialog box closed, the cursor displays a **Loaded Graphic** icon (   ). Move the **Loaded Graphic** cursor to the bleed guide (the red guide) in the upper-left corner of the page. Click to place the graphic on the page.

*With the **Loaded Graphic** cursor ready, you can place a graphic in one of three ways. When you click somewhere in the document, InDesign creates a frame that is the size of the graphic and places the graphic in it. When you click in a frame that already exists, the graphic is placed in the frame. The third way is to click and drag with the **Loaded Graphic** cursor to draw a frame the size you would like, and then InDesign automatically places the graphic into it. Throughout this chapter, you will learn about these three methods, when to choose one over the other, and why.*

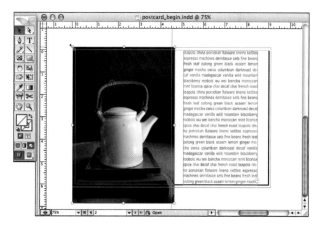

6. With the graphic on the page, InDesign automatically chooses the **Selection** tool. You can tell that the frame is selected because the frame handles appear and the blue outline is visible.

*Note: When you use the click-and-release method to place a graphic, InDesign puts the upper-left corner of the new graphic frame at the point where you clicked the **Loaded Graphic** cursor.*

7. The image you just placed is a little large for the postcard layout. Using the **Selection** tool, with the graphic frame still selected, click the bottom frame handle and drag it up until the bottom of the frame snaps to the red bleed guide. This crops the graphic.

Earlier in this chapter, you learned about how graphics and their frames interact. The Selection tool moves or resizes the frame. Resizing the frame isn't the same as resizing the graphic. You are affecting the image, though, by cropping part of the picture—essentially removing part of the image from view.

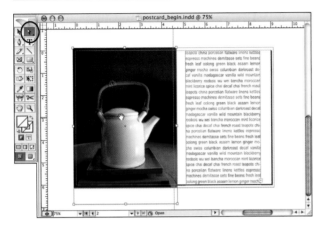

After you click the graphic with the **Direct Selection** tool, a brown frame appears. This is the outline of the graphic itself, not the frame.

The hand that appears as the cursor indicates that the graphic can be "grabbed" and moved within the frame.

8. After resizing the frame to crop the image, you are going to reposition the image in the frame so that it looks more centered in the frame. Choose the **Direct Selection** tool and click the picture. You notice that the cursor turns into a hand when hovering over the graphic. The outline also changes from blue to brown, indicating that you've selected the object inside the frame, rather than the frame itself.

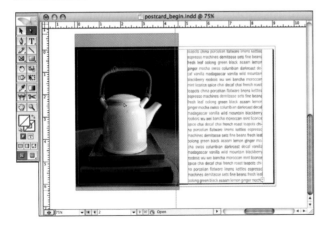

9. To reposition the graphic within the frame, click, hesitate for a second or two, and then begin to move the graphic. Position the image so that it still fills the width of the frame but the teapot is higher on the page.

Note: Hesitating before moving the graphic allows InDesign to show what is being cropped or hidden by the frame as you move the graphic. Not hesitating prevents this "live preview" feature from being available.

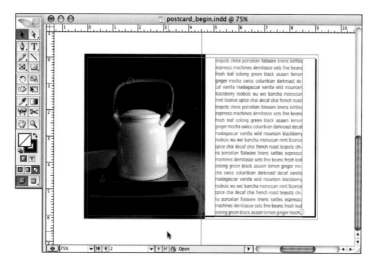

10. Choose the **Selection** tool from the **Toolbox,** and click somewhere off the edge of the page to see the finished product.

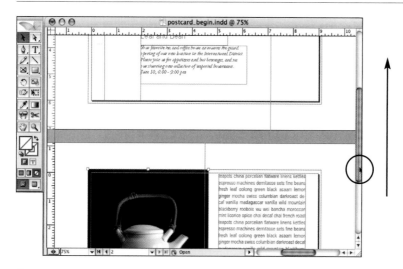

11. Using the **scroll bar** or the **Hand** tool, scroll up to the first page to place another graphic using a different method.

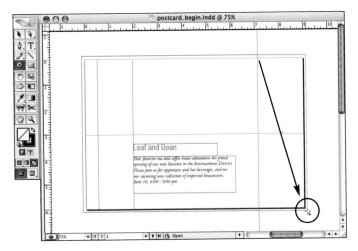

12. On the first page, choose the **Rectangle Frame** tool. On the right side of the page, starting from where the top bleed guide meets the vertical guide located at around **7 in**, drag the cursor down and to the right to draw a frame that covers the area shown in the illustration. Stop at the bleed guides at the lower-right corner of the page. After drawing the frame, choose **File > Place** with the frame still selected.

Note: The graphic on the first page is going to print to the edge of the postcard. Using a bleed allows for the typical margin of error if a printer is going to cut the postcard out of a larger press sheet or your desktop printer can print to the edge of the page. As a result, it is important to make sure that the frame snaps to the lower-right corner of the bleed guides.

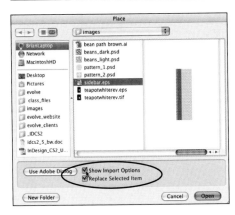

13. With the **Place** dialog box open, from the **chap_08** folder on the **Desktop**, choose the graphic **sidebar.eps** from the **images** folder. Check the box to the left of **Show Import Options** and click the **Open** button.

For this graphic, you will learn how import options can help you when placing a graphic.

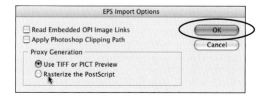

14. Because you selected **Show Import Options** in the **Place** dialog box, the **EPS Import Options** dialog box opens. This dialog box is contextual, so different import options will show depending on the file type being placed. Click **OK** to place the graphic.

*When you're placing an EPS file, the **EPS Import Options** dialog box displays the **Rasterize the PostScript** option. This is useful when placing an EPS file that appears as a big gray box when placed in InDesign. The gray box indicates that when that particular EPS graphic was originally saved, it was saved without a preview (also called a proxy, or FPO). If the gray box appears, try placing the EPS again, but this time choose **Rasterize the PostScript** from the **EPS Import Options** dialog box. This allows InDesign to preview the graphic onscreen (the preview in InDesign will be a raster image, but the original graphic will retain its original properties).*

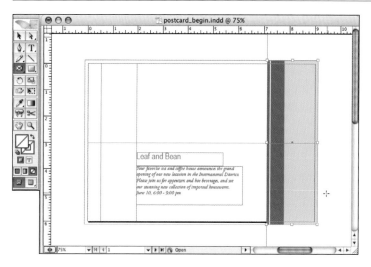

15. On the page, the graphic should appear in the frame you drew with the **Rectangle Frame** tool.

Drawing frames before placing graphics allows you to design the layout before the graphics are available. This is also helpful for setting up a document that will be used repeatedly, like a weekly newsletter. Draw the frames for the graphics and text, and then place all the content at a later date.

16. Save the file and keep it open for the next exercise.

The Adobe Bridge

A very useful feature in InDesign CS2 that comes with the Creative Suite 2 or when you purchase InDesign CS2 alone is the Adobe Bridge. This stand-alone application is used for viewing and organizing your files.

The Adobe Bridge can be accessed from the **Control** palette within InDesign. The **Go to Bridge** button at the right end of the **Control** palette launches the Bridge application.

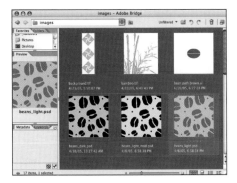

Once launched, the Adobe Bridge allows you to view any folder you can access. You can drag and drop graphics directly from the Bridge into a document or into an existing frame in a document.

 MOVIE | Placing Graphics from the Adobe Bridge

To learn about placing graphics from the Adobe Bridge, check out **bridge.mov** in the **movies** folder on the **InDesign CS2 HOT CD-ROM**.

Resized Graphics and Resolution

At the beginning of this chapter, you learned the basic differences between raster and vector images. Raster images are composed of dots or squares called pixels. The quality and usability of raster images depends largely on the number of **pixels per inch (ppi)**, or dots per inch (dpi), two terms that describe the resolution of the file. For the rest of the chapter, ppi will be used to describe the resolution of a graphic.

Use caution when resizing raster graphics like TIFFs in InDesign CS2. When you increase the size of a raster graphic beyond its original size, the pixels are stretched, and the resolution decreases because the number of inches increases while the number of pixels remains the same. If you make the graphic significantly larger than its original size, the pixels become stretched enough that the graphic appears blurry. On the other hand, when a raster graphic is made smaller than its original size, the resolution increases. While printers' standards can vary widely, general industry standards for print-worthy graphics suggest that a rasterized graphic original that starts as a 300 ppi file can be enlarged to 150 percent of its original size and downsized to 25 percent of its original size.

Because vector files are essentially math based, they are referred to as resolution independent. This means that they have no resolution associated with them. As a result, vector files can be resized (up or down) indefinitely without affecting print quality.

The Info Palette and Graphics

One of the best-kept secrets of InDesign is the **Info** palette. Its main function is to show information like width, height, location, and more for any selected object in a document.

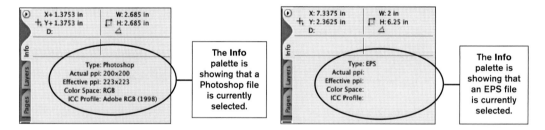

This chart explains some of the options that will appear in the **Info** palette.

Info Palette Options	
Option	**Meaning**
Actual ppi	The original resolution of the graphic when it was placed in InDesign.
Effective ppi	The resolution after the graphic is resized in InDesign. This is the resolution at which InDesign will print the graphic.
Color Space	Also called color mode. This refers to the colors used to create the graphic. Choices are CMYK and RGB.
ICC Profile	A color management term that you can learn more about in Chapter 14, "*Output.*"

Scale Tool Options

When you're scaling, or resizing, graphics, the **Scale** tool is very helpful. The **Scale** tool scales the frame and the graphic simultaneously.

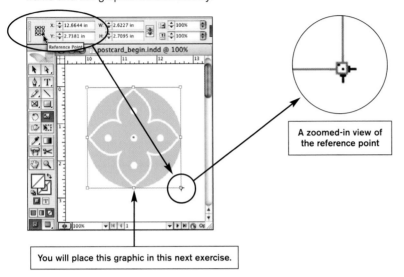

A zoomed-in view of the reference point

You will place this graphic in this next exercise.

With a graphic selected and the **Scale** tool chosen, crosshairs appear in the graphic. The crosshairs shows the **point of origin**, or the point from which the image will scale. By default, graphics scaled with the **Scale** tool are scaled with the point of origin at the center.

On the far-left side of the **Control** palette, a collection of dots appears in the shape of a box. The blackened dot shows the point of origin of the selected graphic frame.

To keep the lower-right corner in place and scale out to the upper left, in the **Control** palette you select the lower-right reference point as the point of origin. The crosshairs on the graphic frame moves to the lower-right corner.

You can also use the crosshairs to select the point of origin by clicking directly on the graphic with the **Scale** tool. If you choose as the point of origin a point other than those in the **Control** palette, none of the boxes in the **Control** palette will be black.

While it may seem easy to click the graphic with the **Scale** tool to choose a point of origin, I recommend using the **Control** palette whenever possible. The more limited options of the **Control** palette can prevent a host of scaling nightmares!

The Control Palette and Graphics

When a graphic is selected, the **Control** palette once again becomes contextual, changing its options to match the attributes of a graphic. This includes attributes like width, height, size, and rotation, among others.

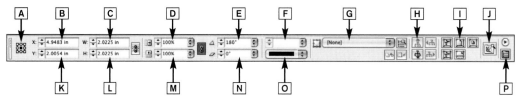

The **Control** palette contains many features for controlling graphics. This chart briefly explains each.

	Feature	Function
	Control Palette Controls	
	Feature	**Function**
A	Point of origin	Indicates the point around which the graphic is being rotated, resized, flipped, and so on.
B	X Position	Where on the page the frame or graphic is located on the x-axis (horizontal).
C	Width	Width of the frame or graphic, depending on which is selected.
D	Scale X Percentage	Percentage of the frame or graphic on the x-axis (horizontal), depending on which is selected.
E	Rotation Angle	Degree of rotation of a frame or graphic, depending on which is selected.
F	Stroke Size	Stroke size of the frame, in points.
G	Object Style	Object style applied, if any. Also, allows you to apply an object style.
H	Select Options	If a graphic or frame is selected, these buttons select either the content or the container (frame) as well as objects within groups.
I	Fit Options	Fit frames and their contents to each other.
J	Adobe Bridge	Launches the Adobe Bridge (see the section titled "The Adobe Bridge" earlier in the chapter for more).
K	Y Position	Location of the frame or graphic on the y-axis (vertical).
L	Height	Height of the frame or graphic, depending on which is selected.

continues on next page

	Feature	Function
	Control Palette Controls *continued*	
M	Scale Y Percentage	Percentage of the frame or graphic on the y-axis, depending on which is selected.
N	Shear X Angle	Allows the graphic to be skewed.
O	Stroke Style	Offers options for the style of the stroke of the frame.
P	Toggle the Stroke and Object Styles palettes	Opens the Stroke palette and the Object Styles palette.

Fitting Options

Working with graphics and frames can be challenging at times, especially when you place a graphic into an existing frame and the existing frame is either too big or too small. The fitting options are found under **Object > Fitting** or, when a frame containing a graphic is selected, at the right end of the **Control** palette in the form of five buttons. In the next exercise, you will learn how to use the **Control** palette buttons to access fitting options.

Fitting Options Explained

The original graphic with oversized frame.

Fit Frame to Content fits the frame to the graphic.

Center Content centers the graphic in the frame.

Fit Content to Frame fits the content of the frame (the graphic) without concern for proportions.

Fit Content Proportionally fits the content of the frame (the graphic) so that it fits the frame either vertically or horizontally while maintaining the graphic's proportions.

Fill Frame Proportionally, new in InDesign CS2, fills the frame with the content (the graphic) while maintaining the proportions of the graphic.

2. —————————————**Cropping and Scaling Graphics**

In this exercise, you will place two more images in the document and then change the sizes of the images by cropping or scaling them to match the design.

1. With **postcard_begin.indd** still open from the previous exercise, and while still on the first page of the document, choose **Edit > Deselect All**, or press **Ctrl+Shift+A** (Windows) or **Cmd+Shift+A** (Mac). Choose **File > Place** to place another graphic. In the **Place** dialog box, choose **pattern_1.psd** from the **images** folder of the **chap_08** folder on the **Desktop**. Make sure that the **Show Import Options** check box is selected, and then click **Open**.

Note: The image you are placing is a raster image created in Photoshop.

*With time, it will become clearer when it is important to select **Show Import Options**. I usually choose this option when placing a native file format such as an Illustrator or Photoshop file.*

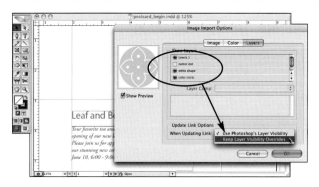

2. The **Image Import Options** dialog box appears. Because **pattern_1.psd** is a native Photoshop file with separate objects on separate layers, this dialog box allows you to turn those layers on and off depending on what you want to print. Click the **Eye** icon to the left of the **center dot** layer name. From the **Update Link Options** pop-up menu, choose **Keep Layer Visibility Overrides**. Click **OK** to activate the **Loaded Graphic** cursor and close the dialog box.

Working with layer options in a Photoshop or PDF file is a new and welcome addition in InDesign CS2. It is no longer necessary to perform this function only in Photoshop, which can save time when a graphic you are placing needs to be adjusted.

Note: *Choosing* **Use Photoshop's Layer Visibility** *from the* **Update Link Options** *pop-up menu ensures that if the file is changed in Photoshop, and InDesign updates the file placed in the document (remember, the graphic in InDesign is linked to the original), any changes to the layers made in the native program (Photoshop) will override any changes made in InDesign. To give top priority to the layer options chosen in InDesign, regardless of any actions taken in Photoshop, choose* **Keep Layer Visibility Overrides.**

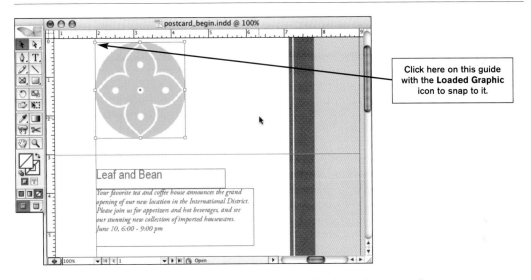

Click here on this guide with the **Loaded Graphic** icon to snap to it.

3. With the **Loaded Graphic** cursor, click to place the graphic above the text on the page.

As explained earlier, InDesign places the upper-left corner of the graphic at the point where you click with the **Loaded Graphic** *cursor.*

Tip: *To edit the layers in the graphic after it is placed, select the graphic and choose* **Object > Object Layer Options.**

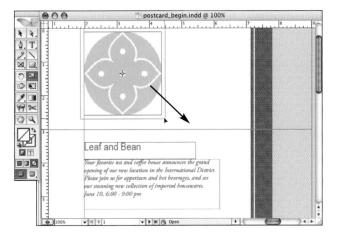

4. The graphic is a little too small. To resize it, choose the **Scale** tool from the **Toolbox**. From any corner on the graphic frame, hold the **Shift** key down and drag away (just a bit) from the center. Holding the **Shift** key down constrains the image so that it keeps its proportions.

*The **Scale** tool resizes the frame and the graphic. This is good, because the frame can't be smaller than the graphic without cropping the graphic.*

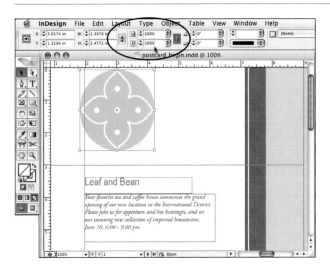

5. Once the graphic is scaled, choose the **Selection** tool from the **Toolbox**, and click the graphic to select its frame. Looking at the **Control** palette, you see two percentages of **100** each. These percentages represent the width and height of the frame, not the graphic. To see the size of the graphic, you need to select the graphic rather than the frame. You will do this in the next step.

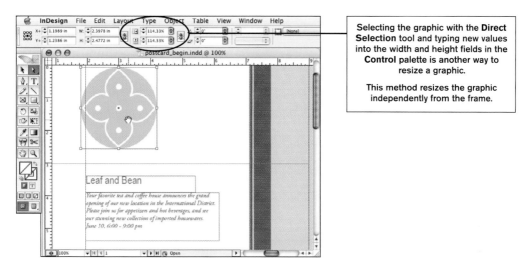

Selecting the graphic with the **Direct Selection** tool and typing new values into the width and height fields in the **Control** palette is another way to resize a graphic.

This method resizes the graphic independently from the frame.

6. Choose the **Direct Selection** tool from the **Toolbox**. Click the graphic on the page. Looking at the **Control** palette, you see the percentages have changed. The sizes are for width and height, respectively. In this example, the graphic is **114.33%**, but yours may be different.

*Selecting the image with the **Direct Selection** tool selects the graphic and not the frame. Always keep an eye on the color of the graphic frame. The blue outline indicates that the frame is selected, and a brown outline indicates that the graphic is selected.*

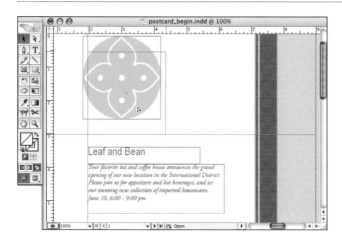

7. With the **Selection** tool, move the graphic so that it snaps into where the horizontal and vertical guides meet. Choose **Edit > Deselect All** to deselect all objects on the page. You are about to place another graphic.

8. Choose **File > Place**, and pick the graphic called **beans_light.psd** from the images folder in the **chap_08** folder on the **Desktop**. Although this is a native Photoshop (PSD) file, it contains no layers, so you can deselect the **Show Import Options** check box. Click **Open** to activate the **Loaded Graphic** icon and close the dialog box.

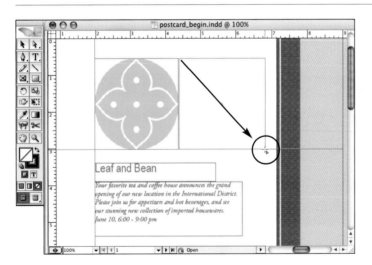

When you place a graphic as you do in these steps, InDesign places the graphic in the upper-left corner of the frame. If the frame is too small, the graphic won't be centered.

9. With the **Loaded Graphic** cursor, hold the **Shift** key down, and then click and drag a frame onto the page just to the right of the graphic you placed in the previous steps. Let the **Loaded Graphic** cursor snap to the horizontal guide.

*Placing a graphic this way allows you to predetermine the size of the frame regardless of the size of the graphic itself. Holding the **Shift** key down creates a perfectly proportioned square frame.*

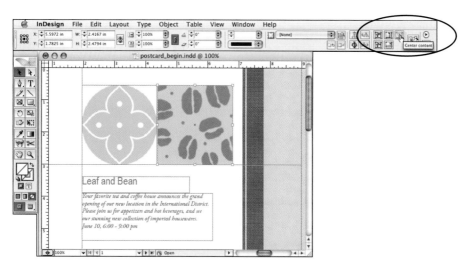

10. Make sure the **Selection** tool and the graphic frame are selected. Five buttons appears at the far-right end of the **Control** palette. Click the **Center Content** button to center the graphic in the frame.

*Tip: Each of the five buttons either fits the frame to the content (graphic) or fits the graphic to the frame (in three ways—proportionally, fill proportionally, and fit to frame). For a more detailed explanation of these options, take a look at the previous section titled "**Fitting Options.**" These buttons are very useful when the frame and graphic don't match in width or height. You can also access the options by choosing **Object > Fitting > (choose an option)** or by **right-clicking** (Windows) or **Ctrl+clicking** (Mac) directly on the graphic and choosing **Fitting** from the contextual menu!*

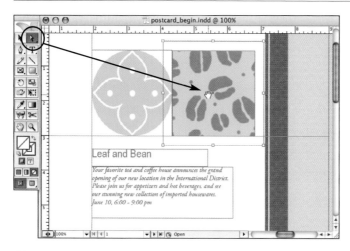

11. With the **Direct Selection** tool, click the graphic to select the graphic itself, not the frame. In the next step, you will resize the image within the frame.

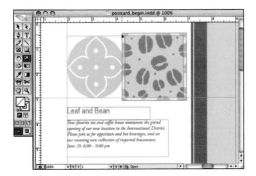

12. With the graphic selected (note the brown outline), choose the **Scale** tool from the **Toolbox**. Select a corner of the brown graphic outline, hold the **Shift** key down, and drag in toward the center to make the graphic a little smaller.

Unlike earlier in this exercise, you are now resizing the graphic, not the frame. Once again, it all depends on what you have selected before scaling the graphic. You get used to this eventually!

Note: *When making a very small adjustment with the **Scale** tool, the graphic can "jump." This may be difficult to visualize, but you'll know it when you see it. Scaling can be easier if you keep the cursor at the corner point of the image or frame as you resize it (depending on what you are scaling). Zooming in can also be helpful when you are making small-scale adjustments.*

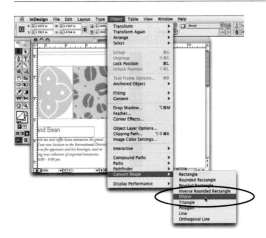

13. The first graphic placed on the page is a circle, so now you are going to change the frame for that graphic into a circle (called an ellipse in InDesign). With the **Selection** tool, click the frame of the new graphic. Choose **Object > Convert Shape > Ellipse**.

Convert Shape *is a great feature for changing any frame selected into another shape. This is a brand-new feature in InDesign CS2 that you will explore a bit more in the next chapter.*

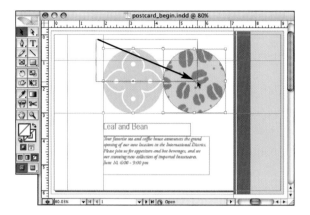

14. As the graphics stand right now, they are too large for the design, so they need to be scaled smaller. Drag a horizontal guide from the horizontal ruler down until it is positioned at **1 inch** from the top of the page. Select both the graphics with the **Selection** tool by dragging from the upper left across the two graphics.

*Note: When dragging with the **Selection** tool, keep in mind that any graphic that is touched will be selected. In most cases, it is best not to surround the entire graphic—it is too easy to select more than you need.*

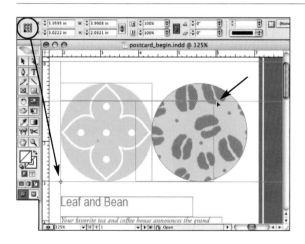

Watch the **point of origin** when scaling images. In this example, scaling should originate in the upper-right corner so the graphics won't need to be moved after they are scaled.

Selecting several graphics at once works just like selecting a single graphic. InDesign basically treats these two graphics as one for the purpose of scaling.

15. With the two graphics selected, choose the **Scale** tool. In the **Control** palette, choose the lower-left reference point. This keeps the lower-left corners of the graphics in place when they are being scaled. With the **Scale** tool, hold the **Shift** key down to maintain the original proportions of the graphics when they are scaled. Click and drag from the upper-right corner of the graphic on the right. The cursor should snap to the guide when it comes close enough.

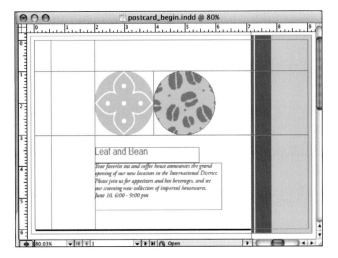

16. Choose **Edit > Deselect All** to deselect all objects. Save this file, and keep it open for the next exercise.

TIP | Another Way to Resize

A fast method for resizing is to use the **Selection** tool. On its own, the **Selection** tool only resizes the frame, but when you hold down **Ctrl+Shift** (Windows) or **Cmd+Shift** (Mac) and then click and drag, the graphic and the frame are resized simultaneously. Holding down the **Ctrl** or **Cmd** key resizes the frame and graphic. The **Shift** key maintains the proportions.

TIP | Display Performance

As you have learned, by default InDesign links to the original graphic file placed in InDesign and displays a low-resolution proxy, or FPO, on the page for viewing. While this lets you move around the page very quickly, placed graphics may look "pixelated," or grainy. Fortunately, InDesign also allows you to view graphics at higher resolution.

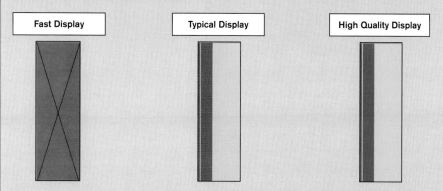

Select a graphic on the page and choose **Object > Display Performance > High Quality Display** to view the file at full resolution (how it should look when printed). This only changes the display performance for the selected image.

There are three settings for viewing graphics onscreen: **Fast Display**, **Typical Display**, and **High Quality Display**. Here's how each setting works.

Display Performance	Action
Fast Display	Graphics are dimmed so that you can move around faster and concentrate on the text or the general placement of objects.
Typical Display	This is the default view setting. All images are 72 ppi low-resolution previews.
High Quality Display	Graphics are shown at full resolution on the screen. Vector artwork (drawings) are especially improved by this view.

Another way to change the view settings is at the document level. This means that you can change all the graphics in the entire document at once. Choose **View > Display Performance > (choose the type of performance you desire)**.

Warning: The more graphics on the page, the slower InDesign will be. To maximize efficiency, I recommend using **High Quality Display** for quick previews only, then going back to **Typical Display** when you are done with the preview.

Rotating and Flipping Graphics

In the next exercise, you will place another graphic, completing the one side of the postcard for the coffee and tea company. The graphic you place will also need to be rotated.

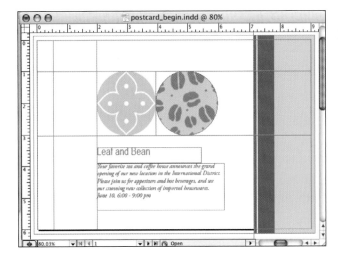

1. With the **postcard_begin.indd** file open from the previous exercise, choose **File > Place** to place a final graphic on this side of the postcard.

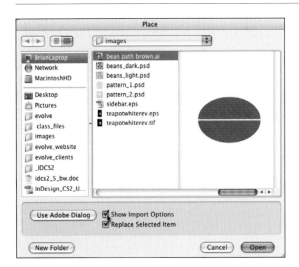

2. In the **Place** dialog box, choose **bean path brown.ai** from the images folder in the **chap_08** folder on the **Desktop**. Select the **Show Import Options** check box to open the import options for the Illustrator file you are about to place. Click **Open**.

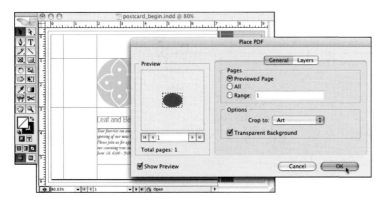

3. In the **Place PDF** dialog box that comes up, select the **Transparent Background** check box. Also, from the **Crop to** pop-up menu, select **Art**.

*Illustrator files are treated just like PDF files when they are placed. You chose **Transparent Background** for this graphic to remove any white background color. Choosing **Art** as the **Crop to** option places just the graphic and none of the area around it. Most people create an Illustrator logo on a letter-size document. When you choose **Art**, InDesign can place just the artwork, not the whole page with the graphic in the middle of it.*

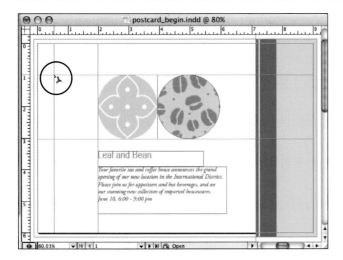

4. With the **Loaded Graphic** cursor, click to place the image at the meeting point of the first vertical guide on the left side of the page and the top horizontal guide.

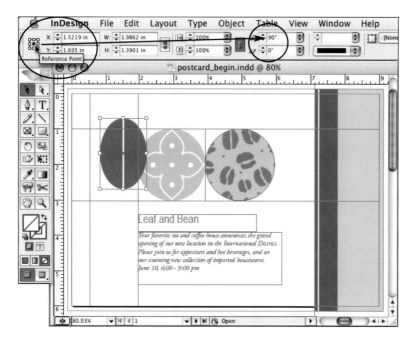

5. Now you are going to rotate the graphic you just placed. With the graphic selected, in the **Control** palette choose the center point as the point of origin so the graphic rotates around the center. In the **Rotation Angle** field, select **90** from the pop-up menu to the right of the field.

Note: The point of origin is very important when rotating or scaling graphics. Always pay attention to it, because once you've changed it for one frame or graphic, it sticks for that document regardless of which graphic or frame you choose next.

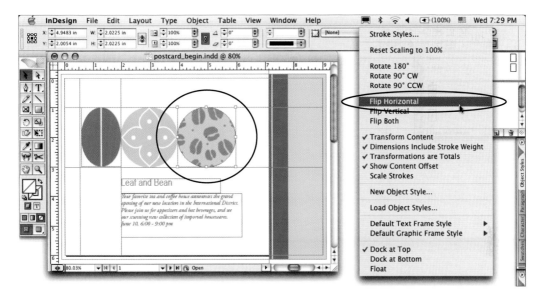

6. With the **Selection** tool, click the third graphic. You are going to flip the graphic horizontally. With the graphic selected, choose **Flip Horizontal** from the **Control** palette menu.

*Note: This flips the frame and the graphic together. If you select the graphic with the **Direct Selection** tool first, only the graphic inside the frame flips.*

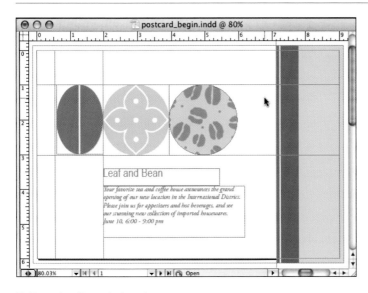

7. Save the file and close it.

The Links Palette

When you're working with linked graphics (which you should be doing most of the time), the **Links** palette becomes especially important when outputting the file. The **Links** palette, which can be found by choosing **Window > Links**, lists all the graphics placed in a document.

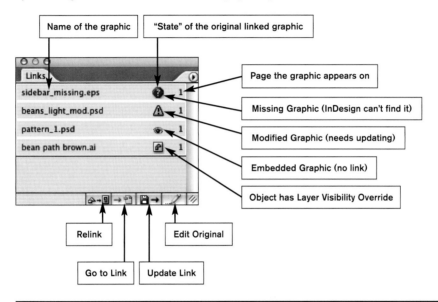

Links Palette		
Option	**Function**	
Relink	Selects an existing graphic and replaces it with another, or if the link to an original graphic is broken, the **Missing Graphic** (icon) icon appears, and a dialog box to find it opens.	
Go to Link	Takes you to the page where the graphic selected in the **Links** palette is located and selects the graphic on the page with the **Direct Selection** tool.	
Update Link	The **Modified** icon (icon) indicates that the original graphic has been changed. This forces InDesign to "look" at the linked image and bring in an updated low-resolution preview (also called a proxy image).	
Edit Original	Selects a graphic and launches the native application so you can edit the graphic and update its link in InDesign automatically. This is sometimes referred to as "round-tripping."	

4. _____Editing and Relinking Using the Links Palette

Keeping track of the location and state of all of the original graphics files placed in an InDesign document would be very difficult without the **Links** palette. In this exercise, you will learn how to use this palette to edit and relink graphic originals to an InDesign document.

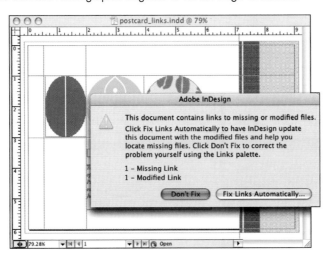

1. Open **postcard_links.indd** from the **chap_08** folder on the **Desktop**. Because there are missing or modified links in the document, InDesign immediately warns you that the links need some attention with the missing or modified links dialog box (labeled **Adobe InDesign**). In most cases, it is best to click **Fix Links Automatically** to help clear up any problems, but for this exercise, choose **Don't Fix** so you can learn how to use the **Links** palette.

*Note: The **Missing Fonts** dialog box may appear when you open this file. If it does, change the font by choosing **Find Font** and replacing the font with a version of Arial or Helvetica. To learn more about this, visit Exercise 1 of Chapter 5, "Typography in InDesign."*

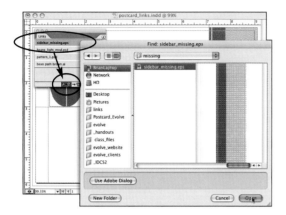

In the **Find** dialog box, choose the graphic **sidebar_missing.eps** from the **missing** folder to relink the file.

2. Open the **Links** palette by choosing **Window > Links**. In the **Links** palette, you should notice a series of graphic names. All these graphic files have been placed in this document. Icons like the stop sign will also appear, indicating that a graphic is missing. Click the graphic called **sidebar_missing.eps** in the **Links** palette to select it. To fix the link, click the **Relink** button at the bottom of the **Links** palette. In the **chap_08** folder on the **Desktop**, go into the **missing** folder and find the graphic **sidebar_missing.eps**. Click **Open** to relink the image and close the **Find** dialog box.

*InDesign is pretty smart about finding missing graphics. To fool it, I had to use two folders nested inside each other. If you open this file and you don't see a **Missing Link** icon, you can try moving the image **sidebar_missing.eps**.*

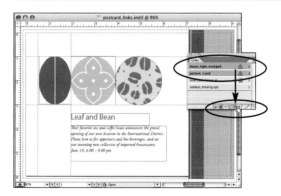

3. To fix the modified link, choose **beans_light_mod.psd** and **pattern_1.psd** by Shift-clicking on the the two names in the **Links** palette. Click the **Update Link** button at the bottom of the **Links** palette to update the links.

Links need to be updated because after the graphic was placed in InDesign, it was edited outside InDesign in a graphics application such as Adobe Photoshop. InDesign continuously checks the modification dates of both placed and original graphics. Relinking instructs InDesign to bring in an updated proxy or FPO graphic.

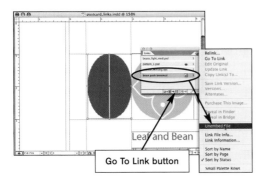

4. The last icon to deal with is the **Embed** icon (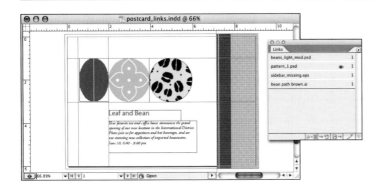). As you learned earlier in this chapter, graphics can be embedded and unembedded in InDesign. Choose **bean path brown.ai** from the **Links** palette, and then click the **Go to Link** button to highlight the embedded graphic. To unembed this graphic, choose **Unembed File** from the **Links** palette menu.

Tip: You can embed graphics by choosing one or more from the **Links** palette and choosing **Embed File** from the **Links** palette menu.

5. A dialog box appears. Click **Yes** to unembed the graphic and create a link between the proxy display in InDesign and the original graphic file in the **images** folder in the **chap_08** folder on the **Desktop**.

*Clicking **Yes** to unembed a graphic works well when the original graphic is in the same location as it was when it was first placed in the document. In other cases, it will prompt you to find the graphic to link to. Clicking **No** is a good idea if the original graphic isn't available. Clicking **No** pulls the graphics that were previously embedded from the InDesign file and saves them in the folder or location that you designate.*

6. Save the file and close it.

The Text Wrap Palette

The **Text Wrap** palette wraps text or runs text around any object. The palette can be found by choosing **Window > Text Wrap**. This palette offers many different ways to wrap text around an object.

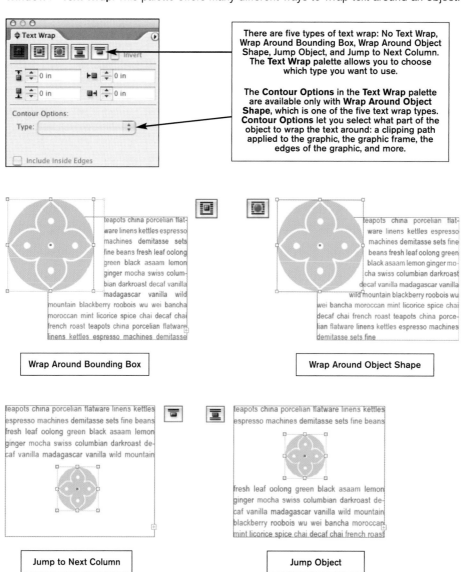

There are five types of text wrap: No Text Wrap, Wrap Around Bounding Box, Wrap Around Object Shape, Jump Object, and Jump to Next Column. The **Text Wrap** palette allows you to choose which type you want to use.

The **Contour Options** in the **Text Wrap** palette are available only with **Wrap Around Object Shape**, which is one of the five text wrap types. **Contour Options** let you select what part of the object to wrap the text around: a clipping path applied to the graphic, the graphic frame, the edges of the graphic, and more.

Wrap Around Bounding Box

Wrap Around Object Shape

Jump to Next Column

Jump Object

**5.**———————————**Text Wrap**

In this short exercise, you will apply text wrap to a graphic that is on top of text.

1. Open the file **postcard_textwrap.indd** from the **chap_08** folder on the **Desktop**. Also, open the **Text Wrap** palette by choosing **Window > Text Wrap**. Select the green graphic in the middle of the page with the **Selection** tool. In the **Text Wrap** palette, click the **Wrap Around Bounding Box** button.

*Note: The **Missing Fonts** dialog box may appear when you open this file. If it does, change the font by choosing **Find Font** and replacing the font with a version of Arial or Helvetica. To learn more about this, visit Exercise 1 of Chapter 5, "Typography in InDesign."*

*Note: The missing or modified links dialog box (labeled **Adobe InDesign**) may appear when you open this file. If it does, choose **Fix Links Automatically** to update any modified graphics automatically. After fixing the links, close the **Links** palette. If the **Find** dialog box opens, navigate to the **chap_08** folder on your **Desktop** and find the graphic in the **images** folder. For a more detailed explanation, look at Exercise 4, "Editing and Relinking Using the Links Palette," earlier in this chapter.*

*Choosing **Wrap Around Bounding Box** tells InDesign to wrap the text around the selected green graphic. Any text that comes within range of touching the graphic will be pushed away. This prevents text from interfering with the graphic.*

2. In the **Text Wrap** palette, in both the **Top Offset** and **Right Offset** fields, use the up arrows to increase the value to **0.1875 in**. The text pushes away from the top and right edges of the graphic by the designated amount.

Tip: When using up and down arrows in InDesign palettes or dialog boxes, holding down the Shift key increases or decreases the value faster.

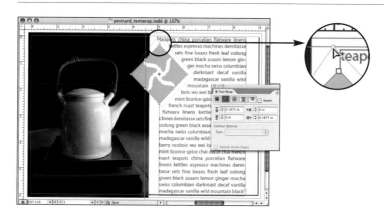

3. You notice that another frame now appears on the top and right side of the graphic frame. This is the text wrap. Regardless of what type of text wrap is applied, the text wrap can be edited. First, zoom in a bit with the **Zoom** tool. With the **Selection** tool, click the top corner point of the text wrap and drag it further toward the top of the page.

Tip: This is a great way to make text flow or wrap around an object in the shape you want. In the next chapter, you will learn about editing shapes using vector-drawing tools like the Pen tool. Any of these tools can be employed to edit the text wrap because every text wrap is actually a path. Also, if you go too far with the shaping and want to start over, turn off the text wrap with the No Text Wrap button and then turn it on again with the Wrap Around Bounding Box.

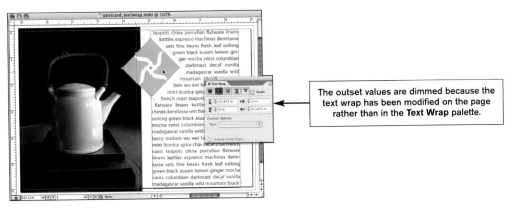

The outset values are dimmed because the text wrap has been modified on the page rather than in the **Text Wrap** palette.

4. Release the mouse. The text follows the line of the text wrap. This is a great way to add unique elements to the way text flows in a document.

5. The text wrap is complete. Save the file, and keep it open if you'd like to experiment with the tips that follow this exercise. Otherwise, close the file and you are done!

TIP | Ignore Text Wrap

Sometimes text wrap gets in the way—for instance, when a picture with text wrap applied to it also needs a caption or headline over it. If the caption or headline text frame touches the image, the text is gone—pushed out of the frame. **Ignore Text Wrap** stops that from happening. After selecting the text frame in question, choose **Object > Text Frame Options**. Select **Ignore Text Wrap** and click **OK**.

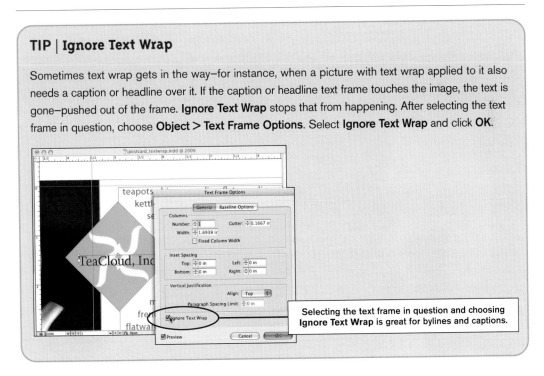

Selecting the text frame in question and choosing **Ignore Text Wrap** is great for bylines and captions.

TIP | Creating a Background Graphic

In Chapter 4, "*Working with Text*," you saw the background images that were already on the page. In this tip, you will learn how to create a background image. It involves placing a graphic, using transparency to make it semitransparent, sending it behind all other objects, and locking it in place.

With **postcard_textwrap.indd** open from the last exercise, choose **Edit > Deselect All** to deselect everything on the page. Place the graphic **background.tif** from the **images** folder in the **chap_08** folder on your **Desktop**. Open the **Transparency** palette by choosing **Window > Transparency**. Change the transparency to **40%** using the arrow to the right of the field or typing the value directly into the field.

Position the graphic by selecting it with the **Selection** tool, clicking, holding down the mouse button and hesitating for a second, and then moving the graphic into position (where you think it looks good). The hesitation, as discussed earlier in this chapter, is a way to preview the graphic as you move it.

Transparency will be discussed in greater detail in Chapter 12, "*Transparency*."

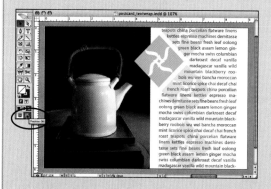

With the graphic still selected, choose **Object > Arrange > Send to Back**. Then choose **Object > Lock Position** to lock it into position behind all other objects. Turn on the preview mode by clicking the **Preview** button at the bottom of the **Toolbox**, and take a look at your fine work!

MOVIE | Using Anchored Objects

Adobe has added a great feature to InDesign CS2. **Anchored objects** are graphics or text frames placed in text. An example of this would be if you placed either a **Tool** icon () in the text (just like in this line of text) or a graphic in a paragraph, as in the example below.

Anchored objects, sometimes referred to as inline graphics, are graphics or text frames that are anchored to text. When the text moves, because you added text above or moved the text frame, the anchored object goes with it.

To learn about using anchored objects, check out **anchored_objects.mov** in the **movies** folder on the **InDesign CS2 HOT CD-ROM**.

MOVIE | Working with Clipping Paths

Clipping paths crop part of the graphic so that only a portion of the graphic shows through the shape you create. You can create clipping paths to hide unwanted parts of a graphic, such as backgrounds. InDesign lets you bring in clipping paths from other programs like Photoshop and allows you to create your own clipping path in InDesign.

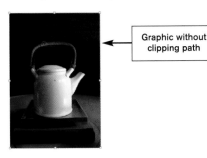

Graphic without clipping path

Graphic with clipping path

To learn about working with clipping paths, check out **clipping_path.mov** in the **movies** folder on the **InDesign CS2 HOT CD-ROM**.

Graphics are a great way to express creativity, and InDesign offers many ways to use them. In the next chapter, you will learn about the drawing and reshaping features in InDesign. Because both InDesign and Illustrator are created by Adobe, and because the Creative Suite is intended to help you work faster and better, InDesign borrows some of Illustrator's more widely used drawing tools.

9
Vector Artwork

| Creating Basic Shapes | Transforming and Converting Shapes |
| Using Pathfinder Operations | Using Stroke and Fill |
| Aligning and Distributing Objects |
| Converting Text to Vector Outlines |
| Creating Shapes with the Pen Tool | Editing Paths |

chap_09

InDesign CS2
HOT CD-ROM

InDesign is best known for its amazing type and graphic control. Few people are aware that it can also create vector artwork. In the last chapter on graphics, you learned the differences between raster and vector artwork. In this chapter, you will concentrate on vector artwork—how to create different types of shapes and control them.

You will be building a poster for an opera with text, vector shapes, and color using many new drawing tools in InDesign CS2. And don't worry, just because I mention drawing, don't think you have to be an artist. InDesign provides many ways to create objects by combining simple shapes or using transformations.

Why Use InDesign for Vector Artwork?

If you have purchased the entire Adobe Creative Suite 2, you probably understand that each of the programs in CS2, which includes at least Photoshop, InDesign, and Illustrator, has a specific purpose. This was discussed in the first two chapters of the book, but a quick recap won't hurt.

Illustrator CS2 is a phenomenal product that creates simple and complex vector artwork. Generically, it is referred to as a drawing program, and it's great for creating a logo, developing a poster–any (single-page) document that involves lots of drawing and shapes. Knowing that, you may be wondering why I am advocating that you learn to create vector artwork in InDesign, which is supposed to be a page layout program, not a drawing program.

In the last few versions, InDesign has "borrowed" some of the simpler functionality from Illustrator to make it possible to create uncomplicated shapes and drawings or make basic modifications to illustrations brought into InDesign from a program like Illustrator. InDesign's vector drawing tools are not intended to take the place of Illustrator's, which offer far more range and flexibility. Instead, the drawing tools in InDesign complement those in Illustrator and can save you time when you need simple vector shapes or quick modifications to existing vector artwork. In this chapter, you will learn how InDesign's drawing tools work and when to use them.

The Chapter Project

In this chapter, you will create a poster for an opera with shapes. After creating shapes, you will learn how to apply stroke and fill, align shapes, work with the **Pen** tool, and edit the shapes you created.

Shapes in InDesign

InDesign CS2 can create three basic shape types—rectangles, ellipses, and polygons. Each of these shape types appears in the "InDesign CS2 Shape and Frame Tools" chart that follows.

Each shape type has a shape tool associated with it. The shape tools—the **Rectangle** tool, **Ellipse** tool, and **Polygon** tool—can be found to the right of the frame tools in the **Toolbox**. Both the frame tools and the shape tools offer the same three shape types, which might be confusing at first, particularly since both the frame and shape tools create frames. Shape tools are usually used for creating vector artwork because they don't have any associations with text or graphics. You create shapes mainly to hold color and create vector artwork.

In earlier chapters, you used the **Rectangle Frame** tool (⊠). When you draw a frame with that tool, by default the frame has no stroke or fill, and an "**X**" appears in the middle of the frame. These frames are called **placeholder graphics frames**. When a frame is created with the **Rectangle** tool (▢) from the shape tools, by default the frame has a 1-pt black stroke, and no "**X**" appears in the middle of the frame.

Although the different names of the frame and shape tools may seem to imply different capabilities, in reality the frame and shape tools share a great deal of functionality and can often be used interchangeably, as you will learn in this chapter.

To see the different shape tools, click and hold down on either the **Rectangle Frame** tool or the **Rectangle** tool to see a tools menu pop out.

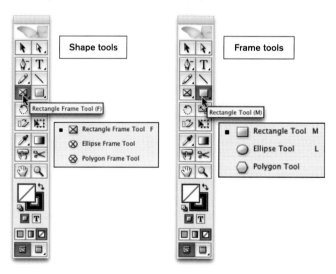

InDesign CS2 Shape and Frame Tools

Shape Tool	Function	Example
Rectangle Frame tool and Rectangle tool	Creates rectangle and square shapes	
Ellipse Frame tool and Ellipse tool	Creates circles and ellipses	
Polygon Frame tool and Polygon tool	Creates shapes that have three sides (triangle) or more (hexagons, stars, etc.)	

Ways to Create Shapes

Click and drag with a selected frame or shape tool	Click on the page with a selected frame or shape tool

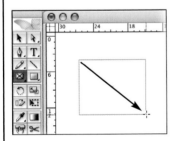

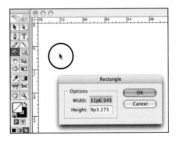

With a frame tool selected, click and drag on the page to size the frame.

To set specific frame characteristics, select a frame tool and click on the page where the frame (shape) is to go. A dialog box appears. The point where you click is the upper-left corner of the shape you create. All three frame tool types have different options for creating shapes, and those options are described in the following chart.

Clicking on the page with a frame tool is a great feature for placing specific sizes of shapes in precise locations. There are three different dialog boxes that are each described in the chart.

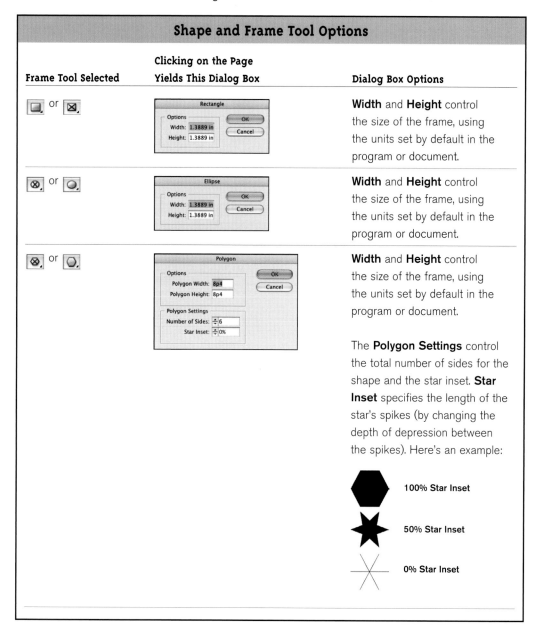

Shape and Frame Tool Options

Frame Tool Selected	Clicking on the Page Yields This Dialog Box	Dialog Box Options
(rectangle icons)	Rectangle dialog box — Options, Width: 1.3889 in, Height: 1.3889 in	**Width** and **Height** control the size of the frame, using the units set by default in the program or document.
(ellipse icons)	Ellipse dialog box — Options, Width: 1.3889 in, Height: 1.3889 in	**Width** and **Height** control the size of the frame, using the units set by default in the program or document.
(polygon icons)	Polygon dialog box — Options, Polygon Width: 8p4, Polygon Height: 8p4; Polygon Settings, Number of Sides: 6, Star Inset: 0%	**Width** and **Height** control the size of the frame, using the units set by default in the program or document. The **Polygon Settings** control the total number of sides for the shape and the star inset. **Star Inset** specifies the length of the star's spikes (by changing the depth of depression between the spikes). Here's an example: 100% Star Inset, 50% Star Inset, 0% Star Inset

Selecting Shapes

Selecting shapes may seem simple, and you will most likely use the **Selection** tool to do so. As you just learned, the frame tools can create the same shapes as the shape tools. A shape that you draw with any of the frame tools (both the shape and the tool have "**X**"s on them) you can easily select by clicking in the middle of the shape or frame. However, shapes created with the **Rectangle**, **Ellipse**, and **Polygon** tools (the shapes and icons without "**X**"s) can be more difficult to select. The following chart explains how to select the various shapes.

Selecting Shapes	
Shape Selection Method with the Selection Tool	**Description**
 Selecting a frame tool shape.	Frames created with a frame tool have no fill or stroke by default. They are also easily selected with the Selection tool by either clicking on the edge of or inside the frame. Watch the cursor! If a black box appears to the right of the arrow, clicking selects the object.
A shape tool shape cannot be selected by clicking inside without a fill color.	Selecting a shape created with any of the shape tools can be a different process, depending on whether or not the shape has a color fill. Shapes created with the shape tools have no fill color by default. You cannot select a shape that does not have color fill by using the Selection tool and clicking in the center of the shape. But you can easily select a shape that does have color fill using this method. Once again, watch the cursor. A black box indicates that the object will be selected if you click. If no black box appears to the right of the arrow, then the object will not be selected.
 Selecting a shape tool shape by clicking on the frame edge.	Clicking on the edge of a shape drawn with a shape tool selects that shape, whether or not it has a color fill.
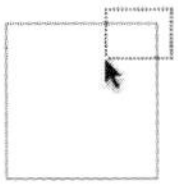 Selecting any shape by clicking and dragging across the object.	With the Selection tool, click and drag across the object to select it. This method works for all objects.

I. —————————**Creating Basic Shapes**

Now that you understand the different types of shapes, it is time to begin creating and working with them.

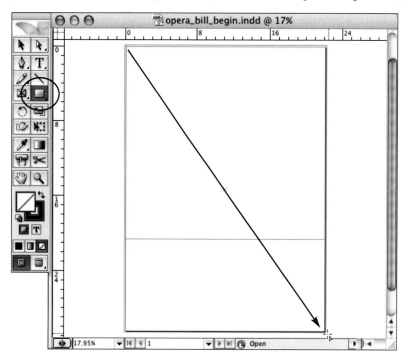

1. From the **chap_09** folder on the **Desktop**, open **opera_bill_begin.indd**. Select the **Rectangle** tool from the shape tools in the **Toolbox**. To start the poster, draw a rectangle the size of the page by starting in the upper-left corner and dragging down diagonally to the lower-right corner. Make sure the frame snaps into the red bleed guides, because the color-filled frame you are creating will cover the page from edge to edge.

Note: It is important to pay attention to the scale of a document. Just because it fits the screen and looks like a letter-size document doesn't mean it is. This document is roughly 22 × 30 inches, which is not immediately evident when you are drawing objects. This is also why, when the page is fit into the window, the bleed guides look like they are too small. I suggest keeping rulers showing (View > Show Rulers) if they're hidden.

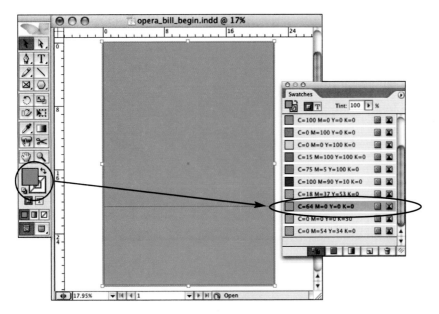

2. Choose the **Selection** tool from the **Toolbox**. With the shape still selected (if not, click its border to select it), open the **Swatches** palette. This document has a number of saved swatches you can choose from. Making sure that the **Fill Box** (from the **Toolbox**) is chosen, click on the light-blue color toward the bottom of the **Swatches** palette. Keep the **Swatches** palette off to the side because you will use it in the next few steps.

---

3. With the frame still selected, choose **Object > Lock Position** to lock it in place. This frame is the background for the poster, and locking it prevents you from accidentally moving it.

A lock icon (🔒) appears when you try to move a frame that is locked. Locking also prevents InDesign from deleting frames accidentally. You can edit the stroke, fill, and content of a locked frame, but you cannot change the frame's positioning and other attributes until you unlock the frame by choosing **Object > Unlock Position.**

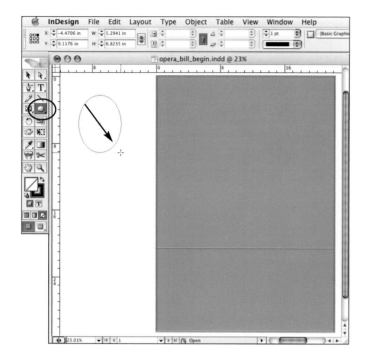

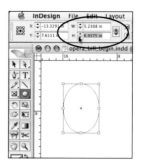

After drawing an ellipse with the **Ellipse** tool, you can change its width and height (displayed in the **Control** palette) while it is still selected.

4. Click and hold down on the **Rectangle** tool to see the three shape tools, and choose the **Ellipse** tool. Bring the cursor onto the page. Move the page over to the right by holding the **spacebar** down (the **Hand** tool appears) and then clicking and dragging the page to the right to reveal the left paste-board. This allows you to draw on the pasteboard. Let go of the **spacebar**, and draw an ellipse by clicking and dragging on the pasteboard. While looking at the **Width** and **Height** fields in the **Control** palette, try to drag the ellipse out to **5.2 in** (width) × **6.8 in** (height). Release the mouse button, and keep the shape selected for the next step.

Note: To create a shape of a certain size, you can also type numbers directly into the **Width** and **Height** fields while keeping the shape selected.

Tip: Often I begin by drawing shapes and other frames on the pasteboard because it makes it easier to select and manipulate them.

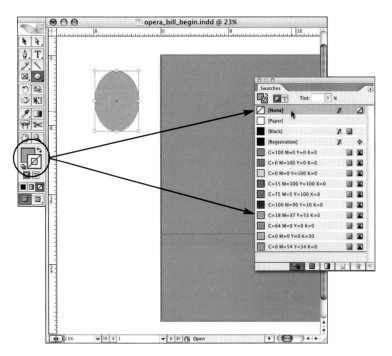

5. With the shape selected from the previous step, choose the **Fill Box** from the **Toolbox** (or from the **Swatches** palette) and choose the light-brown color from the **Swatches** palette for the fill. Also, notice that the stroke has a black color applied. Select the **Stroke Box** from the **Toolbox** (because it's easier to see there than in the **Swatches** palette). Choose **None** as the color from the **Swatches** palette.

Note: When the elliptical shape is selected, a blue rectangular frame appears around it. This is called a bounding box. It is a nonprinting area that facilitates shape transformations, which you will learn about later in this chapter.

*Tip: Another way to apply a swatch color is to drag the swatch from the **Swatches** palette directly on top of the shape you want to apply the color to.*

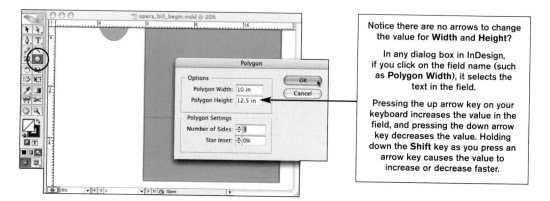

Notice there are no arrows to change the value for **Width** and **Height**?

In any dialog box in InDesign, if you click on the field name (such as **Polygon Width**), it selects the text in the field.

Pressing the up arrow key on your keyboard increases the value in the field, and pressing the down arrow key decreases the value. Holding down the **Shift** key as you press an arrow key causes the value to increase or decrease faster.

6. Select the **Polygon** tool from the shape tools in the **Toolbox**. With the cursor on the page, click the pasteboard somewhere below the ellipse you created in the previous steps. The **Polygon** dialog box appears. Leave the default **Height** and **Width** settings, change the **Number of Sides** setting to **3**, and leave the **Star Inset** at **0%**. You are about to create a triangle. Click **OK** to create the shape.

*Note: If the values that appear in the **Polygon** dialog box are different from the **9.9412 in** width and **12.6176 in** height you see in the illustration of this step, type these values in the **Width** and **Height** fields, or use the method described in the tip to the right of the illustration to adjust them.*

*A triangle with a 1-pt black border appears. The border is hard to see because of the frame edge (blue line). You can turn frame edges off to see the border by choosing **View > Hide Frame Edges** and deselecting the shape. Turn the frame edges back on by selecting **View > Show Frame Edges**.*

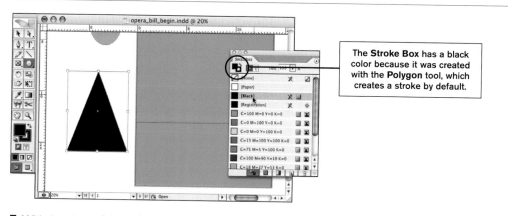

The **Stroke Box** has a black color because it was created with the **Polygon** tool, which creates a stroke by default.

7. With the shape (triangle) still selected, open the **Swatches** palette and, with the **Fill Box** selected, choose the black swatch to apply a black fill. Leave the stroke color on the triangle. Dock the **Swatches** palette if you pulled it off the side or minimize it on the side of your workspace.

8. Save the file and keep it open for the next exercise.

TIP | Frame or Shape Content

Frames and shapes in InDesign can hold any type of content, and they can all be repurposed to hold a different type of content than originally intended.

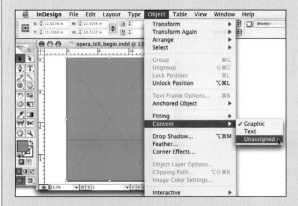

With a frame or shape selected with the **Selection** tool, choose **Object > Content > Graphic, Text** or **Unassigned**.

When working with shapes that are just color-filled objects, **Unassigned** is the default content type. If you accidentally click a shape or frame with the **Type** tool, that shape or frame is automatically converted to a text frame. Even without text in it, InDesign calls for the default font when the document is output.

To avoid headaches, I make sure that **Unassigned** is the chosen content type for shapes.

TIP | Shape Creation Shortcuts

When creating shapes, there are many helpful shortcuts. The following chart lists several of the most commonly used ones.

Shortcut	Outcome
Hold down the **Shift** key while drawing with any shape or frame tool.	Constrains the proportions of the shape (a perfect square or circle for instance).
Hold down the **Alt** (Windows) or **Option** (Mac) key before or during the process of drawing with any shape or frame tool.	Draws the shape from the center. The center is where you first clicked and began to draw.
Hold down **Shift+Alt** (Windows) or **Shift+Option (Mac)** before or during the process of drawing with any shape or frame tool.	Constrains the proportions while you draw from the center of the shape.
While drawing a shape or frame, hold down the **spacebar** and drag with your mouse.	Allows you to reposition the shape *while* you are drawing it onto the page—the trick is to not let go of your mouse button.
With the **Polygon** tool or **Polygon Frame** tool selected, draw a shape by clicking and dragging. While drawing (don't release your mouse button), press the **up arrow** to add one side to the polygon or the **down arrow** to decrease the number of sides by one every time you press the key. *To get this to work, hold down the mouse button and move the cursor constantly back and forth to see the effect. Bizarre, yes— but it's a great shortcut!*	These shortcuts affect how many sides the polygon has.
With the **Polygon** tool or **Polygon Frame** tool selected, draw a shape. While drawing (don't release your mouse button) hold down the **right arrow** key to increase the **Star Inset**, and then hold down the **left arrow** key to decrease the **Star Inset**. *To get this to work, hold down the mouse and move the cursor constantly back and forth to see the effect. Also bizarre, but another useful shortcut!*	Affect the **Star Inset** of the polygon (the higher the percentage, the longer and thinner the spikes appear).

Understanding Transformation Operations

Transformations are changes or edits made to shapes and frames after they are drawn. You can transform shapes in several ways using tools you can access through menus, palettes, or the **Toolbox**. The chart below describes the various ways to access InDesign's transformation operations and what each operation does.

Transformation Options			
Transformation	Toolbox tool	Where to Access	Functionality
Move		**Object > Transform > Move** or the **Selection** tool	The **Selection** tool moves shapes and frames freely around the page. Holding down the **Shift** key constrains movement to a horizontal, vertical, or diagonal direction. Choosing **Object > Transform > Move** opens a dialog box that enables you to move an object by typing a value and choosing an angle (direction) to move in. You can also copy a shape or frame and then move the copy using the dialog box.
Scale		**Object > Transform > Scale** or the **Scale** tool	The **Scale** tool scales any object and its content. Choosing **Object > Transform > Scale** opens a dialog box that enables you to do the same thing, but it also allows you to scale a frame or shape separate from its content (if the frame or shape contains a graphic). Using this dialog box, you can also make a copy of the original frame or shape and scale the copy.
Rotate		**Object > Transform > Rotate** or the **Rotate** tool	The **Rotate** tool rotates any object and its content. Choosing **Object > Transform > Rotate** opens a dialog box that allows you to do the same thing, but it also lets you rotate a frame or shape separate from its content (if the frame or shape contains a graphic). Using this dialog box, you can also make a copy of the original and rotate the copy.

continues on next page

Transformation Options *continued*			
Transformation	**Toolbox tool**	**Where to Access**	**Functionality**
Shear		**Object > Transform > Shear** or the **Shear** tool	The **Shear** tool skews any object and its content. Choosing **Object > Transform > Shear** opens a dialog box that allows you to do the same thing, but it also lets you skew the frame or shape "by the numbers" and separate from its content (if the frame or shape contains a graphic). Using this dialog box you can also make a copy of the original and skew the original.
Free Transform		**Free Transform** tool	The **Free Transform** tool scales, rotates, moves, and shears any object and its content. It is a combination tool. There is no menu item for free transform.
			Note: When using the **Free Transform** tool, you need to hold down **Ctrl+Alt** (Windows) or **Option+Cmd** (Mac) while dragging a side point to shear the object.

What Are Convert Shape Operations?

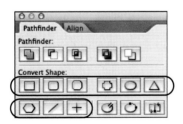

Shapes and frames can also be converted into other shapes—for instance, a square can be turned into a circle, a triangle, or any other shape. Instead of redrawing the shape or frame, InDesign can convert the shape. The **Convert Shape** options can be found under the **Object > Convert Shape** menu or in the **Pathfinder** palette (**Window > Object & Layout > Pathfinder**). To convert a shape, frame, or line using the options, you first select the object.

Convert Shape Options

Convert Option	Outcome
Rectangle	Converts a shape, line, or frame to a rectangle.
Rounded Rectangle	Converts a shape, line, or frame to a rectangle with rounded corners. How rounded the corner is depends on the radius setting in the **Corner Effects** dialog box, which is explained below.
Beveled Rectangle	Converts a shape, line, or frame to a rectangle with beveled corners. How beveled (cut off) the corners are depends on the radius setting in the **Corner Effects** dialog box, as explained in the next section.
Inverse Rounded Rectangle	Converts a shape, line, or frame to a rectangle with inverse rounded corners. How inverse rounded the corners are depends on the radius setting in the **Corner Effects** dialog box, as explained in the next section.
Ellipse	Converts a shape, line, or frame to an ellipse.
Triangle	Converts a shape, line, or frame to a triangle.
Polygon	Converts a shape, line, or frame to a polygon. The **Polygon** tool settings dictate how shapes are converted to a polygon with this option. Before using this option, double-click the **Polygon** tool to set the **Number of Sides** and **Star Inset**.
Line	Converts a shape, line, or frame to a line.
Orthogonal Line	Converts a shape, line, or frame to a straight vertical or horizontal line.

Corner Effects

You will frequently need to edit shapes and frames after you've created them. The **Corner Effects** dialog box offers options to round, bevel, inset, and inverse round a shape as well as create "fancy" corners (I'll let you be the judge of that). You access the **Corner Effects** options by choosing **Object > Corner Effects**.

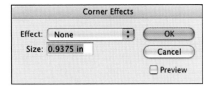

From the **Effect** pop-up menu, you can select the type of corner effect (the options available are shown in the following chart). The **Size** field determines how much the corner effect extends inward from each corner point. Corner effects work on any frame or shape and can only be modified by the Effect and Size options in the dialog box. Corner effects will also affect any text wrap on a text frame.

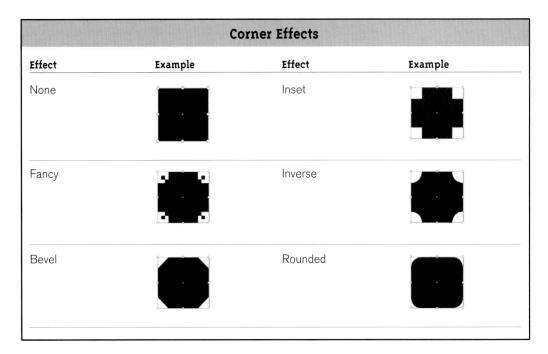

Corner Effects			
Effect	**Example**	**Effect**	**Example**
None		Inset	
Fancy		Inverse	
Bevel		Rounded	

*Tip: If you edit the options in the **Corner Effects** dialog box while you have a document open and nothing selected, InDesign assumes you are setting default corner effects for that document. The next shape you create (with the **Pen** tool, **Pencil** tool, shape tools, and more) will use those corner effect and size settings.*

The **Corner Effects** options affect the **Convert Shape** operations. If you set the size of a corner effect while nothing is selected in the document, the next time you convert a shape, line, or frame to a **Rounded Rectangle**, **Beveled Rectangle**, or **Inverse Rounded Rectangle**, InDesign will apply that same size.

The Transform Palette

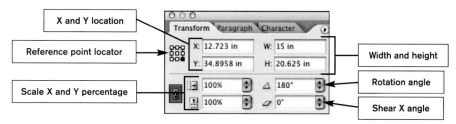

The **Transform** palette—accessed by choosing **Window > Object & Layout > Transform**—is another place to find transform options available in the **Control** palette, menus, and **Toolbox**. What is transformed depends on what is selected. If you select an object with the **Selection** tool, the frame or shape is transformed (along with its content), but if you select a graphic (for instance) using the **Direct Selection** tool, the graphic is the only thing that is transformed. The chart below describes the **Transform** palette options.

Transform Palette Options	
Option	**Use**
Reference Point Locator	All transformations operate from the point selected here.
X and Y Location	Changes the vertical or horizontal position of the selected object.
Width and Height	Changes the width and/or height of the selected object.
Scale X and Y Percentage	Scales the selected object in the x-axis and/or y-axis.
Rotation Angle	Rotates a selected object around the selected reference point.
Shear X Angle	Slants or skews a selected object along its horizontal axis.

2. _____Transforming and Converting Shapes

In this exercise, you will transform several of the shapes you created by rotating, scaling, and converting them.

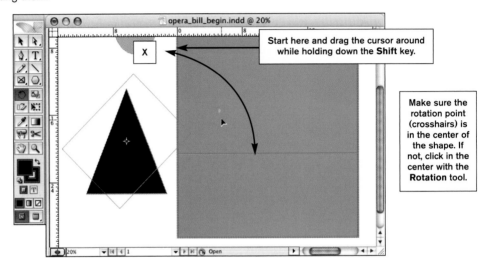

Start here and drag the cursor around while holding down the **Shift** key.

Make sure the rotation point (crosshairs) is in the center of the shape. If not, click in the center with the **Rotation** tool.

1. With **opera_bill_begin.indd** open from the previous exercise, choose the **Rotation** tool from the **Toolbox**. If the triangle is already selected, a crosshairs will appear in the center (✛). If not, deselect everything by choosing **Edit > Deselect All**, and then select the triangle by clicking in it with the **Rotation** tool. With the **Rotation** tool, move the cursor away from the triangle, click, hold down the mouse button and the **Shift** key, and drag the cursor in a circle to the right. The **Shift** key constrains the rotation to 45 degrees. The goal is to rotate the triangle so it appears upside-down (a rotation of 180 degrees). Keep the shape selected.

*Note: As you drag around to rotate the shape, the further you move the cursor from the shape, the finer the control you have over the rotation. Also, make sure that the crosshairs (✛) is in the center of the shape. If not, before you start rotating, make sure the **Rotation** tool and shape are selected and then click in the center of the shape to set the rotation point (crosshairs).*

Note: As you rotate, InDesign might scroll the page. Although this can be beneficial, sometimes it gets out of hand. Be aware that it can happen!

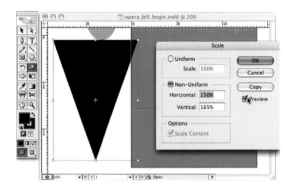

2. Now you will use the **Scale** dialog box to make the triangle bigger. With the triangle fully rotated and still selected, double-click the **Scale** tool in the **Toolbox**. In the **Scale** dialog box, select **Non-Uniform**. Type **150** in the **Horizontal** field and **165** in the **Vertical** field (the % symbol appears automatically). Check the **Preview** box to see the result. Click **OK** to accept. Make sure that the triangle is positioned beneath the ellipse, as in the illustration.

*The **Scale** dialog box, which can also be accessed from the **Object > Transform > Scale** menu, is great for resizing objects using percentages. The **Non-Uniform** option lets you scale the shape with different values for the width and height.*

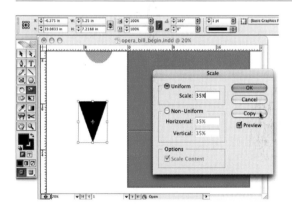

3. Now you are going to make a copy of the black triangle. With the triangle still selected from the previous step, double-click the **Scale** tool again. This time, in the **Scale** dialog box and with **Preview** selected, choose **Uniform** and type **35** in the **Scale** field. You are making a smaller copy of the black triangle so click the **Copy** button.

*Note: This step is a little jarring at first because the **Scale** dialog box will remember the **150%** and **165%** settings from the last time you used the dialog box. It also looks like the black triangle is being scaled, but as soon as you click the **Copy** button, InDesign makes a copy and scales that. This is an easy way to make a copy of an object while scaling it.*

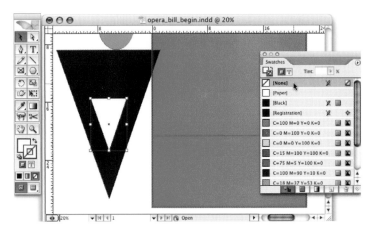

4. With the copied and scaled shape still selected, open the **Swatches** palette. With the **Fill Box** selected from the **Toolbox**, pick **Paper** as the color and make sure the stroke is set to **None**.

*Remember, the color **Paper** may be used for white or to preview any paper or background color you are going to output to. The color **Paper** was discussed in Chapter 7, "Working with Color."*

5. To see how the **Convert Shape** options work, choose the white triangle with the **Selection** tool if it isn't still selected. Choose **Object > Convert Shape > Ellipse** to see what the white triangle looks like as an ellipse instead.

*The **Convert Shape** feature is brand new in InDesign CS2 and can be very helpful when repurposing shapes or frames. It allows any shape or frame to be converted to any of a long list of other shapes. Just know that if you convert a shape or frame to a **Line** or **Orthogonal Line** (straight line), it can only be converted back by choosing **Edit > Undo**.*

***Tip:** If you draw a square, a circle, or even a line and it somehow becomes a bit distorted or slightly rotated, picking the same shape from the **Convert Shape** options will bring it back into line (so to speak).*

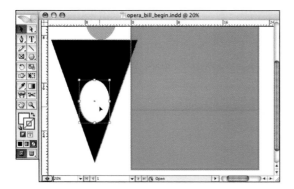

6. You are working on the white shirt for the opera singer, which looks better with a small triangle, rather than the current ellipse. Choose **Edit > Undo** or **Object > Convert Shape > Triangle** to turn the ellipse back into a triangle.

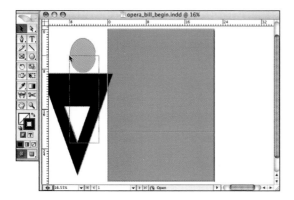

7. With the Selection tool chosen from the Toolbox, starting on the pasteboard, select the black and white triangles and the ellipse you've created so far by clicking, holding down the mouse button, and dragging across all three shapes. Once selected, drag them from the pasteboard onto the page. The next step will show you the rough placement.

***Note:** With the selection box you drag out with the **Selection** tool, you just need to touch the objects. It's not necessary to surround them.*

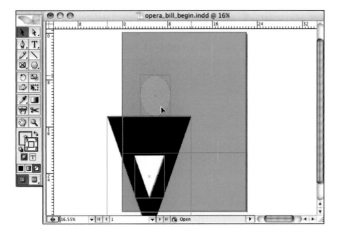

This is how the shapes you just selected should look before you proceed to the next step. You will line them up and position them in an exercise later in this chapter.

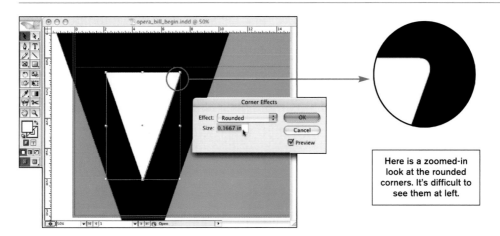

Here is a zoomed-in look at the rounded corners. It's difficult to see them at left.

8. To round the corners of the white triangle, choose **Edit > Deselect All**, and choose the white triangle with the **Selection** tool. Zoom in a bit using the **Zoom** tool so you'll be able to see the effect take place. Choose **Object > Corner Effects**. In the **Corner Effects** dialog box, choose **Rounded** from the **Effect** pop-up menu. The **Size** should be **0.1667 in** by default, but if not, select the field and type the value. Click **OK** to close the **Corner Effects** dialog box and apply the rounded the corners.

9. Save the file and close it.

*Tip: With the white triangle selected, press **Ctrl** (Windows) or **Cmd** (Mac) and the plus key (**+**) to zoom in. This shortcut has the unique attribute of also bringing the selected shape or object—the triangle, in this case—to the center of the page, zooming in every time you press the keys.*

TIP | Transform Again

The **Transform** options offer some great ways to edit shapes. The **Transform Again** options take those options one step further by "replaying" the transform operations onto another shape, so you can repeat transformations, such as moving, scaling, rotating, resizing, reflecting, shearing, and fitting.

By choosing **Object > Transform Again**, you can perform four operations:

1. **Transform Again** applies the last single transformation operation (scale, rotate, resize, reflect, shear, or fit) to the selection.

2. **Transform Again Individually** applies the last single transformation operation to each selected object individually, rather than as a group. (This can be very important if you did a rotate, for example, because with more than one object selected, it would rotate the group around its center point rather than each independently.)

3. **Transform Sequence Again** applies the last sequence of transformation operations to the selection.

4. **Transform Sequence Again Individually** applies the last series of transformation operations to each selected object individually. (This can be very important if you did a rotate, for example, because with more than one object selected, it would rotate the group around its center point rather than each independently.)

The illustration shows two examples of **Transform Again** operations. On the black circle at left, a square shape was drawn and lined up with the center of the circle. The square was then rotated around the center of the circle and duplicated by holding down **Alt** (Windows) or **Option** (Mac) and dragging with the **Rotation** tool. The **Transform Sequence Again** operation was then used. The same type of operation was done to the stars to achieve copies of the original star. The copies were then rotated individually.

What Is a Path?

A path is a vector graphic that is drawn, whether in InDesign or a more involved vector program like Illustrator. For instance, the path of a vector shape like a circle is the curving "line" along which the "pen" draws the shape. Paths are the basic foundation of any vector shape; without a path, a vector shape cannot exist.

There are different types of paths: open and closed paths, and simple and compound paths. Open paths are vector shapes that have an "open" end. A good example is a U-shaped graphic, which opens at the top, or even a straight line drawn from point A to B. A closed path is the opposite. Examples of closed paths include squares, circles, triangles, and rectangles—any path in which the two ends eventually meet.

Simple paths involve one shape, like a circle or square. Compound paths, on the other hand, combine two or more shapes, like two circles that partially overlap.

Pathfinder Operations

Using InDesign's **Pathfinder** operations, you can create complex shapes from simple ones. Consider, for example, a doughnut-shaped object. Using **Pathfinder** and beginning with two separate circles, InDesign can subtract one circle from the other and create a third, combined shape—a doughnut. Because InDesign performs much of this work for you, **Pathfinder** make the process of turning simple shapes into more complex ones both fast and easy.

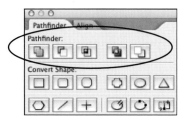

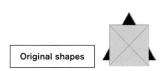

Original shapes

Pathfinder operations work on any two or more selected frames or shapes and can be found under **Object > Pathfinder** or in the **Pathfinder** palette (**Window > Object & Layout > Pathfinder**), which is what you will be using in this exercise. The on the next page below explains the operations that can be performed from the **Pathfinder** palette.

Pathfinder Operations

Pathfinder Operation	Explained	Example
Add	Adds (combines) two or more shapes together to create a single shape. The final shape takes the properties (stroke and fill) of the frontmost shape or frame.	
Subtract	From the selected objects (shapes or frames), all the objects above the bottommost object are subtracted from the bottommost object to create a new shape. The new shape takes the properties of the original bottom-most object.	
Intersect	A new shape or frame is created from overlapping areas. The new shape takes the properties of the frontmost object.	
Exclude Overlap	Creates a shape from areas that do not overlap (knocks out overlapping areas). The new shape takes the properties of the frontmost object.	
Minus Back	Objects in the back knock out of the frontmost object. The new shape takes the properties of the frontmost object.	

3. ————————— Using Pathfinder Operations

In this short exercise, you will create a top hat for the opera figure by combining shapes using **Pathfinder** operations.

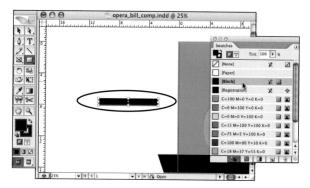

1. Open **opera_bill_comp.indd** from the **chap_09** folder on the **Desktop**. Choose the **Rectangle** tool, and draw a rectangle **8 in** wide and **0.85 in** high. Look in the **Control** palette for the width and height measurements. Open the **Swatches** palette and with the **Fill Box** selected, apply the color **Black**.

Note: The file you are using in this exercise is identical to what you've created up to this point; nothing has changed.

*To change the dimensions of the rectangle, type values into the **Width** and **Height** fields in the **Control** palette after the shape is drawn and is still selected.*

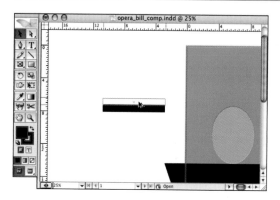

2. With the **Selection** tool chosen from the **Toolbox**, hold down **Shift+Alt** (Windows) or **Shift+Option** (Mac), and click and drag the shape to create a copy above the original. The **Alt** or **Option** key duplicates the object, and the **Shift** key allows the object to move straight up with the two shapes kept in line.

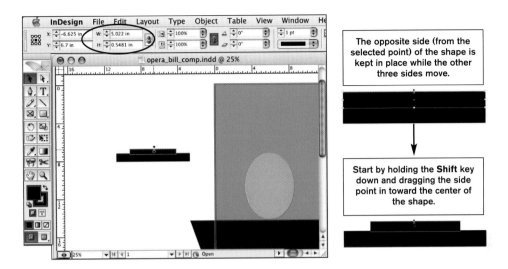

The opposite side (from the selected point) of the shape is kept in place while the other three sides move.

Start by holding the **Shift** key down and dragging the side point in toward the center of the shape.

3. With the **Selection** tool still chosen, make sure the top rectangle is still selected. While holding down the **Shift** key, click and drag the upper-middle handle (square point) toward the center of the shape. Watch the width of the shape in the **Control** palette. Let go when it reaches approximately **5 in**. Keep the shape selected for the next step.

Tip: Zooming in can really help when resizing shapes that are small like this one.

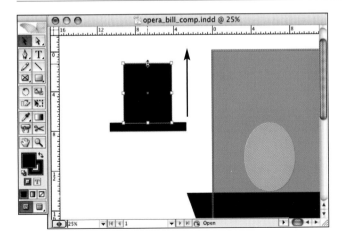

4. With the **Selection** tool still selected, click and drag the upper-middle handle (square point) to make the top part of the hat tall enough for your dapper-looking chap. Looking at the **Control** palette while dragging; a height of **5.75 in** should be suitable.

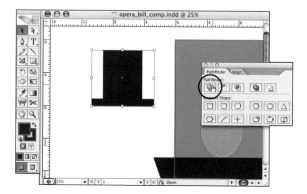

5. Select both objects with the **Selection** tool by **Shift+clicking** them separately or clicking and dragging across the two of them. Open the **Pathfinder** palette under **Window > Object & Layout > Pathfinder**. Click the **Add** button to combine the two shapes.

*You can also choose the **Add** option from **Object > Pathfinder > Add**. When shapes are combined, they take on a single stroke and fill.*

Note: *Using **Pathfinder** operations on shapes (two or more) cannot always be easily undone. You can, of course, choose **Edit > Undo** to undo the operation at that moment, but undoing **Pathfinder** operations later could be challenging.*

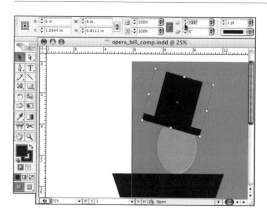

6. Move the "hat" shape on the page with the **Selection** tool. From the **Control** palette, choose **−15°** as the rotation angle by clicking on the down arrow while holding down the **Shift** key. The **Shift** key rotates the object in increments of 5 degrees instead of 1 degree.

InDesign considers a positive (+) rotation value to be counterclockwise, and a negative (−) rotation value to be clockwise.

7. Save the file and close it.

Creating Compound Paths

As you learned earlier in this section, **compound paths** combine several paths into a single object. This is different from the **Pathfinder** operations described earlier. A shape that you create using a **Pathfinder** operation is a single shape. By contrast, a shape you create using compound paths appears and prints as a single shape but is in fact separate shapes that can be "released" to their original shapes at a later point.

Compound paths were originally an Illustrator concept and are one example of an Illustrator feature that InDesign has "borrowed." Here are some examples of when to use compound paths instead of **Pathfinder** operations:

- Add transparent holes to a path and be able to pull the separate shapes back out later (see the following illustration).

- Using the **Create Outlines** command converts text to editable paths. Any letters, such as **o, e,** and **a,** preserve their transparent holes when characters are converted to editable paths because they become compound paths automatically.

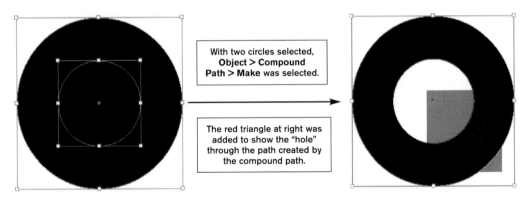

With two circles selected, **Object > Compound Path > Make** was selected.

The red triangle at right was added to show the "hole" through the path created by the compound path.

MOVIE | Compound Paths

To learn about creating and using compound paths, check out **compoundpaths.mov** in the **movies** folder on the **InDesign CS2 HOT CD-ROM**.

Understanding the Stroke Options

The stroke of an object can be so much more than just a border color. Using the **Stroke** palette (**Window > Stroke**), you can unlock features that allow for more creativity. Strokes can be applied to text, frames, shapes, and lines.

Stroke Palette Options

Feature	Function
Weight	The size in points of the stroke.
Cap	For lines or open shapes, these options change the end caps: **Butt** (square ends) ( ), **Round** (rounded ends) ( ), or **Projecting** (square ends that extend beyond the end of the line) ( ).
Join	A Miter join ( ) creates pointed corners that extend beyond the end point when the miter's length is within the miter limit. A **Round** join ( ) creates rounded corners that extend half the stroke width beyond corner points. **Bevel** join ( ) creates squared corners that abut the end points.
Miter Limit	Miter length When you have corners on shapes that are very "pointy," you can set a miter limit that says if the miter length gets too long, miter it or cut it off. The miter limit is determined by the comparing the miter length to the stroke width before a mitered joint becomes a beveled square joint (cut off).
Align Stroke	Three stroke alignments: **Align Stroke to Center, Align Stroke to Outside, Align Stroke to Inside**. These options change where the stroke sits on the line.
Type	InDesign comes with many types of strokes, like dashed or dotted.
Start	The start of the line or open shape can begin with an arrowhead or other object.
End	The line or open shape can end with an arrowhead or other object.
Gap Color	If a dashed or multiple-line type of stroke is chosen, the spaces between the dashes or lines can be filled with a color.
Gap Tint	Creates a tint (percentage) of the gap color.

4. _____Using Stroke and Fill

Applying strokes and fills to shapes adds a much larger creative range to vector shapes in InDesign. In this exercise, you will apply a custom stroke to a shape.

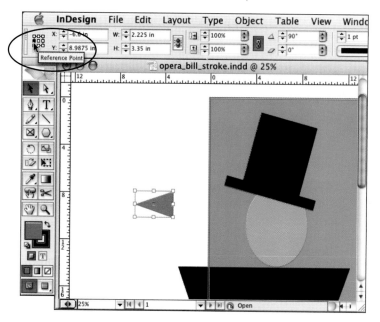

1. Open **opera_bill_stroke.indd** from the **chap_09** folder on the **Desktop**. Select the red triangle on the left pasteboard. I recommend zooming in a bit using the **Zoom** tool in the **Toolbox** to make it easier to see the stroke you will be applying. At the left end of the **Control** palette, choose the leftmost point from the center row (circled in the illustration) as the **point of origin**. In the next step, you will duplicate the triangle to create a bow tie.

Selecting the point of origin allows you to flip the triangle horizontally around that point. While flipping the shape, you will also duplicate it.

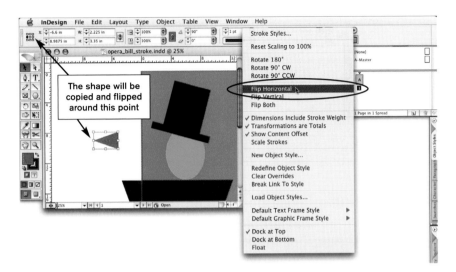

2. Hold down the **Alt** (Windows) or **Option** (Mac) key while you choose **Flip Horizontal** from the **Control Palette** menu, located at the right end of the **Control** palette, under the arrow.

*Note: The **Flip** commands offer an easy way to turn objects around without having to rotate them. The commands flip objects on the **point of origin** set in the **Control** palette. Holding down the **Alt** (Windows) or **Option** (Mac) key is a fast way to duplicate a shape when using the **Flip Horizontal**, **Flip Vertical**, or **Flip Both** commands.*

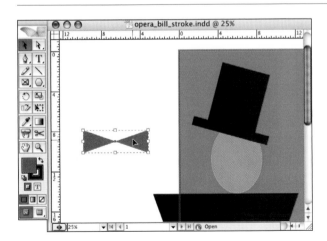

3. Select both the new shape and the original triangle with the **Selection** tool from the **Toolbox**, and choose **Object > Group** to group them together. If they don't look like the shapes in the illustration here, move either one with the **Selection** tool so that they look similar or delete the copied one and try again!

Grouping objects ensures that the shapes stay together when moved.

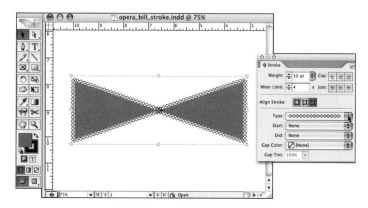

4. Zoom into the grouped shapes with the **Zoom** tool. Open the **Stroke** palette either from the side of the workspace or by choosing it from **Window > Stroke**. In the **Stroke** palette, choose **White Diamond** from the **Type** pop-up menu. Change the **Weight** to **10 pt** by choosing that setting from the **Weight** menu. Click the **Align Stroke to Outside** button to push the stroke outside the edge of the shapes.

*Note: If the **Stroke** palette doesn't show all the options shown in the illustration, choose **Show Options**.*

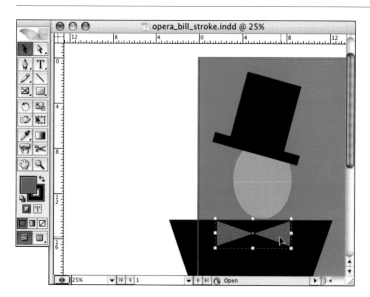

5. With the **Selection** tool, move the "bow tie" shapes onto the page in the position shown here. You will position all the shapes in the next exercise.

6. Save the file and keep it open for the next exercise.

The Align Palette

Aligning objects in InDesign can be done with either the **Control** palette, which is useful for simple alignments, or the **Align** palette (**Window > Object & Layout > Align**), which provides a broader range of alignment options.

The **Control** palette changes when more than one object is selected. The **Align Objects** options will be on the far-right side of the **Control** palette.

The **Align** palette has the **Align Objects** options as well as **Distribute Objects** and **Distribute Spacing** options to affect the alignment and space between objects. The following chart describes all the alignment options. Alignment doesn't affect locked objects and aligns objects to each other, not the document.

Align Palette	
Align Objects	**Function**
Align Left Edges ( )	Vertical alignment of the left edges of objects. All selected objects are aligned to the leftmost object.
Align Horizontal Centers ( )	Vertical alignment of the centers of objects. All selected objects are aligned to the centermost object.
Align Right Edges ( )	Vertical alignment of the right edges of objects. All selected objects are aligned to the rightmost object.
Align Top Edges ( )	Horizontal alignment of the top edges of objects. All selected objects are aligned to the topmost object.
Align Vertical Centers ( )	Horizontal alignment of the centers of objects. All selected objects are aligned to the centermost object.
Align Bottom Edges ( )	Horizontal alignment of the bottom edges of objects. All selected objects are aligned to the bottommost object.

continues on next page

Align Palette *continued*	
Distribute Objects	**Function**
Distribute Top Edges (⬒)	Vertically distributes objects by inserting an equal amount of space between the top edges of all selected objects.
Distribute Vertical Centers (⬒)	Vertically distributes objects by inserting an equal amount of space between the centers of all selected objects.
Distribute Bottom Edges (⬓)	Vertically distributes objects by inserting an equal amount of space between the bottom edges of all selected objects.
Distribute Left Edges (⊫)	Horizontally distributes objects by inserting an equal amount of space between the left edges of all selected objects.
Distribute Horizontal Centers (⬌)	Horizontally distributes objects by inserting an equal amount of space between the centers of all selected objects.
Distribute Right Edges (⊣⊢)	Horizontally distributes objects by inserting an equal amount of space between the right edges of all selected objects.
Use Spacing	Defines the space between the corresponding edges or centers of the selected objects.
Distribute Spacing	**Function**
Distribute Vertical Space (⬓)	Selected objects are evenly spaced between the facing edges vertically.
Distribute Horizontal Space (⬚)	Selected objects are evenly spaced between the facing edges horizontally.
Use Spacing	This option creates a space of specified value between the objects.

5. ——————————**Aligning and Distributing Objects**

So far in this chapter, you've created and manipulated shapes. In this exercise, you will align some of those shapes to each other to get your opera singer looking his best.

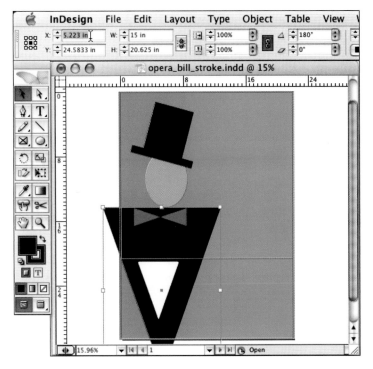

1. With **opera_bill_stroke.indd** open from the previous exercise, choose the **Selection** tool from the **Toolbox**, and select the black triangle. Move the triangle over to the right on the page until you see approximately **5.2 in** in the **X** field at the left end of the **Control** palette. Choose **Object > Lock Position** to lock the triangle into place.

You are locking the black triangle into position because you are going to align the rest of the objects to it. Depending on the alignment method used, when objects are aligned to each other and one is locked, the unlocked objects automatically line up with the locked one.

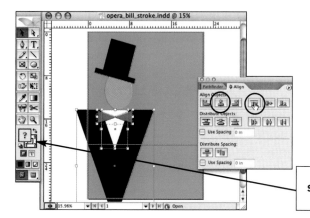

Notice the question marks (?) in the **Fill** and **Stroke** boxes? They indicate that multiple objects with different strokes and fills are selected.

2. Open the **Align** palette from **Window > Object & Layout > Align**. If the palette doesn't look like the palette in the illustration (it's missing the **Distribute Spacing** options), choose **Show Options** from the palette menu. With the **Selection** tool selected, **Shift+click** the black triangle, the white triangle, and the bow tie (red triangles) to select them all. Click the **Align Horizontal Centers** button and the **Align Top Edges** button. When finished, keep the **Align** palette open but move it to the side of the workspace.

*Tip: If you accidentally select too much, you can use the **Shift** key to deselect objects. Just hold the **Shift** key down and click a selected object to remove it from the group of selected objects.*

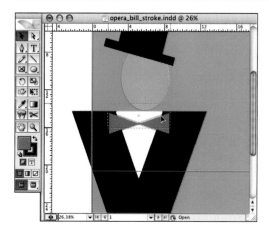

3. Choose **Edit > Deselect All** to deselect all the objects. With the **Selection** tool, click and drag the bow tie (two red triangles) so they are positioned above the black and white triangles a bit, as shown here.

*When objects are grouped, a dotted box appears around them. This is a bounding box surrounding the grouped objects. It means they can be resized as a group with the **Selection** tool. You will also notice a little "x" in the center of the grouped objects. This can be very helpful when you want to line up objects or move them to see the center.*

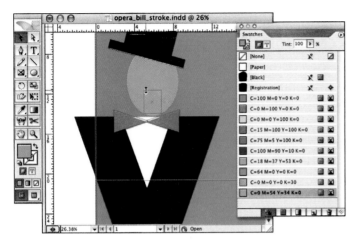

4. Select the brown ellipse with the **Selection** tool, and choose **Edit > Copy, Edit > Paste in Place**. This is great for creating a copy and pasting it in the same location on that or any other page. With the shape selected, open the **Swatches** palette, and with the **Fill Box** chosen, apply the pink color at the bottom of the palette. Resize the shape by holding down the **Shift** key and dragging from the top center handle of the new frame.

This step covered a lot of ground, but these are things that you have already done earlier in this chapter.

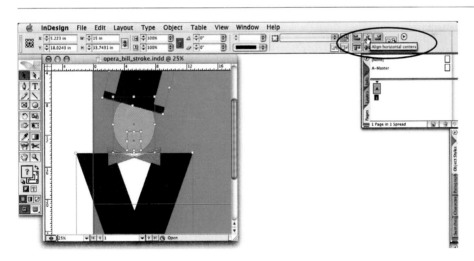

5. With the pink ellipse finished from the previous step, select the brown ellipse, the pink ellipse (it should already be selected), and the top hat (black rectangles) with the **Shift** key and the **Selection** tool. Click the **Align Horizontal Centers** button from the right end of the **Control** palette.

6. Save the file and close it.

What Is the Create Outlines Operation?

In the graphics world, working with type and fonts typically consist of changing font size, scaling the type, colorizing it, among many other operations. However, type that is converted to outlines offers far more flexibility.

The process of converting type to outlines eliminates the need for a font because it converts the type into vector shapes that are completely editable. This can lead to tremendous design possibilities. After selecting the text, or selecting an entire text frame to convert all of the text inside, choose **Type > Create Outlines** to convert to outlines.

So why would you convert type to outlines? Here are a few reasons:

- You want to ensure that the type can be output, in case the font is dropped or not sent with the file.
- You want to reshape the type, creating an artistic headline.
- You want to put a graphic on the page in the shape of text.
- You want the type on your page to have a gradient fill.

There are other reasons to convert text to outlines, but these are some of the most common ones.

Original text converted to outlines. Notice the individual points that make the text completely editable.

Original text with the font Myriad Pro Regular applied.

Note: There are a few things to consider before converting type to outlines. I suggest not turning an entire page of type into outlines because vector art (the shapes that are created when text is converted to outlines) can take longer to print on certain printers. Also, text that uses certain fonts will look different onscreen when converted to outlines at smaller sizes due to the conversion process, and the manufacturers of some fonts do not allow their fonts to be converted to outlines.

Finally, before converting text to outlines, you need to consider that the conversion cannot be undone (once the file has been saved and reopened)! This can prove difficult if you send someone else the file and they need to make text edits but don't know the original font used.

The new Theater is located
adjacent to the old theater

The text at left was converted to outlines. Each line of text is a separate shape and can be manipulated. When the text frame is first converted, each line is grouped together.

You can also convert text to outlines by selecting the text, such as a letter for a large drop cap or the first word in a paragraph, or by selecting a text frame with the **Selection** tool and then converting the whole text frame to outlines. Just know that when a frame of text is converted, each line is a separate shape.

6. ————————Converting Text to Vector Outlines

You are going to open a file that looks similar to the projects you've been working on to this point. The only change is that some text was added to the page. In this short exercise, you will convert that text to shapes by converting it to outlines.

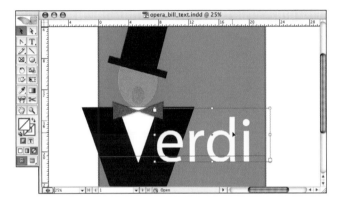

1. Open **opera_bill_text.indd** from the **chap_09** folder on the **Desktop**. Select the text frame with the **Selection** tool by clicking on the text to start. The text in the selected frame is going to be converted to a shape that is editable.

*Note: The **Missing Fonts** dialog box may appear when you open this file, listing **Myriad Pro Regular**. If it does, change the font by choosing **Find Font** and replacing Myriad Pro Regular with a version of Arial or Helvetica. To learn more about this, visit Exercise 1 of Chapter 5, "Typography in InDesign."*

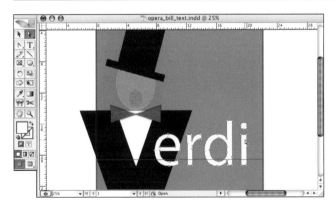

2. With the text frame selected, choose **Type > Create Outlines**. Select the **Direct Selection** tool, and you see all of the editable points that make up the paths. The text was just converted to a compound path. If you select it, you select all the vector paths as one object.

*Tip: If you wanted to select a single "letter" shape, you could select the **"erdi"** shape and choose **Object > Compound Paths > Release**. This releases the shape into all the separate shapes you could edit individually. Watch out, though! The "e" and the "d" shapes will not have a see-through center anymore. For the "e" shape, for example, you would have to select the main "e" shape and the "e" see-through shape and then choose **Object > Compound Paths > Make** to have it look like a letter with a see-through part again!*

In Exercise 8, "Editing Paths," later in this chapter, you will learn how to edit these newly created shapes.

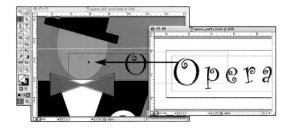

3. In this step, you will drag over some text from another document that has already been turned into outlines. While leaving this file open, choose **File > Open**. In the **Open** dialog box, choose **opera_paths.indd** from the **chap_09** folder on the **Desktop**. With the **Selection** tool, select the "**Opera**" text that has already been converted to outlines and is now a single compound shape, and drag the shape into the **opera_bill_text.indd** file. Click and drag the shape across from one file to the other. This will copy the compound path and place it where you release your mouse in **opera_bill_text.indd**.

*Note: Dragging may prove difficult on the Windows platform, unless you resize the windows. Alternatively, you can select the compound path "**Opera**," copy it, and then click back into the opera_bill_text.indd and paste. That has the same effect as dragging.*

4. With the new compound path on the page, hold down the **Shift** key while you select the pink ellipse and the "**Opera**" shape. Drag them up a bit so that the bottom of the letter "**p**" doesn't hit the red bow tie shape.

Tip: *To move objects, you can also use the arrow keys. The up, down, left, and right arrow keys are great for moving selected objects. To move selected objects farther and faster, hold down the* **Shift** *key while you press one of the arrow keys. To move objects in smaller increments, hold down* **Shift+Ctrl** *(Windows) or* **Shift+Cmd** *(Mac), and press an arrow key to move the shape.*

5. Save the file and keep it open for the next exercise.

TIP | Outline Creativity with Graphics

One of the many reasons to change type into outlines is to avoid having to send the font to the printer when the file is ready for output, but there are also several creative reasons for converting text to outlines.

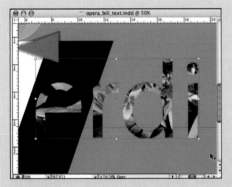

Try placing a picture in the newly created shape. With the **Selection** tool, select the shape "**erdi**." Choose **File > Place**, and pick the image from the images folder in the **chap_09** folder named "**flower.tif**." With the **Direct Selection** tool (white arrow) in the **Toolbox**, click and drag the picture in the shape to position it perfectly! Gradients can also be applied to the new letters shape. Refer to Chapter 7, "*Working with Color*," for details on how to add a gradient.

What Is the Pen Tool?

The **Pen** tool is another feature InDesign has borrowed from Illustrator. In contrast to the drawing tools you have used so far, the **Pen** tool allows for more free-form drawing using points to create paths containing straight and/or curved segments.

The **Pen** tool takes some practice. Those of you who use this tool in other programs like Illustrator, Photoshop, or Macromedia FreeHand may find it easier to use in InDesign. Once you understand the mechanics of drawing shapes with the **Pen** tool, you will learn how to edit them as well.

Pen Tool Paths Explained

The **Pen** tool can be found in the **Toolbox**, along with three path-editing tools, which you will learn about in the "Editing Paths" exercise later in this chapter.

Before using the **Pen** tool, it is important to understand the elements that makes up a path. In this illustration, each of the elements is explained.

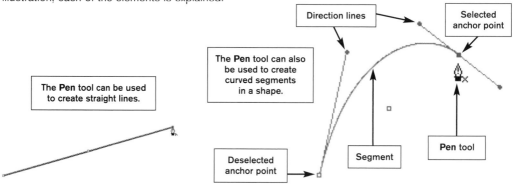

Path Terms	
Path term	**Definition**
Anchor point	Created by clicking with the **Pen** tool. Segments connect anchor points to create the final path. An anchor point can be either a curved or a corner point.
Deselected anchor point	Anchor point that is currently not selected.
Selected anchor point	Anchor point that is currently selected and ready to be edited.
Segment	Connecting path between the anchor points.
Direction line	Controls where and how much to curve a line segment. Direction lines are pulled away from the anchor point by clicking and dragging with the **Pen** tool when the anchor point is created. Think of them as magnets that pull the line toward themselves. The further you pull them out, the more curved the line becomes.

7. ————————Creating Shapes with the Pen Tool

For this exercise, you will get some practice using the **Pen** tool. You will create a tie to go with the bow that is already present in the file.

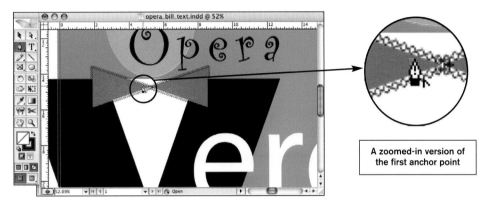

A zoomed-in version of the first anchor point

1. With **opera_bill_text.indd** open from the previous exercise, select the **Pen** tool from the **Toolbox**. Where the two red triangles meet for the center of the bow tie, click off center to the left a bit. This is the first anchor point in the tie you are creating.

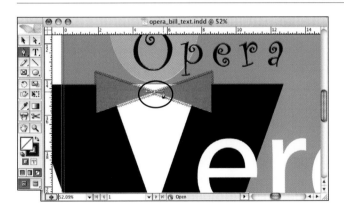

2. With the **Pen** tool selected, move the cursor to the right, into the right red triangle. Hold down the **Shift** key as you click to create the second anchor point of the shape.

*Note: The **Pen** tool easily creates straight lines. Every click and release creates another anchor point. These points control the number of segments in the line or shape. Holding down the **Shift** key creates a perfectly straight horizontal line in this case.*

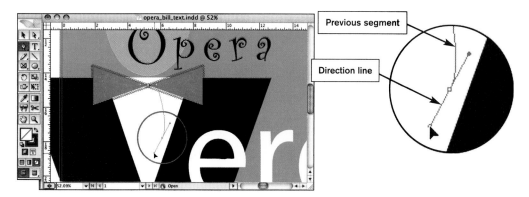

3. With the **Pen** tool, you are now going to create the first curved segment for the bottom of the tie. Move the cursor over the white triangle below the second anchor point you just created. Click, **hold down the mouse button**, and drag away from the anchor point. This creates a curve between the previous anchor point and the new anchor point.

As you drag away, direction lines appear. Always watch how these direction lines affect the previous segment. The further the direction lines are pulled away from the anchor point you just created, the more curved the segments of the path become. In this exercise, you want to drag the direction line to the lower left because the curve is going in that direction next.

*Tip: Make sure you click and **hold down the mouse button** as you drag. Releasing the mouse button while dragging tells InDesign that you are ready to create a new anchor point. If you accidentally release and the anchor point is not up to standards, choose **Edit > Undo** and redraw the anchor point. You can undo one point at a time until the path is gone.*

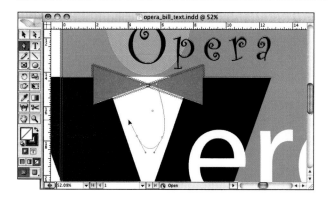

4. With the **Pen** tool, move the cursor to the left, almost even horizontally with the anchor point you just created. Click, hold down the mouse button, and drag away, just as you did for the previous anchor point. This time, the curve needs to go up and to the left a little, so drag the direction line in that direction. You are going to close the shape in the next step.

*Tip: Using keyboard shortcuts, you can edit curves as you draw them with the **Pen** tool. After creating the last anchor point, hold down the **Ctrl** (Windows) or **Cmd** (Mac) key, and bring the end of the **Pen** tool over the end of the direction line pointing upward. With that key held down and the **Pen** tool still selected, you can adjust the direction line, even though you finished drawing the anchor point by letting go of the mouse!*

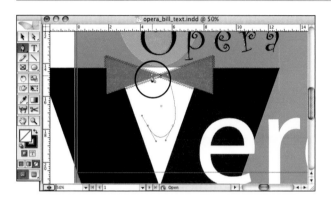
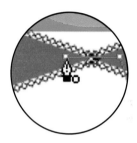

5. With the **Pen** tool, bring the cursor back to the first anchor point you created. When you hover over that point, you see the **Pen** tool cursor change. An "**O**" appears in the lower-right corner of the **Pen** tool icon. The "**O**" indicates that a shape (path) is being closed. Click, and the path becomes a closed shape.

*When working with the **Pen** tool, always watch the **Pen** tool icon, which can change often. Each version of the icon has its own story to tell.*

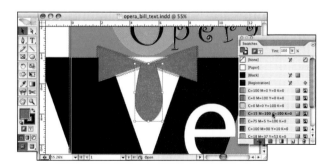

6. The shape should now be complete with a thin black stroke. Choose the **Selection** tool and open the **Swatches** palette. Making sure that the **Fill Box** is selected, click the red color to apply it to the shape.

7. Close the file without saving.

The Direct Selection Tool

The **Direct Selection** tool is used to edit shapes or lines that are already drawn. In conjunction with some of the other shape and path editing tools, which you will learn about in the chart below, you can edit any shape that has anchor points.

As you have seen throughout this book, the **Selection** tool is great for selecting objects, resizing them, and moving them. Notice the bounding box around the circle shape.

The **Direct Selection** tool is used to edit the anchor points of a shape.

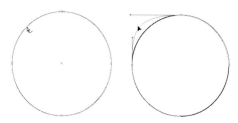

With the **Direct Selection** tool selected, approach a shape segment. You see that a line is added to the cursor. If you click the segment with this cursor and drag, you reshape the segment.

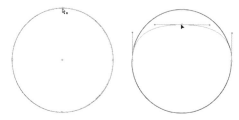

With the **Direct Selection** tool selected, approach an anchor point. Use see that a small box is added to the cursor. If you click the anchor point with this cursor and drag, you reshape the segment by dragging the anchor point.

The Pen Tool Editing Tools

The **Pen** tool has three tools in the menu beneath it that are very useful for editing shapes.

Pen Tool Editing Tools	
Tool and Explanation	**Example**
The **Add Anchor Point** tool adds anchor points to existing shapes. This gives you the ability to create curved and straight segments.	A point was added by clicking on the edge of the shape with the **Add Anchor Point** tool.
The **Delete Anchor Point** tool removes anchor points from a path or shape. When anchor points are deleted, the shape remains as a closed shape.	On the left image the anchor point added is clicked on with the **Delete Anchor Point** tool. The result is on the right.
The **Convert Direction Point** tool changes anchor points from curved to straight and from straight to curved when you click an anchor point in a selected object.	This curved anchor point was converted to a straight anchor point when clicked on with the **Convert Direction Point** tool.

Editing Paths

In this exercise, you will edit a few of the shapes created in the previous exercises using the shape editing tools.

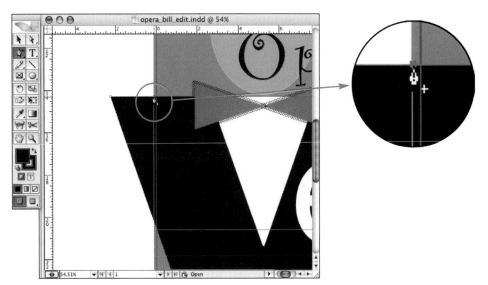

1. Open **opera_bill_edit.indd** from the **chap_09** folder on the **Desktop**. Zoom into the left side of the page with the **Zoom** tool so you can clearly see the left corner of the black triangle. Select the black triangle with the **Direct Selection** tool, and you see its leftmost anchor point. Choose **Object > Unlock Position**, because this object is locked and can't be edited until it's unlocked. Click and hold down the mouse button on the **Pen** tool to access the **Pen Tool** menu. Choose **Add Anchor Point Tool**. Where the bleed guide and the black triangle meet, click with the cursor to add an anchor point.

Why are you doing this? Your goal is to remove the extra black triangle that is outside the bleed guide. It doesn't need that area, so you will add two anchor points and delete the triangle's original corner point to create a "cut off" edge that lines up with the bleed guide.

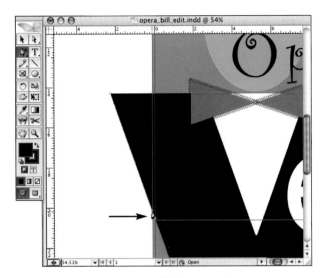

2. With the **Add Anchor Point** tool still selected, bring the cursor to the bottom part of the triangle where it meets the bleed guide. Click to add another point.

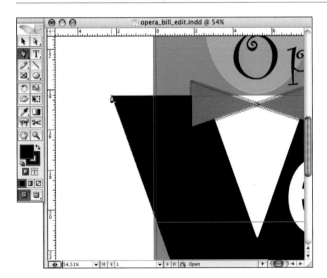

3. Now that the two new points are added, it's time to remove the corner of the triangle. With the triangle still selected, choose **Delete Anchor Point Tool** from the **Pen Tool** menu, and hover over the corner point of the triangle. A minus sign (–) appears. Click, and the point is gone.

*Tip: You can select and delete anchor points with the **Direct Selection** tool, but I don't suggest that. Deleting a point with the **Direct Selection** tool makes the shape an open path, which can have a fill but not a continuous stroke that surrounds the entire shape.*

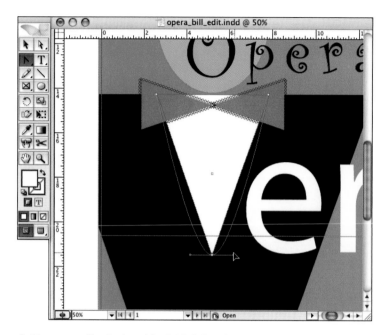

4. Now you will edit the white "shirt." Scroll the page over to the right a bit with the **Hand** tool (hold down the **spacebar** to temporarily see the **Hand** tool) to see the white triangle if you are zoomed in. Choose the white triangle with the **Direct Selection** tool by clicking in the middle of it. The anchor points appear. Select **Object > Unlock Position**, because this object is also locked and cannot be edited as such. Choose **Convert Direction Point Tool** from the **Pen Tool** menu. Click the anchor point at the bottom of the white triangle, hold down the mouse button, and drag the cursor to the right while holding down the **Shift** key to keep the direction lines you pull out perfectly horizontal. This creates direction lines that turn this point into a curve.

Tip: *Clicking back on the same anchor point with the **Convert Direction Point** tool will convert it back to a corner point. Don't do this; otherwise, you will have to drag out the direction lines again!*

5. Close the file without saving.

Placing Graphics into Shapes

One of the more fun things to do in InDesign has to be creating artistic shapes and placing graphics in them. You can place a graphic in any shape using any of a variety of methods. In the Tip titled "Outline Creativity with Graphics," which follows Exercise 6, you learned how to place graphics into text converted to outlines. That is one way to be creative with graphics and shapes. In the following movie, you will learn a few of the methods for placing graphics into shapes.

 MOVIE | Placing Graphics into Shapes

To learn more about graphics and shapes, check out **graphics_in_shapes.mov** in the **movies** folder on the **InDesign CS2 HOT CD-ROM**.

What Are Object Styles?

Object styles are a new feature in InDesign CS2, and a much welcome feature at that. Vector shapes, text frames, and graphic frames can all use stroke, fill, drop shadows, paragraph styles, anchored objects, and more. Object styles are useful for applying the same sets of attributes to several shapes or frames, such as objects with similar formatting or text frames that hold the same style of text formatting (i.e., product descriptions in a clothing catalog). Object styles are similar to type styles because they store formatting as a style that can be used later and controlled from a central location–the **Object Styles** palette. However, object styles are quite different from type styles in the kind of formatting they store.

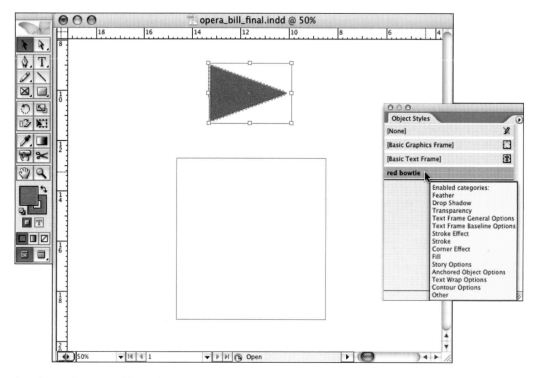

A style can be created based on a selected object, such as the red triangle you added the stroke to earlier in this chapter. By opening the **Object Styles** palette (**Window > Object Styles**) or accessing the **Object Styles** menu from the right side of the **Control** palette, you can, for example, create a style called "**red bowtie.**"

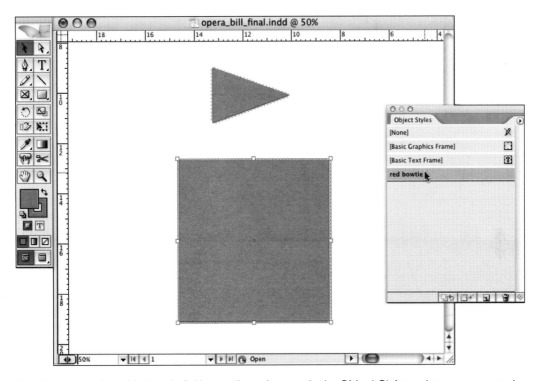

By selecting another object and clicking on the style name in the **Object Styles** palette, you can apply the formatting in the "**red bowtie**" object style to this other object. The **Object Styles** palette is also where you can control the frame tool defaults.

 MOVIE | Object Styles

To learn more about object styles, check out **objectstyles.mov** in the **movies** folder on the **InDesign CS2 HOT CD-ROM**.

Kudos on finishing another chapter! You now know how to create and edit vector drawings in InDesign. Although InDesign's drawing tools will never replace a program like Illustrator, they can add some exciting graphic elements to your designs. In the next chapter, you will learn how to build a more complex document using master pages, multiple pages, and layers.

10

Pages, Master Pages, and Layers

| Adding Document Pages | Working with Nonfacing Master Pages |
| Creating Facing-Page Master Pages and Documents |
| Adding and Changing Automatic Page Numbers |
| Using Text Frames on a Master Page |
| Working with and Overriding Master Objects |

chap_10

InDesign CS2
HOT CD_ROM

Now that you have learned how to work with graphics, type, drawing shapes, and more, you will explore tools for creating long documents with consistent elements such as page numbers and graphics. If you plan to create multipage documents like catalogs, brochures, booklets, and manuals, you will find this chapter especially helpful.

In this chapter, you will learn how to add pages to documents, create and control master pages to apply consistent elements to pages (i.e., page numbers), and edit those elements. You will also become familiar with layers and how they can be used to organize a document.

Facing-Page vs. Nonfacing-Page Documents

InDesign can create two basic types of documents: **facing-page** and **nonfacing-page** documents. It is important to pay attention to what type of document you are working with because it affects how a multipage document functions, particularly a document that uses master pages, as you will learn later in this chapter.

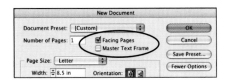

The options for setting up a document with facing or nonfacing pages are found in the **New Document** dialog box, which opens when you choose **File > New > Document**. By default, the **Facing Pages** option is selected. When a check mark appears in the **Facing Pages** check box, InDesign generates a document with two or more pages next to each other—often referred to as a **spread**. Magazines, catalogs, and newspapers are all examples of documents that use facing pages.

A facing-page document (consisting of two pages put together as a spread)

The same document folded to create a newsletter

Facing-page documents are often folded or bound—into a book, pamphlet, or magazine, for instance—using a variety of binding methods (stapled, glued, folded, etc.). They are called facing-page documents because when the page is folded, the two pages face each other. For example, suppose you wanted to create a newsletter that has eight pages, and you want the finished size of the folded newsletter to be 8.5 × 11 inches. You would need to create a document that has two 8.5 × 11-inch pages next to each other for a combined total area of 17 × 11 inches. Together, the two pages make a spread.

When you select the **Facing Pages** option in the **New Document** dialog box, InDesign does two things:

1. Creates a spread composed of two or more pages next to each other.

2. Creates a **Facing Master Page** (a master page consisting of two or more pages, which will be discussed in Exercise 3, "Creating Facing-Page Master Pages and Documents").

Deselecting the **Facing Pages** option generates a document with one or more pages that follow each other vertically on the screen and print as individual pages, such as a multipage proposal or a set of notes to be printed and stapled.

The Pages Palette

In the **Pages** palette, InDesign provides you with the controls and options you need to create long documents, enabling you to work with master pages, check for transparency, and navigate documents.

The **Pages** palette is in the workspace by default. If it doesn't appear, reset the workspace by choosing **Window > Workspace > [Default]**. The **Pages** palette contains master pages (which you will learn about in later in this chapter) and the pages that make up a document. Interestingly, however, much of the power of the **Pages** palette is located in the **Pages Palette** menu.

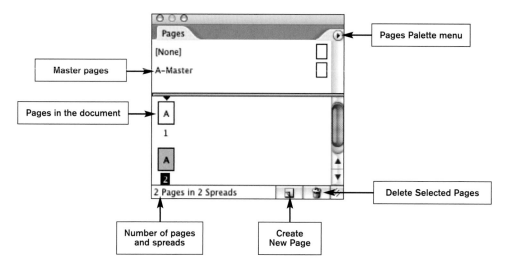

The **Pages** palette in the illustration shows the setup for a nonfacing-page document. The first document you will open in the first exercise is a document with nonfacing pages. The following chart explains the options for the **Pages** palette. In the next section, you will see the **Pages** palette for both a facing-page and a nonfacing-page document. You will also learn about the visual differences between the two types of documents.

Pages Palette Options

Option	Definition
Master Pages	Could be compared to a digital version of stationary, or a template. Consistent elements, such as page numbers, Web addresses, and graphics, usually appear on master pages. When you create a master page, you can apply it to any number of pages in the document. Those pages then "start" with the master objects. If you edit the master page, the associated pages are changed automatically. While the master page does get applied to the pages in the document, it is nonprinting unless you specifically tell InDesign to print the master page by itself.
Pages in the document	Displays the pages in the document. They are shown vertically (as nonfacing pages) in the palette by default. Every page has a number beneath it that indicates its place in the document.
	A page that is gray (or blue, depending on your operating system) is actively selected and can be deleted or moved.
	If the number beneath the page appears white in a black box, it indicates that InDesign considers that to be the page you are working on in the document window.
Number of pages and spreads	Indicates how many pages and spreads are in the document (spreads are defined as two or more pages together, such as a magazine spread).
Create New Page button	Creates new pages.
Delete Selected Pages button	Deletes pages selected in the Pages palette.
Pages Palette menu	Where most of the power in the Pages palette is hidden. As the chapter unfolds, you will learn more and more about the contents of this menu.

How Can You Tell If a Document Is a Facing-Page or Nonfacing-Page Document?

Looking at the **Pages** palette is a dead giveaway for what type of document you are working with.

Nonfacing-Page Document

Facing-Page Document

A nonfacing-page document (the **Facing Pages** option is deselected in the **New Document** dialog box found under **File > New > Document**) has a single page and a single master page called **A-Master**.

A **Facing Page** document (the **Facing Pages** option is selected in the **New Document** dialog box found under **File > New > Document**) has a single page 1 with a line to the left and a folded corner on the page. The master page **A-Master** has two pages and folded corners (sometimes called dog ears).

Note: Leaving the **Facing Pages** option selected when working on a single-page document that doesn't use a master page won't affect the document unless you later need to add pages or use master pages.

I. ——————————Adding Document Pages

In this exercise, you will add a page to a document that begins as a single page. There are many ways to add pages in InDesign. This exercise will lead you through one method.

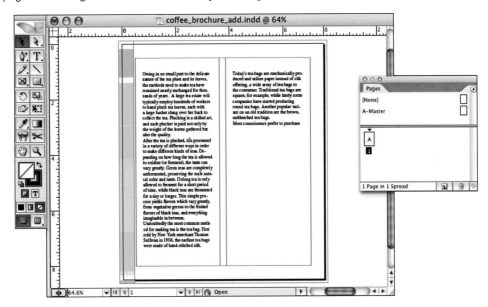

1. From the **chap_10** folder you copied to the **Desktop**, open **coffee_brochure_add.indd**. Also, open the **Pages** palette from the right side of the workspace. Looking at the **Pages** palette, notice that this is a nonfacing-page document (the **Facing Pages** option was deselected in the **New Document** dialog box).

*Note: The **Missing Fonts** dialog box may appear when you open this file. If it does, change the font by choosing **Find Font** and replacing the font with a version of Arial or Helvetica. To learn more about this, visit the Exercise 1 of Chapter 5, "Typography in InDesign."*

2. Choose **Layout > Pages > Add Page** to add a second page to the document. The next illustration will show you what the added page looks like.

*This is a new method for adding pages to an InDesign document in InDesign CS2. It's simple and easy to find. You don't have any control over the number of pages this method adds (it only adds one page every time you choose **Layout > Pages > Add Page**), but you can control where pages are inserted. It adds the new page after the selected page.*

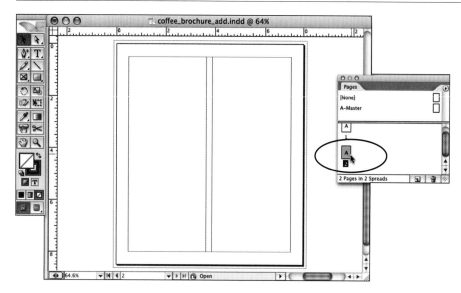

*Looking at the **Pages** palette, you see a second page appear below the original page. After adding the page, InDesign automatically displays the new page in the document window. Pages are listed in order vertically. If you have a document with lots of pages, you have to scroll up and down in the **Pages** palette to find a specific page.*

*The new page is blank, with the column and margin guide settings that were set when the document was originally created (in the **New Document** dialog box found under **File > New > Document**).*

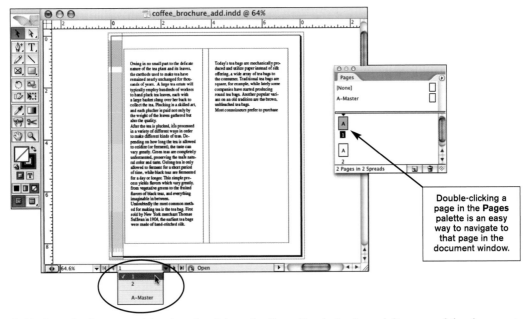

Double-clicking a page in the **Pages** palette is an easy way to navigate to that page in the document window.

3. Navigate back to page 1 by choosing **1** from the **Page Box** in the lower-left corner of the document window. By default, the **Page Box** shows all pages and master pages in the document (master pages will be discussed in the next exercise).

*Notice that page 1 is gray or blue (depending on your operating system), and its number (underneath the icon) is white text in a black box? The white text in a black box for the number beneath the page icon indicates that you are "on" that page (it is displayed in the document window). However, it is important to remember that the page that appears in the document window is not necessarily the selected page. To see which page is selected (and will therefore reflect any edits you make), look in the **Pages** palette. The icons of the selected pages appear gray or blue (depending on your operating system).*

*Tip: To navigate through pages easily, **double-click** a page icon in the **Pages** palette. Be sure to double-click. Clicking a page once in the **Pages** palette just selects that page in the palette; it doesn't show that page in the document window.*

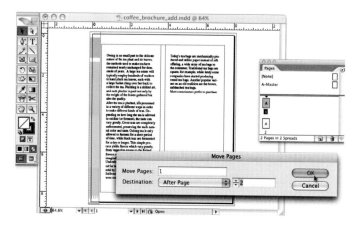

4. Next you will switch the order of page 1 and page 2. Page 2 (the blank page you added in the previous steps), needs to be first because it will be the title page for the document. Check that page 1 is selected in the **Pages** palette, and then choose **Layout > Pages > Move Pages**. The **Move Pages** dialog box appears. The **Move Pages** field should display **1**. In the **Destination** option, **After Page** should be chosen by default; if not, choose it from the **Destination** menu. Make sure **2** is displayed in the field to the right of the **Destination** field, and click the **OK** button to change the page order.

*Note: The page you are moving doesn't have to be selected before you choose **Layout > Pages > Move Pages**. One benefit of selecting the page first, however, is that it automatically enters the page number you are on into the **Move Pages** field. This can be especially helpful when dealing with a long document.*

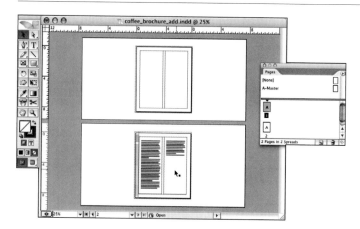

5. Zoom out by pressing **Ctrl+–** (Windows) or **Cmd+–** (Mac) several times. You see the pages as well as the pasteboard (the surrounding gray area). Like the pages listed in the **Pages** palette, the pages in the document window in InDesign are shown vertically. Each page or spread has its own pasteboard as well.

6. Leave the **Pages** palette open and save the file, keeping it open for the next exercise.

TIP | Moving Pages by Dragging in the Pages Palette

In InDesign, an easy way to move a page (change its order in the document) is to drag the page icon in the **Pages** palette to the desired location.

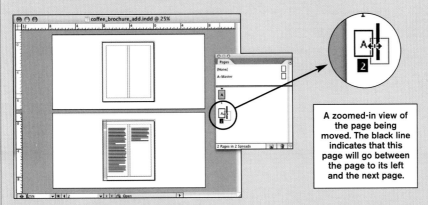

A zoomed-in view of the page being moved. The black line indicates that this page will go between the page to its left and the next page.

With **coffee_brochure_add.indd** still open from the previous exercise and the **Pages** palette open, click the icon of a page you want to move, and drag it to the right of the page icon you want to move it after (it needs to be very close to the right side of the page icon). A black line appears to the right of the page icon, and the cursor changes to a double arrow. The black line indicates that the page is being moved.

Note: As with many tools in InDesign, you need to pay attention to the cursor when you work in the **Pages** palette. As the chapter progresses, you will see several different cursors and what each one means.

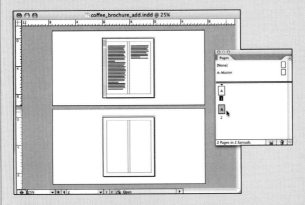

Once you release the mouse button, the page is reordered in the **Pages** palette and in the document window. Choose **Edit > Undo** if you tried this with **coffee_brochure_add.indd** and leave the file open for the next exercise.

What Is a Master Page?

A master page is like a digital version of stationary or letterhead. It creates a template that can be applied to any number of pages before or after the actual content (such as text and graphics) is placed on the individual pages. For instance, the master page for a multipage letter might include the company logo in the header and the company contact information in the footer. These objects automatically appear on the pages you designate.

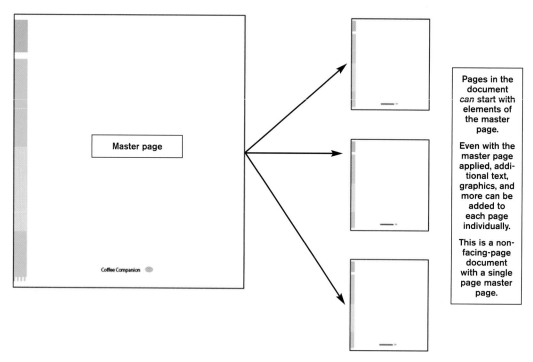

Master page

Coffee Companion

Pages in the document *can* start with elements of the master page.

Even with the master page applied, additional text, graphics, and more can be added to each page individually.

This is a non-facing-page document with a single page master page.

Master pages are great for applying master objects, or objects common to several pages in the document, to multiple pages. The illustration above shows a nonfacing-page document like the one in the **Pages** palette illustration to the right. You will learn about facing-page master pages in Exercise 3, "Creating Facing-Page Master Pages and Documents."

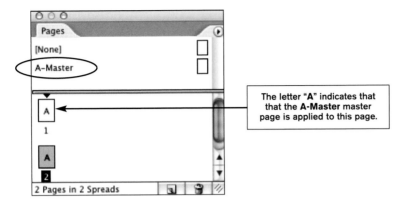

The letter "**A**" indicates that that the **A-Master** master page is applied to this page.

Every document in InDesign starts with two master pages by default. They are called **None** and **A-Master**. By default, the first page of the document has an "**A**" in the middle of the page icon in the **Pages** palette. This indicates that the **A-Master** master page has been applied to that page, so all the master objects on **A-Master** automatically appear on this page.

A-Master is the master page that is applied to every page by default. **None** is a master page that is intentionally blank and useful when a page needs to be blank.

By default, the master page **A-Master** is also blank. The difference between the **A-Master** and **None** master pages is that InDesign allows you to add master objects to **A-Master**, whereas **None** is essentially locked as a blank page.

Master objects can also be added to **A-Master** after a document has been created and worked on. This is useful when a document unexpectedly grows in page count or when you need to add master objects, like page numbers or logos. A document can also contain several master pages, which is helpful when you are creating a long document with several sections, like a clothing catalog that might use one master page for the men's section, and another master page for the women's section. By default, master objects in master pages cannot be moved or edited in the individual pages of the document. They can, however, be edited in the master page itself. Later in this chapter, you will learn how to unlock master objects in individual pages and why you would want to do this.

When creating short documents, adding master objects to **A-Master** is often unnecessary. Often with short documents, it is easier to ignore master pages altogether.

Throughout this chapter, you will use master pages in different situations, helping you to understand how versatile and powerful they can be.

2. ——————————————**Working with Nonfacing Master Pages**

In this exercise, you will create a master page. While master pages may seem confusing or intimidating, rest assured they are a very efficient tool that will make your life easier, not harder. Once you've had a chance to work with them hands-on, you'll see what I mean.

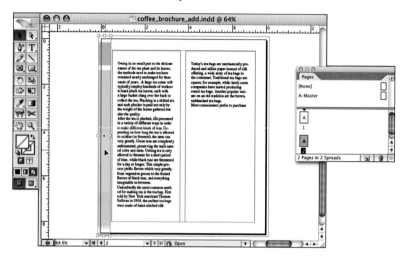

1. With **coffee_brochure_add.indd** open from the previous exercise, and with the **Pages** palette still open, choose the **Selection** tool from the **Toolbox**. Fit the page in the window by choosing **View > Fit Page in Window**, or press **Ctrl+0** (Windows) or **Cmd+0** (Mac). Click the graphic on the left side of page 2 to select it. You are going to move this graphic to the master page called **A-Master** so that it will show up on both pages in the document automatically. Choose **Edit > Cut** to cut the graphic off the page.

*Choosing **Edit > Cut** is necessary because once the graphic is pasted onto the master page, it will display on this page anyway (as a master element). If you don't remove (cut) it from the document page, the graphic will appear on the page twice—as a master element and as a page element.*

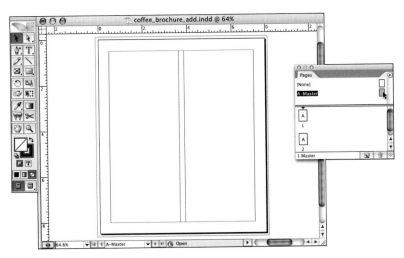

2. To add content to a master page (in this case, the graphic cut from the page in the previous step), you need to go to the master page by double-clicking the **A-Master** page icon or name. A blank page with two columns set for the column guides appears in the document window. This is where you can add master objects. In the next step, you will paste the graphic cut in the previous exercise.

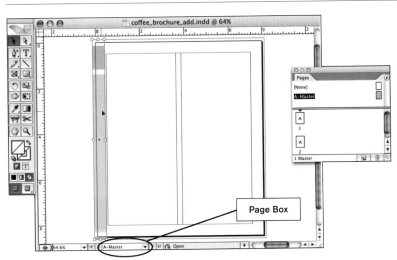

Page Box

3. Once on the master page **A-Master**, choose **Edit > Paste in Place** to paste the graphic cut from the document in step 1 into the same position on the master page.

*Note: When working with master pages, it's important to know what page you are on. Always keep an eye on the **Page Box** (circled in the illustration above) when working with master pages. This indicates which page InDesign considers you to be on.*

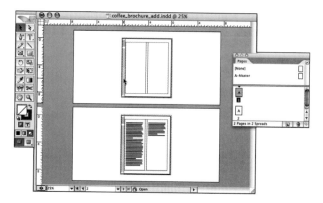

4. Once the master element (the graphic) is in place, double-click the icon for page 1 in the **Pages** palette to return to the document. Zoom out by pressing **Ctrl+-** (Windows) or **Cmd+−** (Mac) until the two pages are visible in the document window. Choose the **Selection** tool from the **Toolbox**. On the first page, click the graphic that now appears on the page. You shouldn't be able to select the graphic because it is a master element and therefore only editable on the master page, not on individual pages. In the next step, you will change the master element on the master page and watch it change on both pages of the document.

Notice that the graphic appears on both pages. Master objects also appear underneath all objects on the pages by default.

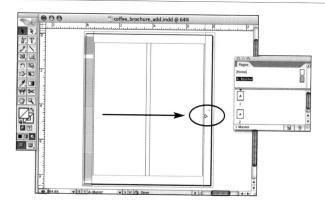

5. To move the graphic, which is a master element, on both pages of the document, you need to return to the **A-Master** page. Double-click the **A-Master** page icon in the **Pages** palette (or choose **A-Master** from the **Page Box** at the bottom of the document window). Choose **View > Fit Page in Window** to zoom into the master page. With the **Selection** tool still selected from the **Toolbox**, hold down the **Shift** key and click/drag the graphic to the right side of the page, lining the graphic up with the bleed guide off the right side of the page. The **Shift** key constrains the movement of the graphic to be exactly horizontal.

Note: Remember to always check that you are on the master page. By default, you won't be able to move master objects, like this graphic, on the pages of the document.

6. Double-click page 1 in the **Pages** palette to return to the first page of the document. You can see the change on both pages by either scrolling down or zooming out by pressing **Ctrl+-** (Windows) or **Cmd+−** (Mac) a few times.

7. Welcome to the power of master pages! Save the document and close it. Leave the **Pages** palette open for the next exercise.

Facing Master Pages

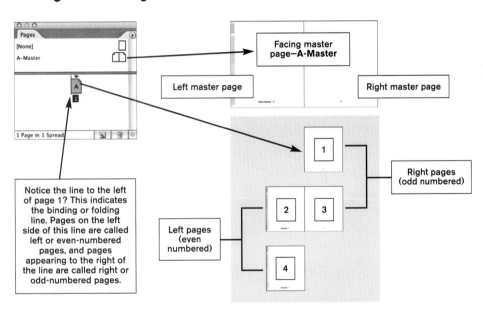

Unlike a nonfacing-page document, which has a nonfacing master page (as you learned in the previous exercise), a facing-page document (a spread or document with two or more pages next to, or facing, each other) has a facing master page. In either case, the name of the master page is **A-Master**.

A facing master page has two pages to it for a reason. It is composed of left and right master pages. Think of it this way: Pick up a magazine, catalog, or book, and more often than not, when you look at a spread, elements like page numbers, company information, and various elements placed in the margins around the pages are different for the left page and the right page. Having a facing-page master page allows you to create a page number in the lower-left and lower-right corners of the spreads. Looking at the illustration above, notice the master page (labeled "**Facing master page – A-Master**"). Looking straight down from the master page, you see four pages, each labeled with a number. Notice the graphic on the left pages (on the left side of the imaginary dotted line). The left master page applies to all the pages to the left of the line in the facing page document in the **Pages** area of the **Pages** palette, and the right master page applies to all the pages on the right side of the line.

3. ———————Creating Facing-Page Master Pages and Documents

Throughout the remaining exercises in this chapter, you will create a facing-page document that will be folded and bound (e.g., stapled). You will also create two facing master pages and work with those masters in the document.

1. Choose **File** > **New** > **Document**.

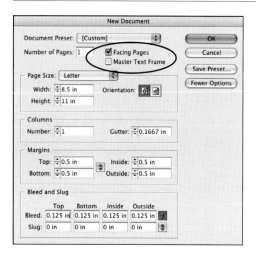

2. In the **New Document** dialog box, leave the **Facing Pages** option checked (if it isn't checked, select it). Leave the **Page Size** field set at **Letter**. (With the **Letter** setting, InDesign automatically sets the **Width**, **Height**, **Columns**, and **Margins** at the default values shown in the illustration above.) Click **More Options** (if you see the **Fewer Options** button instead, the additional fields are already displayed in the dialog box), and set **Bleed** to **0.125 in** (note that you need to type **in** for inches) in the **Top**, **Bottom**, **Inside**, and **Outside** fields. Click **OK** to create the new document.

Note: If the values you see in the New Document dialog box differ greatly from those in the illustration here, you can reset the default values by choosing Default from the Document Preset menu. This will make the values closer to those in the illustration.

3. Once the document is open, choose **File > Save As** and save the document into the **chap_10** folder on the **Desktop** as **coffee_brochure_begin.indd**. The **Pages** palette should still be open from the previous exercise. If not, choose **Window > Pages**, or click the tab on the side of the workspace to open it.

*The **Pages** palette displays a lot of information about the document, including signals telling you that this is a facing-page document. For a refresher on what those signals are, go back to the section titled "How Can You Tell If a Document Is a Facing-Page or Nonfacing-Page Document?" before the first exercise.*

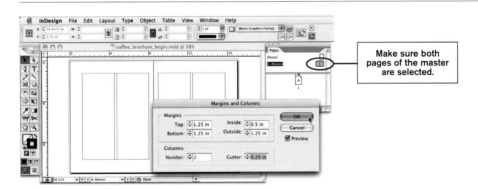

Make sure both pages of the master are selected.

4. This document is going to contain text that flows between pages using text threading. The text will flow into two columns on each page, so two column guides would be a big help. If you recall, column guides are initially set in the **New Document** dialog box when you first set up the document, but often you don't know how many columns you will need at that point. So, while still on the **A-Master** pages, make sure that *both* pages of the master are selected (both page icons in the **Pages** palette should appear gray or blue when selected, depending on your operating system) by clicking the "**A-Master**" name (you could also **Shift+click** on both pages of the master). Choose **Layout > Margins and Columns**. Change the **Number** option in the **Columns** field to **2** and the **Gutter** option to **0.25 in** by either typing the values (you must type **in** for inches) or using the arrows to the left of the fields. This creates two columns for both pages of the master. Change the **Top**, **Bottom**, and **Outside** margin fields to **1.25 in** by typing the value into each field (again, be sure to type **in** for inches) or using the up arrow to the left of the field. Leave the **Inside** margin field at **0.5 in** (type **in** for inches).

You are changing the margins so that the text you place later into this document will fit into those margins. You could leave the margins at the default value of 0.5 inch, but the settings established in Step 4 above leave more room for content around the text you place.

Note: *You can change column guides, margins, gutters, and bleed guides independently for each page of a master spread. You can also set any of the guides to be the same on both pages of the master spread by selecting both the pages in the* ***Pages*** *palette. Before changing the settings, remember to check which page, or pages, are selected. As discussed earlier in this chapter, the pages that are visible in the document window are not necessarily the selected pages. In the* ***Pages*** *palette, the icons of the selected pages appear gray or blue, depending on your operating system.*

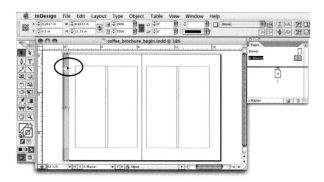

5. Next you will place a graphic that appeared in the previous exercises. Choose **File > Place** and from the **chap_10** folder on the **Desktop**, choose **stripe1.tif** from the **images** folder. Click **Open** to see the loaded graphic cursor. Position the cursor in the upper-left corner of the left master page at the bleed guide. Click to place the graphic on the page.

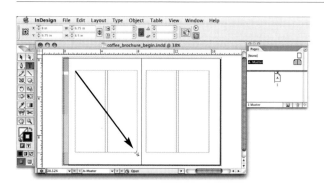

6. Now you will place a text frame on the master page so it will automatically appear on the pages in the document and you can place text in it. Select the **Type** tool from the **Toolbox**. On the left page of the spread, click and drag the cursor starting from the upper-left corner of the margin guide to the lower-right corner of the margin guide.

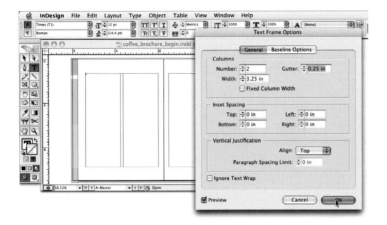

7. Once the text frame is on the left master page, you will change the frame to two columns. With the text frame selected, choose **Object > Text Frame Options**. In the **Text Frame Options** dialog box, change the **Number** field in the **Columns** options at the top of the dialog box to **2** using the arrows to the left of the field. Also, change the **Gutter** field to **0.25 in** (type **in** for inches) so there is a one-quarter-inch space between the columns. Click **OK** to close the **Text Frame Options** dialog box.

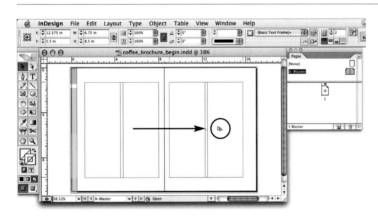

8. To duplicate the text frame, first choose the **Selection** tool from the **Toolbox**. Then hold down the **Alt** (Windows) or **Option** (Mac) key as you click and drag on the frame to create a duplicate and snap it into the margin guides on the right page.

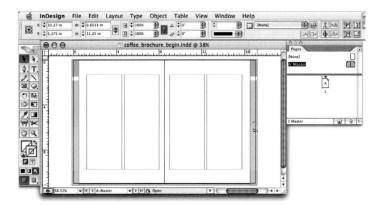

9. With the **Selection** tool chosen from the **Toolbox**, hold down the **Alt** (Windows) or **Option** (Mac) key and click to select the graphic on the left page. Drag the graphic across the spread to the bleed guides on the right page.

*The **Alt** (Windows) or **Option** (Mac) key is used to drag a copy from the original object.*

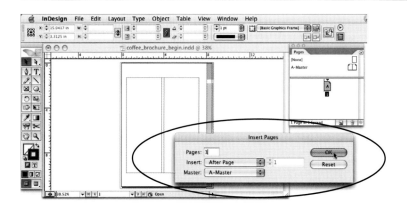

10. With the master objects in place from the previous step, you are going to insert three pages to make a total of four for the document (including the first page already showing). Double-click the first page in the **Pages** palette to see that page in the document window. Choose **Layout > Pages > Insert Pages** to open the **Insert Pages** dialog box. Change the **Pages** field to **3** to add three pages. InDesign will automatically insert the pages after page 1 (the **Insert** field will be dimmed because there is only one page) and apply **A-Master** to the newly added pages. Click **OK** to add the pages.

*The **Master** menu gives you only two options to start with: **None** and **A-Master**. As discussed earlier, the **None** master page is a permanently blank page and can be useful for documents with uncertain layout and content.*

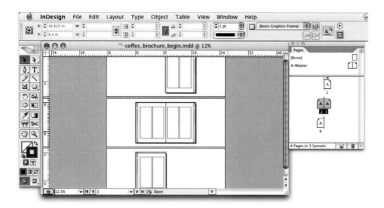

11. Double-click the numbers for pages **2-3** in the **Pages** palette to view the pages in the document. Zoom out by pressing **Ctrl+-** (Windows) or **Cmd+-** (Mac) a few times.

*Throughout this chapter, the **Pages** palette has been removed from the side of the workspace. If it is still collapsed, you can now scroll in the **Pages** area of the palette to see all the pages. If the palette is removed from the side of the workspace, drag the lower-right corner of the palette to open it up and see all the pages.*

12. Save the file and keep it open for the next exercise.

What Are Automatic Page Numbers?

While numbering pages on shorter documents may seem easy enough, the process can become surprisingly complex and time consuming for long documents. Using automatic page numbers, however, can make the task easier.

The first step in creating automatic page numbers is placing the cursor in a text frame and choosing **Type > Insert Special Character > Auto Page Number**. The page numbers are placed either on the pages in the document or, for faster application, on the master page. An automatic page number is a placeholder in a text frame that displays the number that is showing beneath that page icon. That's it. They are very useful because if you ever add a page, the automatic page numbers are always correct.

In this next exercise, you will add automatic page numbers to the **A-Master** page.

4. _____Adding Automatic Page Numbers

In this short exercise, you will add automatic page numbers to the pages of the facing master pages you created earlier.

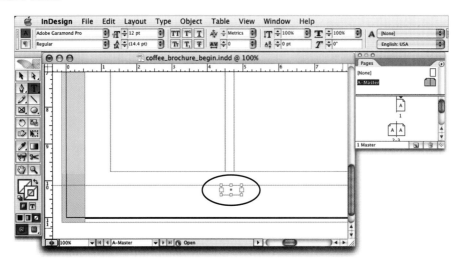

1. With **coffee_brochure_begin.indd** open from the previous exercise, double-click the name "**A-Master**" in the **Pages** palette to open the master in the document window. You may want to zoom in to the bottom of the left master page by selecting the **Zoom** tool from the **Toolbox** and clicking in that area of the document window, since the automatic page number is going on that page at the bottom. While holding down the **Ctrl** (Windows) or **Cmd** (Mac) key, drag a horizontal guide down from the horizontal ruler to around **10.25 in** (look at the **Control** palette to see the **Y** position of the guide). Select the **Type** tool, and create a text frame whose top edge lines up with the newly created guide by dragging out a small frame in the middle of the page at the bottom.

*Note: So far in this chapter, you've been asked to use inches for the units. If the units in your version of InDesign are different, you can change them by choosing **Edit > Preferences > Units & Increments** (Windows) or **InDesign > Preferences > Units & Increments** (Mac).*

*Note: If the rulers are not showing, choose **View > Show Rulers** to see them. Also, holding down the **Ctrl** (Windows) or **Cmd** (Mac) key while dragging a guide creates a guide that goes across the entire spread!*

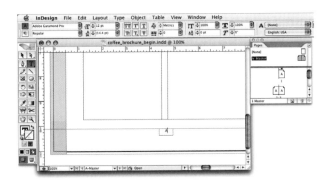

2. With the text frame on the page, it's time to insert the page number. To have InDesign automatically display the correct page number on a page, you need to use an automatic page number. With the cursor in the frame, choose **Type > Insert Special Character > Auto Page Number**. The automatic page number will appear as a letter "**A**." Click the **Align Center** button from the **Paragraph Format Controls** of the **Control** palette to center align the page number.

Why a letter "A"? InDesign looks at the ***Pages*** *palette and sees "A" (for "A-Master") as the page number, so it's displaying "A" as the page number for the* ***A-Master***.

Note: *In previous chapters, you learned about the fitting options found under* ***Object > Fitting*** *or from the right side of the* ***Control*** *palette in the form of buttons. If you attempt to use* ***Object > Fitting > Fit Frame to Content*** *(the only option available), the frame will be too small for the automatic page number.*

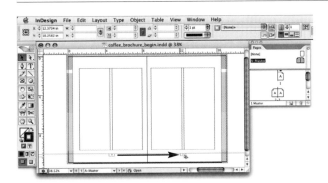

3. With one automatic page number on the page, a second needs to be added to the right page of the master. Fit the spread in the window by pressing **Ctrl+Alt+0** (Windows) or **Cmd+Option+0** (Mac). Choose the **Selection** tool from the **Toolbox**, holding down **Alt+Shift** (Windows) or **Option+Shift** (Mac), click and drag the text frame to the right page of the master. Line the page number up with the middle of the two columns.

Holding down the ***Shift*** *key while dragging off a copy will keep the copied text frame horizontally in line with the original text frame from which you are dragging.*

4. Double-click page 2 in the **Pages** palette to go to page 2 to see automatic page numbering in action (you may need to zoom in using the **Zoom** tool in the **Toolbox**). Looking at all the pages, notice the numbers at the bottom of the pages.

5. Save the file and keep it open for the next exercise. Keep the **Pages** palette open as well.

What Are Numbering and Section Options?

Using the **Automatic Page Numbering** option in InDesign is great for numbering long documents. But what happens when you don't want the pages in the document to be numbered as 1, 2, 3, and so on? For instance, a table of contents may be numbered with lowercase roman numerals (i, ii, iii, etc.) in the beginning of the document. With the automatic numbers in place on the pages (from the master page applied), you can control how the numbering in the document works by choosing **Numbering & Section Options** from the **Pages Palette** menu, which opens the **New Section** dialog box (when a section is first being created) and the **Numbering & Section Options** dialog box (when a section is being edited). In these dialog boxes, sections are created and edited, which are basically page-numbering systems that allow you to determine how the pages in the document are numbered.

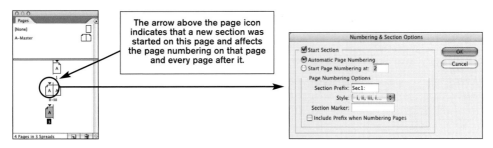

Choosing a page where you want the new section to start is the first step. From the **Pages Palette** menu, choose **Numbering & Section Options** to open the **Numbering & Section Options** dialog box where you set the pagination. InDesign starts the new section (page-numbering system) on that page and continues it through the rest of the document until you start a new section. Once you start a new section on a page, that page has a little black arrow above it to indicate that a new section starts there.

The **Numbering & Section Options** dialog box has many options that are described in the chart below.

Options in Numbering & Section Options Dialog Box	
Option	**Function**
Start Section	Instructs InDesign to start a new page-numbering system, or section, on the page that is selected in the document.
Automatic Page Numbering	Allows InDesign to continue the page-numbering system from the previous pages, and allows you to change the style to roman numerals, letters, and more.
Start Page Numbering at	Changes the page number from the selected page onward.
Section Prefix	Places a prefix on the page in front of the page number. For example, for a table of contents section, the prefix "TOC-" may be used, so the page numbers appear as "TOC-1," "TOC-2," and so on. InDesign places section prefixes by default to differentiate between multiple page numbers (such as two pages numbered 1). The section prefixes start with "SecX," where "X" is the number of the section.
Style	Choose from one of five styles: Arabic numerals (1, 2, 3, etc.), uppercase roman numerals (I, II, III, etc.), lowercase roman numerals (i, ii, iii, etc.), uppercase letters (A, B, C, etc.), and lowercase letters (a, b, c, etc.).
Section Marker	Indicates what text appears in a section marker. See the section titled "Working with Sections" after the next exercise.
Include Prefix when Numbering Pages	Places the text in the Section Prefix field in front of the page number on the pages for this section only.

5. ───────────Changing Automatic Page Numbering

In this exercise, you will change how the automatic numbers that you set up in the previous exercise appear on the pages.

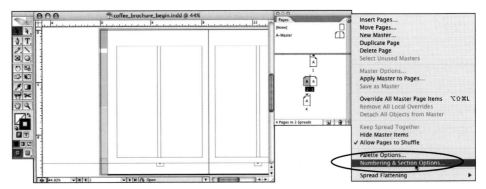

1. With **coffee_brochure_begin.indd** open from the previous exercise, and the **Pages** palette open as well, double-click the page icon for page 2 in the **Pages** palette. From the **Pages Palette** menu, choose **Numbering & Section Options** to open the **Numbering & Section Options** dialog box.

Note: By double-clicking the page 2 icon, you are telling InDesign to start the new section on that page. You can also select the page by clicking once.

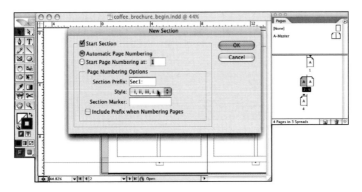

2. When the **New Section** dialog box opens, **Start Section** will be checked by default. By opening this dialog box, InDesign shows that it knows you are going to start a new section. In this example, you are going to change the page numbering style from this page onward to lowercase roman numerals. Choose the lowercase-roman style (i, ii, iii, etc.) from the **Style** pop-up menu. Leave **Automatic Page Numbering** checked so that the numbering continues from the previous section (it will continue to be numbered 2 and 3, but the style will change). Click **OK** to close the **New Section** dialog box.

*Note: When you create a new section, the dialog box that opens when you choose **Numbering & Section Options** from the **Pages** palette menu will be titled **New Section**. If you edit the section later on, the dialog box will be titled **Numbering & Section Options**.*

*Creating a new section can range from changing how the pages in that section are numbered (**Automatic Page Numbering** or **Start Page Numbering At**) to how they look on the page (the style of the number).*

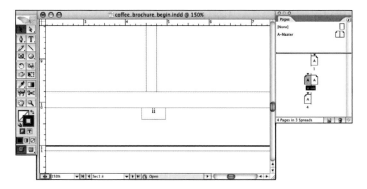

3. Looking at the **Pages** palette, you can see that the new numbering style shows beneath the second page and every page after. The lowercase-roman style also now shows on the pages in the document. On the second page, zoom into the bottom of the page using the **Zoom** tool from the **Toolbox** to see the change. In the next step, you will stop the lowercase-roman style on page four by adding a new section.

*Tip: Notice the black arrow showing above the second page in the **Pages** palette? This indicates that a new section started on this page. Double-clicking this arrow opens the **Numbering & Section Options** dialog box. Although easier than choosing **Numbering & Section Options** from the **Pages Palette** menu again, the black arrow is small and can be difficult to click.*

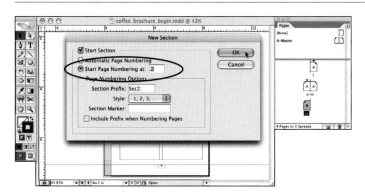

4. To stop the lowercase-roman style on page four, a new section needs to be started. Double-click page 4 in the **Pages** palette to select the page. Choose **Numbering & Section Options** from the

Pages Palette menu to start a new section. In the **New Section** dialog box, select **Start Page Numbering at** and type **2** in the field to the right. This changes the page number to **2** for the page now numbered "**iv**." It also changes the style back to Arabic numbers (1, 2, 3, etc.) by default. Every page after this will use that page-numbering system. Click **OK** to accept the new section and view the new page-numbering system.

*Note the **Section Prefix** value in the **New Section** dialog box. Every time a new section is started, InDesign inserts a new value into this field. You can delete this text if you prefer, but you don't have to. It is there just in case you have two pages numbered **2**, for instance, with the same style applied. If this section prefix is removed, and there are several sections with the same page number and style, InDesign would eventually display a dialog box warning you that two pages have the same page numbers, which may become confusing when printing sections of a document. It's best to number pages uniquely to avoid any potential confusion at a later time.*

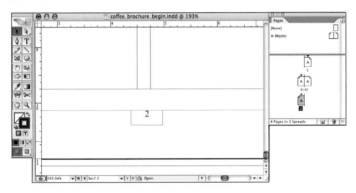

5. Using the **Zoom** tool in the **Toolbox**, zoom into a page number on a right page. The page-numbering system should be working perfectly!

*Tip: To turn off a new section you have created, double-click the black arrow above the page icon where the new section starts. The **Numbering & Section Options** dialog box opens. Deselect **Start Section**, and the numbering section will go away.*

6. Keep the file open without saving (unless you do not want to try the Tip after this exercise, in which case you can close the file without saving). Keep the **Pages** palette open for the next exercise.

TIP | Using Section Prefixes to Your Advantage

In the **Numbering & Section Options** dialog box, the **Section Prefix** allows InDesign to differentiate between different sections when printing, if two section numbers are the same number and style. You can also use **Section Prefix** to your numbering advantage as well.

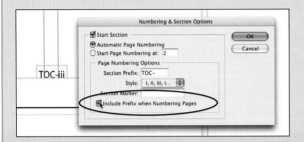

To try it, double-click the black arrow (indicating a section start) above page **ii** in the **Pages** palette. With the **Numbering & Section Options** dialog box open, type "**TOC-**" into the **Section Prefix** field. For the section prefix to appear in the numbers on the pages, you need to choose **Include Prefix when Numbering Pages**. Click **OK**. The section prefix is added in front of the numbers on the pages for this section only. The illustration above shows the dialog box and the changes taking place because the **Numbering & Section Options** dialog box was reopened for illustration purposes only.

Working with Sections

Like automatic page numbering, sections are usually placed on a master page. Sections are useful for information that appears on multiple pages, such as a chapter title, or a magazine section. Section markers can be placed on the master page. **Section markers** are placeholders that are blank on the pages until you tell InDesign what to put in that section marker in the document.

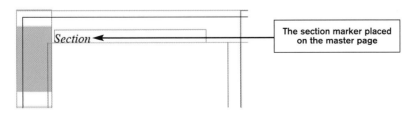

On the master page (**A-Master**, in this example), draw a text frame. With the cursor in the frame, choose **Type > Insert Special Character > Section Marker**. The text "**Section**" appears in the text frame as a placeholder. Apply the styling you would like (character and/or paragraph styling).

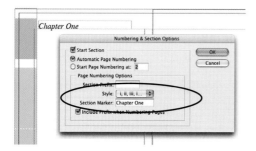

Double-click the black arrow above the icon for page ii in the **Pages** palette. In the **Numbering & Section Options** dialog box, type "**Chapter One**" (or whatever text you want to appear on the page) in the **Section Marker** field, and click **OK** to see it appear on the page. The section marker text frame in the document is empty until you enter the text in the **Section Marker** field.

 MOVIE | Creating Sections

To see an example of how to work with sections, check out **sections.mov** in the **movies** folder on the **InDesign CS2 HOT CD-ROM**.

Why Use More than One Master Page?

A long document with several sections, like a book with multiple chapters, usually needs more than one master page. Each chapter has a chapter name and subtitle that appears on the bottom of the page (called the footer). A master page could be created for every chapter.

A document created with InDesign can have a great many master pages (I have yet to reach the upper limit, creating documents with as many as 200 master pages). Master pages can be created as originals so that they are completely unique, or they can be duplicated from an existing master page or pages and edited as necessary. In the bonus exercise you are going to duplicate the master page **A-Master** and change the positioning of the text.

BONUS EXERCISE | Creating Multiple Master Pages in InDesign

To learn how, check out **multiple_masters.pdf** in the **bonus_exercises** folder on the **InDesign CS2 HOT CD-ROM**.

BONUS EXERCISE | Different Methods for Applying Master Pages

To learn how, check out **apply_masters.pdf** in the **bonus_exercises** folder on the **InDesign CS2 HOT CD-ROM**.

TIP | Using the None Master Page for the Cover

The cover pages on most reports, magazines, or catalogs (for example) have no page numbers and usually have a different appearance than the rest of the document. So it may be beneficial not to have a master page applied to the cover page. In other words, applying the **None** master page to a page will leave that page black to start with and won't add or update master objects because the **None** master page can't have any.

Applying the **None** master page to the first page, using any of the methods described in the previous tip, will leave the first page blank while retaining the margin guides. You are now free to design the cover.

TIP | Sharing Document Pages and Master Pages Between Documents

To share pages or master pages between documents, many people choose **File > Save As** and create a new document, which strips out the unwanted pages and master pages. An easier way to share master pages and pages between documents is to drag them between the two documents.

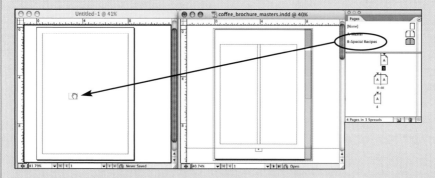

The most efficient way to do this is to tile the two documents next to each other so that both are visible in the document window.

1. With **coffee_brochure_begin.indd** open from the previous exercise, create a new blank document by choosing **File > New**. Make sure that the new document is a facing page document with the same page size (letter).

2. Choose **Window > Arrange > Tile** to tile the two documents side by side.

3. Click in the **coffee_brochure_begin.indd** document window, and open the **Pages** palette if it isn't already open.

4. Click and drag a master spread (by clicking the master name such as "**B-Special Recipes**") into the document window of the new document. That's it! This method allows you to drag selected pages and content as well.

Note: Documents with different page sizes and document types (facing or nonfacing) can share pages and master pages using this dragging method, but be aware when doing this that problems, such as object shifts, can arise.

TIP | Converting a Nonfacing-Page Document to a Facing-Page Document

A document can also be converted from a nonfacing-page to a facing-page document. With the **coffee_brochure_begin.indd** document still open, choose **File > Document Setup**.

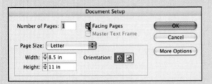

The **Document Setup** dialog box appears. Select **Facing Pages** and click **OK**.

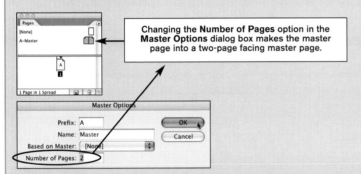

Changing the **Number of Pages** option in the **Master Options** dialog box makes the master page into a two-page facing master page.

The next step is to turn the master page into a facing master page. Click the master name in the **Pages** palette to select the master spread (both pages). **Alt+click** (Windows) or **Option+click** (Mac) the master name, "**A-Master**," to open the **Master Options** dialog box. Change the number of pages to **2** and click **OK**. This converts the master page into a master spread. For a document that has multiple master pages already, you will have to do this to each one.

Note: If you kept **coffee_brochure_begin.indd** open from the previous exercise to attempt these tips, close the file now without saving it.

Basing One Master Page on Another

Like styles, master pages can also be based on one another. This can be helpful for long documents with several master pages that share elements, such as page numbers and text frames.

Suppose you make an original master page (**A-Master**, for example) that you want to change slightly in various ways, saving each variation as a separate master page.

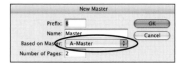

After creating the original, when you create a new master page (called **B-Master**), you can indicate in the **New Master** dialog box that you want to base this new master on **A-Master**. The objects from **A-Master** will appear on the new master page automatically. **A-Master** is the "parent" of **B-Master**. It's like having a master page for a master page, if that doesn't make your head spin.

At that point, any edits made to the "parent" master will be automatically reflected in the "child" master, which is **B-Master** in this example. The **Based on Master** option is a powerful way to maintain consistency for master objects that appear on all master pages, like page numbers or text frames.

MOVIE | Basing One Master on Another

To see an example of how to base one master page on another, check out **based_on_masters.mov** in the **movies** folder on the **InDesign CS2 HOT CD-ROM**.

Master Text Frames

A text frame that is created on a master page and appears on the pages in the document is locked. That doesn't mean that you can't use the text frames in the document, however.

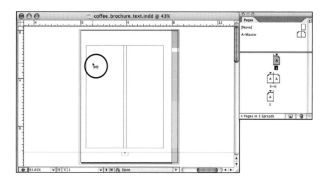

If you place text onto a page in the document and bring the **Loaded Text** cursor over the master text frame, the **Loaded Text** cursor changes to the **Autoflow Text** cursor ( ). If you click with this cursor, the text flows into the master text frame, which then becomes unlocked and usable.

This also means that because text frames will show up on all the pages that have that same master page applied, you can use the semi- and autoflow text placement methods.

6. _____Using Text Frames on a Master Page

In this short exercise, you will place text into a document using master text frames placed on a master page that is applied to the pages. Using text autoflow, you will place four pages of text from a text file into four pages of an InDesign document with one click.

1. Open **coffee_brochure_text.indd** from the **chap_10** folder on the **Desktop**. This has the same content as the file created in Exercise 4.

*Note: The **Missing Fonts** dialog box may appear when you open this file. If it does, change the font by choosing **Find Font** and replacing the font with a version of Arial or Helvetica. To learn more about this, visit Exercise 1 of Chapter 5, "Typography in InDesign."*

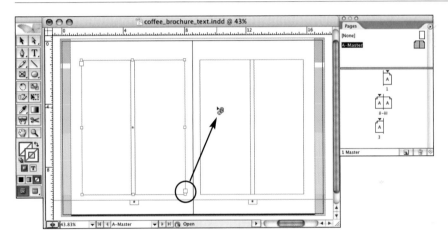

2. Navigate to the master spread by double-clicking the "**A-Master**" label in the **Pages** palette. This should fit the spread into the window. If both pages of the spread aren't visible, choose **View > Fit Spread in Window**. There are two text frames on the pages (as you cre-ated in Exercise 4, "Adding Automatic Page Numbers." With the **Selection** tool from the **Toolbox**, click the text frame on the left page. You are going to thread these two frames together. Click the outport of the left text frame. This gives you the **Loaded Text** cursor. Click the text frame on the right to thread (link) them together.

Note: Threading the two frames together on the master page is setting it up so that when you autoflow text on the pages, InDesign will thread the text between as many pages as it needs to get all the text onto the page.

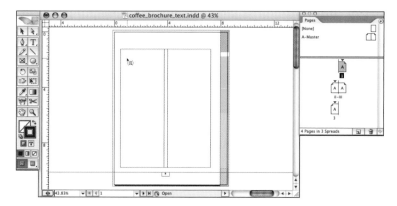

3. Double-click the first master page on the **Pages** palette to show the first page in the document window. Choose **File > Place** to place a text file. From the **chap_10** folder on the **Desktop**, choose **coffee_text.txt** from the **text** folder. Make sure that **Show Import Options** is not selected (it isn't necessary in this case), and click **Open** to see the **Loaded Text** cursor. Hold down the **Shift** key to see the **Autoflow Text** cursor (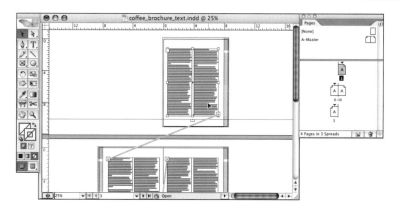). With the cursor over the first column of the first page, click to place the text and have it flow onto the pages.

*Note: When the **Place** dialog box is closed, it may warn you that fonts are missing. If this dialog box appears, choose **Find Font** to see which font it is looking for. Replace any missing fonts with Times Roman or a similar font before opening the file. If the text is highlighted in pink once the document is open, this also indicates that a font is missing. Choose **Type > Find Font** to find and replace the font.*

*Zoom out to see the text and pages. Choose the **Selection** tool from the **Toolbox**, and then click one of the text frames where the text is showing. Choose **View > Show Text Threads** to see how the text frames are linked together.*

4. Save the file and close it.

TIP | Creating Two Pages for the First Spread

When working with facing-page documents, InDesign (and other page layout programs) do something strange to pages. The first page is always alone, and any attempt to drag a page to the left of that first page will be thwarted. There is a way around this, however.

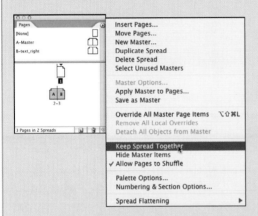

If you want to have a spread instead of a single page, select the second spread by clicking the page numbers (**2-3**, in this example) beneath the page icon in the **Pages** palette. With the pages selected, choose **Keep Spread Together** from the **Pages Palette** menu. This places brackets around the page numbers (**[2-3]**). The pages are now locked together so that InDesign can't split them apart. (This is also another way to make a spread that has three or more pages, for folded pieces and other applications.)

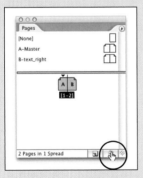

Click the first page to select it, and then click the **Trash Can** icon at the bottom of the **Pages** palette to delete it. The spread in which you set the **Keep Spread Together** command is still together and is now the first spread. Also, notice, in this example that the page numbers have changed to 1 and 2.

TIP | Using the Master Text Frame

When you create a document, InDesign gives you the option in the **New Document** dialog box to create a **master text frame**. A **master text frame** is a text frame that InDesign creates on the master page (facing or not) and is the size of the margin guides. If the document is a facing page, then text frames are created on the left and right master pages and are threaded together.

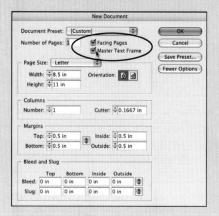

When you create a new document, select **Master Text Frame** in the **New Document** dialog box to start the document with a text frame on the master page. You don't have to use this master text frame, because it is initially locked on the pages in the document. Unless you want to flow text using autoflow, I suggest not selecting **Master Text Frame** when creating a new document.

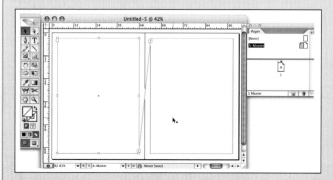

After clicking **OK** to create the new document, go to the **A-Master** master page by double-clicking the name "**A-Master**" in the **Pages** palette (this puts the entire master spread into the document window). Using the **Selection** tool, click in the middle of the left master page to see a text frame appear. Choose **View > Show Text Threads** to see that the selected frame is threaded to a text frame on the right master page. This master text frame is handy when you place a large Word document and want InDesign to make pages for you by using the autoflow feature.

Working with Master Objects

A **master object** is any element that you put inside a master page. When you are working on document pages that are created from a master page, the objects that reside in the master page are not editable in the resulting document. Master objects are locked in the document by default. This doesn't mean, however, that you can't remove or edit them on the pages. Using either menu commands or a shortcut, master objects (such as the page number you added earlier in the chapter) can be edited or removed.

Why would you want to do this? There will be times when a page or spread that is attached to a master page needs something different added, and a master object could be in the way. On that particular page, it would be helpful to remove the master object that is in the way and leave the remaining master objects in place.

There are two ways to "unlock" master objects: overriding master page objects and detaching objects from their master. Both techniques are explained in the sections that follow.

Overriding Master Objects

Using an **override**, you can change the attributes of a master object but leave that master object associated with the master page. For example, there may be a graphic in one spread of a long document, like a magazine, that needs to be different on one page. An override is specific to each attribute of a master object. In other words, if you override a master object, such as a graphic, by changing the color of that graphic in the frame, InDesign defines the override of that master object as pertaining specifically to the object's color but not to any of its other attributes. As a result, if you move that overridden master object on the master page, after you changed the color, the graphic will still move because all the attributes of the object that were not changed continue to update with the master. Attributes of a master object that you can change include stroke, fill, content of a frame, and any transformations (such as rotating, scaling, or skewing).

Detaching Objects from Their Master

On a document page, you can detach (disassociate) a master object from its master. When master objects are detached from their master, it's as if they were created directly on that page. They are no longer associated with the master they started on and won't update if the master object is edited on the master page.

7.————————**Overriding Master Objects**

In this short exercise, you will learn how to edit master objects by changing their association with the master pages.

> **1.** Open **coffee_brochure_final.indd** from the **chap_10** folder on the **Desktop**.
>
> *Note: The **Missing Fonts** dialog box may appear when you open this file. If it does, change the font by choosing **Find Font** and replacing the font with a version of Arial or Helvetica. To learn more about this, visit Exercise 1 of Chapter 5, "Typography in InDesign."*
>
> *Note: A dialog box that indicates **Missing or Modified** graphics may appear when you open this file. If it does, choose **Fix Links Automatically** to update any modified graphics automatically. After fixing the links, close the **Links** palette. If the **Find** dialog box opens, navigate to the **chap_10** folder on the **Desktop** and find the graphic in the **images** folder.*

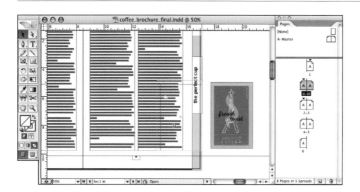

> **2.** Double-click page **iii** of the document in the **Pages** palette. Using the **Hand** tool from the **Toolbox** (or holding the **spacebar** down to temporarily show the **Hand** tool), click and drag the page so you can see the right pasteboard. A graphic is on the pasteboard already. Choose the **Selection** tool from the **Toolbox**. Click and drag the graphic to the left until the right edge of the graphic snaps to the bleed guide. Align the bottom of the graphic with the bottom of the text frame.

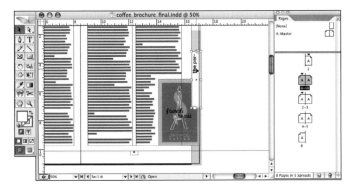

3. Notice the white vertical text frame that is now partly covered with the graphic. This is a master object that now needs to be moved or removed. To remove the text frame from the page, hold down **Ctrl+Shift** (Windows) or **Cmd+Shift** (Mac) and click the text frame. This overrides the master object so that you can make a change to its attributes.

*Note: This is one way to override master objects. The **Pages** palette also has menu options for overriding master objects for an entire page. See the movie at the end of this exercise for more information.*

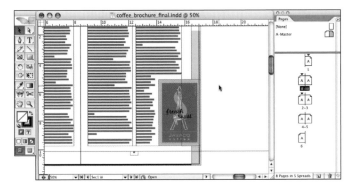

4. Press **Ctrl+Shift+A** (Windows) or **Cmd+Shift+A** (Mac) to deselect all objects. With the **Selection** tool from the **Toolbox**, click on the text frame. Press **Backspace** or **Delete** to remove the text frame completely.

5. Close the file without saving.

 MOVIE | Working with Master Objects

To see an example of how to work with master elements, check out **master_elements.mov** in the **movies** folder on the **InDesign CS2 HOT CD-ROM**.

What Are Layers?

Layers are like transparent pieces of paper that are stacked on top of each other. InDesign documents by default come with a single layer. By adding layers to the document, you can separate content like text, images, and master objects, making it easy to move, manipulate, and turn the visibility on and off for objects on the page.

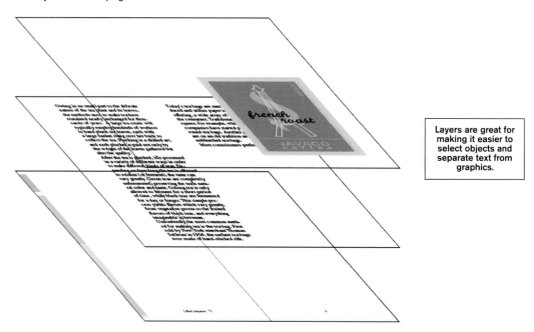

Layers are great for making it easier to select objects and separate text from graphics.

Why would you use layers in an InDesign document? Suppose a team of designers is working with a copy editor on a brochure that has a lot of graphics within several pages of text. The designers can create the document so that the text is on one layer and the graphics are on another. That way the copy editor can turn off the visibility for the graphics layer and concentrate on the text.

I've also created documents with multiple languages (say French and English). You can create one InDesign file with one layer for the English text and another layer for the French text.

The Layers Palette

The **Layers** palette (**Window > Layers**) is where the layers are found. One thing to remember is that you don't have to use layers in InDesign. I know many people who don't because they don't need to separate content.

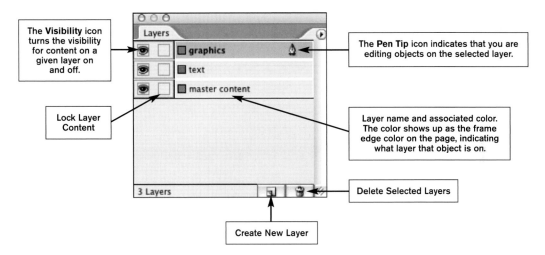

The **Visibility** icon turns the visibility for content on a given layer on and off.

The **Pen Tip** icon indicates that you are editing objects on the selected layer.

Lock Layer Content

Layer name and associated color. The color shows up as the frame edge color on the page, indicating what layer that object is on.

Delete Selected Layers

Create New Layer

MOVIE | Working with Layers

To see an example of how to work with layers in InDesign, check out **layers.mov** in the **movies** folder on the **InDesign CS2 HOT CD-ROM**.

You'll find yourself working often with master pages as you become more experienced with InDesign. I hope this chapter gave you a good foundation in understanding their use and purpose! Professional layout artists couldn't live without this feature, and you'll find it invaluable as you build your own future projects.

11

Working with Tables

| Creating Tables Manually | Editing and Formatting Tables |
| Editing Table Strokes and Fills |
| How Tables and Frames Work Together |
| Placing Tables from Excel |

chap_11

InDesign CS2
HOT CD-ROM

Tables are useful for conveying data in a graphic format, and InDesign provides tools that allow you to create tables of different sizes, shapes, and colors. In this chapter, you are going to learn how to create tables using different methods. Once a table is in place, you will learn how to add design elements to the table by editing its stroke, fill, and content; splitting the table; adding header and footer rows; and more.

What Is a Table in InDesign CS2?

Tables organize information into rows and columns in a gridlike structure. InDesign tables offer similar functionality to Microsoft Word and Excel tables. An InDesign document can include tables created in various ways: you can place a table created in Microsoft Word or Excel (as a Word or Excel document), create a table from scratch in InDesign, or convert text from the InDesign document into a table. In this chapter, you will use all three methods to create tables. The different methods are useful in different situations, and as you proceed through this chapter, it will become clear when each method is appropriate.

First, let's take a quick look at a table.

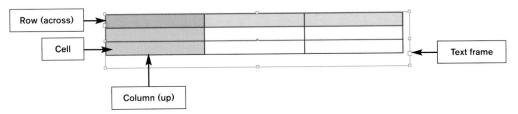

Tables are composed of columns, rows, and cells. Each cell can contain graphics, text, color, or a combination of these elements. Tables are contained within a text frame. They are not considered graphics because they are fully editable inside InDesign CS2, even when placed from other applications. This is one reason they have so many purposes. Tables are usually reserved for data, often the sort of information Excel is great at manipulating, but InDesign tables can be useful for enhancing designs or even laying out pages.

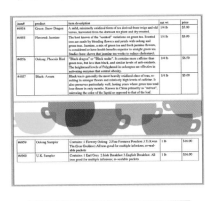

Table that looks like a grid

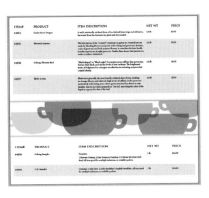

Table with a less obvious grid

A table can contain any number of rows and columns, but it can also be formatted so that the typical grid you see in a program like Excel melts away and you are left with a less obvious, more visually appealing, structure.

When you create a table manually, you can determine the number of rows and columns. This is the easiest way to create a table when you are working with small amounts of text. To do this, you need to use the **Insert Table** dialog box, which is accessed by choosing **Table > Insert Table**. The options in the **Insert Table** dialog box are explained in the chart below.

Insert Table Dialog Box Options

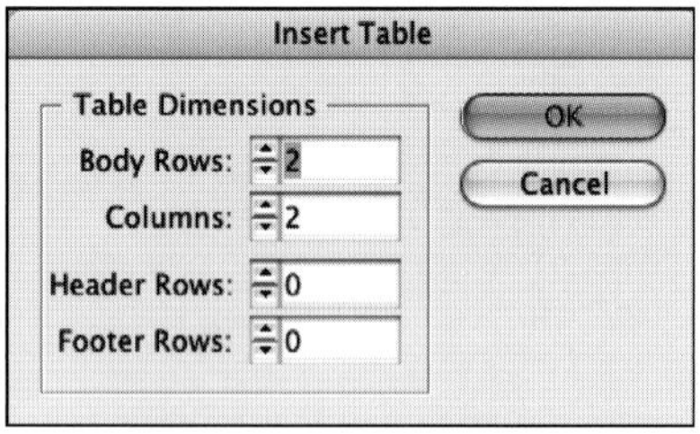

All tables in InDesign documents must be placed into text frames. Therefore, when creating a table, you must first create a text frame, place the cursor in the text frame, and then choose **Table> Insert Table**. The **Insert Table** dialog box is where you will set up the table.

Tables have body rows and columns. The number of each is up to you (you can add or remove rows and columns after the table is made as well).

Header and footer rows are rows at the top and bottom of the table, respectively. They are used for long tables—those spanning multiple text frames or pages—to repeat information at the top or bottom of the table.

I. ————————Creating Tables Manually

In this first exercise, you will create a table by first inserting an empty table and then typing the content into the cells.

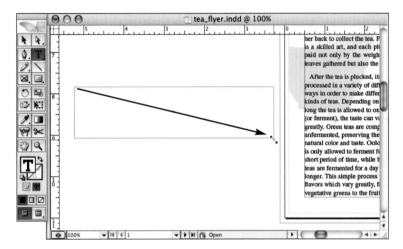

1. From the **chap_11** folder you copied to the **Desktop**, open **tea_flyer.indd**. To create a table on the page, choose the **Type** tool from the **Toolbox**. On the pasteboard to the left of the page, click and drag to create a text frame that will contain the table. It should be about 5 inches in width, but it doesn't have to be exact.

Note: If this file looks familiar, it's because you worked with it in Chapter 4, "Working with Text."

*Note: The **Missing Fonts** dialog box may appear when you open this file. If it does, change the font by choosing **Find Font** and replacing the font with a version of Arial or Helvetica. To learn more about replacing fonts, visit Exercise 1 of Chapter 5, "Typography in InDesign."*

Note: To insert a table, you need a text frame on the page. In this case, you created that frame on the pasteboard because it is easier to work with the table there than on the page. You will move it onto the page later.

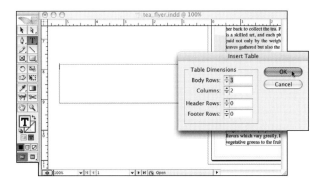

2. The cursor appears in the text frame automatically. Next you will insert the table. Choose **Table >
Insert Table** to open the **Insert Table** dialog box. Use the arrows to the left of the fields to change
the **Body Rows** value to **3** and the **Columns** value to **2**. Click **OK** to insert the table.

*Note: When you create a table, it is automatically made to be the width of the text frame. For a larger
table, make a larger text frame to start. You can always edit any attributes after the table is made.*

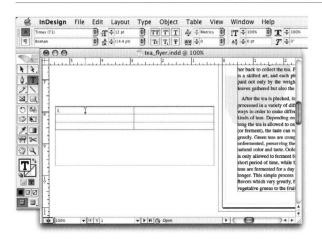

3. Now that you've created the shell of the table, you need to add the content. With the **Type** tool still
chosen from the **Toolbox**, click the upper-left cell to insert the cursor, if the cursor is not already there.
Type "**1**" in the cell.

*Note: Pink may appear in the table, indicating that your machine does not have the default font for
this document. If this happens, you need to change the font by selecting the text and changing the
font in the **Control** palette or by choosing **Type > Find Font**.*

*The height of the cells (rows) is dictated by the default font size set in InDesign, allowing the text to
fit in the cells. By default, all cells have left alignment, just like a text frame, and have borders of 1pt.
around them. As you'll see in the next exercise, you can change all these defaults to suit your needs.*

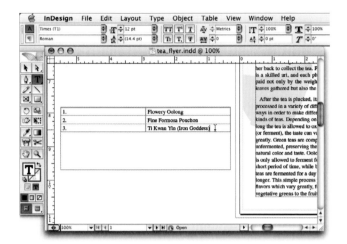

Pressing the **Tab** key when the cursor is in a cell moves the cursor to the next cell to the right. If there are no more cells in the row, the cursor moves to the first cell in the next row.

4. Next you will add content to the rest of the cells. With the cursor in the first cell, move to another cell by pressing the **Tab** key. This moves the cursor through the cells from left to right, top to bottom. In the second cell to the right, type "**Flowery Oolong**." Press the **Tab** key to move to the first cell of the next row, and type "**2**." Press the **Tab** key again to move to the next cell and type "**Fine Formosa Pouchon**." Continue to the last row by pressing **Tab** and typing "**3**." Press **Tab** one last time and type "**Ti Kwan Yin (Iron Goddess)**."

Tip: *When tabbing through cells, you may need to go back to a cell you already passed. Press* ***Shift+Tab*** *to move the cursor backward through the cells. Of course, you can just click in a cell to place the cursor in it!*

Note: *Be careful when tabbing through cells! When you reach the very last cell of a table, if you press the* ***Tab*** *key again, InDesign adds a new row. This can be good or bad, depending on what you are expecting.*

5. Save the file and keep it open for the next exercise.

The Control Palette

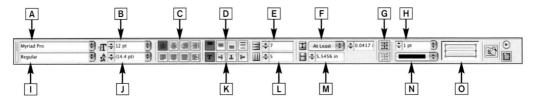

The chart below describes the features in the **Control** palette that appears when a cell is selected, or when any part of the table is selected.

	Option	Function
Control Palette Options for Tables		
A	Font Family	Determines the font family for the selected text or cell(s).
B	Font Size	Determines the font size for the selected text or cell(s).
C	Horizontal Alignment	Determines the horizontal alignment of content of cells.
D	Vertical Alignment	Determines the vertical alignment of content of cells.
E	Number of Rows	Determines the number of rows in a selected table.
F	Row Height	Determines the height of the selected row(s). The associated pop-up menu has two choices: **At Least** and **Exactly**. Rows expand to fit text vertically when **At Least** is chosen. **Exactly** maintains the row height as content is added.
G	Merge Cells	Merges selected cells together.
H	Stroke Size	Determines the size of the stroke on selected cell(s).
I	Font Style	Determines font style (bold, italic, and more).
J	Font Size	Determines font size.
K	Rotate Text	Rotates content of selected cell(s).
L	Number of Columns	Determines the number of columns in a selected table.
M	Column Width	Determines exact width of selected column(s).
N	Stroke Style	Determines the stroke style (dashed, dotted, and more) for selected cell(s).
O	Proxy Preview Area	Determines which strokes (borders) of selected cell(s) will be affected when the stroke style and size are changed.

The Table Palette

The **Table** palette (accessed by choosing **Window > Type & Tables > Table**) contains much of the basic formatting for the structure of a table, including the number of rows and columns, width and height of rows and columns, alignments of cell content, inset spacing, and more. The **Table** palette and the **Control** palette share a lot of formatting options. I don't use the **Table** palette as much as the **Control** palette, but it's your choice. To change table properties in the **Table** palette, the cursor must be placed in one of the cells of the table.

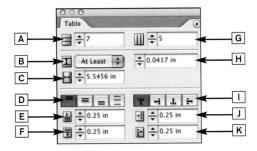

The chart below explains each of the options in the **Table** palette.

Table Palette Options		
	Option	**Description**
A	Number of Rows	Determines the number of rows in the table.
B	Row Height	Determines the height of the selected rows. When the cursor is in one cell of the table, this option determines the row height for that row only. Also, the pop-up menu offers the options of **At Least** and **Exactly**. The field to the right of the pop-up menu determines the height. Every row defaults to at least the height of the text size. Cells expand to fit text vertically when **At Least** is chosen. **Exactly** maintains the row height as content is added.
C	Column Width	Determines the width of the selected columns. When the cursor is in one cell of the table, this option determines the column width for that one column.
D	Alignments (Vertical)	**Top**, **Center**, **Bottom**, and **Justified** vertical alignments of the contents of selected cells.
E	Top Cell Inset	Insets the content a set amount from the top edge of the cell.
		continues on next page

	Table Palette Options *continued*	
	Option	**Description**
F	Bottom Cell Inset	Insets the content a set amount from the bottom edge of the cell.
G	Number of Columns	Determines the number of columns in the table.
H	Row Height field	This field, to the right of the pop-up menu, also determines the height of the selected row. A number is typed into this field determining whether the row height is exactly or at least that measurement.
I	Rotate Text	Rotates text within selected cells by 0, 90, 180, or 270 degrees.
J	Left Cell Inset	Insets the content a set amount from the left edge of the cell.
K	Right Cell Inset	Insets the content a set amount from the right edge of the cell.

Selecting Rows, Columns, and Cells in a Table

Selecting tables, cells, rows, and columns is made easier with some shortcuts. When editing tables, you will need to be able to select portions of a table or the whole thing. For more information on this, check out **table_selection.pdf** in the **bonus_exercises** folder on the **InDesign CS2 HOT CD-ROM**.

2. —————————**Editing and Formatting Tables**

In this exercise, you will learn how to edit and format the table that you created in the last exercise by changing the widths and heights of rows and columns as well as cell alignments, adding rows and columns, and merging cells. Remember, once you've created a table, you can always modify it.

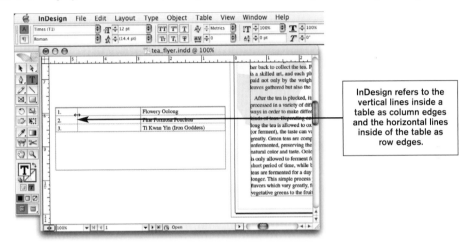

1. With **tea_flyer.indd** open from the previous exercise, you will now edit the table. With the **Type** tool still selected from the **Toolbox**, hover the cursor over the vertical line separating the two columns. A double arrow appears ( ), indicating that you can drag the column width to change it. This also works for row heights. Hold down the **Shift** key, and click and drag the column edge to the left. The **Shift** key keeps the table the same width while you are changing the width of the columns to the left and right of the column edge you are dragging.

*Note: If you just drag a column edge without holding down the **Shift** key, the width of the table will change.*

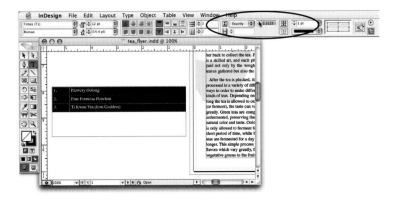

2. Next you will change the height of the rows to a set value and to give the text a little "breathing room" in the cells. With the **Type** tool, click in the first cell, and drag the cursor across diagonally through the table. By dragging through cells, you select them. In the **Control** palette, the table formatting options will appear after you've selected one or more cells. From the **Row Height** pop-up menu, choose **Exactly**. To the right of the pop-up menu is the **Row Height** field. Use the arrows to the left of the field to increase the height of the rows to **0.3125 in**.

*By default, the row heights in a table are set to **At Least**. This means that the row heights are always at least as high as the type size that is set as the default. Cells automatically expand vertically when more text is added. Setting the **Row Height** to **Exactly** sets the height at a fixed value, which means that InDesign will not automatically increase the height of the selected rows as more content is added to a cell in that row.*

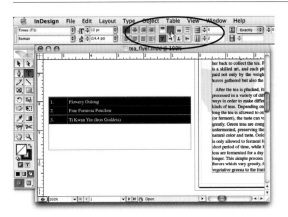

3. With the cells still selected, you will change the vertical alignment within the cells. This will affect all of the content (which is just text right now). In the **Control** palette, click the **Align Center** button.

Every cell could have a different horizontal or vertical alignment. By selecting them all, you will change them all at the same time.

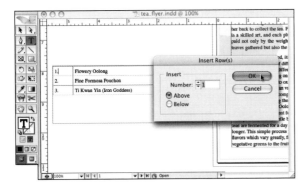

4. Now you will add a row at the top of the table to give the table some context. Click in the first cell in the upper-left corner of the table. Choose **Table > Insert > Row**. In the **Insert Row(s)** dialog box, leave the **Number** field at **1** and leave the **Above** option selected. With these settings, InDesign inserts a new row above the row the cursor is in.

Tip: When you insert a row or column this way, the new row or column copies the formatting of the row or column the cursor is in. This means that the new row or column has the same alignment, row height, font, and more.

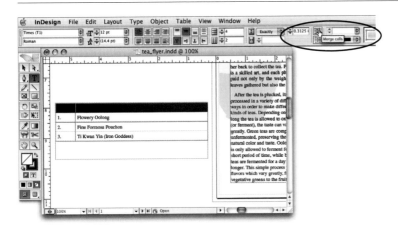

5. Next you will merge the cells together to form a single cell so that you can type a headline above the other three rows. With the **Type** tool selected from the **Toolbox**, click and drag from the first cell through the second cell to select them both. In the **Control** palette, click the **Merge Cells** button to merge the selected cells.

6. In the newly merged cell, type "**Nationally Ranked Teas (America's Favorites)**."

7. Choose the **Selection** tool from the **Toolbox**, and click and drag the table text frame onto the page until the left edge snaps to the left margin guide. Exact vertical placement is not important right now.

Note: *When the table is moved onto the page, it appears above the text in the first few columns.*

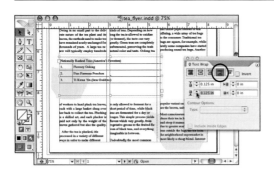

8. Open the **Text Wrap** palette by choosing **Window > Text Wrap**. The frame the table is in can have text wrap applied. With the table's frame still selected, in the **Text Wrap** palette, click the **Jump Object** button (circled in the illustration above). Change the both **Top Offset** and **Bottom Offset** to **0.125 in** so that the text pushes away from the table at the top and bottom.

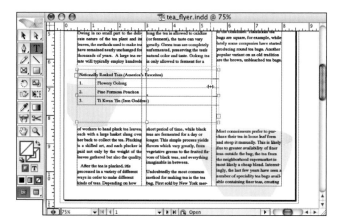

9. Select the **Type** tool from the **Toolbox**, and click and drag the right edge of the table to make it fit into the column guide as shown in the illustration above. The column edge snaps to the column guide, and only the column to the left of the column edge is resized.

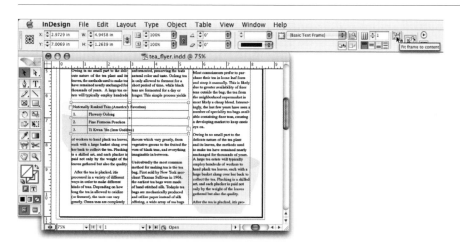

10. Choose the **Selection** tool from the **Toolbox**, and with the table's frame still selected, click the **Fit Frame to Content** button in the **Control** palette. The frame should now fit snugly around the table.

11. Save the file and close it.

NOTE | Overset Cells

When you set the row height to **Exactly**, as you did in Step 2, the rows remain that height and will not expand automatically when new content is added.

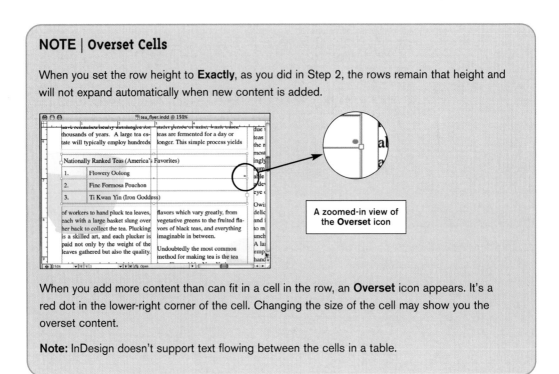

A zoomed-in view of the **Overset** icon

When you add more content than can fit in a cell in the row, an **Overset** icon appears. It's a red dot in the lower-right corner of the cell. Changing the size of the cell may show you the overset content.

Note: InDesign doesn't support text flowing between the cells in a table.

Understanding Table Options

In addition to editing and formatting tables to ensure that the content of the cells fits properly and the table is the correct proportion and size, you will also want to change the strokes and fills of the cells to make the table both functional and attractive.

With the cursor in a cell, choosing **Table > Table Options > Options** and then selecting one of the five options, such as **Table Setup**, opens the **Table Options** dialog box. This dialog box is full of formatting options for the entire table. The options control the look and feel of the whole table and are organized within five tabs. The names of the tabs correspond to the options available in the **Table > Table Options** menu, and when you choose, for instance, **Table > Table Options > Table Setup**, the **Table Options** menu opens with the **Table Setup** tab displayed.

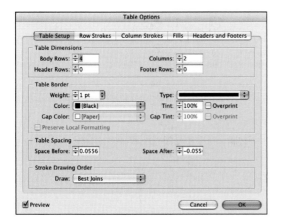

Each tab in the **Table Options** dialog box performs specific functions, as described in the chart below.

Table Options Dialog Box	
Tab	**Function**
Table Setup	Contains many of the formatting options available in the **Control** palette and **Table** palette, such as the number of rows and columns and the number of header and footer rows.
	You also have the ability to control the border of the table (the perimeter or outside border), as well as table spacing before and after the table if you paste or place into the middle of text in a frame.
	The **Stroke Drawing Order** option determines the order in which the strokes are applied to columns and the rows are drawn.
Row Strokes	Changes the strokes of the rows or horizontal edges of the cells. Stroke patterns (every other row, and more) or custom strokes may be applied with ease to the entire table.
Column Strokes	Changes the strokes of the columns or vertical edges of the cells. Stroke patterns (every other row, and more) or custom strokes may be applied with ease to all of the column strokes in the table.
Fills	Determines the fills of the rows or columns for the entire table. Fill patterns (every other row, and more) or custom fills may be applied with ease to all of the rows or columns in the table.
Headers and Footers	Creates new first and last rows in a table, respectively, that repeat information across threaded tables.

Understanding Cell Options

Selecting one or more cells and choosing **Table > Cell Options** and then selecting one of the four options (such as **Text**) opens the **Cell Options** dialog box with the tab corresponding to the option you chose displayed. This dialog box is full of formatting options for selected cells. The formatting options include text alignments and insets, strokes and fills, row and column height and width, as well as the placing of diagonal lines in any selected cells.

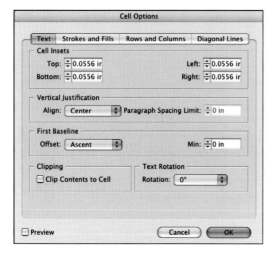

Each tab in the **Cell Options** dialog box performs specific functions, as described in the chart below.

Cell Options Dialog Box	
Category	**Function**
Text	Controls the cell insets and vertical justification for selected cells (as explained in Exercise 2), and allows you to clip the content of a cell (helpful when a graphic is too big) and rotate the content (text and graphics) in a selected cell.
Strokes and Fills	Allows you to control the stroke of a selected cell (each cell edge independently) and the fill color of the selected cell(s).
Rows and Columns	Determines the row height or column width for a selected cell.
Diagonal Lines	Places diagonal lines in cells in a variety of ways to indicate such things as blank cells or as a placeholder for showing which cells will contain graphics (for example).

The order in which you apply either the table options or the cell options can be important. If you first apply table formatting and then select a cell or cells and apply cell options, the cell options override any options that conflict with the table options. If you apply cell options to a cell or cells first, the table options will override any options that conflict with the cell options.

Row Strokes vs. Column Strokes

However obvious it may seem, before beginning the next exercise, it is important to have a crystal clear understanding of the difference between row strokes and column strokes.

The illustration below shows examples of each.

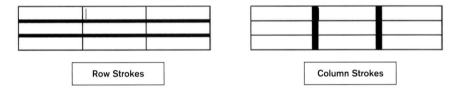

Row Strokes   Column Strokes

Both row strokes and column strokes are added using the **Table Options** dialog box. The row strokes and column strokes that the **Table Options** dialog box will affect are contained within the border of the table. The outer perimeter, or border, of the table is not affected. The border can be changed on the **Table Setup** tab of the **Table Options** dialog box.

3. _____Editing Table Strokes and Fills

In the previous exercises, you set up the table to fit into a two-column area with the text on the page flowing around the table. In this exercise, you will change the appearance of the table by editing the strokes and fills of individual cells and the entire table, beginning with changing the cell inset for specific cells.

> **1.** Open **tea_flyer_final.indd** from the **chap_11** folder on the **Desktop**. This file looks exactly like what you should end up with at the end of the last exercise. To more easily see the table formatting options in this exercise, choose **View > Hide Frame Edges** (if they are not already hidden) so that you can preview the formatting without seeing the blue borders associated with a frame.

> _Note: The **Missing Fonts** dialog box may appear when you open this file. If it does, change the font by choosing **Find Font** and replacing the font with a version of Arial or Helvetica. To learn more about replacing fonts, visit Exercise 1 of Chapter 5, "Typography in InDesign."_

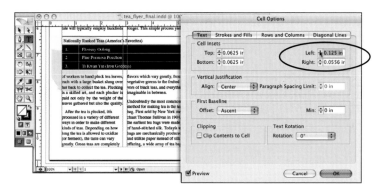

> **2.** Select the **Type** tool from the **Toolbox,** and click and drag across the second, third, and fourth rows in the table to select those cells (see the arrow in the illustration above). Choose **Table > Cell Options > Text** to open the **Cell Options** dialog box with the **Text** tab displayed. In that dialog box, increase the value of the left cell inset to **0.125 in** by clicking on the arrows to the left of the **Left** field. Click **OK** to close the dialog box.

> _The cell inset pushes the content of the cells in from the cell edges. All the cell edges can be controlled independently._

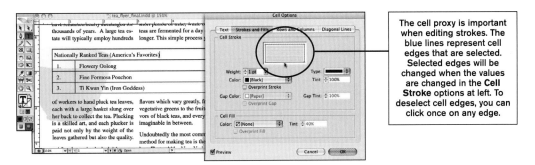

The cell proxy is important when editing strokes. The blue lines represent cell edges that are selected. Selected edges will be changed when the values are changed in the **Cell Stroke** options at left. To deselect cell edges, you can click once on any edge.

3. With the **Type** tool, click in the top cell of the table. This allows you to change the cell options for that single cell. Choose **Table > Cell Options > Strokes and Fills** to open the **Cell Options** dialog box again, this time with the **Strokes and Fills** tab displayed. The top cell has a stroke on all four edges. You are going to remove the stroke from the left, top, and right edges of the cell. To do this, click once on the bottom edge of the cell proxy (circled in the illustration above). This deselects the bottom edge and allows you to edit the other three edges. When the stroke is deselected, it turns from blue (selected) to gray (deselected). Leave this dialog box open for the next step.

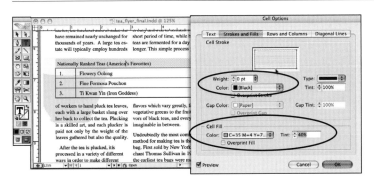

4. Change the weight of the three selected cell edges in the **Cell Stroke** options to **0 pt** by choosing **0 pt** from the **Weight** pop-up menu. Make sure that **Preview** is checked so you can see the changes take place. Also, change the color of the cell in the **Cell Fill** options by choosing the light green at the bottom of the **Color** pop-up menu. Change the tint of the color fill to 40 percent by pressing the **Shift** key and clicking several times on the down arrow to the left of the **Tint** field until **40%** appears (unless already set). Click **OK** to accept the changes and close the **Cell Options** dialog box.

*The cell options you are using are only affecting the cell that the cursor is in. In the next step, you will control formatting for the entire table at once using the **Table Options** dialog box.*

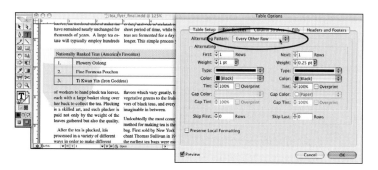

5. With the cursor still in the first cell, you will now change the formatting for the entire table. Choose **Table > Table Options > Alternating Row Strokes** to open the **Table Options** dialog box with the **Rows and Strokes** tab displayed. From the **Alternating Pattern** pop-up menu, choose **Every Other Row**. With this option you can change the strokes of all the rows in the table (the horizontal cell edges). Check **Preview** to see the changes happen.

*Using the **Table Options** dialog box is a great way to apply formatting to the table as a whole, rather than selecting cells and applying formatting bit by bit. I see a lot of tables with every other row or every other column a different color, forming a pattern. For tables that contain a lot of repetitive formatting like that, the **Table Options** dialog box is very useful.*

*Note: You need to plan how the table you are editing is going to look. It's usually easiest to apply the overall formatting for the table with the **Table Options** dialog box first. Then you can go to any cells that need special formatting and edit those with the **Cell Options** dialog box. That way, the table options don't override the cell options. In a few steps, you will learn a trick to overcome the override problem.*

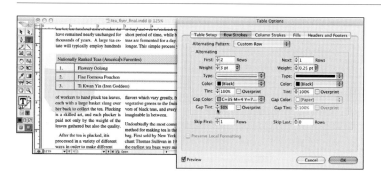

6. Now it's time to change the row strokes. The row strokes affect the row edges inside the table border only. Change the **First** field to **2** by clicking the arrows to the left of the field. This tells InDesign which rows to affect (starting at the row edge below the first row). Change **Weight** to **3 pt** and **Type** to **Thin – Thin**. Change **Gap Color** to the light green you chose in Step 4, and change **Gap Tint** to **50%** so the color between the lines isn't too dark. Finally, in the **Skip First** field, change the setting to **1** to tell InDesign to skip the row stroke for the row containing the text that begins "**Nationally Ranked**."

Among their many uses, row strokes are a very effective way of separating content like a header row from the body of the table. You may find that, although you understand the theory of using strokes, in practice you still need to try several different formats before you can decide on the best one. You can always come back into this dialog box later to edit any of the row strokes you have chosen.

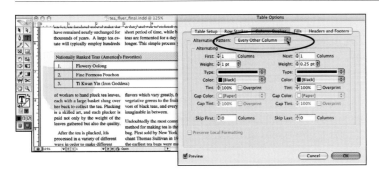

7. The next step is to change the column strokes to visually separate the number column from the tea name column. Click the **Column Strokes** tab, and choose **Every Other Column** from the **Alternating Pattern** pop-up menu. This option affects the column strokes (vertical cell edges inside of the table border). Leave this dialog box open for the next step.

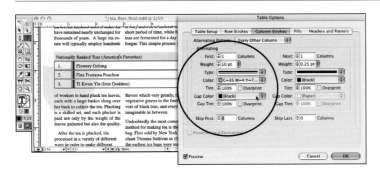

8. Only one column stroke in this table will be affected, so leave **1** in the **First** field. Change the weight of the column stroke to **10 pt** by choosing **10 pt** from the pop-up menu to the right of the **Weight** option. Change the type of stroke by choosing **Thick – Thin** from the **Type** pop-up menu. Change **Color** to the light green used previously, and choose **Black** from the **Gap Color** pop-up menu. Leave the **Table Options** dialog box open for the next step.

*At this point, the **Preview** option should still be selected. Column strokes, just like row strokes, can be set up in patterns (such as every second column). The **Next** options in the **Column Strokes** and **Row Strokes** tabs (on the right side of the dialog box) control what would happen with the next column stroke (for instance) after the first was applied. InDesign applies the column strokes starting from the leftmost column edge and working its way to the right, depending on how you set it up.*

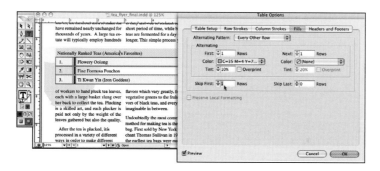

9. To fill the cells with color, click the **Fills** tab. In this dialog box, InDesign allows you to fill the rows with color, starting with the top row in the table. From the **Alternating Pattern** pop-up menu, choose **Every Other Row**. In the **Alternating** section of the dialog box, you have two color areas to work with: **First** and **Next**. **First** dictates the color of the first row, and **Next** is the color of the next row. The alternating pattern then repeats the colors for every other row. In the **First** field, leave the setting at the default of **1**, and change **Color** to the light green color used elsewhere in the table. Also, change the tint to **10%** by holding down the **Shift** key and clicking the down arrow to the left of the **Tint** field. Under the **Next** field, make sure **Color** is **None**. To skip the first row of the table (since you already applied formatting to it in Step 4), change the **Skip First** field to **1**. Leave the **Table Options** dialog box open for the next step.

*Once again, the options available under the **Fills** tab are a great way to apply formatting to a table quickly and uniformly. Tables can almost always be read more easily when alternating rows have different fill colors. Besides, this can be fun to experiment with!*

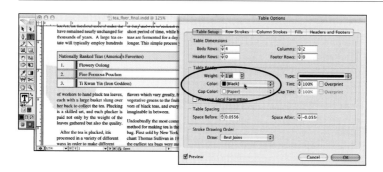

10. Click the **Table Setup** tab. Now you will change the border of the table. In the **Table Border** options, change **Weight** to **1 pt** and make sure **Color** is set to **Black**. This applies a 1 pt black border to the outside of the table (the perimeter). Leave the **Table Options** dialog box open for the next step.

Note: The table border you apply here overrides the cell edges you set to 0 pt in Step 4 of this exercise. In the next step, you will learn how to retain previously applied formatting.

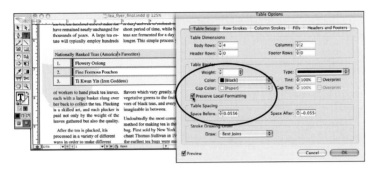

11. Click the **Preserve Local Formatting** option. You will notice that the border remains on the table, except around the top cell. Click **OK** to accept the changes you've made and close the **Table Options** dialog box.

*You will notice the **Preserve Local Formatting Option** in almost all the tabs in the **Table Options** dialog box. This is your secret weapon when you've gone through the process of applying cell formatting first (or formatting you did with the **Table** or **Control** palette before coming into the **Table Options** dialog box). It will honor that formatting, which would otherwise be removed.*

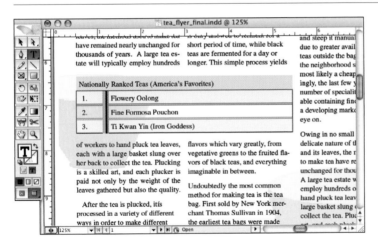

12. The table should be complete. Save the file and close it.

MOVIE | Editing Strokes and Fills

To see an example of editing the strokes and fills for a table, check out **tables.mov** in the **movies** folder on the **InDesign CS2 HOT CD-ROM**.

TIP | Using the Stroke Proxy More Effectively

The **Control** palette, the **Stroke** palette, and the **Table** and **Cells Options** dialog boxes all include a proxy you can use to select cell edges. When the lines are blue in the proxy, they are selected. When they are gray in the cell proxy, they are deselected.

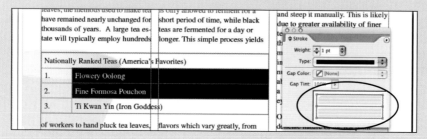

On the cell proxy, double-click any outside line to select the entire outer rectangle. Double-click any inside line to select the inside lines. Triple-click anywhere in the cell proxy to select or deselect all lines.

BONUS EXERCISE | More on Tables

You can create tables from text. To learn how, check out the **text_to_table.pdf** in the **bonus_exercises** folder on the **InDesign CS2 HOT CD-ROM**.

You can also thread tables across pages. To learn how, check out the **threading_tables.pdf** in the **bonus_exercises** folder on the **InDesign CS2 HOT CD-ROM**.

InDesign also lets you add header and footer rows to tables. To learn how, check out the **header_footer.pdf** in the **bonus_exercises** folder on the **InDesign CS2 HOT CD-ROM**.

How Tables and Frames Work Together

When you create a table using the **Insert Table** command (**Table > Insert Table**, which you used in the first exercise) or by converting text, the table is the width and height of the text frame. For example, a table with five columns will appear with five evenly spaced columns spread across the width of the text frame. The fact that tables are always in text frames by default can lead to some interesting effects. As with text, a table within a text frame can be overset, meaning that the table may not fit into a single text frame.

Once the table is created, resizing the text frame width has no effect on the table. As shown in the illustration above, a table can literally hang outside the text frame. But, if the text frame that contains a table is too short (in vertical height), the rows that fall outside the height of the text frame will be overset, and the red plus will appear in the lower-right corner of the frame.

If you extend the frame to meet, or exceed, the height of the table, the remainder of the table will appear, and the red plus will disappear.

Placing Tables from Other Programs

Tables can be placed or copied into InDesign text frames from Microsoft Excel and Word. More often than not, you will receive an Excel spreadsheet that you then need to use in InDesign. The easiest way to get the table into InDesign is to place the spreadsheet directly.

You can also copy and paste a table from Word or Excel. By default, the table that you select in either of those applications is pasted as unformatted tabbed text. But if you plan to cut and paste from either of those programs and want to keep the formatting, you can change the format in which InDesign pastes the table (tabbed text or formatted table). To learn more about this, see the **Tip** titled "Changing Table-Pasting Options."

When you place Word documents with tables in the text, the tables are placed in the same position in the text in InDesign as they were in Word. This places a text frame that contains a table inside the main text frame. It is still fully editable and can be cut out if you don't want it to appear.

Excel Table Import Options

When placing Excel files, it is a good idea to check **Show Import Options** in the **Place** dialog box (**File > Place**). This opens the **Microsoft Excel Import Options** dialog box. You can then decide both what portions of the table to place as well as whether or not to retain the table's original formatting.

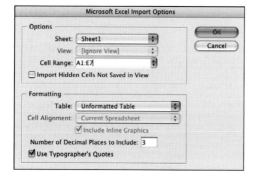

The **Microsoft Excel Import Options** dialog box options are described in the chart on the next page.

Microsoft Excel Import Options	
Option	**Function**
Sheet	An Excel spreadsheet can be brought in one worksheet at a time. This is where you choose which sheet to place in InDesign.
View	Only activated when a custom view was saved in the Excel file. (custom view is an option in Excel).
Cell Range	You can specify the range of cells to place. All cells with content are included in that range by default.
Table	Specifies the format in which the table will be placed. Options are **Unformatted Table** (still a table with no fills or strokes), a **Formatted Table** (maintains formatting applied in Excel), or **Unformatted Tabbed Text** (no table, just text with tabs to indicate where the columns were).
Cell Alignment	Changes the default alignment in the cells to left, right, or center when the **Formatted Table** option is selected.
Include Inline Graphics	Determines whether to keep or remove any graphics placed in the table cells when the **Formatted Table** option is selected.

Word Table Import Options

When you're importing Word documents, tables included in the documents are brought in. How they are brought in (as formatted tables or tabbed text) depends on the options set in the **Microsoft Word Import Options** dialog box. This dialog box appears when you place a Word document and select **Show Import Options** in the **Place** dialog box (**File > Place**).

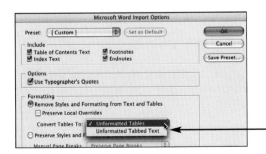

Word tables are brought in with formatting by default. To remove the table formatting, you select **Remove Styles and Formatting from Text and Tables**, which strips the table formatting or turns the table into unformatted text.

5. ——————————**Placing Tables from Excel**

In this short exercise, you will place a table from Excel into a document.

1. Open **product_excel.indd** from the **chap_11** folder on the **Desktop**.

*Note: A dialog box that indicates **Missing or Modified** graphics may appear when you open this file. If it does, choose **Fix Links Automatically** to update any modified graphics automatically. After fixing the links, close the **Links** palette. If the **Find** dialog box opens, navigate to the **chap_11** folder on the **Desktop** and find the graphic in the **images** folder.*

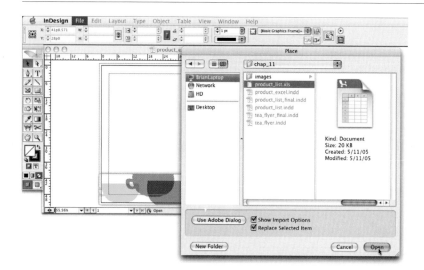

2. With the file open, choose **File > Place** to open the **Place** dialog box. Navigate to the **chap_11** folder on the **Desktop** and select **product_list.xls**. Select **Show Import Options** and click **Open** to see the import options for an Excel file.

*Note: On the Windows platform, if you don't see the file in the list, choose **All Files** from the **Files of Type** pop-up menu.*

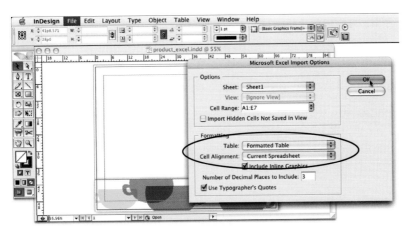

3. The **Microsoft Excel Import Options** dialog box opens. In the **Formatting** section, choose **Formatted Table** from the **Table** pop-up menu. Click **OK** to see the **Loaded Text** cursor in the next step.

*Note: The **Missing Fonts** dialog box may appear when you place this file. If it does, change the font by choosing **Find Font** and replacing the font with a version of Arial or Helvetica. To learn more about replacing fonts, visit Exercise 1 of Chapter 5, "Typography in InDesign."*

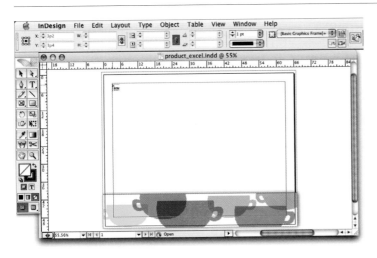

4. Move the **Loaded Text** cursor icon to the upper-left corner of the margin guides. Click to place the table, which you will see in the next step.

5. With the table on the page, select the **Type** tool from the **Toolbox**. Click in the text frame to the right of the table. From the **Paragraph Formatting Controls** in the **Control** palette, click the **Align Center** button to align the table in the center of the text frame.

6. Save the file and close it.

TIP | Resizing Tables

InDesign offers two techniques for changing the size of a table. First, using the **Selection** tool, position the pointer over the lower-right corner of the table frame so the pointer becomes an arrow. Hold down **Ctrl+Shift** (Windows) or **Cmd+Shift** (Mac), and drag to increase or decrease the table size.

This will not only change the table size but scale the content as well. Holding down the **Shift** key ensures that all the content and the table are scaled proportionally.

Here's another method. Using the **Type** tool, position the pointer over the lower-right corner of the table so that the pointer becomes a double arrow, hold down the **Shift** key, and drag to increase or decrease the table size.

This will change the table size, but the content (type, in this case) won't change in size.

TIP | Changing Table-Pasting Options

As mentioned earlier, when you place a Word table in InDesign (**File > Place**), the formatting applied in Word comes into InDesign with the table by default. However, when you copy a table from Word or Excel and paste it into an InDesign document, the formatting is lost by default.

Before choosing **Paste**, choose **Edit > Preferences > Type** (Windows) or **InDesign > Preferences > Type** (Mac) to open the **Text** options of the **Preferences** dialog box.

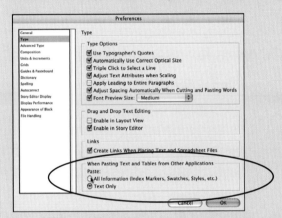

In the **Preferences** dialog box, select the **All Information (Index Markers, Swatches, Styles, etc.)** option to paste all the table formatting.

NOTE | Placing or Pasting Charts and Graphs from Excel or Word

Graphs or charts will not come into InDesign as part of an Excel or Word document you place. You can copy/paste these items from those applications, but they are converted to low-resolution graphics that are embedded. To place a graph or chart that is part of an Excel document you are placing into an InDesign document, I suggest creating a PDF of the graph or chart from the Excel document and placing that into InDesign. Excel has a function that takes a chart or graph from a file and puts it into a separate worksheet. You can then make a PDF from that worksheet. To place a graph or chart from Word, just copy and paste the chart or graph into a new document and create a PDF from that.

Another chapter down! You now have a basic understanding of working with tables. Since tables come in many forms and from several applications, understanding how InDesign handles them, and how you can manipulate them, is important.

I2

Transparency

| Applying Drop Shadows | Using Blending Modes |
| Applying Transparency | Feathering in InDesign |
| Placing Transparent Graphics from Photoshop |

chap_12

InDesign CS2
HOT CD-ROM

Before InDesign CS, using transparency in page layout programs typically required workarounds, because few, if any, page layout programs could handle transparency natively. For instance, transparent overlays and text could be saved as TIFF or EPS files and placed into a page layout program as images. While this works and is still useful for complex pieces that include multiple layers of transparency, the transparency built into InDesign offers a remarkable time-saver for the simpler features, such as applying a drop shadow to a graphic.

In this chapter, you will learn all about the various methods InDesign offers for creating transparency, including object transparency (with blending modes), drop shadows, feathering, and native transparency from programs like Adobe Photoshop and Illustrator. You will also learn the best practices for using transparency that can be output effectively.

The Chapter Project

In this chapter, you will apply different types of transparencies and apply them across multiple objects.

To see the finished product, from the **chap_12** folder on the **Desktop**, open **flowershow_final.indd**. Each flower has a different type of transparency applied. Close the file after looking at it.

What Is Transparency?

Transparency is often defined as changing the opacity of objects (making objects partially or completely see-through), which can include text, graphics, and shapes. Although this is correct, InDesign expands on that definition by adding drop shadows and feathering. In addition, InDesign can work with opacity changes (transparency) made directly in InDesign or created in other Adobe applications, like Photoshop, and brought in as native file formats (such as PSD files).

InDesign has the ability to apply transparency (such as drop shadows or changed opacity) because the program can support what is called **native transparency**. This essentially means that InDesign understands and can display and output transparency created within InDesign or imported from a program like Photoshop in a transparent graphic or shape.

Note: Keep in mind that InDesign's native transparency support doesn't negate the potential for disaster when outputting complex transparencies—transparencies applied to multiple objects, objects with several layers of transparency, and more. In this chapter, you will learn how to check for transparency as well as learn the tools involved in properly outputting that transparency.

How Can You Tell That Transparency Is Present in a Document?

Before sending a document for output, it is important to understand whether transparency has been applied and where.

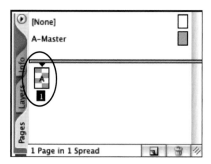

To see where transparency is applied in a document, open the **Pages** palette, which may be docked on the side of the workspace. If the palette is not docked, choose **Window > Pages** to open it. In the palette, you can scroll to find a page with a checkerboard pattern in it. This checkerboard indicates that transparency is applied somewhere on that page. For documents with facing pages (spreads), InDesign applies the checkerboard pattern to the entire spread in the **Pages** palette, even if only one of the pages in the spread contains a transparent object. Remember, InDesign considers objects with drop shadows, feathering; placed transparent objects; and objects in which transparency or opacity has been changed to be transparent objects, so pages that use any of those features will show the checkerboard as well.

To view transparent objects in a document, open **flowershow_transparent.indd** from the **chap_12** folder on the **Desktop**.

*Note: The **Missing or Modified** dialog box may appear when you open this file. If it does, choose **Fix Links Automatically** to update any modified graphics automatically. After fixing the links, close the Links palette. If the **Find** dialog box opens, navigate to the **chap_12** folder on the **Desktop** and find the graphics in the **images** folder.*

Open the **Pages** palette from the side of the workspace or by choosing **Window > Pages**. Notice the first-page icon has a checkerboard pattern. This indicates that transparency in some form is applied to something on the first page. Close the document when done.

While this is a very useful way of locating transparency, InDesign offers other ways as well. In the last few exercises of this chapter, you will learn about other ways to view where transparency is being used.

What Is a Drop Shadow?

A drop shadow is shading that appears behind a selected object to make it look as though it is three-dimensional. Most drop shadows are gray to black in color and somewhat see-through, or semitransparent (you will learn about opacity changes in transparency in the second exercise).

The drop shadows created in InDesign closely resemble those made in Photoshop. Because InDesign supports transparency, the shadows look and print remarkably well. In the illustration of the red flower above, both the yellow glow around the red petals and the dark shadow beneath the yellow shape in the center of the flower were applied using InDesign's Drop Shadow feature.

Next, you will learn how to apply drop shadows in InDesign. Later in the chapter, you will learn how to output them and how to recognize some potential trouble spots.

The Drop Shadow Dialog Box

A drop shadow can be applied to any object, including graphics, frames, shapes, text, and lines. The **Drop Shadow** option can be found by choosing **Object > Drop Shadow**.

To apply a drop shadow, your first step is to select the object.

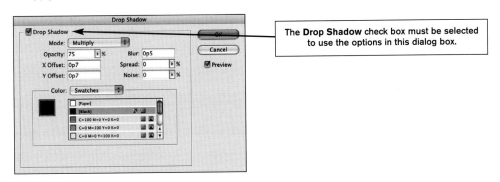

The **Drop Shadow** check box must be selected to use the options in this dialog box.

The **Drop Shadow** dialog box provides a wealth of options for creating drop shadows. These options are explained in the chart below.

Drop Shadow Dialog Box Options	
Option	**Description**
Mode	Applies a blending mode to the object. See the beginning of the next exercise to fully understand blending modes.
Opacity	Sets the amount of transparency (how see-through the drop shadow is) applied to the shadow. The range is from **0%** (completely transparent) to **100%** opaque.
X Offset	Offsets the shadow along the x-axis (horizontally). A positive value offsets the shadow to the right, and a negative value offsets the shadow to the left.
Y Offset	Offsets the shadow along the y-axis (vertically). A positive value offsets the shadow down, and a negative value offsets the shadow up.
Blur	Determines the size of the blur and how blurred the edge of the shadow becomes. A larger **Blur** value pushes the shadow edge further away from the object to which the drop shadow is applied.
Spread	Sets the opacity of the shadow within the range of the blur. A **Spread** value of **100%** makes the shadow a solid, and a **Spread** value of **0%** makes the shadow less visible.
Noise	Adds noise, or artifacts, to the shadow. Noise breaks apart the shadow into specks or dots.
Color	Determines the color of the shadow. Colors can be chosen from three color modes: RGB, CMYK, and Lab. By default a list of existing swatches from the Swatches palette appears.

I. ———————————————Applying Drop Shadows

In this first exercise, you will use a document that has several graphics already on the page to begin to learn how to apply different methods of transparency to graphics, shapes, and text.

1. Open **flowershow_begin.indd** from the **chap_12 folder** on the **Desktop**.

Note: A dialog box that indicates **Missing** or **Modified** graphics may appear when you open this file. If it does, choose **Fix Links Automatically** to update any modified graphics auto- matically. After fixing the links, close the **Links** palette. If the **Find** dialog box opens, navigate to the **chap_12** folder on the **Desktop** and find the graphics in the **images** folder.

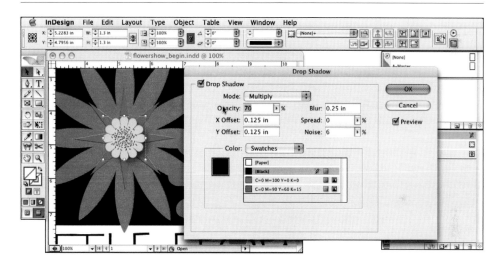

2. You may want to zoom in a bit to the red flower with the yellow center by using the **Zoom** tool in the **Toolbox**. With the **Selection** tool selected from the **Toolbox**, click the yellow cen- ter of the red flower (as shown in the illustration). This graphic was brought in from Photoshop. With the yellow graphic selected, choose **Object > Drop Shadow** to open the **Drop Shadow** dialog box. Turn on the drop shadow (always the first step) by clicking the **Drop Shadow** option at the top of the dialog box. Keep the **Drop Shadow** dialog box open to set up the drop shadow in the next step.

*The **Preview** option in the **Drop Shadow** dialog box is not checked by default. Checking the **Preview** option is sticky, which means it stays the next time you open the dialog box. As long as the dialog box is not obstructing the object, **Preview** enables you to see any changes to the drop shadow as you are making them.*

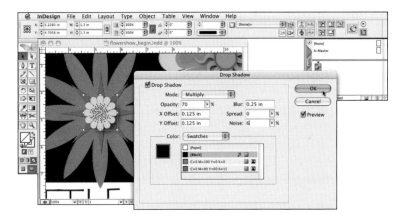

3. With the **Drop Shadow** dialog box open from the last step, change the **Opacity** setting to **70%** by either typing the number in the field or by selecting the arrow to the right of the **Opacity** field and moving the slider that appears. Leave **Offset** at its default setting, change **Blur** to **0.25 in** (type the number into the **Blur** field), and set **Noise** at **6%** (by typing the number into the field or using the slider to the right of the field). Leave the color of the shadow as **Black**. Click **OK** to accept the shadow and close the **Drop Shadow** dialog box.

*Note: To edit a drop shadow, select the graphic and choose **Object > Drop Shadow** to open the **Drop Shadow** dialog box and make changes.*

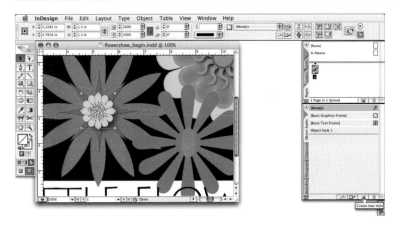

4. With the dialog box closed and the yellow graphic still selected, open the **Object Styles** palette. You learned about **Object Styles** at the end of Chapter 9, "*Vector Artwork*." In this exercise, you are going to create an object style so that the drop shadow you created in the last step can easily be shared with other objects (in this document, the pink center of the purple flower on the page). In the **Object Styles** palette, click **Create New Style** at the bottom of the palette. This creates **Object Style 1** in the palette.

5. Double-click the style named **Object Style 1** to edit the settings for the style.

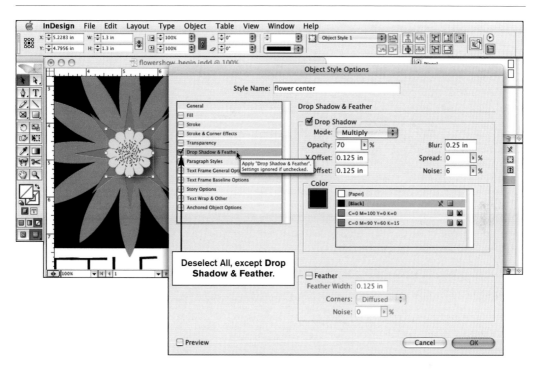

6. In the **Object Style Options** dialog box that opens, all the features that can be saved in an object style are listed. The only feature you want to save in this style is the drop shadow you just created. Deselect all the check boxes to the left of the option names except for **Drop Shadow & Feather**. Then click the **Drop Shadow & Feather** name to see the settings on the right side of the dialog box. InDesign has "picked up" or copied the drop shadow settings from the selected yellow graphic. Change the **Style Name** to "**flower center**," and click **OK** to close the dialog box and create the object style.

*Note: There are many options that can be saved in an object style. Often you need only a few options to create the desired object style. Turning off all the options except **Drop Shadow & Feather** is helpful in this case because it ensures that the style you are creating includes only the drop shadow.*

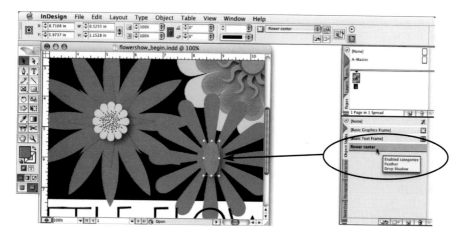

7. With the **Selection** tool, click the pink center of the purple flower. You are going to apply the object style you created in the previous step to that selected graphic. In the **Object Styles** palette, click the **flower center** object style to apply it.

In the next step, you will open the object style, change the shadow definition, and watch how the change affects the two graphics to which you've applied the object style!

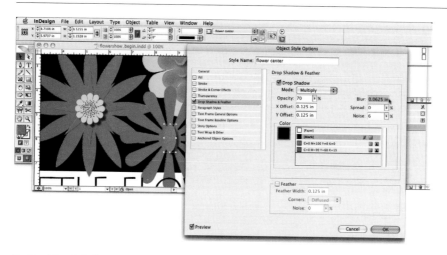

8. Double-click **flower center** in the **Object Styles** palette to reopen the **Object Style Options** dialog box. Click the **Drop Shadow & Feather** option on the left side of the dialog box to see the drop shadow options on the right side of the dialog box. With **Drop Shadow & Feather** checked, change the **Blur** setting to **0.0625 in**, and click the **Preview** option to see the change applied to the drop shadow of both graphics! The change you made is going to be small, so if you like, try increasing the spread to see a more dramatic change. Click **OK** to close the dialog box and accept the changes.

9. Save the document and keep it open for the next exercise.

TIP | Transparency Viewing Preferences

When drop shadows are used several times on a single page, or when one is applied to a large object, InDesign may slow down and prevent you from navigating efficiently. To avoid this, InDesign provides a **Preferences** setting that changes the quality of the shadow (and all transparency) previews onscreen. This setting only changes the preview and doesn't affect output. I usually leave this setting at **Medium Quality**, unless I have a document that uses a lot of transparency, in which case I set it to **Low Quality**.

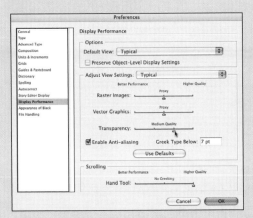

You can change the transparency preview settings by choosing **Edit > Preferences > Display Performance** (Windows) or **InDesign > Preferences > Display Performance** (Mac). This setting affects the level of quality for previews of all transparencies, including drop shadows. The following chart shows an example of a graphic viewed at each of the four available settings.

Drop Shadow (Transparency) Quality Preference Settings

Off	Low Quality	Medium Quality	High Quality

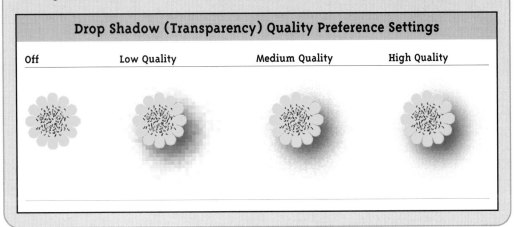

TIP | Changing Field Values Easily

Some fields in the **Drop Shadow** dialog box require you to type values. You can quickly change values in these fields by selecting an object (graphic) on the page and opening the **Drop Shadow** dialog box by choosing **Object > Drop Shadow.** The following illustrations show how to select text in a field quickly and change it.

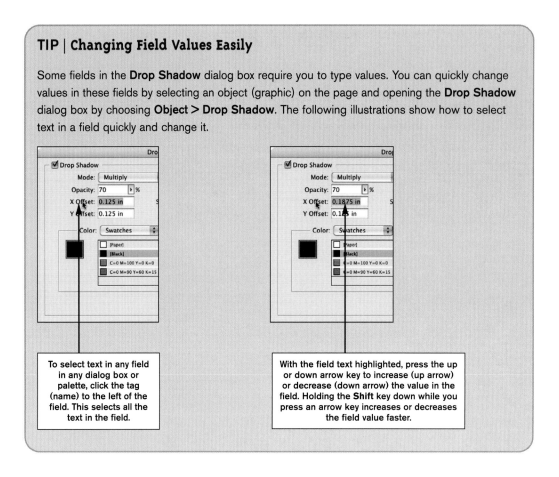

To select text in any field in any dialog box or palette, click the tag (name) to the left of the field. This selects all the text in the field.

With the field text highlighted, press the up or down arrow key to increase (up arrow) or decrease (down arrow) the value in the field. Holding the **Shift** key down while you press an arrow key increases or decreases the field value faster.

The Transparency Palette

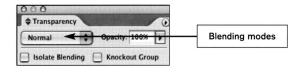

Blending modes

The **Transparency** palette, which can be accessed from **Window > Transparency**, is where you can apply transparency and blending modes to an object. The options in the **Transparency** palette are explained in the chart below, and blending modes are defined in the section that follows.

Transparency Palette Options

Feature	Function
Blending modes	Determines how the color of a selected object (called the **blend color**) interacts with the color of an underlying object (called the **base color**). The color that results is called the **resulting color**. For more information on blending modes, please refer to the next section.
Opacity	Determines the amount of transparency (how see-through) an object is (settings range from **0%** to **100%**).
Isolate Blending	Blends only the color within a selected group of objects (the objects must be grouped).

The yellow square on top has **Multiply** blend mode applied. It is affecting everything underneath it.

The yellow square and circle beneath were grouped, and the **Isolate Blending** option was checked.

Feature	Function
Knockout Group	**Knockout Group** will "knock out," or hide, grouped objects if transparency is applied and objects in the group overlap.

Objects with transparency applied to each (except for the black box behind)

Objects are grouped and the **Knockout Group** option is selected (except for the black box).

Blending Modes

Using **blending modes** can give you a great deal of creative flexibility when you are working with over-lapping colored objects because blending modes control how the colors of overlapping objects interact. Blending modes in InDesign work similarly to those in Photoshop and Illustrator in that they determine how InDesign blends the color of a selected object (called the **blend color**) into the color of an under-lying object (called the **base color**). The **resulting color** is the color that is produced by the blend. You can apply blending modes to various types of objects, including shapes, graphics, frames, lines, and text. The modes, described in detail in the following chart, blend the colors in different ways.

Blending modes are accessed from the **Transparency** palette. Although you can apply blending modes to objects that don't use transparency, using them on objects that do have transparency often produces unique and interesting results.

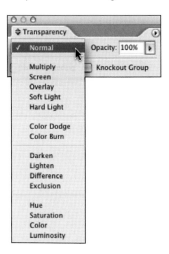

Clicking the **Normal** button in the **Transparency** palette reveals all the blending modes in the palette. The chart below explains each type of blending mode, along with an accompanying example.

Blending Modes

Blending Mode	Example	Blending Mode	Example
Normal: Two objects (text, shapes, graphics, frames, or lines), one on top of another, have different fill colors that are not blended.		Darken: Whichever color is darker, the **base color** or the **blend color**, becomes the **resulting color**. Areas lighter than the blend color are replaced, and areas darker than the blend color do not change.	
Multiply: The **base color** (the color of the object underneath) is multiplied by the **blend color** (the color of the selected object). The result is usually a darker color.		Lighten: Whichever color is lighter, the **base color** or the **blend color**, is the **resulting color**. Areas darker than the blend color are replaced, and areas lighter than the blend color do not change.	
Screen: Multiplies the inverse (opposite) of the **blend** and **base** colors. The **resulting color** is usually lighter.		Difference: Subtracts either the **blend color** from the **base color** or the **base color** from the **blend color**, depending on which has the greater brightness value.	
Overlay: Multiplies or screens the colors, depending on the **base color**. The **base color** is not replaced but is mixed with the **blend color** to reflect the lightness or darkness of the original color.		Exclusion: Creates an effect similar to, but lower in contrast than, the **Difference** mode. Blending with white inverts the **base color** components. Blending with black produces no change.	

continues on next page

Blending Modes *continued*

Blending Mode	Example	Blending Mode	Example
Soft Light: Darkens or lightens the colors, depending on the **blend color.** The effect is similar to that produced by shining a diffused spotlight on the object.		**Hue:** Creates a color with the luminance and saturation of the **base color** and the hue of the **blend color.**	
Hard Light: Multiplies or screens the colors, depending on the **blend color.** The effect is similar to that produced by shining an intense spotlight on the image.		**Saturation:** Creates a color with the luminance and hue of the **base color** and the saturation of the **blend color.**	
Color Dodge: Brightens the **base color** to reflect the **blend color.**		**Color:** Creates a color with the luminance of the **base color** and the hue and saturation of the **blend color.**	
Color Burn: Darkens the **base color** to reflect the **blend color.**		**Luminosity:** Creates a color with the hue and saturation of the **base color** and the luminance of the **blend color.** This mode creates an inverse effect from that of the **Color** mode.	

2. —————————**Applying Transparency**

In this short exercise, you will apply transparency to one of the flowers on the page. This will change the opacity of the object, making it more see-through.

1. With **flowershow_begin.indd** open from the previous exercise, choose the **Selection** tool from the **Toolbox**. Open the **Transparency** palette (if it's not on the right side of the workspace, open it by choosing **Window > Transparency**). Select the purple flower with the **Selection** tool. In the **Transparency** palette, change the **Opacity** to **70%** by either typing **70** into the **Opacity** field or clicking the arrow to the right of the field and using the slider to change the value. If you use the slider, the effect will take place as soon as you release the mouse button.

*After typing a value into the **Opacity** field, you need to click anywhere on the page or press **Enter** or **Return** to accept the change.*

2. With the transparency set (by changing the opacity), try a blending mode to see the effect on the objects underneath. The purple flower is on top of all the other objects it touches except the pink center, so those other objects should be affected when you apply a blending mode. From the **Blending Mode** menu, choose **Lighten** to see the effect. The change should take place immediately.

Note: When you apply a blending mode to an object that is on top of a black object, such as the black background shape in this file, the blending mode will usually "blend away" the areas of the flower that touch the black. For most of the blending modes, the effect is that any object that is not black looks as if it disappears.

*Note: Be careful when applying a blending mode to an object that contains a spot color. When the transparency is viewed onscreen, InDesign substitutes CMYK or RGB equivalents for the spot colors depending on the how **Transparency Blend Space** is set under **Edit > Transparency Blend Space**. This means that when outputting files with spot colors that have blending modes applied, you may encounter unexpected results. To avoid this, use either CMYK colors in objects with blending modes or avoid using blending modes with spot colors. Adobe suggests avoiding the Difference, Exclusion, Hue, Saturation, Color, and Luminosity blending modes with spot colors.*

3. Set the blending mode to **Normal** to keep the flower purple. A blending mode isn't necessary for this flower. Save the file and keep it open for the next exercise.

What Is Feathering?

Feathering softens the edges of objects by the amount specified in the **Feather** dialog box. You used to have to have Photoshop to apply feathering, but now you can do it in InDesign as well. To access the feathering options, select an object and choose **Object > Feather.**

Feathering can be applied to almost any object, including text. It's great for softening the edges of a photo to give an old-time photo look or for hiding sharp edges on shapes such as the star above.

The Feather Dialog Box

The **Feather** dialog box only has a few options. Each one is described in the chart below.

Feather Dialog Box Options	
Option	**Description**
Feather Width	Determines the width of the feather. The edges fade from transparent to opaque, forming a gradient feather around the object.
Corners	There are three feathering corner options available: **Sharp, Rounded,** and **Diffused. Sharp** feathers the object following the contour exactly. **Rounded** rounds the corners of the object using feathering. **Diffused** makes the edges of the object fade from opaque to transparent.
Noise	Adds a specified amount of noise, or artifact, to the feathered area.

3. ——————Feathering in InDesign

In this short exercise, you will feather one of the flower graphics. The graphic is a placed Photoshop file that is rasterized.

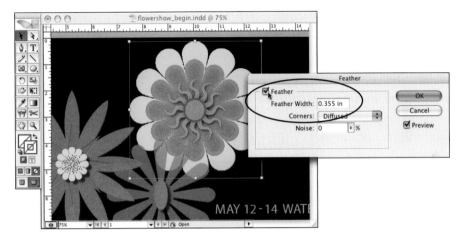

1. With **flowershow_begin.indd** open from the last exercise, choose the **Selection** tool from the **Toolbox**, if it isn't already chosen. You may need to zoom out (using the **Zoom** tool) or scroll the page up and to the right to see the yellow and pink flower. Select the yellow and pink flower (as shown in the illustration above). Choose **Object > Feather** to open the **Feather** dialog box and set the feathering. Turn on the feathering options by clicking the **Feather** check box. Also, select the **Preview** option to see the changes take place as they are made. Leave the dialog box open for the next step.

Note: *When setting feathering options, make sure that you first select an object. Setting feathering with no object selected tells InDesign to apply feathering to every shape or line created from that point forward.*

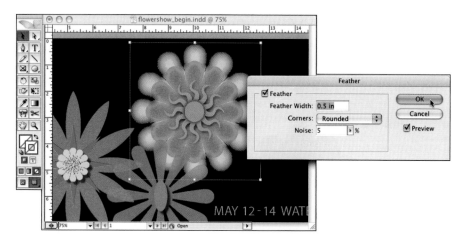

2. In the **Feather** dialog box, change the **Feather Width** to **0.5 in** by typing the value into the field. To see the changes take place, either press the **Tab** key or click another option in the **Feather** dialog box. Next, choose **Rounded** from the **Corners** menu to create a rounded feather effect on the yellow petals in the graphic. Add **5%** noise by typing the value into the **Noise** field or by clicking the arrow to the right of the field and dragging the slider to the left. This adds just a touch of graininess to the gradient created. Click **OK** to close the **Feather** dialog box and accept the feathering settings.

*Experiment a little with the settings in the **Feather** dialog box. Feathering can create some interesting design effects on this raster image.*

*Tip: Changing the **Display Performance** of this image to **High Quality Display** will give you a better idea of how this image will print after feathering is applied. With the graphic still selected, choose **Object > Display Performance > High Quality Display** to preview the feathering. Remember to change the **Display Performance** back to **Typical Display** (the default) so InDesign doesn't slow down as you navigate around the document.*

*Note: You can always go back and either turn off the feathering or edit the feathering by selecting this graphic and choosing **Object > Feather.***

3. Save the file and keep it open for the next exercise.

Transparency from Photoshop and Illustrator

Note: *To navigate this section, it is recommended that you have some prior working knowledge of Photoshop in particular. Because some terms used throughout this section—such as* masks, clipping paths, *and* alpha channels—*are large topics unto themselves, it is out of the scope of this book to define them.*

InDesign CS2 knows what transparency is and can display and output transparent objects (with specific output settings that you will learn about later in the chapter). This is good for placing native file formats, such as native Photoshop (PSD) or Illustrator (AI) files. When PSD files that contain alpha channels, masks, or paths are placed in InDesign, the alpha channels, masks, or paths are treated as transparencies in InDesign. For example, if the background of a PSD is deleted, the file is not flattened and its layers are intact. Once brought into InDesign, the deleted background area will be treated as a transparent object. This can be a huge time-saver, especially compared with using clipping paths to clip out areas of a graphic.

Not all printers or print service providers are going to like using native Photoshop or Illustrator files, so be sure to check with them or print a test proof whenever possible.

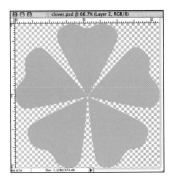

This is how the graphic appears in Photoshop. The checkerboard pattern behind the graphic indicates **transparency.**

The same file (saved as a PSD file) placed in InDesign. The **transparency** from Photoshop is maintained.

In the next exercise, you will place a native Photoshop file that has a transparent background (the area around or behind the graphic has been deleted). Once placed in InDesign, the **transparency** that was in the graphic in Photoshop is retained, and the background doesn't show because InDesign understands the transparency from the PSD file.

When a Photoshop file (either a PSD or the newer **Layered TIFF** file format in Photoshop CS+) that has a layer mask is placed in InDesign, the mask is automatically treated as a transparent object. If a path is saved with a PSD file and brought into InDesign, the path needs to be selected from the **Clipping Path** dialog box in InDesign by selecting the graphic and choosing **Object > Clipping Path**. Once the path is selected from the **Clipping Path** dialog box, it is interpreted as a transparent object. Clipping paths were discussed in Chapter 8, "*Bringing in Graphics.*"

4. ─────────────**Placing Transparent Graphics from Photoshop**

Now that you have applied drop shadows, changed opacity, and applied feathering, you will learn how
to place a native Photoshop (PSD) file to see the effects of native file transparency.

1. With **flowershow_begin.indd** open from the previous exercise, you are going to place a
clover graphic under the pink center object of the purple flower. Scroll down the page so that
the purple flower is close and at the center of the document window (if you are zoomed in).
Choose **File > Place**. From the images folder inside the **chap_12** folder on the **Desktop**,
choose **clover.psd**. Deselect the **Replace Selected Item** check box so that this graphic
won't replace anything that may be selected on the page (instead of deselecting everything
on the page). Check the **Show Import Options** check box. Click **Open**.

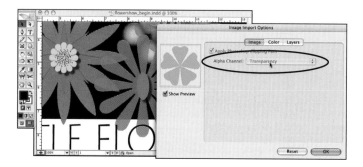

2. In the **Image Import Options** dialog box that opens, click the **Image** tab to see the image
settings. The **Alpha Channel** pop-up menu has **Transparency** selected and dimmed. This
indicates that this file has transparency in some form (mask, alpha channel, or path). Click **OK**
to get the **Loaded Graphic** cursor.

Note: *If an alpha channel is saved in Photoshop (a saved selection in Photoshop), InDesign
provides the option to select it in the **Alpha Channel** menu (it will not be dimmed) when
you are placing the graphic in InDesign.*

Click here with
the **Loaded
Graphic** icon.

3. Position the **Loaded Graphic** cursor above and to the left of the pink ellipse at the center of the purple flower, and click to place the Photoshop file onto the page. The transparency should appear automatically around the clover graphic. Choose the **Selection** tool in the **Toolbox** if it isn't already selected. Click in the middle of the new graphic, and choose **Object > Arrange > Send Backward** to send the new graphic behind the pink ellipse that is the center of the flower. The next step shows the result.

Note: Choosing **Object > Arrange > Send Backward** *sends the graphic behind one object at a time. Every new object (text frame, graphic, etc.) added to the page goes on top of everything else, so you may need to send an object backward several times.*

Tip: With the green clover chosen, you can **right-click** *(Windows) or* **Ctrl+click** *(Mac) directly on the shape to open a contextual menu. Send the shape backward by choosing* **Arrange > Send Backward.**

4. The new green clover graphic should be behind the pink ellipse. Now the objects need to be lined up. With the **Selection** tool still selected from the previous step, click the pink ellipse. Choose **Object > Lock Position** to lock it in place. With this shape locked, you will align the green graphic, the pink ellipse, and the purple flower graphic. Keep the pink shape selected for the next step.

Note: If multiple objects are aligned and one of the objects is locked in position, the unlocked objects will align to the locked objects.

5. With the **Selection** tool, **Shift-click** each of the three objects to select them all. At the right end of the **Control** palette, click the **Align Horizontal Centers** and the **Align Vertical Centers** buttons.

6. The green Photoshop graphic with transparency is now placed. Save the file.

TIP | Placing Transparent Graphics from Illustrator

An Illustrator file placed in InDesign is placed as a PDF. InDesign recognizes transparency in PDFs and Illustrator files just as it does with Photoshop files.

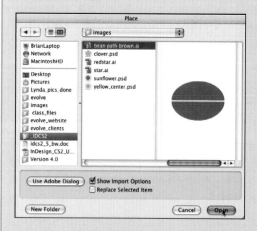

To place an AI or PDF file into an InDesign document, choose **File > Place**, and then select **Show Import Options** in the **Place** dialog box and click **Open**. The same **Place PDF** dialog box opens whether you are placing an AI or PDF file.

continues on next page

TIP | **Placing Transparent Graphics from Illustrator** *continued*

Selecting the **Transparent Background** option in the **Place PDF** dialog box will retain the transparency in the file. By default, this option should be checked. When placing a PDF file, it makes the page behind the PDF content transparent.

*Note: When you attempt to place a PDF file with security in InDesign, the **PDF Security Password** dialog box opens, asking you to supply a password before placing the file.*

Previewing Transparency and Blends

When working with InDesign files that have transparency of any kind (opacity changes, feathering, drop shadow, and transparency within placed files), you will want to pay attention to several options to prevent difficulty during the output process. Previewing transparency is great for checking for trouble spots that may arise when printing.

Note: As stated earlier in the chapter, when sending a file that contains transparency for output in high resolution, check with your service provider to find out any limitations or special settings that you will need to address prior to output.

BONUS EXERCISE | **Previewing Transparency and Blends in an InDesign Document**

To learn how, check out **transparent.pdf** in the **bonus_exercises** folder on the **InDesign CS2 HOT CD-ROM**.

Congrats! You have another chapter under your belt. Although transparency can be fun and great for design, you do have to pay attention to how you use it and how often it occurs in a single document. In the next chapter, you will learn about handling long documents.

13

Long-Document Tools

| Creating and Using a Library | Updating Library Items |
| Creating a Footnote | Formatting a Footnote |

chap_13

InDesign CS2
HOT CD-ROM

As InDesign has evolved from version 1.0, Adobe has added capability for handling long documents, which can be loosely defined as documents that require a table of contents or have roughly more than 50 pages. In this chapter, you will learn about some of the tools in InDesign that simplify tasks involving long documents, including creating a library to reuse objects consistently, working with footnotes, building a table of contents, and forming a book.

What Is a Library in InDesign CS2?

Often a long document will repeatedly use consistent elements, like text, objects, or graphics. For instance, certain pages in a chapter might use a common tagline inside a text frame. Instead of copying and pasting to add that text frame to each appropriate page, you could save time by adding the text frame (which contains the tagline) to a library.

A **library** is an organized collection of frequently used elements, which can include objects, graphics, guides, grids, grouped objects, and even pages. In InDesign, a library is a file with an extension of .indl. Although it opens and closes like a regular document, a library appears as a palette in the workspace. The palette is opened automatically once the library is created, and it carries the name you assign to the library. Many users can share a library across a network, but only one person can have a library open at any one time. A library is created by choosing **File > New > Library**. Once created, a library is not tied to any one document. It is open as long as InDesign is open. This allows you to easily share elements among documents.

A Library Palette

Dragging objects from an InDesign document into an open library creates a library item.

The library item is stored in the library file. Graphics, lines, shapes, and text frames can all be dragged into a library.

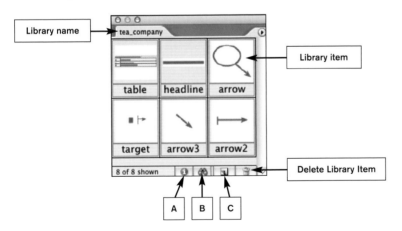

The following chart describes the features of a library palette.

Library Palette Options

Option		Definition
A	Item Information	Allows you to edit information about the library item using options such as **Item Name**, **Object Type** (category), and **Description**. All this information can be searched to pinpoint a library item.
B	Show Subset	Opens the **Show Subset** dialog box, where you can search the library to show a subset of the library items. It searches all the information supplied in the **Item Information** dialog box and more.
C	New Item	When you select an object on a document page, this button is undimmed and usable. By clicking the button, you save a copy of that object into the library.

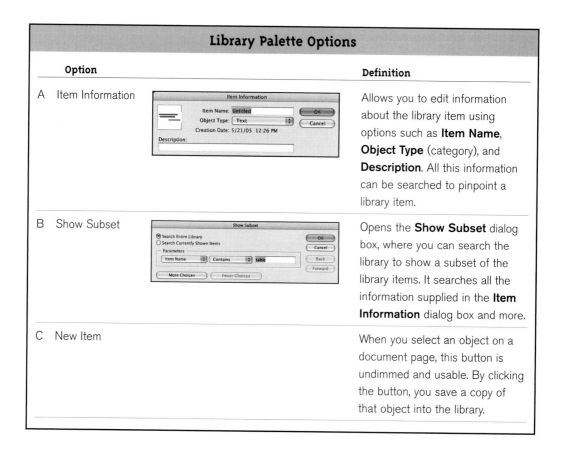

I. ————————**Creating and Using a Library**

In this exercise, you will create a library and add a few objects to it.

1. Open **tea_flyer_final.indd** from the **chap_13** folder you copied to the **Desktop**.

Note: *When the InDesign file opens, it may warn you that fonts are missing. If this dialog box appears, choose **Find Font** to see which font it is looking for. Before opening the file, replace any missing font with Times Roman or a similar font. You can select several fonts at once in the **Find Font** dialog box by **Shift+clicking.** If the text is highlighted in pink, this also indicates that a font is missing. Choose **Type > Find Font** to find and replace the font if you do not replace the missing font while opening the file. To learn more about this, visit Exercise 1 of Chapter 5, "Typography in InDesign."*

Note: *A dialog box that indicates missing or modified graphics may appear when you open this file. If it does, choose **Fix Links Automatically** to update any modified graphics automatically. After fixing the links, close the **Links** palette. If the **Find** dialog box opens, navigate to the **chap_13** folder on the **Desktop** and find the graphic in the **images** folder.*

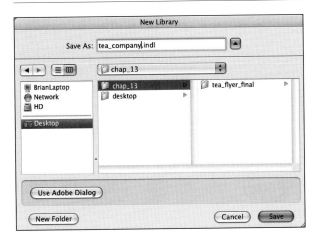

2. With the file open, you are going to create a new library. Choose **File > New > Library**. The **New Library** dialog box opens. Choose the **chap_13** folder on your **Desktop**, and type "**tea_company.indl**" into the **File Name** (Windows) or **Save As** (Mac) field. Click **Save** to save the library and open the library palette in the workspace.

Tip: *Name the library according to its purpose or with a project name. When you come back to it later, you will have some idea of the elements it contains.*

Note: *When you open a library from an earlier version of InDesign, a warning dialog box appears, asking you to rename the library.*

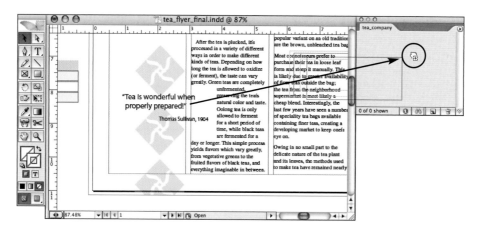

3. Choose the **Zoom** tool from the **Toolbox**, and zoom into the lower-left corner of the first page. Choose the **Selection** tool from the **Toolbox**. Click the text frame with the pull quote in the lower-left corner. Drag it into the **tea_company** library palette to save a copy of the text frame.

Tip: When you drag an object into a library, all the formatting of that object, including styles and swatches, are preserved. The library item you created in Step 3 preserved the text wrap and text for-matting of the original text frame. Saving library items is a great way to share paragraph and character styles as well as swatches among documents.

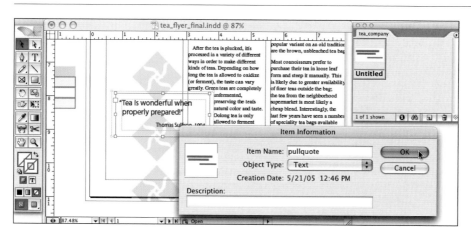

4. Double-click the library item you just created in the **tea_company** library palette. This opens the **Item Information** dialog box. In the **Item Name** field, type "**pullquote**." Leave the **Object Type** pop-up menu at **Text**, and click **OK** to close the dialog box.

*Note: All the information in this dialog box is useful if you perform a search using the **Show Subset** (⚙) option at the bottom of the library palette.*

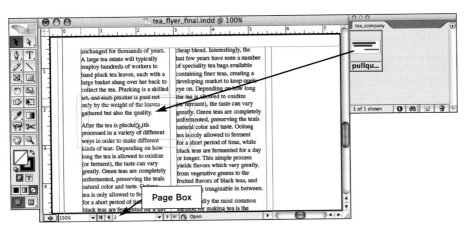

5. Go to the second page of the document by choosing **2** from the **Page Box** at the bottom of the document window. From the **tea_company** library palette, click and drag the **pullquote** item onto the left side of the page. Notice that the text wrap and formatting is still there.

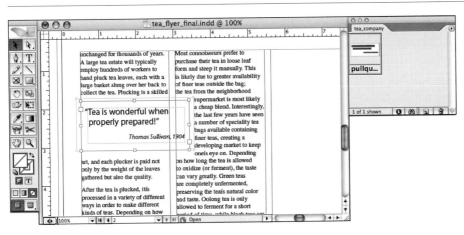

6. With the library item on the page, save the file and keep it open for the next exercise.

2. —————————Updating Library Items

In this short exercise, you will update the library item created in the previous exercise.

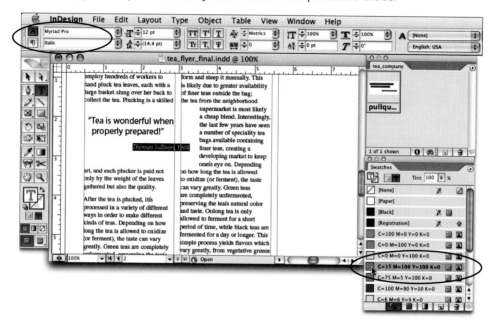

1. With **tea_flyer_final.indd** open from the previous exercise, choose the **Type** tool from the **Toolbox** and select the text "**Thomas Sullivan, 1904**." From the **Character Formatting** controls of the **Control** palette, choose italic from the **Font Style** pop-up menu (if available for the font chosen). Also, open the **Swatches** palette by choosing **Window > Swatches**. With the **Fill Box** chosen from the **Toolbox**, choose red from the **Swatches** palette.

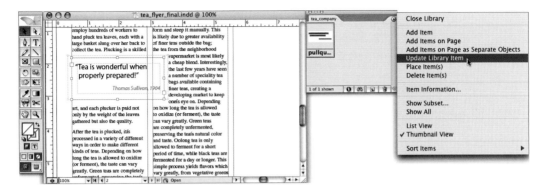

2. Now you are ready to update the library item. Choose the **Selection** tool from the **Toolbox**. The text frame should automatically be selected; if not, click it to select it. With the text frame selected, click the **pullquote** library item in the library palette to make sure it is selected as well. From the **tea_company** library palette menu, choose **Update Library Item**.

The library item doesn't look very different when you update the file, but the next time you drag the library item out onto the page, it will look like the text frame in this step.

3. Save the file and close it.

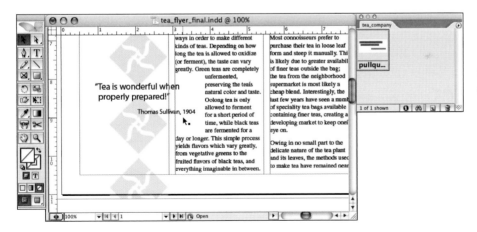

Note: When you update a library item, the library item changes to match the object selected on the page. However, any other copies of the library item you previously dragged onto the document will not be updated along with the library item. Updating a library item is just a way to change what will be placed onto the page the next time you use the library item.

TIP | Saving a Page as a Library Item

The contents of an entire page, including the guides, can be saved as a library item. This is a new feature in InDesign CS2.

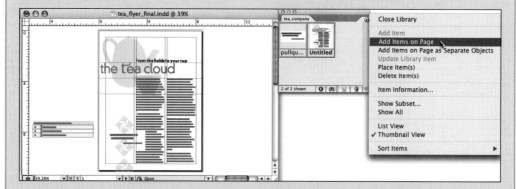

Go to any page in a document (the illustration above shows the first page of the document from the last exercise). From the **tea_company** library palette menu, choose **Add Items on Page**. The contents of the page are added to the library as a single library item. This is a great way to copy a page design to another document or to another page within the same document.

Note: To place this new library item onto a page, you cannot drag it. Instead, InDesign displays a dialog box telling you to choose **Place** item(s) from the library palette menu. The items maintain their positioning relative to each other, but you can place them on the pasteboard and then just move them onto the page.

Choosing **Add Items on Page as Separate Objects** creates one library item from each element on the page.

Footnotes in InDesign CS2

Footnotes are usually used to credit sources of research data or any material that is borrowed, summarized, or paraphrased. In numerical order, footnotes are placed at the bottom of the page or column that contains the research or externally sourced material.

A footnote consists of two linked parts: the footnote reference number (or other symbol) placed in the body text and the footnote text placed at the bottom of the column. In InDesign CS2, footnotes can be created or imported from Word or RTF (Rich Text Format) documents. Footnotes are automatically numbered as they are added, although you can control the appearance of footnotes for the document as a whole.

Footnote Options

When you create footnotes, you have complete control over their appearance in the text. From the **Footnote Options** dialog box, which you access by choosing **Type > Document Footnote Options**, you can choose options that apply to the entire document.

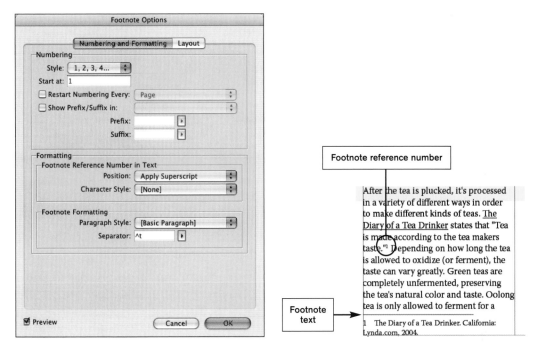

Footnote reference number

After the tea is plucked, it's processed in a variety of different ways in order to make different kinds of teas. The Diary of a Tea Drinker states that "Tea is made according to the tea makers taste."[1] Depending on how long the tea is allowed to oxidize (or ferment), the taste can vary greatly. Green teas are completely unfermented, preserving the tea's natural color and taste. Oolong tea is only allowed to ferment for a

Footnote text

1   The Diary of a Tea Drinker. California: Lynda.com, 2004.

The footnote options are described in the chart below.

	Options in the Footnote Options Dialog Box
Option	**Definition**
Numbering	Assigns a numbering style to the footnote reference number and footnote text. You can control the style, the number to start at, and whether or not a prefix or suffix (such as "TOC-" for table of contents) appears.
Formatting	Formats the footnote reference number by assigning a character style and positioning (superscript, subscript, or normal).
Footnote Formatting	Formats the footnote text by assigning a paragraph style and a separator between the number and the text (tab is the default default, **Em Space** and **En Space** are options).

3. ——————Creating a Footnote

In this exercise, you will create a footnote for several pieces of footnote-worthy text in a document.

1. Open **coffee_brochure_final.indd** from the **chap_13** folder on the **Desktop**.

*Note: When the InDesign file opens, it may warn you that fonts are missing. If this dialog box appears, choose **Find Font** to see which font it is looking for. Before opening the file, replace any missing font with Times Roman or a similar font. You can select several fonts at once in the **Find Font** dialog box by **Shift+clicking.** If the text is highlighted in pink, this also indicates that a font is missing. Choose **Type > Find Font** to find and replace the font if you do not replace the missing font while opening the file. To learn more about this, visit Exercise 1 of Chapter 5, "Typography in InDesign."*

*Note: A dialog box that indicates missing or modified graphics may appear when you open this file. If it does, choose **Fix Links Automatically** to update any modified graphics automatically. After fixing the links, close the **Links** palette. If the **Find** dialog box opens, navigate to the **chap_13** folder on the **Desktop** and find the graphic in the **images** folder.*

2. Navigate to page 2 of the brochure (which is actually the fourth page of the document) by choosing **Sec1:2** from the **Page Box** in the lower-left corner of the document window (if that page is not already displayed in the document window).

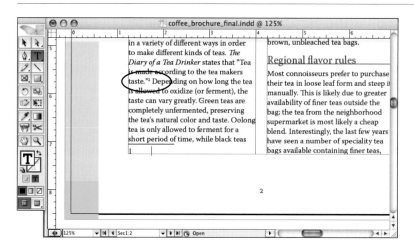

3. Choose the **Zoom** tool from the **Toolbox**. Zoom into the lower-left corner of the page, and look for the text that contains "**The Diary of a Tea Drinker.**" Choose the **Type** tool from the **Toolbox**, and place the cursor in the text after the quote that ends "**the tea makers taste.**" Choose **Type > Insert Footnote** to insert a footnote reference number where the cursor is.

Note: Inserting a footnote is relatively easy in InDesign CS2. As soon as the footnote reference is placed in the text, footnote text automatically appears at the bottom of the column or frame that contains the footnote reference number. A line separating the footnote text from the body text in the column also appears. You will learn how to control the formatting of the footnote reference number and text in the next exercise. As you add footnotes to the body text, InDesign numbers them according to their position in the text. The footnote that appears closest to the beginning of the text will have the smallest number.

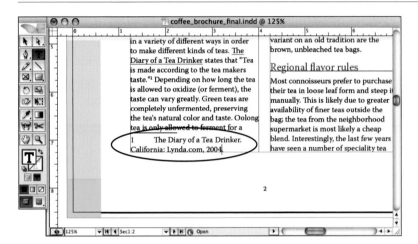

4. The footnote text should appear at the bottom of the column. The cursor should have automatically been placed in the footnote text from the previous step. Type, "**The Diary of a Tea Drinker, California: Lynda.com, 2004**." for the footnote text.

Note: When placing footnotes, InDesign uses the default font. If you see pink text, you will need to choose **Type > Find Font** to change the font.

The footnote text area will grow to accommodate as much text as you want to type or paste into it. Also, if the column has multiple footnotes, the text for each footnote appears one after the other in this footnote text area.

Tip: You can always insert a footnote reference number into text by placing the cursor and **right-clicking** (Windows) or **Control+clicking** (Mac) to choose **Insert Footnote** from the contextual menu. If you use footnotes often, you might want to add your own shortcut for the **Insert Footnote** command by choosing **Edit > Keyboard Shortcuts.**

Tip: Footnotes are easily deleted. By selecting the footnote reference number in the body text (not in the footnote text) and pressing **Backspace** or **Delete**, you can remove both the footnote reference number and the footnote text associated with it.

5. Save the file and keep it open for the next exercise.

4. ——————————Formatting a Footnote

In this short exercise, you will control the formatting of the footnote placed in the previous exercise. The formatting you will apply will appear on all the footnotes throughout the entire document.

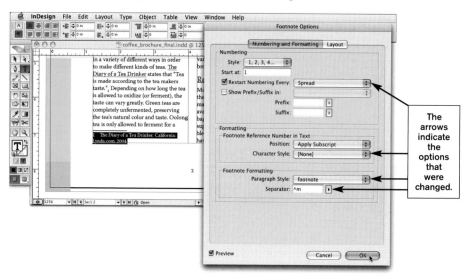

1. With **coffee_brochure_final.indd** open from the previous exercise, place the cursor in the footnote text. Choose **Type > Document Footnote Options** to open the **Footnote Options** dialog box. Select the **Preview** option if it is not already selected. Select the **Restart Numbering Every** option, and choose **Spread** from the pop-up menu to the right of that option. This restarts the footnote numbering to 1 on every spread. To change the formatting of the footnote reference numbers, choose **Apply Subscript** from the **Position** pop-up menu. Finally, to change the footnote text formatting, choose **footnote** from the **Paragraph Style** pop-up menu, and choose **Em Space** from the **Separator** pop-up menu. (When you choose the **Em Space** option, "^t^m" is displayed in the **Separator** field. Select and delete "^t," which indicates a tab.) Leave this dialog box open for the next step.

Note: The footnote text in the illustration above is highlighted. You do not have to highlight the text to apply footnote formatting. It is highlighted here only to make it is easier to see.

*The footnote paragraph style you chose was created ahead of time and saved with the document. Otherwise, there would only be **No Paragraph Style** and **Basic Paragraph Style** to choose from.*

Tip: The formatting changes you made in Step 1 affect the formatting of every footnote in the document. This can be useful, unless you decide that one or more footnotes needs to look different. You can apply paragraph and character formatting and styles to the footnote reference numbers and footnote text in the document to override this formatting if you choose.

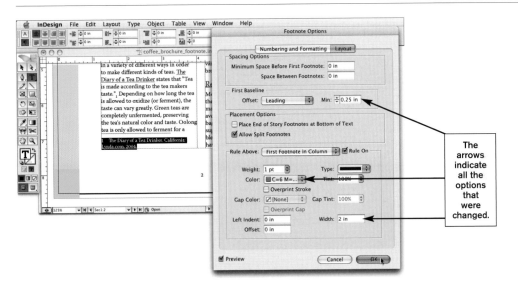

2. Next you will change the layout options for the footnote reference number and footnote text. Click the **Layout** tab in the **Footnote Options** dialog box. In the **First Baseline** section, change **Min** to **0.25 in**. This pushes the rule (in the illustration above, the red line between the body text and the footnote text) up, along with the text in the column, by one-quarter inch. To give the rule a different look, change **Color** to red (if not already selected) and **Width** to **2 in**. Click **OK** to accept the changes.

*In the **Spacing Options** section, you can put space before all the footnote text and the text in the column or between the footnotes as they appear. Also, when you select the **Allow Split Footnotes** option, very long footnote text can span more than one column. With this option selected (which it is by default), if you keep typing footnote text, eventually the bottommost footnote in the text will split and carry over to the bottom of the column to the right.*

3. Save the file and close it.

TIP | Working with Footnotes

Here are a few guidelines for working with footnotes that you might find helpful:

- Placing the cursor in the footnote text area, you can use the arrow keys to navigate among footnotes.

- You can select and apply character and paragraph formatting to footnote reference numbers and footnote text. This will override the formatting applied to all the document footnotes when you use the **Footnote Options** dialog box (accessed by choosing **Type > Document Footnote Options**) to edit the appearance of the footnotes. It is best to use the document footnote options to apply formatting to the footnote text and footnote reference numbers.

- If a footnote number is accidentally deleted from the footnote text (which happens more often than you might think), you can put it back in by placing the cursor at the beginning of the footnote text and choosing **Insert Special Character > Footnote Number**.

- If you cut and copy body text that includes a footnote reference number, the footnote text moves with the body text when it is pasted. If footnoted body text is moved to a different document, the pasted footnote automatically takes on the formatting of the footnotes in the new document.

- Text wrap has no effect on footnote text.

How Is a Table of Contents Made?

If you have ever worked with a long document that requires a table of contents, you will be overjoyed to learn that, with the proper amount of forethought on your part, InDesign can generate a table of contents for for you, and allow you to edit it as well.

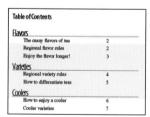

BONUS EXERCISE | Creating and Editing a Table of Contents

To learn how to create a table of contents, check out **create_toc.pdf** in the **bonus_exercises** folder on the **InDesign CS2 HOT CD-ROM**.

To learn how to edit a table of contents, check out **edit_toc.pdf** in the **bonus_exercises** folder on the **InDesign CS2 HOT CD-ROM**.

What Are Baseline Grids?

Baseline grids are a less widely used feature in InDesign because they play a very specialized role.

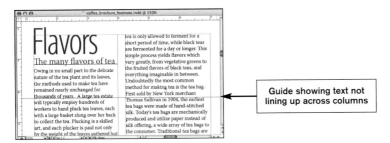

Guide showing text not lining up across columns

When working with multiple columns of text, applying formatting to the text can affect how the text wraps between columns. Sometimes the lines of text no longer line up across the columns. In the illustration above, the brown guide that runs across the two columns of text shows you that the text across the columns doesn't line up vertically.

All text in a document sits on imaginary baselines. This is how leading, paragraph spacing, and more are determined.

You can control baselines and snap or align the text to them.

A **baseline grid** is a network of parallel lines (sort of like ruled or lined paper) to which the lines of text in a paragraph "snap" (InDesign CS2 calls it "aligning to" the baseline grid). This forces text in different columns to sit on the same baseline. The illustration above shows the baseline grid (which runs through both columns on the page) and how text aligns to that grid.

In previous versions of InDesign, the baseline grid was the same through the whole document, and you controlled the grid's size (distance between the baseline lines), color, and other attributes by choosing **Edit > Preferences > Grids** (Windows) or **InDesign > Preferences > Grid** (Mac). In InDesign CS2, you can also change how the grid looks in individual text frames. The following movie will lead you through using baseline grids.

 MOVIE | Using Baseline Grids

To learn more about baseline grids, check out **baseline_grids.mov** in the **movies** folder on the **InDesign CS2 HOT CD-ROM**.

What Is an InDesign Book?

A book in InDesign is a collection of InDesign documents that either share common features, like type styles and swatches, or comprise a larger document broken into smaller documents. A book is generally used for one of two reasons. First, a book allows you to share swatches and type styles among a collection of documents (a spring catalog series, for example). Each catalog within the book can be synchronized so that all the swatches and styles are based on a document you deem as the "master" document. Second, you can create a book from a long document, like a manual, that several people—copywriters, designers, and production teams, for instance—can access at the same time. If the manual is a single document, only one person can open it at a time. But if the spreads or sections are split apart into several documents, and those documents are associated with a book, multiple users can access different parts of the book simultaneously.

coffee_brochure.indb

A book is created by choosing **File > New > Book**. The book is saved as an INDB file somewhere on a network or on your local machine (depending on who needs access to it).

The book acts like a library in that when it is open, it looks like a palette. It stays open as long as InDesign is open, regardless of what document is open. Unlike a library, however, a book file (with the extension .indb) can be open and used by more than one person at any one time. InDesign lists all the documents associated with that book (the documents still need to be created separately from the book, however). To open one of the book documents, you can double-click its name in the book palette. InDesign also shows you whether anyone has that book open at that particular time.

BONUS EXERCISE | Creating a Book and Synchronizing Documents in a Book

To learn how to create a book in InDesign CS2, check out **create_book.pdf** in the **bonus_exercises** folder on the **InDesign CS2 HOT CD-ROM**.

To learn how to synchronize documents in a book, check out **synchronize_book.pdf** in the **bonus_exercises** folder on the **InDesign CS2 HOT CD-ROM**.

What Is an Index?

An **index** is a list of words and terms that appears at the back of a book. An index allows the reader to look up certain words and terms to see where they appear in the document. To create an index, you first place index markers in the text of the document. You associate each index marker with the word, called a **topic**, that you want to appear in the index. This association is done in the **Index** palette by choosing **Window > Type & Tables > Index**.

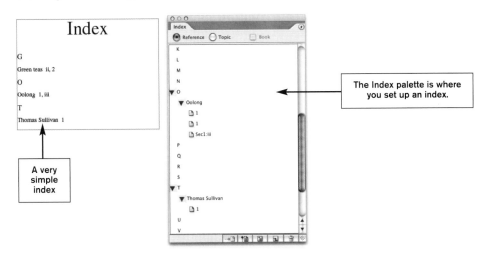

A very simple index

The Index palette is where you set up an index.

When you generate the index, InDesign lists each topic with the page reference on which it was found. The topics are sorted alphabetically, but you can change the appearance of the generated index if you want. You can also create cross-references (a "see also" reference). Once you set up the markers and determine how the index will look, InDesign generates it automatically. The following movie will take you through the process of creating an index.

MOVIE | Creating an Index

To learn more about creating an index, check out **index.mov** in the **movies** folder on the **InDesign CS2 HOT CD-ROM**.

Well done on yet another chapter finished! This chapter took you through some of the more mundane, but necessary, tasks involved in the care and feeding of long documents. Now that you have this under your belt, it's time to move on to the final chapter of the book, which deals with output and exporting of InDesign files.

I4
Output and Export

| Preflighting and Packaging a Document |

| Saving a File as an InDesign Template |

| Exporting as PDF | Creating PDF Presets | Exporting as EPS |

| Exporting to Earlier Versions of InDesign |

chap_I4

InDesign CS2
HOT CD-ROM

First and foremost, congratulations on making it this far. There are just a few final topics to cover—file output and export.

Output used to refer to printing, but with the Web, the scope of output has changed. In this chapter, you will prepare files for output by checking links and fonts and doing general file cleanup—all important ways of working better with print service providers and keeping production costs lower.

You will also learn how to go through the output process, including packaging for printing and the Web, so you will be able to hand off your files easily, and exporting from InDesign to create an EPS, an InDesign document compatible with InDesign CS, and a PDF. Finally, you will learn about InDesign CS2's color management features, which may help to produce more accurate color output.

Preflighting Options

Preflighting can be a great way to save time and lower production costs. In general, preflighting means checking the file for problematic links, colors, and fonts before output. Preflighting in InDesign is a feature under **File > Preflight** that's also useful for taking a step back—to check the status of links, colors, and fonts—while you are working.

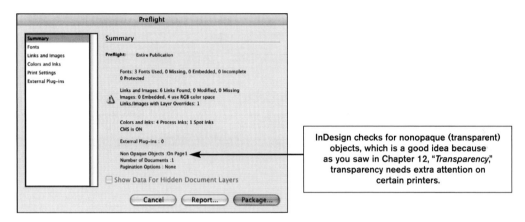

InDesign checks for nonopaque (transparent) objects, which is a good idea because as you saw in Chapter 12, "*Transparency*," transparency needs extra attention on certain printers.

The **Preflight** dialog box, found under **File > Preflight**, has many options. They are described in the chart below.

Preflight Dialog Box Options	
Option	**Function**
Summary	Summarizes the preflight results. A yellow yield sign ⚠ may appear to the left of one of the categories. This indicates that a possible problem was detected. Watch for this.
Fonts	Checks for fonts that are missing, embedded, incomplete (fonts with two parts may have one part missing), or protected (copyrighted and can't be sent to a print service provider). The **Find Font** dialog box can be opened during preflighting.
Links and Images	Indicates when links are missing or modified and whether graphics are embedded, have Photoshop layer overrides (or PDF files, as discussed in Chapter 8, "*Bringing in Graphics*"), and what color space they are in (RGB, CMYK, etc.). The color space option is most often flagged because images are in RGB and not CMYK.
	continues on next page

Preflight Dialog Box Options *continued*	
Option	**Function**
Colors and Inks	Checks to see which colors are used in the document and whether they are spot or process.
Print Settings	Shows the print settings (which you will learn about in the section titled "Print Options in the Print Dialog Box") currently set in InDesign.
External Plug-ins	Shows any external plug-ins (programs added on to InDesign) that were used. This can be important if you are sending the file to a printer that doesn't have the plug-in.
Cancel button	Closes the **Preflight** dialog box without making a change.
Report button	Creates a report of the information found in the **Preflight** dialog box. The report is a text (TXT) file that shows to service providers, at a glance, what the file package contains and all the preflight findings associated with it.
Package button	Copies all the pieces of the document (linked graphics, fonts, etc.) into a comprehensive "package" for final output or archiving. This is the last step in sending a file to a service provider or anyone else who will be working on the file.

Packaging Options

When a file has been preflighted, it is almost ready to be handed over to an external partner or print service provider. First, the "pieces" of the file—the original InDesign document and any linked files like graphics and fonts—need to be collected, or packaged, into a single folder for easy transport. Packaging is also useful for archiving files. Packaging allows other people to open and use the file without encountering the problems of broken links and missing fonts.

Packaging in InDesign performs four basic but critical functions: it copies all the pieces into a single folder; organizes files into subfolders by category, like fonts and graphics; updates the links to the collected graphics in the InDesign document copy it generates; and creates an instruction text file for the service provider that includes any contact information the sender wishes to provide.

Choosing **File > Package** runs the package command on the open and active file. The **Create Package Folder** options are described in the chart below.

Create Package Folder Options	
Option	**Function**
Copy Fonts (Except CJK)	All fonts used in the document that are located on the computer are copied into the package folder. The "CJK" exception refers to Chinese, Japanese, and Korean. It will copy only necessary font files, not the entire typeface.
Copy Linked Graphics	All graphics that are properly linked (it will warn you during the process if a link is broken or missing) will be copied into a links subfolder within the package folder.
Update Graphic Links in Package	When all the graphics and the document are copied into the package folder, InDesign changes the links in the document to link to those in the package subfolders.
Use Document Hyphenation Exceptions Only	If you create any hyphenation exceptions in the document's dictionary, you will most likely want to check this to keep them with the document.
	continues on next page

Create Package Folder Options *continued*	
Option	**Function**
Include Fonts and Links From Hidden Document Layer	With this option selected, InDesign copies any fonts or links from hidden layers. (Hidden layers are layers with visibility turned off.)
View Report	When the package is complete, InDesign opens the text file that accompanies it. The report contains all relevant document information as well as any contact information supplied during the packaging process.
Instructions	Opens the **Printing Instructions** dialog box, where you can enter any contact information that you want the person receiving the package to see.

Warning: The **Create Package Folder** *options can make you very lazy about file organization. Although InDesign will pull copies of correctly linked files into a single folder during the packaging process, this is not a reason to stop organizing and tracking files. Not paying attention to file organization often leads to multiple copies of files, which is a problem InDesign may not be able to detect!*

I. ——————Preflighting and Packaging a Document

In this exercise, you will preflight and package a document that will be printed by an external service provider.

1. Open **postcard_output_clean.indd** from the **chap_14** folder on the **Desktop**.

*Note: A dialog box that indicates missing or modified graphics may appear when you open this file. If it does, choose **Fix Links Automatically** to update any modified graphics automatically. After fixing the links, close the **Links** palette. If the **Find** dialog box opens, navigate to the **chap_14** folder on the **Desktop**, and find the graphics in the **images** folder.*

*Note: You may come across the **Missing Fonts** dialog box. If you do, change the font by choosing **Find Font** and replacing the font with a version of Arial or Helvetica. For a refresher on this, see Chapter 5, "Typography in InDesign."*

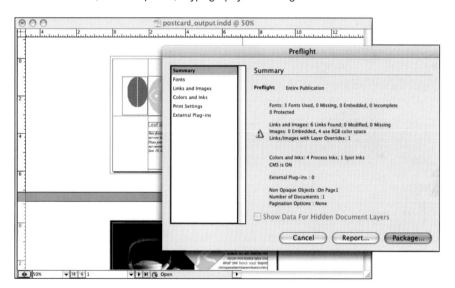

2. With the file open, choose **File > Preflight** to begin the preflight process. The **Preflight** dialog box appears. Leave it open for the next step.

*The yellow yield sign in the **Preflight** dialog box indicates that there are possible problems with the links and images. In the next step, you will see what is wrong.*

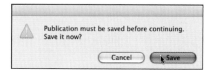

*When you first begin the process by choosing **File > Preflight**, InDesign may ask you to save the file. Respond to the prompt by saving the file before you continue.*

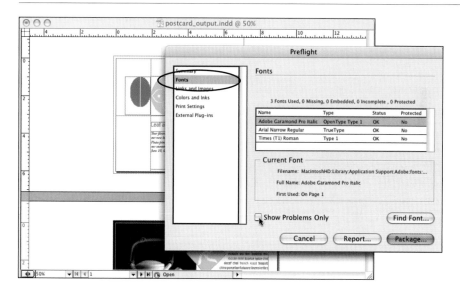

3. In the **Preflight** dialog box, select the **Fonts** category on the left side. InDesign lists all the fonts used in the document, as well as information such as the type of each font (Open Type, True Type, PostScript), the status of each font (whether it's missing), and whether each font is protected (certain fonts have licensing restrictions that prevent you from sending them to a print service provider). Keep the **Preflight** dialog box open for the next step.

*A great feature of this dialog box is the **Show Problems Only** check box. Selecting this option can make it easier to pinpoint a missing font, for instance, instead of scrolling through the list of fonts. A list of fonts that are protected, missing, or incomplete appears in the **Fonts** section of the **Preflight** dialog box.*

*The **Find Font** option is also accessible from the **Font** options of the **Preflight** dialog box. This enables you to find missing fonts.*

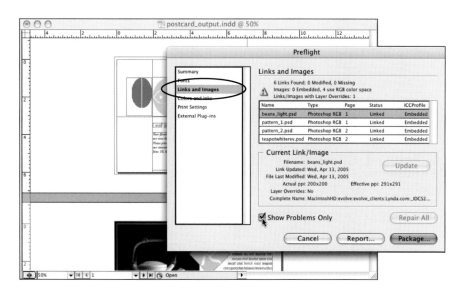

4. With the **Preflight** dialog box still open, click the **Links and Images** section on the left. Every link in the document is listed in this section. Click the **Show Problems Only** check box to sort the list of images that have problems. For example, a graphic may be missing, modified, or embedded or in an RGB color space (something other than CMYK). Click the **Package** button to accept the RGB images and gather a copy of the original document, its links, and fonts into a single folder.

Note: The problem with the graphics in this file is that they are in the RGB color space. In Chapter 7, "Working with Color," you learned that the best color space for printing is CMYK. RGB images can be output, but InDesign alerts you because they will need to be converted to CMYK at some point before being printed, usually at the printer. I recommend doing the conversion to CMYK yourself, rather than seeing the results in the printed piece or proof (unless your workflow calls for RGB specifically). It is much easier (and often less costly) to control the conversion during preflighting than during the final output process, or at a service provider. Changing the graphics to CMYK has to be done in a program like Photoshop, however, since InDesign won't directly convert to CMYK using this process.

*Note: The **Repair All** button in the **Preflight** dialog box can be deceiving. Although it looks and sounds like the answer to all your graphic-linking woes, the button does not make it that easy. If you click **Repair All** and links are missing, InDesign still asks you to locate the graphics, so there's no real magic here. But it is still a useful button. The **Update** button automatically updates any of the modified links and pulls in the updated image. It is a good idea to click **Update** if there are any modified links or images in the document.*

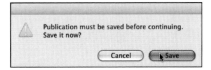

5. When you click the **Package** button in the **Preflight** dialog box, InDesign often asks you to save the file. You may not see this dialog box if nothing has changed or you saved the file just before you started the preflighting process. If you do encounter this dialog box, click **Save** to save the file, and then continue to the next step.

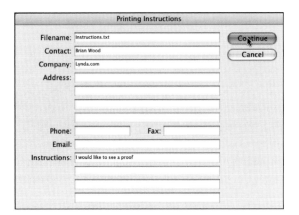

6. Next, the **Printing Instructions** dialog box appears. The printing instructions you enter here are put into a text file created automatically by InDesign during the preflight process. The instructions contain a summary of the information found in the **Preflight** dialog box as well as any contact information supplied here. After filling in whatever you think is the most pertinent information, click the **Continue** button to close this dialog box and continue to the next step.

I usually leave this information blank out of habit. I found out that my print service provider doesn't look at this file, and because I use that printer exclusively, it's not necessary for me. Leaving the **Printing Instructions** *dialog box blank won't stop the package process from happening, but the person or service provider who will be handling the file may find the information helpful.*

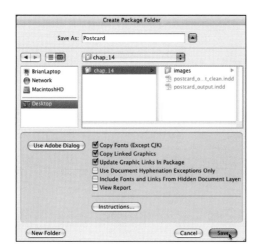

7. With the **Printing Instructions** dialog box gone and the **Package Publication** (Windows) or **Create Package Folder** (Mac) dialog box showing, navigate to the **chap_14** folder on the **Desktop**. Type "**Postcard**" into the **Folder Name** (Windows) or **Save As** (Mac) field. This is the name of the folder that will contain the packaged copies of the files you are packaging. Leave the **Copy Fonts**, **Copy Linked Graphics**, and **Update Graphic Links in Package** options checked (they should be checked by default). Click **Package** (Windows) or **Save** (Mac) to begin copying the files into the single folder that InDesign will create.

*Note: You need to click the **Use Document Hyphenation Exceptions Only** check box if you added any hyphenation exceptions to the dictionary (these are created by choosing **Edit > Spelling > Dictionary**). When you select this check box, InDesign uses the dictionary in the document and hyphenates according to the hyphenations you created. You may want to select **Use Document Hyphenation Exceptions Only** when packaging a document to be printed by an external party, like a service provider.*

8. The **Font Alert** dialog box appears when you select the **Copy Fonts** option in the **Create Package Folder** dialog box, as you did in the last step. It is warning you of font restrictions due to licensing for some of the fonts used. Click **OK** to package the document.

9. You return to the InDesign file after the packaging process has completed. Save the file and close it.

*The illustration above shows what the package folder will contain (Mac). InDesign organizes all the fonts into a **Fonts** subfolder and all the links into a **Links** subfolder. The InDesign file (**postcard_output_clean.indd**) and the **Instructions.txt** file are in the main **postcard** folder. Remember, these are copies of the files, not the originals, so you now have two copies of all of these files. The graphic links in this new InDesign file copy should link to the graphics in the **Links** subfolder.*

Note: *The content of your packaged folder may be different from the illustration because of font replacements.*

All that someone has to do to begin working on this set of files is install the fonts in the appropriate font folder on the hard drive.

Previewing Separations

Before printing an InDesign CS2 file or outputting any type of file (PDF, EPS, etc.), you need to think about a few elements of the file. One of the most important considerations is what colors are used in the document. If you are designing for print, you should be using CMYK graphics (unless your output situation deems otherwise), CMYK swatches, and the occasional spot color if necessary. But every once in a while, an RGB graphic or an extra spot color that you weren't aware of finds its way into the file. That's why it's good practice to check the document separations.

> ### BONUS EXERCISE | Previewing Separations in InDesign
>
> To learn how, check out **separations.pdf** in the **bonus_exercises** folder on the **InDesign CS2 HOT CD-ROM**.

Packaging for the Web (to GoLive CS2)

InDesign has the amazing capability of repurposing print-ready files for use on the Web. Using InDesign's **Package for GoLive** feature, found under **File > Package for GoLive**, you can create a package composed of XML files and either images you supply later or images that InDesign optimizes from the print-ready graphics in the document.

The package InDesign creates when you use the **Package for GoLive feature** is intended to be opened in GoLive CS2 (Adobe's Web development tool), not in earlier versions of GoLive. It is also not intended to be used easily with other Web applications, such as Macromedia Dreamweaver. The package file that InDesign creates contains the following:

- An **Assets folder** that contains the graphics, movies, and sounds (yes, you can add movies and sounds to an InDesign document).

- A **PDF** that is opened directly in GoLive. From this package PDF, you can drag pieces onto an HTML page or save as HTML once you are in GoLive.

- An **XML** file that contains the content information.

The **Package for GoLive** feature can also convert paragraph and character styles into CSS (Cascading Style Sheets) styles to be used in GoLive for text formatting. All in all, the feature is very useful for moving a print piece to Adobe GoLive CS2. Instructions for how to use the **Package for GoLive** feature will be covered in the following movie.

 MOVIE | Package for GoLive

To see an example of how to create a package using the **Package for GoLive** feature, check out **golive_package.mov** in the **movies** folder on the **InDesign CS2 HOT CD-ROM**.

Printing in InDesign

Although the concept of printing a file may seem straightforward, features like transparency, spot colors, and gradients in documents created in InDesign CS2 make greater control over the printing process a necessity. Before getting into InDesign's various print options, it is helpful to understand some basic concepts related to printing—specifically, the difference between PostScript and non-PostScript printers and the two main ways printers handle color.

The two major types of printers are PostScript and non-PostScript. A PostScript printer processes PostScript information, also known as a PDL (Page Description Language), which describes the document in the PostScript language to a printer. PostScript is one of the most widely used printer languages. The print driver (software) installed on the computer acts as an intermediary, effectively translating the document's information to the printer in a format, or language (such as PDL), that the printer can understand.

Non-PostScript printers work similarly, although they expect to be sent a non-PostScript language. Several major manufacturers of desktop printers produce non-PostScript printers. When printing InDesign documents that use EPS (Encapsulated PostScript) files, it is important to understand that non-PostScript printers cannot interpret EPS graphic files, which are, of course, PostScript-based. The trick for getting EPS files to print to non-PostScript printers is to change the **View** setting to **High Quality Display** by choosing **View > Display Performance > High Quality Display**. What you see onscreen in preview mode (by clicking the **Preview Mode** button at the bottom of the **Toolbox**) should be what prints.

If you type letters, draw simple graphs, or print photographs, you may not need to use the PostScript language or a PostScript printer. For simple text and graphics, your non-PostScript printer driver may be adequate for outputting the files. You can check the manufacturer's information for the desktop printer you are using to see if it does in fact support the PostScript language.

As with so many topics, when it comes to printing, a little knowledge is dangerous. When outputting for a commercial press, it can be best to let the service provider perform tasks like making color separations. Each press is different and requires its own settings, so the process can get complicated very quickly.

Print Options in the Print Dialog Box

Choosing **File > Print** in InDesign CS2 opens the **Print** dialog box. Although the **Print** dialog box can seem mysterious, it's important to get an idea of the functions of at least some of its options. More often than not, the defaults will be sufficient, but there may be times when you need to adjust a few of the settings.

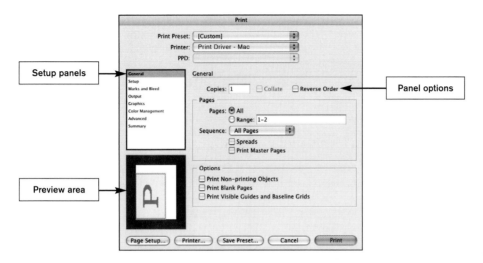

Setup panels

Panel options

Preview area

The **Preview** area is great for viewing how the document is positioned on the paper (or media), as well as document dimensions, color information, and more. This chart explains the various options available in the **Preview** area.

Preview Area Options

In the **Preview** area of the **Print** dialog box, click with the cursor to cycle through three windows. The options are described below.

This is the default **Preview** area. You can see if the document will fit on the paper (media). It also shows bleed, printer's marks, orientation, tiling, and more.	Click once to display this **Preview** area. Here you can see information contained in the **General** and **Setup** areas of the **Print** dialog box.	Click a second time to display this **Preview** area. InDesign shows the **Output** options in the **Print** dialog box: Separations (▣), CMYK Composite (▣), RGB Composite (▣), Gray Composite (▣), or Composite Leave Unchanged (▣- nothing). Click once more to return to the default **Preview** area.

The **General** panel in the Print dialog box includes options that most of us will be using to output our files. The chart below describes in some detail what each of these options determines.

General Panel Print Settings	
Option	**Function**
Print Preset	Saves settings created in the **Print** dialog box as named sets that can be chosen at a later date from this pop-up menu. Each saved preset is associated with the printer that is used when the preset is created.
Printer	Designates the print driver. This tells InDesign which printer features to use when printing to this particular printer. Having the correct driver ensures that you have access to all the features that a particular printer supports.
PPD	PPD (PostScript Printer Description) is a text file that installs with a PostScript print driver. When you designate a printer driver (in the **Printer** field), you need to choose the matching PPD. This text file instructs InDesign on the setup options that are displayed, such as paper sizes the printer can handle. Non-PostScript printers typically do not use PPDs.
Copies	Specifies how many copies of the file are to be printed. **Collate** allows multiple copies to be printed as sets. **Reverse Order** prints from the last page of the document forward.
Pages	Prints page ranges (**1-4** for example) or **All** pages. The **Sequence** options include **All Pages**, **Even Pages**, or **Odd Pages**. The **Spread** check box enables you to print facing pages together as spreads. **Print Master Pages** is a feature that prints the master pages of the document only—excellent for sharing design ideas!
Options	Selecting **Non-printing Objects** prints any objects that were designated as nonprinting in the **Window > Attributes** palette. **Print Blank Pages** is useful for printing placeholder pages, such as the inside cover of a book. **Print Visible Guides and Baseline Grids** is useful for training or instruction purposes.

continues on next page

General Panel Print Settings *continued*

Option	Function
Setup button (Windows) or button (Mac)	Opens device-specific options. These are settings that are Page Setup associated with each output device. When you choose a different printer, these options change. In most cases, it's good to use the options available in the **Print** dialog box, but in some instances, the printer-specific settings are necessary.

> **Warning**
>
> If the desired print setting is available in InDesign's Print dialog box, please set it there to avoid printing conflicts.
>
> ☐ Don't show again
>
> OK

	Clicking the **Setup** button (Windows) or **Page Setup** button (Mac) opens a dialog box that indicates that some of the options are the same between the printer-specific options and those in the **Print** dialog box. This warning appears on both Mac and Windows platforms.
Printer button (Mac)	Available only on the Mac platform, this button opens the **OSX Print** dialog box that contains printer-specific options.

The Save Preset Button

Saving the settings you've selected in the **Print** dialog box as presets is particularly helpful for repeat-edly printing the same types of documents to one output device. Once you've saved the presets, you can choose them from the **Print Preset** pop-up menu in the **Print** dialog box at a later date.

After selecting the print settings for a document, click the **Save Preset** button to open a dialog box that prompts you to save the settings, or preset, with a name. Name it according to the output device it is going to (if you have several) and a general description. I often include document dimensions in the name. Click **OK** to create the preset.

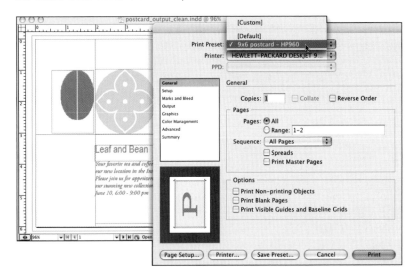

The next time you open the **Print** dialog box by choosing **File > Print**, all you have to do is choose the preset from the **Print Preset** menu and then click the **Print** button!

Note: This works especially well for printing the same types of documents constantly, like spreads in a catalog or a monthly newsletter.

*Tip: If you find yourself visiting the printer-specific options often, you can save time by changing the default settings in the print driver, which is in the operating system. Click the **Setup** button (**Windows**) or the **Page Setup** or **Printer** button (**Mac**) to save settings in the print driver. You will only have to do this once. On the Mac platform, open the **Print Setup Utility** under **MacintoshHD:Applications/ Utilities/Printer Setup Utility (Mac OS 10.3)** or in the **Control Panel** under the **Start** menu on **Windows**.*

Print Dialog Box Options

The **Print** dialog box contains many options. To learn more about them, open the PDF titled **PDF_printsettings.pdf** in the **bonus_exercises** folder on the **InDesign CS2 HOT CD-ROM**.

TIP | Editing Print Presets

Print presets that you have saved by clicking the **Save Preset** button in the **Print** dialog box (see the previous section, "The Save Preset Button," for more information) can be edited, deleted, or shared with others when you choose **File > Print Presets > Define**. The **Print Presets** dialog box opens.

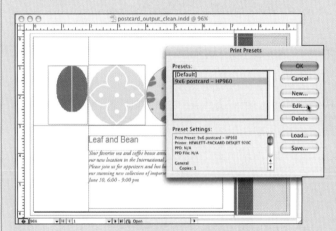

In the illustration, you can see the print preset saved earlier in the chapter: "**9x6 postcard – HP960.**" You can edit or delete this print preset directly in the **Print Presets** dialog box. You can also create and save new presets from the dialog box. Finally, you can share print presets by clicking **Load**, which imports a preset from someone else, or **Save**, which exports a preset to e-mail to others. The file format used for exchanging preset files is PRST (Print Preset).

What Is Imposition?

When printing with a commercial printer, often your document is output on a press sheet. Press sheets come in various sizes (there are industry standards, of course), so when the printer prints your document, as many of the pages as possible are squeezed onto a single press sheet. The pages need to be printed in the correct order as well.

When you build a facing-page (spread) document in InDesign, most of us build it using **readers spreads**. This means that you design the document so that page 2 is next to page 3 (in the same spread), 4 is next to 5 (in the same spread), 6 is next to 7 (in the same spread), and so on. When you send this file to a commercial printer, they have to move the pages into a different order, called **printers spreads**. The process of reordering the pages in the spreads is called **imposition**, and a commercial printer will usually take care of this process. The following illustration shows the difference between readers and printers spreads.

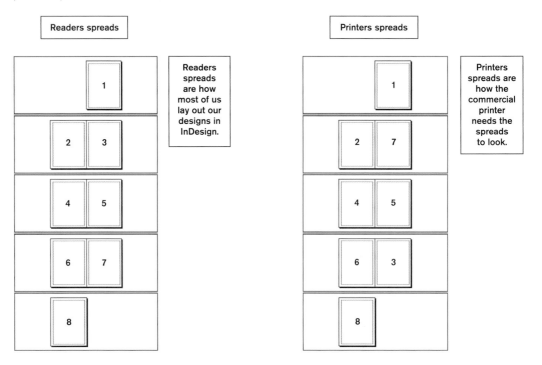

The reason why the page order needs to change is that as documents are printed and cut out of the press sheet, they are cut out in spreads printed on the front and back of the sheet. These are referred to as **signatures**. A signature then, consists of four pages in the document. The signatures are folded into each other and bound to create a magazine, newspaper, newsletter, book, etc.

Take a magazine, for example. If it's stapled at the center (glued is harder!), find the center two pages and remove them by pulling them out. (Obviously, you'd better conduct this experiment at home; the dentist's office or bookstore wouldn't appreciate this.) If the pages are numbered, you will get a sense of why they need to be numbered and reordered through the process of imposition. A newspaper also is a good test of this.

MOVIE | Imposing with InBooklet SE

To see an example of how to impose a document for output with a commercial printer using InBooklet SE, check out **imposition.mov** in the **movies** folder on the **InDesign CS2 HOT CD-ROM**.

What Is a Template?

I work with a lot of designers who design brochures and marketing pieces for companies that want to use that same documents and designs over and over, replacing only the contents to produce new pieces. You could accomplish such a task by saving the original InDesign document over and over. But a more efficient method is creating a template from the original document. That way you never have to worry about harming the original file.

A template, on the surface, is nothing more than an InDesign document with the extension of .indt, but it's more than that. Templates are used so that whenever someone attempts to open the original design file (saved as a template), a copy is opened instead. This saves the original template file from being changed in any way. Of course, you can change a template file, but it requires getting through a few safety measures.

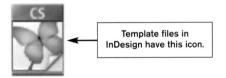

Template files in InDesign have this icon.

2. ————————Saving a File as an InDesign Template

In this short exercise, you will save a file as a template.

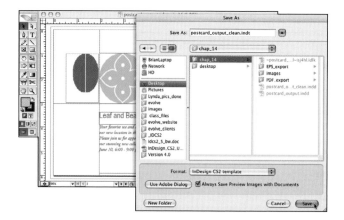

1. Open **postcard_output_clean.indd** from the **chap_14** folder on the **Desktop**. Choose **File > Save As**. From the **Save as Type** menu (Windows) or **Format** menu (Mac) located near the bottom of the dialog box, choose **InDesign CS2 template**. Check that the file will be saved into the **chap_14** folder on the **Desktop**, and then click **Save** to save the template file. Once saved, close the file (which is now a template) by choosing **File > Close**.

Note: A dialog box that indicates missing or modified graphics may appear when you open this file. If it does, choose **Fix Links Automatically** *to update any modified graphics automatically. After fixing the links, close the* **Links** *palette. If the* **Find** *dialog box opens, navigate to the* **chap_14** *folder on the* **Desktop**, *and find the graphics in the* **images** *folder.*

Note: You may come across the **Missing Fonts** *dialog box. If you do, change the font by choosing* **Find Font** *and replacing the font with a version of Arial or Helvetica. For a refresher on this, see Chapter 5, "Typography in InDesign."*

Note: The extension of the file changes to .indt (indicating it is an InDesign template).

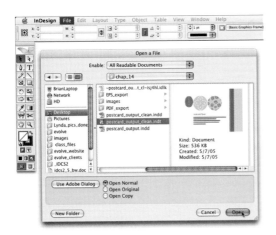

2. Next you will open the template file and see it at work. Choose **File > Open** and open the template file called **postcard_output_clean.indt**, which you just saved into the **chap_14** folder on the **Desktop**.

*Note: A dialog box that indicates missing or modified graphics may appear when opening this file. If it does, choose **Fix Links Automatically** to update any modified graphics automatically. After fixing the links, close the **Links** palette. If the **Find** dialog box opens, navigate to the **chap_14** folder on the **Desktop**, and find the graphics in the **images** folder.*

*Note: You may come across the **Missing Fonts** dialog box. If you do, change the font by choosing **Find Font** and replacing the font with a version of Arial or Helvetica. For a refresher on this, see Chapter 5, "Typography in InDesign."*

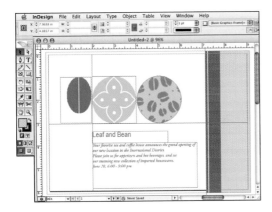

*The file that opens should not be the original template but an untitled document. Your document most likely will have a different number than the **Untitled-2** document in the illustration. Every time you open a template in the same session of InDesign, the number in the document name increases. Normally, at this point you would save the file by choosing **File > Save As** and saving the new document somewhere you plan to work with it. In this case, however, close the file and don't save it.*

Tip: When working with templates, make sure that you either embed the graphics or make the users aware of any graphic links that they need to pay attention to. Otherwise, the links might break and the users wind up calling you asking why the graphics don't look right! For a refresher on graphic links, visit Chapter 8, "Bringing in Graphics."

Tip: When creating a template, you may not want the graphics in the template, only the frames as placeholders. Before you save an InDesign document as a template, select the **Direct Selection** tool (the white arrow). Click in the graphic frames to select the graphics. Press **Backspace** or **Delete** to remove the graphic and keep the graphic frame. Then save the file as a template using the steps in this exercise.

What Is a PDF and Why Use It?

The Adobe PDF format is commonly used these days. People exchange them as attachments in e-mails and even use them to fill out IRS tax forms. PDF, which stands for Portable Document Format, is meant to be an exchange file format. In other words, PDFs can be easily exchanged because anyone who has free Adobe Reader software (downloadable from Adobe's Web site) can view a PDF file exactly as the author had intended it to be viewed.

Adobe asserts that PDF files can be created from anything you can see. That means that any file you have (with a few very minor exceptions) can be turned into a PDF file. PDFs can be used for quick previews (a designer sending a design concept, for instance) or for printing a file (on a commercial press or a local desktop printer). They can even be prepared for use on a Web site. PDF files are generally smaller than the original file they were created from, and they contain the document and all its content—fonts, links, and more. To create a PDF file from InDesign, you do not need the Adobe Acrobat application. InDesign has PDF creation capability built in. This means you can create a PDF simply by choosing **File > Export** within InDesign. PDF files are especially useful for outputting to a service provider because they are a self-contained document with all of the elements already inside.

Creating PDF files from InDesign is a relatively simple process, but it's important enough to require at least a general understanding of the PDF creation process.

PDF Presets

The first step in creating a PDF is to define its purpose. A PDF that you want to e-mail to someone for a quick review should be as small as possible, while a PDF that you will send to a commercial press will be larger to meet appropriate standards of quality. During the PDF creation process in InDesign, key features—how the PDF treats fonts and graphics, for instance—can be controlled to achieve output goals.

InDesign offers five options, or **Adobe PDF presets**, for you to choose from when generating a PDF from the program. These options are predefined settings that you can use to generate a PDF for a particular purpose, like sending to a commercial printer or optimizing it for the Web.

The five PDF presets are in the **Export Adobe PDF** dialog box, which you can access by choosing **File > Export**, then selecting **PDF** from the **Save as Type** (Windows) or **Format** (Mac) pop-up menu, and clicking the **Save** button. You will use that dialog box in the next exercise, "Exporting as PDF." The presets are **High Quality Print**, **PDF/X-1a:2001**, **PDF/X-3:2002**, **Press Quality**, and **Smallest File Size**. Each one is described in the chart below.

PDF Presets	
PDF Preset	**Function**
High Quality Print	Creates Adobe PDF documents for quality printing on desktop printers and/or proofers.
PDF/X-1a:2001	Creates Adobe PDF documents that must conform to PDF/X-1a:2001, an ISO standard for blind exchange of PDF files (for example, a PDF file being output to a service provider when you don't know their print settings). For more information on PDF/X, download an informational PDF file from Adobe's Web site at **http://www.adobe.com/products/acrobat/pdfs/acr6_pdfx_faq.pdf**.
PDF/X-3:2002	Creates Adobe PDF documents that are to be checked by or must conform to PDF/X-3:2002, another ISO standard for blind exchange of PDF files. Again, for more information on PDF/X, download an informational PDF file from Adobe's Web site at **http://www.adobe.com/products/acrobat/pdfs/acr6_pdfx_faq.pdf**.
Press Quality	Creates PDF files intended for high-quality prepress printing.
Smallest File Size	Creates Adobe PDF documents for onscreen display in presentations, on the Internet, and for sending via e-mail.

PDF Preset Options

Before creating a PDF from InDesign, you need to choose a PDF preset. Usually, the settings within the **Adobe PDF Presets** dialog box are sufficient, but when necessary, the settings can be edited in the **Export Adobe PDF** dialog box to optimize the file for its intended use. To learn more about the PDF preset options (such as **General**, **Compression**, or **Security**), open the PDF titled **PDF_presets.pdf** in the **bonus_exercises** folder on the **InDesign CS2 HOT CD-ROM**.

3. ——————————Exporting as PDF

In this exercise, you will walk through how to create a PDF that can be sent to a print service provider for output.

1. Open **postcard_output_clean.indd** from the **chap_14** folder on the **Desktop**.

*Note: A dialog box that indicates missing or modified graphics may appear when you open this file. If it does, choose **Fix Links Automatically** to update any modified graphics automatically. After fixing the links, close the **Links** palette. If the **Find** dialog box opens, navigate to the **chap_14** folder on the **Desktop**, and find the graphics in the **images** folder. It is important to fix any missing or modified graphics when creating a PDF.*

*Note: You may come across the **Missing Fonts** dialog box. If you do, change the font by choosing **Find Font** and replacing the font with a version of Arial or Helvetica. For a refresher on this, see Chapter 5, "Typography in InDesign."*

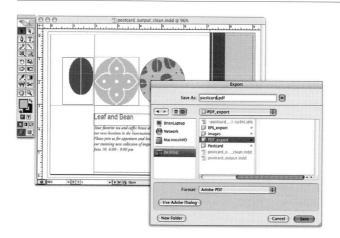

2. Choose **File > Export**. In the **Export** dialog box, choose **Adobe PDF** from the **Save as Type** menu (Windows) or the **Format** menu (Mac). Navigate to the **Desktop** and open the **chap_14** folder. Once inside that folder, select the **PDF export** folder and click **Open** (Windows) or select the **PDF_export** folder (Mac). In the **File name** (Windows) or **Save As** (Mac) field, type **postcard.pdf**. Click **Save** to open the **Export Adobe PDF** dialog box.

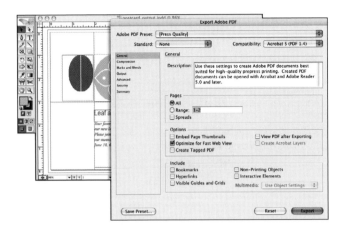

3. In the **Export Adobe PDF** dialog box, choose **Press Quality** from the **Adobe PDF Preset** pop-up menu. This preset can be used for sending the file to a commercial printer. Leave all settings in the **General** panel at their defaults.

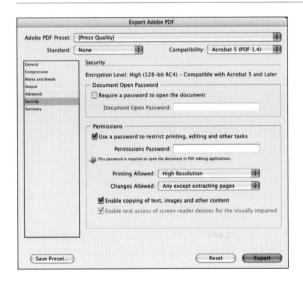

4. Click **Security** on the left side of the dialog box to open the **Security** panel. You will set permissions security on the file to limit what the user can do to it. Click the **Use a password to restrict printing, editing and other tasks** check box to turn on security. In the **Permissions Password** field, type "**class**." From the **Printing Allowed** pop-up menu, choose **Low Resolution (150 dpi)**. This enables the user to print the PDF, but only with low-resolution graphics; the PDF is intended only as a preview. Choose **None** from the **Changes Allowed** pop-up menu to prevent changes to the document. Deselect the **Enable copying of text, images and other content** check box (this is why you apply security most of the time!). Click **Export** to create the PDF file.

Note: Don't forget the password! It's almost impossible to remove security once a password has been forgotten. In most cases, the PDF has to be re-created. Also, keep in mind that security pass-words for PDFs are case sensitive.

*Tip: If you changed any of the settings (in most cases you won't have to), by clicking the **Save Preset** button in the **Export Adobe PDF** dialog box, you can save the new settings with a name for later use. Next time you export from InDesign to create a PDF, you can choose the saved preset from the **Adobe PDF Preset** menu.*

5. The **Password** dialog box appears, asking you to resupply the password. Type the password "**class**" again, and click **OK** to create the PDF file. Once the PDF file is created, leave the InDesign file open for the next exercise.

Once the PDF file is created, it will look like the illustration above. The amount of time it takes to create a PDF can vary, depending on the size of the original InDesign document.

*Note: Because you did not select the **View PDF after Exporting** check box in the **General** panel of the **Export Adobe PDF** dialog box, the PDF will not open automatically.*

4. _____Creating PDF Presets

As discussed in the last exercise, Adobe InDesign CS2 has five built-in PDF presets. Although these presets are not editable, you can create your own presets for various PDF creation purposes. In this exercise, you will create a new PDF preset to make the file size the smallest it can be for use on the Web.

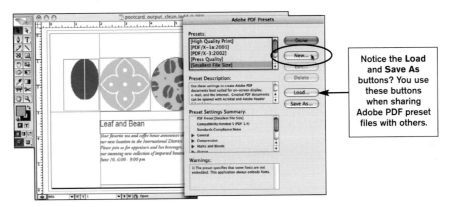

Notice the **Load** and **Save As** buttons? You use these buttons when sharing Adobe PDF preset files with others.

1. With **postcard_output_clean.indd** open from the previous exercise, choose **File > Adobe PDF Presets > Define** to open the **Adobe PDF Presets** dialog box. Click the **Smallest File Size** preset in the **Presets** list. It is one of the presets that come with InDesign. That means you cannot edit it, but when you create a new preset, it will base the new PDF preset on the chosen one. Click **New**.

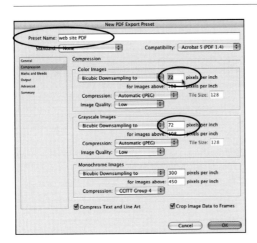

2. The **New PDF Export Preset** dialog box opens. Change the **Preset Name** to **web site PDF**, and select **Compression** on the left side of the dialog box. Change the sampling resolution for **Color Images** and **Grayscale Images** to **72**, and click **OK** to accept the new preset. Close the **Adobe PDF Presets** dialog box.

By setting **Compression** at 72 pixels per inch (ppi), you are lowering the resolution to the lowest that you want to go for use on the Web. This helps make the PDF file the smallest size it can be. Once again, you can change any of the PDF preset options and save the settings so that you can use them later. It may take some testing on your part to get the perfect PDF for the intended use, but it will be worth it.

Note: The **Smallest File Size** PDF preset is not the smallest file size you can get. That PDF preset seems to be created to that you can e-mail a PDF, but it will still print decently.

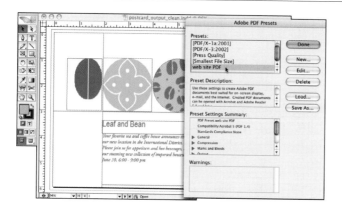

3. The preset will now appear in the **Adobe PDF Presets** dialog box. Click **Done** to close the **Adobe PDF Presets** dialog box.

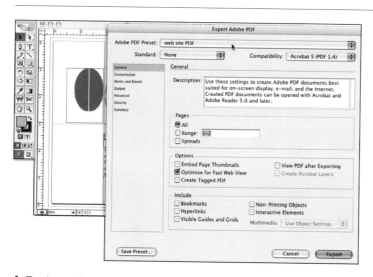

4. To show where you will use this PDF preset, you will go through the motions of creating another PDF (as in the previous exercise). Choose **File > Export**. In the **Export** dialog box, choose **Adobe PDF** from the **Save as Type** menu (Windows) or the **Format** menu (Mac). Click **Save** without minding where the PDF will be saved, because you won't actually create it. In the **Export Adobe PDF** dialog box, choose **web site PDF** from the **Adobe PDF Preset** pop-up menu. Anytime you make a PDF from here on out, you will see this preset. Click **Cancel** so that you don't have to make the PDF. Leave the file **postcard_output_clean.indd** open for the next exercise.

Tip: This preset is also going to show up in other Creative Suite 2 products when you create a PDF.

NOTE | Confirming the Print Service Provider's PDF Presets

When preparing to create a PDF for output (printing), always check with the print service provider for their preferred settings. Some service providers also supply a PDF options file, which may have an extension of .joboptions, that you can load into the **Adobe PDF Presets** dialog box (found under **File > Adobe PDF Presets > Define**). This is much better than going through the options with the service provider one by one.

Exporting as an EPS

InDesign offers several export options, and EPS is one of them. Why export as an EPS? There are several reasons, but the main one is to save an InDesign file as a graphic so that it can be placed in another InDesign file. EPS is a common cross-application file format for printing. Unlike TIFFs, however, EPS files are typically used for vector images, such as logos or illustrations drawn in Adobe Illustrator or Macromedia FreeHand. EPS files can contain text and graphics, preserving the individual qualities of each component on the exported page. For example, a monthly newsletter might include a picture of the previous newsletter. Exporting the first page of the old issue as an EPS allows you to place it as a graphic in the current issue of the newsletter.

EPS can be chosen as the export format through **File > Export**. Exporting an EPS contains many options. To learn more about them, open the PDF titled **eps_options.pdf** located in the **bonus_exercises** folder of the **InDesign CS2 HOT CD-ROM**.

5. ——————————Exporting as EPS

In this exercise, you will export the first page of the **postcard_output_clean.indd** from the previous exercise as an EPS file.

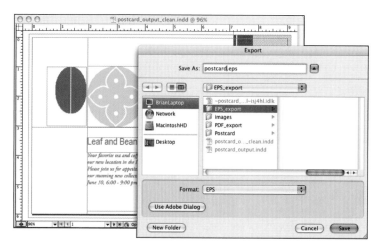

1. With **postcard_output_clean.indd** open from the previous exercise, choose **File > Export**. Select **EPS** from the **Save as Type** menu (Windows) or **Format** menu (Mac) from the **Export** dialog box. In the **Export** dialog box, navigate to the **chap_14** folder on the **Desktop** and open the folder named **EPS_export** inside. In the **File Name** field (Windows) or **Save As** field (Mac), type "**postcard.eps**" and click **Save** to open the **Export EPS** dialog box. This is where you set the options for EPS export.

*Note: If you are just joining this chapter, open **postcard_output_clean.indd** from the **chap_14** folder on the **Desktop**. The **Missing Fonts** dialog box may appear when you open this file. If it does, change the font by choosing **Find Font** and replacing the font with a version of Arial or Helvetica. For a refresher on this, see Chapter 5, "Typography in InDesign."*

*Note: A dialog box that indicates missing or modified graphics may appear when you this file. If it does, choose **Fix Links Automatically** to update any modified graphics automatically. After fixing the links, close the **Links** palette. If the **Find** dialog box opens, navigate to the **chap_14** folder on the **Desktop**, and find the graphics in the **images** folder. It is important to fix any missing or modified graphics when creating an EPS.*

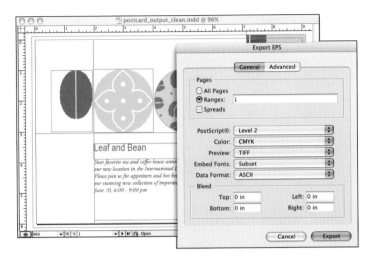

2. With the **General** tab chosen by default, click the **Ranges** option and type **1** into the field. This creates an EPS of only the first page. The rest of the default settings are fine. Click **Export** to create the EPS and return to the InDesign document.

*Note: The document you are creating the EPS from has a bleed. The **Export EPS** dialog box didn't call for a bleed because the EPS image is going to be used as a smaller graphic (you will resize it after it is placed). If it were to be placed onto a page as a full page, the bleed would be necessary.*

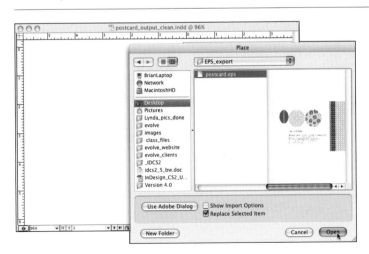

3. Once you are back in **postcard_output_clean.indd**, choose **File > Place** to place the newly created EPS you created in the last step. From within the **chap_14** folder on the **Desktop**, choose **postcard.eps** from the **EPS_export** folder. Make sure that **Show Import Options** is deselected and click **Open** to place the EPS.

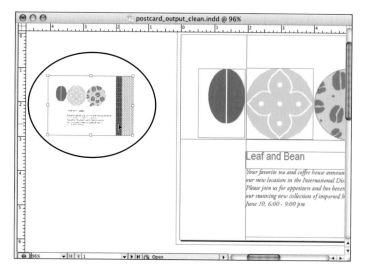

4. Click the **Loaded Graphic** icon on the pasteboard to the left of the document to see the EPS graphic you created in Step 2. When placed, it will be the size of the page.

*The EPS graphic in the illustration has been resized using the **Scale** tool to show how the EPS looks. When resizing a placed EPS like this one, remember that an EPS made from an entire page can contain raster graphics, so you need to be cautious when resizing. Making the EPS larger decreases the resolution of any raster graphics within the EPS, and making it smaller increases the resolution of those graphics.*

5. Save the InDesign file and keep it open for the next exercise.

6. _____Exporting to Earlier Versions of InDesign

InDesign CS2 allows files to be exported to InDesign CS using **File > Export** and saving as an **InDesign Interchange (INX)** file with an extension of .inx. This file format is not compatible with versions of InDesign older than CS.

In this short exercise, you will save the file to be backward compatible with InDesign CS by exporting to the INX format.

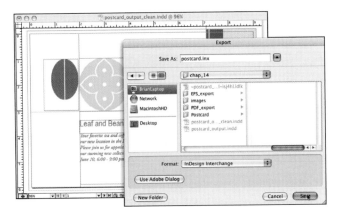

1. With **postcard_output_clean.indd** open from the last exercise, choose **File > Export** once again. Select **InDesign Interchange** from the **Save as Type** (Windows) or **Format** (Mac) menu. Navigate to the **chap_14** folder on the **Desktop**. In the **File Name** field (Windows) or **Save As** field (Mac), type "**postcard.inx**" ("**inx**" should appear by default, but make sure it stays in the name to be safe). Click the **Save** button to create the interchange file.

2. Close the file **postcard_output_clean.indd** when the interchange file has been created.

postcard.inx

*An INX file should show up in the **chap_14** folder on the **Desktop**. This file is now ready to be opened in InDesign CS (only).*

Note: Be careful when saving back as an INX file. If you used any new features, like object styles or footnotes, the formatting for those new features may still show up in InDesign CS. For instance, an object style in CS2 with a color fill will show up as a color fill in InDesign CS, but there will be no object style to use.

Exporting Text from InDesign

One feature that allows you to repurpose content to another program or InDesign file is to export text from an InDesign document. The trick to exporting text to be used elsewhere is to place the cursor in text first and then choose **File > Export**. In the **Save as Type** (Windows) or **Format** (Mac) menu, you can choose from three text file types: **Adobe InDesign Tagged Text** (TXT), **Rich Text Format** (RTF), or **Plain Text** (TXT). The export will create a text file that you can place into another InDesign document or open in a text editor.

 MOVIE | **Export Text from InDesign**

To learn more about exporting text, check out **text_export.mov** in the **movies** folder on the **InDesign CS2 HOT CD-ROM**.

What Is Color Management?

Color management is a way to control color throughout a workflow. To learn more about color management, go to the Adobe Web site at **http://www.adobe.com/products/creativesuite/pdfs/ cscolormgmt.pdf** to view a white paper titled **"Color Consistency and Adobe Creative Suite."** It's a bit dated but still good for understanding what a color management process can accomplish.

BONUS EXERCISE | **Working with Color Management**

To learn how, check out **color_manage.pdf** in the **bonus_exercises** folder on the **InDesign CS2 HOT CD-ROM**.

What Is Soft Proofing?

When printing in a typical print workflow, you usually make sure the document looks right either by receiving a proof from your print service provider or printing a copy from your desktop printer. Called **proofing**, this process requires time and resources. If you have a color-managed system in place with InDesign, however, you can use your monitor and a proofing space to preview or proof the output right on your monitor. For soft proofing to be effective, your workflow needs to be color managed, starting with a monitor properly calibrated to the correct profiles. Soft proofing is only as good as any of those pieces.

BONUS EXERCISE | Soft Proofing InDesign files

To learn how, check out **soft_proof.pdf** in the **bonus_exercises** folder on the **InDesign CS2 HOT CD-ROM**.

Kudos on making it through this entire book! I hope InDesign CS2 contributes as much to your creative workflow as it has to mine. You've learned an incredible amount of new information, so remember to use this book as a reference when that "how do you do that again?" feeling overtakes you. I hope you've enjoyed getting your hands into the program. Now, go create!

Index

THIS SOFTWARE LICENSE AGREEMENT CONSTITUTES AN AGREEMENT BETWEEN YOU AND LYNDA.COM, INC. YOU SHOULD CAREFULLY READ THE FOLLOWING TERMS AND CONDITIONS. COPYING THIS SOFTWARE TO YOUR MACHINE OR OTHERWISE REMOVING OR USING THE SOFTWARE INDICATES YOUR ACCEPTANCE OF THESE TERMS AND CONDITIONS. IF YOU DO NOT AGREE TO BE BOUND BY THE PROVISIONS OF THIS LICENSE AGREEMENT, YOU SHOULD PROMPTLY DELETE THE SOFTWARE FROM YOUR MACHINE.

TERMS AND CONDITIONS:

1. GRANT OF LICENSE. In consideration of payment of the License Fee, which was a part of the price you paid for this product, LICENSOR grants to you (the "Licensee") a non-exclusive right to use the Software (all parts and elements of the data contained on the accompanying CD-ROM are hereinafter referred to as the "Software"), along with any updates or upgrade releases of the Software for which you have paid on a single computer only (i.e., with a single CPU) at a single location, all as more particularly set forth and limited below. LICENSOR reserves all rights not expressly granted to you as Licensee in this License Agreement.

2. OWNERSHIP OF SOFTWARE. The license granted herein is not a sale of the original Software or of any copy of the Software. As Licensee, you own only the rights to use the Software as described herein and the magnetic or other physical media on which the Software is originally or subsequently recorded or fixed. LICENSOR retains title and ownership of the Software recorded on the original disk(s), as well as title and ownership of any subsequent copies of the Software irrespective of the form of media on or in which the Software is recorded or fixed. This license does not grant you any intellectual or other proprietary or other rights of any nature whatsoever in the Software.

3. USE RESTRICTIONS. As Licensee, you may use the Software only as expressly authorized in this License Agreement under the terms of paragraph 4. You may physically transfer the Software from one computer to another provided that the Software is used on only a single computer at any one time. You may not: (i) electronically transfer the Software from one computer to another over a network; (ii) make the Software available through a time-sharing service, network of computers, or other multiple user arrangement; (iii) distribute copies of the Software or related written materials to any third party, whether for sale or otherwise; (iv) modify, adapt, translate, reverse engineer, decompile, disassemble, or prepare any derivative work based on the Software or any element thereof; (v) make or distribute, whether for sale or otherwise, any hard copy or printed version of any of the Software nor any portion thereof nor any work of yours containing the Software or any component thereof; (vi) use any of the Software nor any of its components in any other work.

4. THIS IS WHAT YOU CAN AND CANNOT DO WITH THE SOFTWARE. Even though in the preceding paragraph and elsewhere LICENSOR has restricted your use of the Software, the following is the only thing you can do with the Software and the various elements of the Software: THE ARTWORK CONTAINED ON THIS DVD-ROM MAY NOT BE USED IN ANY MANNER WHATSOEVER OTHER THAN TO VIEW THE SAME ON YOUR COMPUTER, OR POST TO YOUR PERSONAL, NON-COMMERCIAL WEB SITE FOR EDUCATIONAL PURPOSES ONLY. THIS MATERIAL IS SUBJECT TO ALL OF THE RESTRICTION PROVISIONS OF THIS SOFTWARE LICENSE. SPECIFICALLY BUT NOT IN LIMITATION OF THESE RESTRICTIONS, YOU MAY NOT DISTRIBUTE, RESELL OR TRANSFER THIS PART OF THE SOFTWARE NOR ANY OF YOUR DESIGN OR OTHER WORK CONTAINING ANY OF THE SOFTWARE on this DVD-ROM, ALL AS MORE PARTICULARLY RESTRICTED IN THE WITHIN SOFTWARE LICENSE.

5. COPY RESTRICTIONS. The Software and accompanying written materials are protected under United States copyright laws. Unauthorized copying and/or distribution of the Software and/or the related written materials is expressly forbidden. You may be held legally responsible for any copyright infringement that is caused, directly or indirectly, by your failure to abide by the terms of this License Agreement. Subject to the terms of this License Agreement and if the software is not otherwise copy protected, you may make one copy of the Software for backup purposes only. The copyright notice and any other proprietary notices which were included in the original Software must be reproduced and included on any such backup copy.

6. TRANSFER RESTRICTIONS. The license herein granted is personal to you, the Licensee. You may not transfer the Software nor any of its components or elements to anyone else, nor may you sell, lease, loan, sublicense, assign, or otherwise dispose of the Software nor any of its components or elements without the express written consent of LICENSOR, which consent may be granted or withheld at LICENSOR's sole discretion.

7. TERMINATION. The license herein granted hereby will remain in effect until terminated. This license will terminate automatically without further notice from LICENSOR in the event of the violation of any of the provisions hereof. As Licensee, you agree that upon such termination you will promptly destroy any and all copies of the Software which remain in your possession and, upon request, will certify to such destruction in writing to LICENSOR.

8. LIMITATION AND DISCLAIMER OF WARRANTIES. a) THE SOFTWARE AND RELATED WRITTEN MATERIALS, INCLUDING ANY INSTRUCTIONS FOR USE, ARE PROVIDED ON AN "AS IS" BASIS, WITHOUT WARRANTY OF ANY KIND, EXPRESS OR IMPLIED. THIS DISCLAIMER OF WARRANTY EXPRESSLY INCLUDES, BUT IS NOT LIMITED TO, ANY IMPLIED WARRANTIES OF MER-CHANTABILITY AND/OR OF FITNESS FOR A PARTICULAR PURPOSE. NO WARRANTY OF ANY KIND IS MADE AS TO WHETHER OR NOT THIS SOFT-WARE INFRINGES UPON ANY RIGHTS OF ANY OTHER THIRD PARTIES. NO ORAL OR WRITTEN INFORMATION GIVEN BY LICENSOR, ITS SUPPLIERS, DISTRIBUTORS, DEALERS, EMPLOYEES, OR AGENTS, SHALL CREATE OR OTHERWISE ENLARGE THE SCOPE OF ANY WARRANTY HEREUNDER. LICENSEE ASSUMES THE ENTIRE RISK AS TO THE QUALITY AND THE PERFORMANCE OF SUCH SOFTWARE. SHOULD THE SOFTWARE PROVE DEFECTIVE, YOU, AS LICENSEE (AND NOT LICENSOR, ITS SUPPLIERS, DISTRIBUTORS, DEALERS OR AGENTS), ASSUME THE ENTIRE COST OF ALL NECESSARY CORRECTION, SERVICING, OR REPAIR. b) LICENSOR warrants the disk(s) on which this copy of the Software is recorded or fixed to be free from defects in materials and workmanship, under normal use and service, for a period of ninety (90) days from the date of delivery as evidenced by a copy of the applicable receipt. LICENSOR hereby limits the duration of any implied warranties with respect to the disk(s) to the duration of the express warranty. This limited warranty shall not apply if the disk(s) have been damaged by unreasonable use, accident, negligence, or by any other causes unrelated to defective materials or workmanship. c) LICENSOR does not warrant that the functions contained in the Software will be uninterrupted or error free and Licensee is encouraged to test the Software for Licensee's intended use prior to placing any reliance thereon. All risk of the use of the Software will be on you, as Licensee. d) THE LIMITED WARRANTY SET FORTH ABOVE GIVES YOU SPECIFIC LEGAL RIGHTS AND YOU MAY ALSO HAVE OTHER RIGHTS, WHICH VARY FROM STATE TO STATE. SOME STATES DO NOT ALLOW THE LIMITATION OR EXCLUSION OF IMPLIED WARRANTIES OR OF INCIDENTAL OR CONSEQUENTIAL DAMAGES, SO THE LIMITATIONS AND EXCLUSIONS CONCERNING THE SOFTWARE AND RELATED WRITTEN MATERIALS SET FORTH ABOVE MAY NOT APPLY TO YOU.

9. LIMITATION OF REMEDIES. LICENSOR's entire liability and Licensee's exclusive remedy shall be the replacement of any disk(s) not meeting the limited warranty set forth in Section 8 above which is returned to LICENSOR with a copy of the applicable receipt within the warranty period. Any replacement disk(s)will be warranted for the remainder of the original warranty period or thirty (30) days, whichever is longer.

10. LIMITATION OF LIABILITY. IN NO EVENT WILL LICENSOR, OR ANYONE ELSE INVOLVED IN THE CREATION, PRODUCTION, AND/OR DELIVERY OF THIS SOFTWARE PRODUCT BE LIABLE TO LICENSEE OR ANY OTHER PER-SON OR ENTITY FOR ANY DIRECT, INDIRECT, OR OTHER DAMAGES, INCLUDING, WITHOUT LIMITATION, ANY INTERRUPTION OF SERVICES, LOST PROFITS, LOST SAVINGS, LOSS OF DATA, OR ANY OTHER CONSEQUENTIAL, INCIDENTAL, SPECIAL, OR PUNITIVE DAMAGES, ARISING OUT OF THE PURCHASE, USE, INABILITY TO USE, OR OPERATION OF THE SOFTWARE, EVEN IF LICENSOR OR ANY AUTHORIZED LICENSOR DEALER HAS BEEN ADVISED OF THE POSSIBILITY OF SUCH DAMAGES. BY YOUR USE OF THE SOFTWARE, YOU ACKNOWLEDGE THAT THE LIMITATION OF LIABILITY SET FORTH IN THIS LICENSE WAS THE BASIS UPON WHICH THE SOFTWARE WAS OFFERED BY LICENSOR AND YOU ACKNOWLEDGE THAT THE PRICE OF THE SOFTWARE LICENSE WOULD BE HIGHER IN THE ABSENCE OF SUCH LIMITATION. SOME STATES DO NOT ALLOW THE LIMITATION OR EXCLUSION OF LIABILITY FOR INCIDENTAL OR CONSEQUENTIAL DAMAGES SO THE ABOVE LIMITATIONS AND EXCLUSIONS MAY NOT APPLY TO YOU.

11. UPDATES. LICENSOR, at its sole discretion, may periodically issue updates of the Software which you may receive upon request and payment of the applicable update fee in effect from time to time and in such event, all of the provisions of the within License Agreement shall apply to such updates.

12. EXPORT RESTRICTIONS. Licensee agrees not to export or re-export the Software and accompanying documentation (or any copies thereof) in violation of any applicable U.S. laws or regulations.

13. ENTIRE AGREEMENT. YOU, AS LICENSEE, ACKNOWLEDGE THAT: (i) YOU HAVE READ THIS ENTIRE AGREEMENT AND AGREE TO BE BOUND BY ITS TERMS AND CONDITIONS; (ii) THIS AGREEMENT IS THE COMPLETE AND EXCLUSIVE STATEMENT OF THE UNDERSTANDING BETWEEN THE PARTIES AND SUPERSEDES ANY AND ALL PRIOR ORAL OR WRITTEN COMMUNICA-TIONS RELATING TO THE SUBJECT MATTER HEREOF; AND (iii) THIS AGREE-MENT MAY NOT BE MODIFIED, AMENDED, OR IN ANY WAY ALTERED EXCEPT BY A WRITING SIGNED BY BOTH YOURSELF AND AN OFFICER OR AUTHO-RIZED REPRESENTATIVE OF LICENSOR.

14. SEVERABILITY. In the event that any provision of this License Agreement is held to be illegal or otherwise unenforceable, such provision shall be deemed to have been deleted from this License Agreement while the remaining provisions of this License Agreement shall be unaffected and shall continue in full force and effect.

15. GOVERNING LAW. This License Agreement shall be governed by the laws of the State of California applicable to agreements wholly to be performed therein and of the United States of America, excluding that body of the law related to conflicts of law. This License Agreement shall not be governed by the United Nations Convention on Contracts for the International Sale of Goods, the application of which is expressly excluded. No waiver of any breach of the provisions of this License Agreement shall be deemed a waiver of any other breach of this License Agreement.

16. RESTRICTED RIGHTS LEGEND. Use, duplication, or disclosure by the Government is subject to restrictions as set forth in subparagraph (c)(1)(ii) of the Rights in Technical Data and Computer Software clause at 48 CFR § 252.227-7013 and DFARS § 252.227-7013 or subparagraphs (c) (1) and (c)(2) of the Commercial Computer Software-Restricted Rights at 48 CFR § 52.227.19, as applicable. Contractor/manufacturer: LICENSOR: LYNDA.COM, INC., c/o PEACHPIT PRESS, 1249 Eighth Street, Berkeley, CA 94710.